THE INTELLIGENCE ARCHIPELAGO

*The Community's Struggle to Reform
in the Globalized Era*

I0442074

Melanie M. H. Gutjahr

JOINT MILITARY
INTELLIGENCE COLLEGE

WASHINGTON, DC
May 2005

CONTENTS

ACKNOWLEDGMENTS

The author gratefully acknowledges the following individuals who made this research project possible.

The senior leadership of the National Geospatial-Intelligence Agency who selected me as the NGA participant in the FY2004 Intelligence Research Fellows Program at the Center for Strategic Intelligence Research (CSIR) at the Joint Military Intelligence College (JMIC), and colleagues in my assigned organization, NGA/Enterprise directorate (Information Management), who promoted my application.

Mr. Art Grant, LTC (U.S. Army, Ret.), former House Intelligence Committee staff member and currently Vice President, National Intelligence, Space and Geospatial Programs for the Raytheon Company; and Russ Travers, Deputy Director, National CounterTerrorism Center, who reviewed the manuscript and provided commentaries.

Dr. Russell Swenson, Director of the CSIR. His editorial comments and direction have been invaluable to the completion of this project.

The library research staffs at the Defense Intelligence Agency and the National Geospatial-Intelligence Agency, who provided source assistance. An anonymous NGA analyst, who provided map reconstruction assistance.

Lastly, the author would like to express a heartfelt appreciation to my family— Hannah and Joshua Gutjahr—for their continued support and encouragement.

COMMENTARIES

In her research project, *The Intelligence Archipelago: The Community's Struggle to Reform in the Globalized era*, Ms. Melanie Gutjahr has made a significant contribution to our understanding of how Intelligence is conducted, the future implications for our national security if changes do not occur, and the role the recently enacted "Intelligence and Terrorism Prevention Act of 2004" will play in helping to determine the future of U.S. Intelligence. Her diligent research combined with her personal knowledge of the arcane and esoteric world of intelligence provides the basis for her clear analysis and strong conclusions. This is an excellent body of work, worthy of study by anyone interested in U.S. Intelligence and interested in making a world class Intelligence Community even more effective than it is today.

Her description of the history of the U.S. Intelligence Community and efforts to reform it since World War II provides the necessary context for understanding the Community's current organization and the public and private calls for change. She describes in detail the most significant attempts to reform U.S. Intelligence and the responses of career Intelligence officers. Her descriptions show recurring themes throughout the period suggesting that important shortcomings have repeatedly not been addressed. It is this repetitive resistance to change that makes her historical narrative both troubling and sad. In many instances, it appears that career intelligence officers respond to criticisms by asserting that change has occurred after the critiques were developed and therefore suggestions for reform apply to a Community that no longer exists. It certainly is true the intelligence domain is very dynamic and today is different than yesterday, this week is rather different than last week, and this month is very different than six months ago. But it is quite clear that the recurring themes demonstrate a failure to acknowledge problems and to create a future that addresses the fundamental shortcomings of today, yesterday, last month, last year–and tomorrow. The career intelligence officer response to arguably the nation's worst strategic surprise on September 11th appears to be no different than responses in the past: you don't understand intelligence, leave us alone, we will fix it on our own. Ms. Gutjahr's work provides the essential understanding of this context.

Her analysis of the implications if changes do not occur is very important. Moreover, her understanding of the effects of "globalization" and the significance of the digital age are of great value in appreciating the urgency for reform. She assesses the imperfect "Intelligence Reform and Terrorism Prevention Act of 2004" and the opportunity it gives the nation to "get it right." Unfortunately, she does not reveal unbridled optimism about the future of intelligence reform. Career intelligence officer responses to the new law—and other agents for change—so far appear to be no different than they have been in past. Nonetheless, as she advises:

> Reform must be construed as a Community-wide, never-ending series of process improvement tasks. Processes and procedures that guarantee success against our opponent today will be ill-advised as we face tomorrow's enemy. The Community must maintain a constant watch against complacency.

As Ms. Gutjahr notes, much remains to be done and the only people who can get it done are the career intelligence officers who are never seen publicly and have devoted their lives to keeping us all safe. The intelligence archipelago must become a sea without islands.

Art Grant
*Vice President, National Intelligence, Space and
Geospatial Programs, the Raytheon Company*

Ms. Gutjahr makes a valuable contribution to what has been, thus far, a woefully inadequate discussion of intelligence reform. Despite high profile Commissions, legislative initiatives, and more focus on the Community than has existed in many years, the quality of the debate remains shallow and confused. Unfortunately, the various external efforts to date have done a far better job of chronicling intelligence failures (a valuable contribution to be sure) than they have of recommending workable solutions. From all appearances it will fall to practitioners who actually understand the workings of this very complicated Community to lay out a way ahead. This book will be a valuable reference to support that effort.

Ms. Gutjahr's effort is particularly important because the ability of the IC to successfully deal with globalization is *the* single most important issue confronting the new DNI. It has implications for the structure, culture, training and very nature of what we do and how we do it. The topic will dominate any sophisticated discussion of intelligence reform for at least the next decade and Ms. Gutjahr is on the leading edge of that discussion.

Russ Travers
Deputy Director, National CounterTerrorism Center

REVIEW ESSAY

Failures, Fallacies and Fixes: Posturing Intelligence for the Challenges of Globalization

Russell E. Travers[i]

Six decades ago, in the aftermath of the Second World War, the United States struggled to develop a security strategy to confront the Soviet Union. After two years of debate and indecision, the National Security Act of 1947 established the intelligence and security architecture that eventually won the Cold War. Modified over time, that national intelligence apparatus served us well against a monolithic enemy; a talented workforce, extraordinary technical capabilities, and the sheer brute force attendant to spending immense sums on intelligence, gave rise to many successes.

We're now 15 years past the end of the Cold War. We've suffered a series of intelligence failures, and we've seen myriad still-born reform efforts. With the political imperative generated by the 9/11 Commission, we have "The Intelligence Reform and Terrorism Prevention Act of 2004" (the Legislation). And more recently we have the "Report of the Commission on the Intelligence Capabilities of the United States regarding Weapons of Mass Destruction" (WMD Commission). Are we on the road to "fixing" intelligence, or are we at risk of making it worse? In truth, either outcome is entirely possible. Intelligence reform has become such a cottage industry that the debate is confused, and good ideas are routinely interspersed with those that are ill conceived. Certainly we will need to fight the inclination to check the "fix intelligence" block and move on to other issues; if we're going to get this right, we are in the very opening stages of a protracted and complicated series of changes to the Intelligence Community. But how should we be moving forward? Are we focusing on causes or symptoms? What problems are we trying to correct? And how do we go about fixing them? We need to take a very clinical approach to these questions as we implement the Legislation and continue efforts to reform an Intelligence Community that remains ill equipped for the challenges of the 21st Century.

---

[i] Russ Travers works for the Defense Intelligence Agency and is assigned as a Deputy Director of the National CounterTerrorism Center (NCTC). The views expressed in this article are those of the author and do not reflect the official policy or position of the Department of Defense or the United States Government.

Looking back over the past fifteen years, our critics will, with varying degrees of justification, point to our failure to project the demise of the Soviet Union, the unanticipated Indian nuclear test, the inadvertent strike on the Chinese Embassy, the surprise launch of the North Korean Taepo Dong-1, the incorrect assessments of Iraqi WMD, and, of course, 9/11. What do these failures–these symptoms— have in common? In actuality: virtually nothing. The reasons run the gamut: a mismatch between taskings and resources, technical collection inadequacies, a lack of HUMINT sources, inadequate validation of sources, gaps in databases, analytic blinders, substandard analytic art, and shortfalls in information dissemination to analysts and operators. This is in no way a blanket indictment of the Community: there are many brilliant people doing wonderful work. But there are systemic problems that permeate all aspects of our business. Fixes will be neither easy nor fast, and it is not at all clear that either the Legislation or the WMD Commission envisions the necessary remedies.

While intelligence reform is cast in terms of avoiding more failures, we should not lose sight of the historic context. The current imperative should be to ensure that the Intelligence Community is up to the challenges of globalization–where an economic problem in one region can quickly affect conditions around the globe, or technology controls are easily circumvented, or information about the deadliest weapons known to mankind are available at a keystroke, or military capabilities can be either rented or bought, or radical ideologies can be pushed from a cave in Afghanistan to a worldwide audience, or, in a huge challenge to our constitutional order, the foreign and domestic divide simply doesn't mean much anymore. In such an environment, we need to help the policy community build on the many opportunities provided by the upsides of globalization, while accurately forecasting and dealing with the very serious downsides.

The essence of our mission hasn't changed very much; we need to get the facts straight, provide them when/where needed, and be regarded as a source of objective analytic expertise that will keep the policy debate intellectually honest and help inform the country's risk equation. So why are we struggling with such age-old tasks? The answer, unfortunately, is much more complicated than the discussion leading up to either the Intelligence Reform Act or the WMD Commission Report would suggest. This commentary addresses the nature of the IC's problems, debunks some of the conventional wisdom, and suggests a series of principles that could serve as a road map for some of the reforms that need to be pursued.

As we think about reform of the Community, we need to start with a sound understanding of the underlying problems, after which improvements will begin to suggest themselves. Thus we begin with the proposition that the Community's problems can be clinically explained in the simplicity (and tyranny) of the Intelligence Cycle. By doctrine the process of "doing" intelligence is divided into a cycle: the policy community provides general direction, and from that we do our planning; we determine whether we need new collection to address the relevant issues; we utilize the data—newly collected and/or resident in databases to perform analysis; we then disseminate that analysis to our consumers who provide us feedback—and the cycle begins again. While the Intelligence Cycle is much maligned these days, and there are clearly many instances where such a structured approach doesn't apply, it still offers a useful framework for dissecting the problems that have developed over the past 15 years.

Reform Through The Lens of The Intelligence Cycle

Planning and Direction

Because the Planning and Direction portion of the Intelligence Cycle sets in train an inescapable logic for virtually everything that follows, it is difficult to overstate its importance. And unfortunately it is also difficult to communicate how badly it is broken. There are two issues at work: the development of national security policy, and the management of the IC to best inform that policy. Both are in flux.

First, an uncertain, difficult world has bedeviled those responsible for national security strategy. We came out of the Cold War indisputably "number one," but woefully unprepared for the discontinuity attendant to losing the Soviet Union as our organizing principle. As a country we are well into our second decade of geopolitical confusion. While trite, it is true that we don't yet have our George Kennan article for an era of globalization. With no consensus about the nature of our interests or how best to defend them, we have been in a prolonged transition since the early 1990s. The Executive Branch coined its share of buzz words: "engage," "enlarge," "assure," "dissuade," and the like, but from an intelligence perspective there has simply been no actionable way to prioritize resources.

Internal management of the IC matched geopolitical confusion with its own. Faced with the demand for a peace dividend, the Community absorbed 20-25 percent cuts and embarked on a host of flawed prioritization schemes (throughout the 1990s our international challenges always seemed to occur in the lowest priority countries–Somalia, Haiti, the Balkans). Because there was no stomach for reorganization, the Community largely kept the existing structure and forced IC core missions to fit it–in essence "function" followed "form" rather than the other way around. This was most clearly seen in the fundamentally flawed effort to divide analysis into political, economic, and military subcomponents and divide analytic responsibilities around the Community; anyone interested in the roots of analytic intelligence failures need not look much further. Finally, the Community gravitated to the only thing that could support resource demands at the time: intelligence "support to military operations." DoD, anxious about fixing short-comings of DESERT STORM, provided ample justification through the National Military Strategy requirements. This focus on support to the military proved responsible for skewing intelligence resources away from a more balanced view of national security.

Collection

The basic flaws in the Planning and Direction portion of the Intelligence Cycle gave rise to subsequent problems in collection throughout the 1990s–in ongoing as well as planned collection. The immediate problem was associated with being whip-sawed from crisis to crisis. Almost invariably crises occurred in relatively low-priority countries and required a massive surge effort to build a sufficient base of knowledge; clearly some collectors surge better than others, but overall the Intelligence Community can be justifiably proud of the way it marshaled col-lection resources. There was, however, an opportunity cost of surging and that was reflected in diminished work on target development and basic database main-tenance; the mistaken attack on the Chinese Embassy in Belgrade reflected just such neglect. Moreover, the collection community was confronted with an increasingly complex environment as a result of the dizzying pace of information technology advances; it was being run ragged by current crises and was falling farther behind the technology curve.

In the near-term, the collection picture was oriented toward reacting to an ad hoc national security policy, and the future collection picture was overwhelm-ingly oriented toward support to the military. The demand to support two nearly simultaneous large-scale contingencies and the information dominance require-ments of Joint Vision 2010 and JV2020 were consuming programmed resources. We had inadvertently created the proverbial self-licking ice cream cone; the national security strategy (the Planning and Direction portion of the Intelligence Cycle) and its heavy emphasis on total military superiority, gave the IC its guid-ance: the IC needed to support this level of military planning, so, in effect, the collection community had license to steal. The very demanding (expensive) key performance parameters and the composition of the ultimate constellation flowed directly from the military strategy; we are still feeling the financial squeeze—the Future Imagery Architecture shortfalls epitomize the problem. Finally, forgotten in much of the discussion of technical collection was human intelligence; it wasn't deemed very relevant to the 1990s discussion of intelligence support to two major regional contingencies. While HUMINT is all the rage today, we can trace the under-investments of the last decade directly to the focus on support to military operations and the perceived greater relevance of the more technically oriented disciplines of IMINT, SIGINT, and to a lesser degree, MASINT.

Analysis

While the Community invested in collection to support an apparently endless supply of requirements, analysis was inevitably short-changed. For any number of reasons we would find ourselves woefully unable to deal with an increasingly complex world. There is no question that a number of our key analytic problems were the result of self-inflicted wounds. More on that later. However, at least four significant problems that undermined the relevance and quality of our analysis were set in train by the intelligence cycle–indeed, they can all find their lineage in Planning and Direction shortcomings. The first, and perhaps most obvious problem was the near-term, reactive orientation of U.S. national security strategy. With an *ad hoc* foreign policy that had little long-term vision, there was virtually no interest in or patience for longer-term intelligence analysis. As a country we operated from day to day, and our Community analysis reflected that reality; unfortunately, when trend analysis focuses on weeks and months instead of years and decades, we are in trouble. The next two problems acted in concert and further undermined sophisticated, contextual analysis. Because Community investments were oriented primarily toward supporting military operations, we focused more on counting and reporting than analyzing; we operated at the "data end" of the spectrum rather than the "knowledge end." But of even more import, the Community, with Congressional prodding, adopted a management philosophy that divided up analytic responsibilities and parceled them out between and among Departments and Agencies. Now think about this: globalization represents, by definition, the growing interrelationship among politics, religion, culture, economics, technology and security. And at that precise moment in history, the Intelligence Community was, as a matter of conscious design, embarking on a self-imposed Balkanization–divvying up among production centers these various analytic disciplines as if they were unrelated. Contextual analysis never had a chance.

To top matters off, a further side-effect of trying to manage and de-conflict the efforts of a dozen national-level agencies was the introduction of a significant level of bureaucratic friction—it became very difficult to get things done; managers across the IC found themselves focused more on alleviating that friction, fighting for scarce resources, or being assigned to mind-numbing tiger teams, working groups, steering committees or process action teams. As a result they were less focused on the business of knowledge. In the final analysis, desk analysts were often left to operate without adequate substantive supervision, and we were developing, and expanding, a cadre of managerial functionaries with abysmal substantive expertise; they largely measured success in their careers by being managers of intelligence rather than doers of intelligence.

And so, at a time when globalization was confronting the Intelligence Community with the most complicated world in human history, the structure was ill conceived, analysts were ill prepared and managers were increasingly divorced from substance. We had hard-wired failure into the system, and didn't even realize it.

Dissemination and Feedback

Mediocrity was winning by default in our core analytic function, but the Intelligence Community's ability to piggyback on technological innovation in support of dissemination was, and is, a huge success story. The movement of electrons instead of paper revolutionized dissemination. And thanks to the vision of those focused on weaning the Community off proprietary solutions and on to off-the-shelf approaches, the future is bright. However, there are serious challenges. We are moving unevaluated information at the speed of light not only to analysts, but also to a very broad range of consumers; we are empowering those who wish to create their own "intelligence shops," thereby enabling them to search out intelligence (no matter how questionable or badly sourced) to support preconceived notions. The increasing power and reach of our dissemination network will only exacerbate that problem.[ii]

Faced with a flood of information, consumers often perceive intelligence assessments as just one more stream of information–a stream that may not be as timely, as sophisticated, or as aesthetically well packaged as other sources (we don't tell a story very well). Moreover, dissemination and feedback are further complicated by the times in which we find ourselves. An *ad hoc* security strategy implies that policymakers at all levels are increasingly tactical in their outlook. As a result, we see an insatiable appetite for information in which almost no detail is too trivial. Further, in an era of globalization, Executive Branch Departmental responsibilities are blurred and policymakers' interests expand beyond traditional "lanes in the road." As they look to their organic intelligence elements to meet ever-expanding interests, these organizations are being pushed into areas they are ill-equipped to address. The IC finds itself spending an inordinate

---

[ii] This is not merely a problem with policy consumers. Some intelligence analysts, overwhelmed with the amount of available information, do the same thing–search massive data holdings in a manner that inadvertently provides information to support a preconceived hypothesis but doesn't highlight contradictory material. Indeed, this mirrors a broader societal problem; portions of the U.S. body politic deal with information overload by searching out newspapers, cable channels, websites or even movies that support their own political views. This general tendency toward self-selection is undermining everything from objective intelligence analysis and reasoned policy making to informed political debate.

amount of time chasing down meaningless details, debunking erroneous reports that policy has embraced, pursuing angles that are not relevant to the problem at hand, or navigating a steep learning curve trying to address unfamiliar issues. Of course we must go the extra mile and address consumer interests. But intelligence isn't a "free good"; the IC must do a better job of managing consumer expectations and explaining the opportunity costs of indulging off-the-wall "science projects."

Finally, feedback is critically important to ensure that the Intelligence Community gain policy insights–particularly in a rapidly changing world. Unfortunately, perceived sensitivities on both sides may limit the access of intelligence officers into policy deliberations. In addition, it is a rare policymaker who will make time to provide a backbrief to analysts, and their sensitive reporting cables will often stay in policy channels, never making it to the desk analyst.

So, having gone full circle, the lack of feedback further undermines the broken Planning and Direction component of the Intelligence cycle, and the vicious circle begins anew.

The Intelligence Community's Self-inflicted Wounds

The logic of the Intelligence Cycle explains many problems and reflects the fact that within the U.S. Government are many shared failures. But the IC has had some control over its own destiny and has much to answer for. Analysis is the clearest case in point. In the 1990s the analytic component of the Intelligence Community was beginning to lose its competitive advantage and simply wasn't adapting rapidly enough. With the collapse of the Soviet Union our ability to hide behind classification markings was eroding; we could still stamp things "secret," but we had lost the monopoly on information and were increasingly second-guessed by academics, journalists, and even policymakers who had access and expertise rivaling ours.

In the marketplace of ideas, ours were no longer compelling, and we were not training people to compete. As the WMD Commission and others have noted, analysts weren't sufficiently inquisitive when it came to questioning what a source said or why he said it; and the collection community was loathe to let the inquisitive analysts get their noses too far under the collection tent. Ask a young analyst to discuss the role of "assumptions" or "rules of evidence" or "hypotheses" and you would be just as likely to get a blank stare as a coherent discussion of analytic art.

We had created a generation of reporters rather than analysts. Unfortunately, even getting the "facts" straight in a world of web sites, instantaneous communication, and circular reporting can be problematic. Analysts are generally better at the "who," "what," and "where," somewhat worse at the "how" and "when," and often miserable at the "why" and the "so what." We simply haven't brought in and trained sufficient numbers of analysts equipped to handle the latter kinds of contextual questions; how many cultural anthropologists have we hired over the past decade? The corollaries are endless, but two stand out. First, we are generally bad at dealing with uncertainty–the standard fare of the intelligence analyst; despite the fact that the single greatest uncertainty may be the role the U.S. chooses to play in the world, Intelligence Community analysts are tempted to consider the future in terms of three-digit accuracy when we have, at best, one-digit confidence. And second, we tend toward "worst case analysis," piling assumption on top of dubious report on top of speculation. There appears to be no penalty for over-warning, and we have done it often.

Other factors have magnified the impact of inadequate analyst training. The IC remains conflicted about the essence of analysis–what it is, and who does it. On the one hand we tend to blur the distinction between those organizations that should have a truly analytic mission, and those that have more of a situational awareness function. Terrorism analysis remains the perfect example. By taking a relatively anarchic approach, we have had an explosion of "fusion centers." A lack of critical mass and something resembling seven-year-old soccer ensues; with too many organizations chasing the latest intelligence report, and far too many enthusiastic amateurs doing the analysis, the work product can be shallow and the Community is sub-optimized. On the other hand we may need to rethink the meaning of "all-source" intelligence, relative to Signals or Imagery Intelligence. Clearly the "single INT" Agencies must make their "take" available to the broader Community. However, many NSA and NGA analysts routinely, and appropriately, use other disciplines to inform their work, and they often know their target at least as well as their all-source colleagues. As a Community we need to make the best use of our collective talent. This almost invariably means building teams of analysts from across the Community; it has worked every place it's been tried.

The Horizon For "Fixes"

Before focusing on "fixes," it is best to examine the future security environment. As we look out over the next 5-10 years, we can't separate intelligence reform, and the IC's claim on resources, from the global security picture and the U.S. domestic political debate.

On the security side we can be assured that the Middle East will remain in turmoil, that North Korea is at least a near-term problem, that China is a long-term challenge, and that Russia will pose some unique security concerns. Certainly it is true that nation-state development of WMD and long-range missiles will always be a concern.[iii] But beyond such long-standing issues, the principal challenges will continue to be those associated with the downside of globalization–particularly the threat posed by international terrorism and the potential use of WMD against the homeland.

The likelihood and timing of this threat manifesting itself are huge uncertainties. There is no question that the extraordinary efforts of the CIA's Counterterrorism Center, coupled with those of the U.S. military and other USG elements involved in the offensive war against terrorism, have inflicted huge losses on Al Qaeda. But global conditions are a veritable petri dish for jihadists, and we are not going to succeed by killing these people until they like us. The smart money almost certainly says that terrorists are being created faster than we are killing or capturing them. They are more junior, less experienced and more prone to making mistakes. But the new generation is more computer-savvy, and as their experience grows and they become ever more empowered by information and technology, the threat will grow more complex.

Timing, however, is critical as we go about planning to confront such a threat. Absent a clear and present threat perception, democracies don't plan well for future security challenges. And the longer we go without a major attack on the homeland, the greater the likelihood that there will be a recalibration away from the traditional national security accounts and toward the concern about deficits and a host of domestic challenges. One wonders how long the country is going to support continued growth in the defense and intelligence budgets.

Information Sharing—a Red Herring

If the Intelligence Community is not well postured to deal with such an extraordinarily complex security environment, how do we fix it? For those in search of simple solutions to complex problems the latest nominee appears to be "information sharing." Clearly there is much work to be done, though by any objective standard the Community has made huge strides in this area since 9/11. However, it is also critical to recognize that the complex range of policy, technical, security, and legal challenges attendant to information sharing belies any simple solutions. More importantly, while information sharing is critical, it's just not the answer to all our problems. A number of observations are warranted:

[iii] While the IC is coming in for its share of criticism, it is instructive to note that the IC's own mid-1990s assessment of Iran's development of ICBMs is proving to be far more accurate than that of the late 1990s Commission to Assess the Ballistic Missile Threat to the U.S.

—Information Sharing - Necessary (But not Sufficient): It is certainly true that some doctrinal tenets like "need to know" must be reexamined in a globalized world. The cadre of analysts who work many of the transnational problems is going to need much broader access than has traditionally been the case because of the potential nexus between and among terrorism, proliferation, crime and narcotics. The Community hasn't come to grips with this fact.

—Balance is Critical: There will always be legitimate constraints on the free flow of information. Source sensitivities are real: Imagine how much better off we'd be if the fact of UBL's use of SATCOM had not made it into the press several years ago. Special Access Programs, ongoing operations, liaison-provided information, and U.S. persons' privacy rights will all serve to properly limit the free flow of information.

—Dots Do Not Get Randomly Connected: Some seem to believe that if we just "open our doors"–to potential federal, state, local and private sector authorities— "the answer" will appear. Unfortunately analysis just doesn't work that way; the amount of daily terrorism "intelligence" that is completely erroneous, utterly irrelevant or absolute nonsense is already overwhelming. We really don't want everyone free to render an opinion. Rather, we want to ensure, for example, that analysis regarding jihadist interest in airplanes is circulated so that FBI offices in Phoenix or Minneapolis know to be on the lookout for, or have the context to, the dot they've uncovered.

—Effective Information Sharing a Growing Concern: If an organization posts something to its webpage, it can claim to have shared information. Whether the right people know the information/analysis is there, and actually make use of it, is entirely another matter. Indeed, we'll almost certainly be dealing with precisely this problem in the post mortems of our next intelligence failure; the relevant intelligence will have been posted, but the right analysts never found it among the terabytes of available information. XML tagging will certainly prove of some use, but as we move up the complexity chain from data to information to knowledge to wisdom, its utility may be open to question.

—Finally... Information-Sharing is no Panacea: Conventional wisdom seems to suggest that as soon as we fix information-sharing we've fixed intelligence. Even the 9/11 Commission has stated that "the greatest impediment to all-source analysis.... is the human or systemic resistance to sharing information."[iv] If only it were true. In actuality, information-sharing generally operates at the data end of the data/knowledge spectrum—where pieces of information are discrete. In some

---

[iv] *The 9/11 Commission Report: Final Report of the National Commission on Terrorist Attacks Upon the United States.* Official Government Edition, 416.

cases having that data might be extraordinarily important, but most of the intelligence failures of the last 10 years have occurred at the knowledge end of the spectrum and had little to do with sharing a particular piece of information. In the final analysis, without appropriate business process changes, we could find that pushing more electrons to more organizations will simply result in these same organizations being wrong faster.

Principles For Reform—an Insider's View

If information-sharing won't fix all our problems, what do we do? Assuming the depiction of the IC's problems is reasonably accurate, it is not at all clear what the fact of a Director of National Intelligence alone does to fix them. Our problems developed over decades and will not be fixed by moving a few boxes around or transferring some money between accounts. Indeed the answer is not to throw more money or more people at the problem. The fixes will need to be structural, systemic and cultural; they are going to be difficult to implement and progress will be slow in coming. The following ten basic principles map back to the major problems and are intended to help evaluate prospective changes:

—*Address the Major National Security Issue First:* Even assuming agreement on the evaluation of the problems, reasonable people will disagree on the solutions. As the complexity of the IC overhaul increases, so too will the number of moving parts and the potential for serious disarray. Accordingly, our initial focus should be on terrorism and devoted to ensuring that the IC is optimally postured; for instance, the National Counter Terrorism Center must be empowered and must have a critical mass of the best analysts and other necessary capabilities to confront terrorism. Only then should the DNI move on to other major initiatives.

—*Achieve Unity of Purpose:* While superficially straightforward, this blinding flash of the obvious extends well beyond the IC and is not guaranteed by the appointment of a DNI. Who is responsible for what? How many task forces, operations centers and "redundant" efforts are appropriate? Do we need a "lead federal Agency" approach in different regions overseas to counter terrorism? Do we need other "joint" structures domestically to synchronize an array of homeland security, law enforcement, intelligence and military efforts? Unless and until we address these kinds of very difficult questions, Departmental and Agency prerogatives will be confused with, or substituted for, the national interest and the government will remain badly sub-optimized.

—*Form Should Follow Function:* The logic is simple: Determine, in broad strokes, what the IC needs to address and structure it accordingly, ensuring an appropriate balance between resources committed and the relative need/importance of the consumer. The required changes are fundamental: In an era of globalization few analytic issues of any consequence are one-dimensional. As such we need to focus on structures that promote analytic integration; analysis is simply not additive and as a result the entire approach of parceling out discrete pieces of the same problem set must be reexamined. The foreign/domestic angle will be particularly problematic.

—*Tend to the Military:* With the exception of a small policy support shop within the Office of the Secretary of Defense (OSD) and the Services, military intelligence should be narrowly focused on supporting near-term military operations and contingency plans. This would, for example, argue against a separate all encompassing "China Center" subordinate to the DNI. Military intelligence should have primary responsibility for current Chinese military capabilities. Long-term "futures" work—because it inherently involves broader geopolitical trends, economics and so forth, would be largely outside the domain of Defense Intelligence.

—*Maximize the Potential for Objectivity.* With regard to collection, as is painfully evident from the WMD Commission, we need to broaden the evaluation of sources beyond the potentially myopic collectors; this is particularly true for HUMINT where analysts themselves must evaluate sources with an eye to weighing value and credibility of sources with respect to the question at hand. At the same time, with regard to analysis, when Cabinet-level officials such as Department heads have preconceived notions, and yet they have direct control over intelligence organizations that in effect speak for the country on substantive issues, with huge policy and budgetary implications, we can expect to see analytic bias.

—*Focus on Knowledge.* Far too many managers spend the bulk of their time in non-substantive meetings, de-conflicting production responsibilities, trying to apply metrics to inherently non-measurable subjects, dissecting prioritization schemes and the like. They often play virtually no role in the analytic work product. Clearly we need to focus on the training of our analysts, but in addition, by streamlining the analytic configuration such that a single manager has primary responsibility for the major regional and functional issues of concern to the USG, we could dramatically reduce the managerial functionary component within the Community. Analytic quality would quickly rise.

—*The State/INR Model to Competitive Analysis:* A strong central "intelligence factory" should produce analysis for the country with much smaller departmental structures free to track critical issues and ensure alternative analysis is allowed to flourish.[v] INR reflects a model for conducting such analysis with small numbers of high quality analysts; NIEs would continue to be the venue to bring together such views. Two related issues: first, too much competitive analysis would be abdicating IC responsibility, simply resulting in policymakers choosing from the conclusion they liked best; second, while "red cell" work is important, care must be taken to prevent analytic "imagination" from running amok and becoming a "sum of all our fears" approach–connecting dots that aren't really there.

—*Achieve Balance in the Intelligence Cycle:* Once we optimize the structure so that we are, in fact, configured to confront the major security challenges of this millennium, we then need to establish balance between collection and analysis. Research and development is critical to developing future collection capabilities. But we must limit the unfunded mandates associated with these new capabilities; we need to more fully appreciate the attendant downstream costs of processing and exploitation. And within the collection domain, are allocations being made in rough proportion to the relative importance of the threat against which they are best postured to collect?

—*Develop A System of Systems Approach:* At the risk of buying into the buzzword bingo approach to intelligence reform, there are three fundamental changes that would vastly increase system-wide effectiveness: first, a single personnel system for intelligence officers, and an attendant IC University to provide world class cradle-to-grave professional development; second, an IT infrastructure allowing database interoperability that is so self-evidently important; and third, programmatic simplification to reduce the massive bureaucracy associated with our Byzantine programmatic and budgetary processes. Each of these relatively straightforward concepts masks massive complexity.

—*Be Careful:* The notion that we can implement major reform and "do no harm," at least in the short run, is ludicrous. Even if we "get it right," the transition from "where we are" to "wherever we are going" will be extraordinarily tricky. The disruption will be substantial, potentially dangerous, and must be mitigated and phased in properly to avoid significant risk to the Country. The DNI ought to assemble the best minds, give them six months to report back on the ten-plus-year plan (yes, it's going to take at least that long) to address the second-,

---

[v] This will be an extremely emotive subject, but if we accept the integration imperative and the need to bring managers back into the substantive equation, in addition to an NCTC and a WMD Center, the optimal solution for the country may be a consolidation of some parts of the Directorates of Intelligence of the CIA and DIA. The science and technology (S&T) component of the current military service centers would be subordinated to the strategic S&T office found in the consolidated DIA/CIA Directorate for Intelligence, under the DNI. Smaller staffs would remain within DoD to be in direct support of OSD and the Service Secretaries. Clearly the need to ensure support to the Combatant Commanders would be a key concern. DoD's Under Secretary of Defense for Intelligence and the Joint Staff would need ample tasking authority to ensure such demands could be met. An active-duty four-star military officer as Deputy DNI should certainly help.

third-, and fourth-order issues necessary to fix a Community ill-postured to deal with the problems of the 21st Century.

Limits to Reform

The desired end-state just isn't that difficult to envision. Don't be misled by the commentators, academics, and many other self-proclaimed experts who have no clue what it means to be a collector or desk analyst. We do not need a "revolution" in intelligence or any one of the many other slogans that are being bandied about. We just need to ensure relevance in this extraordinarily complicated era of globalization. To do so, we need to get the facts straight and produce high-quality analytic products that make it to the appropriate consumer, when they need it, and in a manner they desire; once we do, and when our assessments begin standing the test of time, we won't have to worry about our analysis being cavalierly dismissed, or policy organs forming their own "intelligence shops"–the political cost of doing so would simply be too high. The principles laid out above are designed to address the IC's various systemic problems and get us to precisely that end state. They would allow us *eventually* to reestablish the essential expertise and credibility, without which we will continue to flounder.

However, when all is said and done, there is still one major problem that intelligence reform will not fix–the drift in, and lack of consensus about—U.S. national security policy. Because we are so terribly under-invested in all levers of power other than the military, we can apply the adage "When all you've got is a hammer, every problem looks like a nail." As we think about the challenges of globalization, the Intelligence Community has a huge role to play in informing our country's risk equation, but the IC is almost never going to compensate for policy shortcomings. Unless and until we figure out who we are as a country, and how we are going to relate to the rest of the world–and then build consensus around that vision–we will continue to see intelligence failures—and policy failures that get dressed up and presented as the former.

AUTHOR'S PREFACE

> Would you tell me please which way I ought to go from here? asked Alice. That depends a good deal, on where you want to get to, said the Cat. I don't care much where..., said Alice. Then it doesn't much matter which way you go, said the Cat. ...so long as I get somewhere, Alice added as an explanation. Oh, you're sure to do that, said the Cat, if you only walk long enough.
>
> —**Lewis Carroll**
> *Alice's Adventures in Wonderland*

A colleague once emphatically asserted that people are inflexible beings who only change at the margins; they do not stray from the core of who they are. This is not to say that individuals cannot change through self-actualization but rather that individuals are "who they are,"—"what you see, is what you get" and significant change is difficult if not impossible. The author believes this phenomenon is even truer for institutions. Institutions do not stray from their initial design constructs. Countless reorganizations attest to this; at some point, once again—the organization looks comparable to an earlier design. Hence, if an organization is poorly designed from its conception it is likely to remain a poorly functioning organization. The leading "best practices" will provide minimal improvement. Management alone cannot provide seminal change in a poorly designed organization.

Regrettably, the U.S. National Foreign Intelligence Community (IC), with the Central Intelligence Agency (CIA) at its hub, has been the foremost example of poorly designed organization—an organization that may truly have been "Flawed by Design."[vi] Since its inception with the passage of the National Security Act of 1947 (P.L. 80-253), the CIA and its Community have been the subject of over 300 reform initiatives. A mere five weeks after "opening for business" in October 1946, the Secretary of Defense demanded a meeting to discuss the "present and widespread belief that our Intelligence Group [sic] is entirely inept."[vii] Shortly thereafter, less than two years later, two executive branch commissions examined

---

[vi] Amy B. Zegart, *Flawed by Design: The Evolution of the CIA, JCS, and NCS* (Stanford: Stanford University Press, 1999)

[vii] Memo for the files by John H. Ohley, 24 October 1947; Department of Defense File—Subject File, 1947: Central Intelligence Agency, Papers of John H. Ohley, HSTL (citation as noted in Rudgers), 152.

the intelligence and operational missions of the CIA, and identified fundamental administrative and organizational loopholes in the initial legislation.[viii] There have been Presidential "Blue Ribbon" Commissions, House and Senate Intelligence Committee Commissions, noted scholarly reviews, inter-agency and intra-agency reviews, as well as major syndicated news organizations all hammering for intelligence reform, mostly to no avail. William E. Odom, LTG (Ret), former Director of the National Security Agency (NSA), believes "structural reform has largely been ignored" [by multiple responsible principals]. First, Congress has proved reluctant to delve into structural issues. Second, the CIA and most directors of central intelligence have also resisted serious review of structural problems. Thus, according to Odom, a quiet and informal consensus that nothing structurally is wrong has prevailed, not only in Congress and in the Intelligence Community itself but in the most recent presidential commission as well. The third point is that private intelligence reform studies have followed suit.[ix]

With the exception of the creation in 1996 of the National Imagery and Mapping Agency (NIMA), now known as the National Geospatial-Intelligence Agency (NGA),[x] there has not been any *major* structural intelligence reform despite countless recommendations for it to happen. In the NGA case, initially, the concept of a national imagery agency surfaced as one of the recommendations from the Boren (Senate) and McCurdy (House) Committees in 1992—"Creating a National Imagery Agency within the Department of Defense (DOD) to collect,

---

[viii] Richard A. Best, Jr., "Appendix C, IC21: The Intelligence Community in the 21st Century," *CRS Report for Congress* (Washington, D.C.: Congressional Research Service, Library of Congress, 28 February 1996), 4, URL:<http://www.access.gpo.gov/congress/house/intel/ic21/ic21018.html>, accessed 11 May 2004. Cited hereafter as CRS Report, Appendix C, February 1996.

[ix] William E. Odom, Fixing Intelligence for a More Secure America (New Haven: Yale University Press, 2003), 3.

[x] The National Imagery and Mapping Agency (NIMA) was created on 1 October 1996 by the 1997 Intelligence Authorization Act. This is only the second agency to be created by a legislative act, with the CIA being the first. This unique origin means that unlike the National Security Agency (NSA) or Defense Intelligence Agency (DIA), which could be eliminated by the President, or the Secretary of Defense, NIMA could only be eliminated by an act of congress. It combined the following organizations: Defense Mapping Agency (DMA), CIA's National Photographic Interpretation Center (NPIC), Central Imagery Office (CIO), National Reconnaissance Office (NRO) Imagery Processing, Defense Airborne Reconnaissance Office (DARO), Defense Intelligence Agency's (DIA) Photographic Interpretation Section (DIA/PGX), Defense Dissemination Program Office (DDPO) and CIA's imagery-related elements/programs. For a more in-depth review of this process, see Anne Daugherty Miles, Joint Military Intelligence College, The Creation of the National Imagery and Mapping Agency: Congress's Role as Overseer, Occasional Paper Number Nine (Washington, D.C.: Joint Military Intelligence College, 2002). In November 2003, the 2004 Intelligence Authorization Act renamed NIMA, the National Geospatial-Intelligence Agency (NGA).

exploit, and analyze imagery."[xi] However, it was not until DCI Candidate John Deutch's confirmation hearing that the concept of consolidating the "management of all imagery collection, analysis, and distribution" received wider consideration[xii] and eventual legislation. Interestingly, Leo Hazlewood, the Deputy CIA Director for Science and Technology and later Deputy Director, NIMA, indicated Deutch's announcement [consolidating imagery functions] "came as a complete surprise to the bureaucracy at Langley" [CIA Headquarters].[xiii] This process exemplifies intelligence reform directed at improving the efficiencies and effectiveness of intelligence via structural and organizational change. In contrast, historically, since the enactment of the National Security Act of 1947, intelligence reform of any note has focused mostly on correcting perceived abuses of power.

Although the Department of Homeland Security (DHS),[xiv] created in December 2002, is a member of the Intelligence Community, its creation was not primarily an intelligence reform initiative as much as it was a domestic security initiative. DHS is primarily a consumer of intelligence; it does not have an intelligence collection responsibility. Similarly, the accretion to the community of the U.S. Coast Guard in 2002 was merely an expansion of the list of diverse organizations that make up the Intelligence Community, and was not intended to alter the information flow or any longstanding practices of the Community.[xv]

Intelligence oversight has not burdened the Community. For decades its components operated not only in secrecy but with expectations of impunity. There were few instances of activist oversight even though intelligence oversight was an explicit charge of Senate and House Armed Services and Appropriations committees,

---

[xi] CRS Report, Appendix C, February 1996, 29.

[xii] U.S. Congress, Senate, Select Committee on Intelligence, Confirmation Hearings of John Deutch, 104th Cong, 1st sess., 26 April 1995, 1, 8 and 9.

[xiii] Miles, 1.

[xiv] Congress created the Department of Homeland Security (DHS) to oversee the government's effort to prevent terrorist attacks on American soil. This was the largest reorganization of the federal government since the creation of the Department of Defense. In the desire to create a better-coordinated domestic security program, DHS was given control over 22 executive branch agencies to include the Customs Service, the Immigration and Naturalization Service and Secret Service. (Philip Shenon, "9/11 Panel is Said to Urge New Post for Intelligence," *New York Times*, online ed., 17 July 2004, URL: http://www.nytimes.com/2004/17/politics/17panel.htm, accessed 19 July 2004.)

[xv] Section 105 of the *Intelligence Authorization Act of 2002* amended the National Security Act of 1947, making the U.S. Coast Guard a member of the National Foreign Intelligence Community despite the objections of the Director of Central Intelligence. For more information, see Kevin E. Wirth, *The Coast Guard Intelligence Program Enters the Intelligence Community: A Case Study of Congressional Influence on Intelligence Community Evolution,* MSSI thesis (Washington, D.C.: Joint Military Intelligence College, 2002).

respectively. As an example, the subcommittees were very supportive when CIA overthrew the governments of Iran in 1953 and Guatemala in 1954. Surprisingly, the subcommittees were not appalled when former DCI Director Dulles briefed them after the fact about the overthrow of the Iranian Prime Minister Mossadegh. Not only did these committees support this action but also they were surprised at "how very cheaply" they had been able to accomplish the mission.[xvi] Congressional oversight responsibility was exercised predominantly as "advocacy oversight." Former Congressman Robert F. Ellsworth reflected on the conciliatory atmosphere that prevailed between Congress and the IC:

> When you think back to the old days, it was a different world and a different perception of us and our role in the world. The political zeitgeist of the time was the CIA was wonderful. In politics, anybody who wanted to make trouble for the CIA was seen to be a screwball and not to be countenanced.[xvii]

Change is not inevitable within the Intelligence Community. At best, however, change within the Community has been marginal. By the mid 1970s, congressional oversight had evolved to be one of public interest—if the public is interested *loudly enough*, Congress will investigate. For example, the creation of the two Congressional oversight committees—Senate Select Committee for Intelligence (SSCI) in 1975 and the House Permanent Select Committee for Intelligence (HPSCI) in 1977—was not a major intelligence reform initiative although initially each was heralded to be just that. These committees were established as a result of the Pike and Church Committees investigating "illegal, improper or unethical activities" by any agency of the federal government.[xviii] These investigations began in the aftermath of the Vietnam War, Watergate and the resignation of President Nixon. Congress regulates through two actions—the power of the purse and the power to investigate. Legislative initiatives from these two oversight committees was merely a logical extension of their responsibility. From the period 1947-1974, oversight by Congress in essence involved only a "keep in touch" relationship with the executive branch, rather than vigorous monitoring.

[xvi] Frank J. Smist, Jr., *Congress Oversees the United States Intelligence Community*, 2nd ed. (Knoxville: The University of Tennessee Press, 1994), 5.

[xvii] Smist, 5.

[xviii] The U.S. Senate appointed a select investigative committee under the leadership of Senator Frank Church on 27 January 1975. The House created a select investigative committee under the chairmanship of Representative Lucien Nedzi on 19 February 1975 but this committee never coalesced and a second committee under the chairmanship of Representative Otis Pike convened on 17 July 1995.

The Intelligence Community quite often becomes the lightning rod for "perceived intelligence failures." Often, this criticism is thoughtful and well deserved. Lack of substantive reform within the Community is legendary. Steadfast parochialism, inflexible corporate culture, and stonewalling[xix] are often cited as barriers to change. George Tenet, former Director of Central Intelligence (DCI) and head of the CIA, when called before the National Commission on Terrorist Attacks Upon the United States, stated "...if I failed or made a mistake, I've been evolutionary in terms of [managing] the community. Maybe I should have been more revolutionary."[xx]

However, not all impediments to change belong incestuously to the Intelligence Community: Partisan politics, an inflexible fiscal apparatus, ambiguous national security policy, rivalries among and between the military services and influential lobbying groups are but a few of the many reasons why effective intelligence reform has not occurred in over six decades. Additionally, quite frequently in cases of intelligence failure, according to Richard Betts, "the most crucial mistakes have seldom been made by collectors of raw information, occasionally by professionals who produce finished analyses, but most often by the decision makers who consume the products of information...intelligence failure is political and psychological more often than organizational."[xxi] For significant change to occur it will require a coordinated vision/partnership involving the Executive Branch, Congress, the Intelligence Community and the American free press to serve as the guardian of public trust. Without the involvement of all, change will remain marginal.

[xix] *Webster's II New College Dictionary,* 2001, page 1086, defines "stonewalling" as 2a. To engage in delaying tactics: STALL <"*Stonewalling* for time to close the missile gap" –James Reston> b. To refuse to answer or cooperate <"I want you to *stonewall* it, let them plead the Fifth Amendment..." –Richard M. Nixon>.

[xx] George Tenet, "Transcript: 9/11 Commission Hearing on Intelligence," *Washington Post,* online ed., 14 April 2004, URL: http://www.washingtonpost.com/ac2/wp-dyn/A11115-2004Apr14?>, accessed 15 April 2004.

[xxi] Richard K. Betts, "Analysis, War and Decision: Why Intelligence Failures Are Inevitable," in *Intelligence and Military Misfortunes,* chap.11 of *Strategic Intelligence: Theory and Application,* 2d rev ed., eds. Douglas H. Dearth and R. Thomas Goodden (Carlisle Barracks: United States Army War College Center for Strategic Leadership, 1995), 295. Originally published in *World Politics* 31, No. 1 (October 1978): 61-89.

Nonetheless, since the end of the Cold War and the Community's subsequent loss of focus and clarity with the demise of the Soviet problem,[xxii] the Community, according to Gregory Treverton, "appears to be drifting, unsure of what it does and for whom. It remains mired in institutions, processes and habits of mind that may have been appropriate to the Cold War but manifestly are not now."[xxiii] Our 21st Century intelligence organizations need to be as flexible and astute as our 21st Century adversaries are because the United States does not have an institutional alternative to the Intelligence Community. As Jordan and others remind us, "Intelligence is an inherent function, whether performed ill or well, of every state; the governing authority must provide itself with intelligence in order to be effective and to protect itself.[xxiv]

Within these pages, the author explains why the Intelligence Community was not set up, nor has it evolved, to assess the rapidly globalizing world. Nonetheless, she contends that the Community must change to reflect the current national security environment. Acting CIA Director and former Deputy CIA Director John E. McLaughlin, recalling that he has lived through several national debates about the future of intelligence, remarked, "National initiatives to change intelligence tend to be a mix of pain and gain, but there appears to be an appetite for it again, in both parties and among key segments of the public."[xxv] History, however, favors the status quo.

Alice, dear, your longest walk is still to come!

[xxii]Robert Gates indicated it was a myth that the Intelligence Community was "totally dominated by the Soviet problem" during a Georgetown colloquium hosted by John H. Hedley in late 1994 and early 1995. Gates also thought the community had been unfairly criticized for failing to adjust its priorities since the end of the Cold War; he felt the IC had made a continuing effort to do so. For more detail, review John H. Hedley, *A Colloquium: The Intelligence Community: Is It Broken? How to Fix It?* URL: http://www.cia.ic.gov/dci/csi/studies/ 96unclass/hedley.htm.

[xxiii]Gregory F. Treverton, *Reshaping National Intelligence in an Age of Information* (Cambridge: Cambridge University Press, 2001), 1.

[xxiv]Amos A. Jordan and others, *American National Security*, 5th ed. (Baltimore: The Johns Hopkins University Press, 1999), 144.

[xxv]Walter Pincus, "McLaughlin Defends CIA, Cites Reform in Speech: Deputy Director Rejects Idea of Intelligence Czar," *The Washington Post*, 7 July 2004, A21.

Chapter One

INTRODUCTION

> If 9/11 was not an event sufficient to jolt the status quo, what is it going to take? How can he [President Bush] have great confidence in our intelligence community after it has proven confused before September 11 and completely wrong on the threat posed by Iraq?
>
> **—Senator Robert Graham (D-FL)**
> *Former Chairman of the Senate Select Committee on Intelligence*

The events of 11 September 2001 visited against the American homeland exposed the raw vulnerability of the United States. The very organization—the Central Intelligence Agency (CIA)—created by the National Security Act of 1947 to prevent "another strategic surprise attack"[1] stands accused of failing to do just that.

Subsequently, after the March 2003 U.S. invasion of Iraq, the Senate Select Committee on Intelligence (SSCI) began a formal review of U.S. intelligence estimates concerning Iraq's WMD programs, the presumed existence of which had been the pretext for the invasion. David Kay was tapped by DCI George Tenet to head a 1,400-strong WMD search party, known as the Iraq Survey Group (ISG). "I'm confident, he said, "that we will reach the goal of understanding Iraq's weapons of mass destruction program, including where weapons are, where weapons may have been removed and the exact status of that program at the time the war commenced."[2]

However, seven months later, Kay admitted "Let me begin by saying, we were almost all wrong. It is highly unlikely that there were large stockpiles of deployed, militarized, chemical and biological weapons there."[3] The Senate Select Committee completed its investigation and concluded that flawed intelligence had led to the presumed WMD. Senator Pat Roberts, co-chair of the committee, declared "This

---

[1] The Japanese attack on Pearl Harbor became the raison d'etre for establishment of the U.S. Intelligence Community—prevent the recurrence of strategic surprise.

[2] Michael Duffy, "So Much for The WMD," *Time*, 9 February 2004, 42.

[3] Duffy, 42-46.

was a global intelligence failure."[4] Once again, the Intelligence Community and specifically the CIA, was caught in this latest maelstrom.

"The Intelligence Community will never bat 1.000; it can't get there," declared Representative Porter Goss (R-FL), former Chairman of the House Intelligence Committee and former CIA employee. "We've been watching too many James Bond movies, to think it always comes out all right in the end. It doesn't."[5] Indeed, according to Mark M. Lowenthal, "intelligence is not about truth....Truth is such an absolute term that it sets a standard intelligence rarely would be able to achieve. It is better—and more accurate—to think of intelligence as 'proximate reality.'"[6]

While recognizing that the nature of intelligence makes it an imperfect science at best, it is reasonable to expect a high level of efficacy after fifty plus years of refining tradecraft. Acting DCI[7] and former Deputy DCI John E. McLaughlin sought to pre-empt criticism of the failings of the Intelligence Community's performance before the 11 September 2001 attacks and the U.S.-led invasion of Iraq in 2003 when he declared:

> What shortcomings there were—and there were shortcomings—were the result of specific discrete problems that we understand and are well on our way to addressing or have already addressed...Experiences and impressions that are just a few years old [referring to the period since 11 September 2001] may be seriously out of date. There has been a real revolution in intelligence—from recruiting and technology to interagency cooperation and morale.[8]

The present author contends that the decades of failing to institute effective intelligence reform has seriously crippled the Intelligence Community's ability to tackle aggressively the challenges of the 21st Century. Unless reform initiatives address the fundamental structural problems that have plagued the Community since its inception, change will not be revolutionary, as McLaughlin suggests, but rather marginal at best. Lee H. Hamilton, Vice-Chair of the

---

[4] Sen Pat Roberts (R-KS), "Perspectives," *Newsweek*, 19 July 2004, 19.

[5] Sen Porter Goss (R-FL), "An Inquiry That's Awash in Disputes at the Outset," Interview by Douglas Jehl in *New York Times* online ed., 2 February 2004, URL *www.nytimes.com/2004/02/02/international/middleeast/02ASSE.htm*, accessed 2 February 2004.

[6] Mark M. Lowenthal, *Intelligence: From Secrets to Policy* (Washington, D.C.: CQ Press, 2003), 6. Cited hereafter as *From Secrets to Policy*.

[7] DCI George Tenet resigned on 11 July 2004 and John E. McLaughlin, the former Deputy DCI became Acting DCI on that date.

[8] Walter Pincus, "McLaughlin Defends CIA, Cites Reform in Speech: Deputy Director Rejects Idea of Intelligence Czar," *Washington Post*, 1 July 2004, A21.

National Commission on Terrorist Attacks upon the United States, commonly known as the 9/11 Commission, in a spirited response to the question, Who's in charge now? [in charge of intelligence], replied "…you can't argue that the DCI is in charge!"[9]

The world of intelligence has been upended by both politics and technology.[10] Given the problem sets of the Cold War—nation-states aligned with either the United States or the Soviet Union—it followed that collection against these adversaries would be static, deliberate, and regimented. Moreover, because information was not readily available and sources limited, the business of the Cold War was secrets. Whereas the intelligence world of the Cold War could be considered a world of small quantities of information regarded as reliable—spy reports and satellite photos; the intelligence world of tomorrow is the Web—enormous amounts of often unreliable information.[11]

Even our national technical means, a euphemism for satellite collection systems, now yield data vastly exceeding our processing and analytical abilities to extract timely and "actionable" intelligence. As an example, while "NSA had no SIGINT [signals intelligence] suggesting that al-Qai'da was specifically targeting New York and Washington, D.C., or even that it was planning an attack on U.S. soil," according to LtGen Michael V. Hayden, Director NSA, "NSA did obtain two pieces of information suggesting that individuals with terrorist connections believed that something significant would happen on September 11th." Unfortunately, "Because of the processing involved," stated Hayden, "we [NSA] were unable to report the information until September 12th."[12] As Odom proclaims, "The communications revolution alone provides grounds for suspecting that major structural reforms in the IC are long overdue."[13]

Finally, whereas the grand strategy of containment provided a successful, narrow definition of the relationship between two Superpowers and all others for nearly fifty years, now, almost fifteen years since the end of the Cold War, no such shorthand adequately captures the relationship between the United States and Others. "We had won the Cold War, but there would be no

---

[9] Lee H. Hamilton in Government Affairs Committee Hearing, *C-SPAN*, airdate 30 July 2004.

[10] Gregory F. Treverton, *Reshaping Intelligence in an Age of Information* (Cambridge: Cambridge University Press, 2001), 6.

[11] Treverton, 34.

[12] LtGen Michael Hayden, Director, National Security Agency, "Testimony before the Joint Inquiry of the Senate Select Committee on Intelligence and the House Permanent Select Committee, 17 October 2002." URL: http://www.fas.org/irp/congress/2002_hr/ 101702hayden.html.

[13] William E. Odom, *Fixing Intelligence for a More Secure America* (New Haven, CT: Yale University Press, 2003), 4.

parade,[14] reflected former DCI Robert Gates. In the words of former DCI James Woolsey, "We have slain the bear, but there are still a lot of serpents around."[15] There was to be no "peace dividend." Issues such as terrorism, globalism, weapons proliferation, pandemics, environmentalism, WMD, international narcotics trafficking and organized crime, the growth of multinational organizations and the emerging prominence of non-governmental organizations (NGOs) have become the escalating global intelligence threats and nascent challenges of the 21st century. Some Cold War threats to national security from such adversaries as North Korea, Iran, and China remain; however, these have been overshadowed by the transnational threats.

The Issue

This study addresses the future of the Intelligence Community in light of 21st century issues/challenges/threats. In addressing this issue, the author reviews many of the chief intelligence reform proposals or legislative activities during the early years of the U.S. intelligence service and throughout the Cold-War era, to include the turbulent mid-1970s, on into the 1990s, and concludes with a review of the recommendations from the Joint Inquiry Report and the 9/11 Commission Report leading to the Intelligence Reform and Terrorism Prevention Act of 2004. At issue is whether these ongoing schemes for reform, including the new legislation, are sufficient for the effective operation of the Community in a globalized environment.

Methodology and Limitations

The methodology used in this study is principally historical analysis and review of primary and secondary source documents interpreted through the lens of the author, who has over two decades of experience in the Intelligence Community, as a tactical and strategic Army signals intelligent (SIGINT) officer, DOD contractor, and federal government systems engineer. The analysis is informed by interviews with select military and civilian professionals, academics, and other professionals. The author also attended numerous symposiums and briefings during fiscal year 2004 to gain additional perspectives from a variety of academic and intelligence professionals.

This research was limited by several factors. Predominantly, this study was limited by the realization that the voluminous amount of primary sources avail-

---

[14]Robert M. Gates, From the Shadows: The Ultimate Insider's Story of Five Presidents and How They Won the Cold War (New York: Simon and Schuster, 1996), 552.

[15] John H. Hedley, "A Colloquium The Intelligence Community: Is It Broken? How to Fix It?" *Studies in Intelligence* 39, no. 5 (1994): 12.

able on the subjects of intelligence reform and globalization were beyond the abilities of this author to gather and absorb in their entirety within the period allotted. Instead, this author distilled the published perceptions of established luminaries within their respective fields as well as intelligence-related congressional testimony and investigatory panel recommendations.

Furthermore, although the author attended many outstanding seminars hosted by such prominent agencies as NSA, The Heritage Foundation, National Military Intelligence Association (NMIA), Armed Forces Communications and Electronics Association (AFCEA) and DIA, most of these presentations were not-for-attribution. This condition facilitated forthright and at times, lively discussions of the subject matter, which are reflected in the author's presentation; however, she could not make reference to specific, illuminating comments. Additionally, many of the presentations were caveated with a special information handling instruction, "For Official Use Only" which prohibits their inclusion *verbatim*.

Understandably, U.S. government intelligence is inherently linked to policy. In the words of Sherman Kent, "Certainly intelligence must not be the apologist for policy, but this does not mean that intelligence has no role in policy formulation."[16] However, in this study the author did not scrutinize the complexities of American domestic and foreign policy; this task is better left to the policymakers themselves, to the political scientists, and to the armchair diplomats who are given interpretive allowances not accorded a U.S. government employee expressing herself in a written record.

Significance of Research

The author's intent is that this study further stimulate debate on the future of the Intelligence Community and its primacy in assessing current and future threats to our national security. In September 2003, the Center for the Study of Intelligence (CSI) sponsored a conference with 85 experts to discuss the implications for this new world [post 9/11]. Following are two selected, anonymous comments on restructuring the Community, which were recorded in the conference report:

> Whatever management philosophy you may think is good, you wouldn't come up with the Intelligence Community the way it is. Almost any change, even random change, would probably improve it.[17]

---

[16] Sherman Kent, *Strategic Intelligence for American World Policy* (Princeton: Princeton University Press, 1949), 201.

If we assume a rate of change in national security affairs over the next 10 years at least equal to what we've seen in the previous 10 years, we had better be prepared to make radical changes in the way we do intelligence.[18]

If the Community is unwilling to make visible changes that are recognizable and understandable to the "talking heads" and more importantly to the American public, then a wake-up notice will come from outside the Community—through executive order or congressional legislation. This study presents an argument for rational, professionally based, but overdue intelligence reform.

[17] Central Intelligence Agency, *Intelligence for a New Era in American Foreign Policy*, presented in Center for the Study of Intelligence Conference Report, January 2004, 15. Cited hereafter as *Intelligence for a New Era*.

[18] *Intelligence for a New Era*, 15.

Chapter Two

FUNDAMENTAL CONCEPTS

> The necessity of procuring good intelligence is apparent and need not
> be further urged--all that remains for me to add, is that you keep the
> whole matter as secret as possible. For upon Secrecy, Success depends
> in most enterprises of the kind, and for want of it, they are generally
> defeated, however well planned and promising a favorable issue.
>
> **—George Washington to Colonel Elias Dayton**
> *26 July 1777*

What is Intelligence?

Intelligence holds distinct meanings for different people. To the typical American, it conjures up "cloak and dagger activities" in a distant land or "Big Brother activities" within our borders. To a military commander it is knowledge of the enemy over the horizon. To the analyst, it is information awaiting clarification. To the policymaker, it is information that meets stated or understood needs. To the resource manager, it is the respective components that carry out all the above functions. Intelligence is all those things sheltered under the umbrella of national security—defense and foreign policy and certain aspects of internal security. In the words of Sherman Kent, former Chairman of CIA's Office of National Estimates:

> Intelligence means knowledge...it means an amazing bulk and assortment of knowledge...the kind of knowledge our state must possess regarding other states in order to assure itself that its cause will not suffer nor its undertakings fail because its statesmen and soldiers plan and act in ignorance.[19]

Kent asserted that intelligence can be thought of as a process, a product as well as an organization. Mark M. Lowenthal, a prominent intelligence scholar, offers this formulation:

---

[19] Sherman Kent, *Strategic Intelligence for American World Policy* (Princeton: Princeton University Press, 1949), 3.

7

Intelligence is the process by which specific types of information important to national security are requested, collected, analyzed, and provided to policymakers; the products of that process; the safeguarding of these processes and this information by counterintelligence activities; and the carrying out of operations as requested by lawful authorities.[20]

Generally, intelligence has been placed into two categories—tactical and strategic. This delineation was driven primarily by the principal consumer—military commanders or policymakers. Operational (tactical) intelligence is knowledge about the immediate situation and is based almost entirely on straightforward observation. Strategic intelligence has a wider base and broader objective, integrating economics, politics, social studies, and the study of technology.[21] Strategic intelligence provides policymakers with the "big picture" whereas tactical intelligence provides the "front yard" view. The main difference between strategic and tactical warning is the time horizon. According to Charles "Charlie" E. Allen, Assistant Director of Central Intelligence (ADCI) for Collection, the cynic would say that strategic warning is far enough away that we don't have to worry about it, and that tactical warning means we don't have time to do anything about it because it's too late. [22]

Intelligence differs from information in that information is anything that can be known, regardless of how it may be discovered. Intelligence, on the other hand, is a subset of information; it responds to specific policy requirements and exists as a capability for policymakers. Any other activity is either wasteful or illegal. "All intelligence is information; not all information is intelligence,"[23] Lowenthal states. Intelligence is distilled knowledge created by people.[24]

Regardless of its definition, while the best information cannot guarantee sound policy in a complex and dangerous world, policy made without intelligence collusion, or at least with too little of it, can succeed only by accident.[25] If intelligence does not change prevailing mindsets, what good is it?[26]

---

[20] *From Secrets to Policy,* 8.

[21] Bruce D. Berkowitz and Allan E. Goodman, *Strategic Intelligence for American Security* (Princeton: Princeton University Press, 1989), 4.

[22] Charles E. Allen, "Intelligence: Cult, Craft, or Business?", briefing presented at Center for Information Policy Research, Harvard University, Guest Presentations ,Spring 2000, Incidental Paper: Seminar on Intelligence, Command and Control, July 2001, URL: *http://pirp.harvard.edu/pubs_pdf/allen/allen-i01.pdf,* accessed 1 April 2004.

[23] Lowenthal, From Secrets to Policy, 2.

[24] Jordan and others, *American National Security,* 5th ed. (Baltimore: The Johns Hopkins University Press, 1999), 143.

[25] Jordan and others, 144.

[26] Treverton, 5.

What is Intelligence Reform?

Throughout the years, intelligence reform has become a catch-all phrase for any "change" proposed to the Intelligence Community. Efforts to tweak the community have been proposed regardless of which political party is in the White House, which party has the majority in Congress or who sits as the Director of Central Intelligence. Proposals generally have fallen into three broad chronological categories of proposals:

- To improve the efficiency of the Intelligence Community in the context of the Cold War
- In response to specific intelligence failures or improprieties
- Post-Cold War efforts to refocus Intelligence Community requirements and structures.[27]

During the mid-1970s, intelligence reform initiatives were proposed and in most instances enacted to correct abuses. For example, concerned with the allegations of CIA involvement in Chilean presidential elections, Congress in 1974 passed the Hughes-Ryan Amendment, which required that the president, prior to the expenditure of CIA funds for noncollection activities in foreign countries, had to issue a "finding" that declared the activity in question to be "important to the national security" of the United States. This finding was to be reported to the House Foreign Affairs and Senate Foreign Relations committees.[28] An interesting note: The passage of this amendment and its replacement, the Intelligence Oversight Act of 1980, has not hampered CIA operations. There has not been reported any instance of a CIA operation not being conducted for lack of a presidential finding. However, a former House Intelligence Committee staffer indicated that, in view of this requirement, some operations have been modified.

R.T. Gooden traces three epochs of the modern United States Intelligence Community beginning with the creation of the CIA. He notes that each of these periods, 1947-1976, 1977-1986, and 1987-1995, has ended with fundamental change imposed by Congress. For example, during the first so-called epoch as a result of the Church and Pike Commissions, two Congressional oversight committees were created. His conclusion is that the existence of a related, underlying crisis between the executive and the Congress can be modeled. His model consists of the following criteria for crisis. First, there is a latent Congressional dissatisfaction with IC performance. Second, there is a triggering event of sufficient

---

[27] CRS Report, Appendix C, February 1996, cited in Mark M. Lowenthal, *Intelligence: From Secrets to Policy* (Washington, D.C.: CQ Press, 2003), 223-224.

[28] Mark M. Lowenthal, *U.S. Intelligence* (New York: Praeger, 1984), quoted in Amos A. Jordan and others, *American National Security,* 5th ed. (Baltimore: The Johns Hopkins University Press), 157.

magnitude to spark public interest. Third, there must be an egregious lack of candor on the part of the executive so that a perceived "cover-up" inflames the public. Fourth, the President should be of the opposite party with respect to the majority in Congress.[29]

It could be argued that if any event was a catalyst for significant change, it was what occurred on 11 September 2001. The 9/11 actions spurred congressional and public outcry, thereby instigating two major congressionally mandated investigations. Furthermore, the allegation that Iraq possessed weapons of mass destruction (WMD) became the premise for a U.S. preemptive offensive attack on that nation. However, this premise was based on faulty, distorted intelligence estimates. Weapons inspectors as well as a congressional investigation concluded that Iraq did not possess WMD. These examples satisfy the first three criteria of Goodden's model. However, the current president, George W. Bush, is a Republican elected for a second term with a Republican-controlled Congress. If Goodden's model is correct, there will not be fundamental change imposed by Congress. However, the acrimonious debates that raged over the passage of an intelligence reform bill between the Senate and the House, as well as between many members of the same chambers in the fall of 2004, underscores the validity of Goodden's fourth criterion. Although an intelligence reform bill, the Intelligence Reform and Terrorist Prevention Act of 2004, was passed in the waning days of the 108th Congress, as of this writing it had not been fully implemented. While some lawmakers hailed this Act's passage as the rightful measure needed to prevent another terrorist attack against the United States, others such as Republican Representative Dana Rohrabacher, (R-CA) thought otherwise. "It's an illusion of legislation," stated Rohrabacher. "It is trying to make people feel better because they think something is being done. It will be duplicative and an impediment to getting things done in the Intelligence Community."[30]

What is Intelligence Oversight?

The term oversight has two distinct but related definitions. The first: an unintentional omission or mistake that implies neglectfulness. Within the Intelligence Community, this definition conveys the sense of analytical failure. As an example, the failure of the community to detect India's resumed nuclear testing in May 1998 is an oversight. "We did not get it right. Period,"[31] George Tenet revealed.

---

[29] R. T. Goodden, "Legislative Control of Intelligence", in *Intelligence and the Law*, 2ed., chp.7 of *Strategic Intelligence: Theory and Application*, eds. Douglas H. Dearth and R. Thomas Goodden (Carlisle Barracks: United States Army War College Center for Strategic Leadership, 1995), 169.

[30] Martin Kady II and John Donnelly, "Many Decisions Ahead After Intelligence Bill Clears," CQ TODAY, 7 December 2004.

Failures in strategic intelligence are usually more a matter of simple error or misfeasance, not malfeasance. Nonetheless, the categorization of an intelligence failure as an oversight does not provide repudiation of responsibility nor absolution. The second definition: watchful care or management or supervision, which implies a custodial relationship. The ensuing discussion centers on the custodial definition of intelligence oversight.

The U.S. Constitution was written to separate the executive, legislative, and judicial powers and it provides a series of checks and balances. The resultant tension is often referred to as "the invitation to struggle." The Founding Fathers sought to give each of the branches "the necessary means and personal motives to resist encroachments of the others."[32] One of the most significant tasks assigned to Congress is the responsibility to oversee the activities of the executive branch. The concept of congressional oversight is established by Article 1, Section 8, paragraph 18, United States Constitution which states: "Congress shall have Power…To make all Laws which shall be necessary and proper for carrying into Execution the foregoing Powers, and all other Powers vested by this Constitution in the Government of the United States, or in any Department or Officer thereof."[33]

Accordingly, there are three questions which should be addressed in discharging this responsibility. First, Is the executive branch obeying the law and conducting activities in accord with the mandate provided by the United States Constitution and legislation passed by Congress? Second, Are there any abuses that have arisen or any deficiencies that have been uncovered that need to be corrected? Third, in light of time and events, How can the performance of a function of government deemed essential and entrusted to the executive branch be improved and strengthened?[34]

Despite this longstanding responsibility enshrined in the constitution, intelligence oversight is relatively new in Congress. The executive branch dominated intelligence policy from the passage of the National Security Act of 1947 until 1974. Although Congress could have played a much stronger role in oversight during this period, it chose to exercise its oversight responsibilities predominantly through its appropriation authority. Congress elected to delegate its oversight

---

[31]Treverton, 1.

[32] *The Federalist* (Indianapolis: Modern Library, 1937), 337, quoted in Frank J. Smist, Jr., *Congress Oversees the United States Intelligence Community,* 2nd ed. (Knoxville, The University of Tennessee Press, 1994), 1.

[33]Lowenthal, *From Secrets to Policy,* 156.

[34] Frank J. Smist, Jr., *Congress Oversees the United States Intelligence Community,* 2nd ed. (Knoxville, The University of Tennessee Press, 1994), 12.

responsibilities to executive-branch leadership during this period. This lackadaisical approach to oversight reflects the thinking of those like Senator Leverett Saltonstall, (R-MA), a member of the Senate Armed Services Committee, who notes that "There are things that my government does that I would rather not know about."[35] A former CIA legislative counsel during this time observed that "We allowed Congress to set the pace. We briefed in whatever detail they wanted. But one of the problems was you couldn't get Congress to get interested."[36]

Congress vigorously reasserted itself in the mid-1970s, amid an upwelling of government mistrust and allegations of incompetence. This was the tumultuous period of executive branch improprieties—Watergate break-in, aftermath of Vietnam, domestic spying on Vietnam anti-war protestors and other dissident groups, and CIA involvement in foreign presidential elections and indirect human rights abuses to mention a few. During this time the Church and Pike Committees were formed to look into the abuses. A consequence of this oversight action was the creation of the Senate Select Committee for Intelligence in 1976 and of the House Permanent Select Committee for Intelligence in 1977. The formation of these committees was unique: In the history of Congress there had never before been a permanent select committee.[37]

Congress discharges its oversight responsibility through a variety of congressional measures, the first and foremost being control over the entire federal budget. Article I, section 9, paragraph 7 of the constitution explicitly states: No money shall be drawn from the Treasury, but in consequence of appropriations made by law; and a regular statement and account of the receipts and expenditures of all public money shall be published from time to time."[38]Other measures include congressional hearings, senate confirmations, treaty ratifications, levying executive branch reporting requirements, congressional investigations and reports, hostage taking,[39] and requiring prior notice of covert action.[40]

The executive branch, on the other hand, discharges its oversight responsibility via the National Security Council (NSC) Office of Intelligence Programs, which is the highest-level organization within the executive branch that provides day-to-

---

[35] Lowenthal, *From Secrets to Policy*, 161.

[36] Smist, 5.

[37] Smist, 11.

[38]Lowenthal, *From Secrets to Policy*, 156.

[39] Taking hostages refers to Congress withholding action on issues that are important to the executive branch. According to Mark M. Lowenthal, critics argue that hostage taking is a blunt and unwieldy tool; supporters of Congress argue it is used only when other means of reaching agreement with the executive have failed.

[40] Lowenthal, *From Secrets to Policy*, 156-161.

day oversight and policy direction of intelligence. The President also relies on the President's Foreign Intelligence Advisory Board (PFIAB) to carry out oversight actions.[41]

What is Globalization?

Globalization is *the* emotionally charged expression of the 21st Century. Often, its mere mention invokes images of its encompassing an often-brutish nature: Americanization of culture, loss of national identity, sweatshops, outsourcing, and at the extreme, the prostitution of young children and women. However, flash forward to another image and globalization means worldwide accessibility, transparency, and cooperation, presenting the opportunity for economic growth and the reduction of poverty. "The term [globalization] all at once provides an allegedly objective diagnosis of world conditions; encapsulates a doctrinal preference; precipitates a counter-creed (or antithesis) that rejects that preference; and generates a pointed political-cultural critique designed to alter the existing global power hierarchy,"[42] according to Zbigniew Brezinski.

Three definitions of globalization expounded below illustrate different professional perspectives.

> Every generation, at least in the 20th century, has some kind of symbolic ideology that gives them a map of the world. For 50-odd years up to 1990, the Cold War gave you the map of the world and impacted upon virtually everything. The word that gives us the map of the world after 1990 is the concept of globalisation [sic]…the term refers to the integration of the economy at a global level and involves two main features. Most trades take place among multinational corporations [that] are an enormous part of the economic activity of the world. The second feature is that where the world economy used to be dominated by physical commodities and goods, now the major activity taking place in the global economy is the flow of money in the form of derivatives, foreign investments and the like.[43]

—Dr. Ian Linden

School of Oriental and African Studies at the University of London

---

[41] Lowenthal, *From Secrets to Policy*, 154.

[42] Zbigniew Brezinski, *Choice: Global Domination or Global Leadership* (New York: Basic Books, 2004), 140.

[43] Ian Linden, "What is Globalisation?" *Geographical*, October 2003, 44.

Globalization has one overarching feature—integration. Globalization: it is the inexorable integration of markets, nation-states, and technologies to a degree never witnessed before—in a way that is enabling individuals, corporations and nation-states to reach around the world farther, faster, deeper, cheaper than ever before, and in a way that is enabling the world to reach into individuals, corporations and nation-states farther, faster, deeper, cheaper than before. This process of globalization is also producing a powerful backlash from those brutalized or left behind by the new system.[44]

—Thomas Friedman
New York Times columnist

Globalization is a dynamic process of the economic integration of virtually the entire world. At least four aspects of this increased economic integration are worth bearing in mind...first, increased international trade...second, increased interpenetration of markets by capital flows...third, globalization of economic products...and fourth, increasing institutional harmonization of economic policies, legislation, and structure.[45]

—Jeffrey D. Sachs
Director of the Center for International Development at Harvard University

In its simplest forms, globalization is defined by two complementary terms. As a phenomenon, *globalization* is defined as a substantial "expansion of cross-border networks and flows."[46] Undoubtedly, this definition is the one that is most familiar—the borderless flow of goods and monies made possible by a vast array of technological advancements. Processes flow throughout the world without regard to the physical boundaries of the nation-states. Geographical location, for the most part, has become irrelevant. Globalization is a long-term process leading to *globality*—a more interconnected world system in which interdependent networks and flows surmount traditional boundaries (or make them irrelevant).[47]

---

[44] Thomas L. Friedman, *The Lexus and the Olive Tree* (New York: Farrar, Straus and Gioux, 1999), 8.

[45] Jeffrey D. Sachs, *The Geography of Economic Development* (Newport: National War College, 2000), URL:< *http://www.nwc.navy.mil/press/review/2000/autumn/art6%2Da00.htm*>, accessed 29 June 2003.

[46] Ellen L. Frost, "Globalization and National Security: A Strategic Agenda," in *The Global Century: Globalization and National Security,* ed. Richard Kugler and Ellen L. Frost (Washington, DC: National Defense University Press, 2000), 37,

[47] Frost, 37.

Numerous indices rank countries according to specific variables, thus measuring "globalization." Two of these indices, the A.T. Kearny/Foreign Policy Globalization Index and the Index of Economic Freedom, published by the Heritage Foundation and *The Wall Street Journal,* as well as two scholarly characterizations of the globalized world, one by Jeffrey D. Sachs and one by Thomas P.M. Barnett, will be discussed in subsequent chapters. Not surprisingly, these studies reflect certain common threads—while globalization is not necessarily a zero-sum game, the consummate winners are those nations that have participatory government, advanced technology, and the highest level of economic freedom; that is, healthy capital flows, foreign investment, strong records of equality, and the like. These are just a few of the characteristics that facilitate successful integration or globalization.

Systemic globalization reigns as the dominant element of the current security environment. Globalization can be seen as the defining aspect of the current post-post-Cold War international system, and therefore an appropriate title for the system itself.[48] Logically, any discussion of a grand strategy for the United States, and for the Intelligence Community's role in its formulation, must include globalization.

---

[48] Sam J. Tangredi, "Introduction," in *Globalization and Maritime Power,* ed. Sam J. Tangredi (Washington, D.C.: National Defense University Press, 2002), xxv.

Chapter Three

PAST: HISTORICAL PERSPECTIVE: SHAPERS OF THE INTELLIGENCE COMMUNITY DURING THE COLD WAR (1945–1989)

> We have two great lessons from World War II. One was we could never again be without a permanent operating intelligence agency. The different branches of government received volumes of information that would come in daily. No central location was there where all the information could be centered, collated, and studied. If we had such an operation, we could have very well had a naval base prepared at Pearl Harbor. The information was never centralized and studied. Second was that we could never go through another war with the Navy Department and the War Department as separate operations in competition with one another. If the army or navy had given as much time to defeating the enemy as they gave to fighting each other, the war could have ended a good deal sooner.
>
> **—President Harry S. Truman to Clark Clifford**

National Security Act of 1947

The end of World War II saw the U.S. emerge as the most powerful nation on earth. Its homeland was untouched by war, and its enormous industrial potential had produced wartime machinery not only for its own armies and navies but for those of its allies as well. The collapse of Germany and Japan meant total victory. Technologically, the country was in an unchallenged position. American development of the atomic bomb was probably the most important single event to affect postwar international relations.[49] The nation's economic strength was unfathomable for the other countries emerging from a protracted war. As an example, in 1945 the United States possessed two-thirds of the world's gold reserve, and its gross national product (GNP) had

---

[49] Amos A. Jordan and others, *American National Security,* 5th ed. (Baltimore: The Johns Hopkins University Press, 1999), 66.

increased by more than half since 1939 in a period when all other industrial economies were in ruins.[50]

In the mid 1940s, in recognition of its acquired global position and the accompanying challenges, the United States began to reorganize many aspects of its government. As Clark Clifford[51] noted, "It was not accident that government reorganization coincided with the development of the Truman Doctrine, the Marshall Plan, NATO, Point Four, and the policy of containment: these policies required new machinery."[52]

Discussions concerning the role of centralized U.S. intelligence in peacetime— while not the center of the debate, as was the military unification issue— did engage prominent, post-World War II government and military leaders:

> [W]e need to adjust our intelligence system to the broad basic factors which move and control people and nations, and to conceive it on a global basis. Our intelligence needs to interpret these factors, aware of but not confused by their outward manifestations in governments.[53]

> —Harold Smith
> *Director, Bureau of the Budget 18 May 1944*

> [W]e should know as much as we possibly can of the possible intent and capacity of any other country in the world....Prior to entering the war we had little more than what a military attache could learn at dinner, more or less over coffee cups....Today I think we see clearly we must know what the other fellow is planning to do, in our defense....The important point is that the necessity applies equally outside the armed forces. It includes the State Department and other functions of Government and it should therefore be correlated on that level.[54]

---

[50]David Jablonsky, *Paradigm Lost? Transitions and the Search for a New World Order* (Westport, CT: Praeger, 1995), 22.

[51] Clark Clifford was a lawyer during Truman's administration who came to Washington initially to work in the White House Map Room (President Roosevelt's wartime operations center). He helped draft the legislation that became the National Security Act of 1947.

[52] David F. Rudgers, *Creating the Secret State: The Origins of the Central Intelligence Agency, 1943-1947* (Lawrence: University Press of Kansas, 2000), 1.

[53] U.S. House of Representatives, Select Committee on Post-war Military Policy, *Proposal to Establish a Single Department of Armed Forces: Hearings...*, 78th Cong., 3d sess. (Washington, D.C.: USGPO, 1944), 303-304 (citation as noted in Rudgers, 94).

[54] U.S. Senate, Committee on Military Affairs, *Department of the Armed Forces, Department of Military Security: Hearings...*, 79th Cong., 1st sess. (Washington, D.C.: USGPO, 1945), 61 (citation as noted in Rudgers 95).

Detailed moment-by-moment knowledge of all aspects of civilian and military activity within the territory of an enemy is essential to sound planning in times of peace or war…There is a great need for a permanent national organization which not only deals with broad questions of policy but also collects, evaluates and disseminates a continuous stream of intelligence data.[55]

In our government today there is no permanent agency to take over the functions which OSS will have ceased to perform. These functions…are in reality essential in the effective discharge by this nation of its responsibilities in the organization and maintenance of peace.[56]

And so it was with the passage of the National Security Act of 1947--the Joint Chiefs of Staff (JCS), the National Security Council (NSC) and the Central Intelligence Agency (initially known as the Central Intelligence Group (CIG)), as well as the Department of the Air Force[57] came into being. This Act created the framework and institutional structures that dominate American national security decisionmaking today. The act popularized a term—"national security"—that was to be the province of no single agency of the United States government, and established a cabinet-level committee charged with advising the president on the "integration" of the various aspects of national security policy.[58]

While the United States remained painfully aware of the attack at Pearl Harbor and was united in its desire to prevent another strategic attack, its protectors were fer-

---

[55] General Henry Arnold, *Third Report of the Commanding General of the Army Air Forces to the Secretary of War* (n.p., 1945), 65, 67 (cited as noted in Rudgers 95).

[56] Donovan to Smith, 25 August 1945, "Strategic Services Unit as of 1 October 1945," 004.7 SSU, Office of Assistant Secretary of War, RG 107, Records of the Secretary of War, NA (citation as noted in Rudgers 42).

[57] The National Security Act of 1947 provided for many things other than just the creation of the aforementioned organizations. For more detailed information, consult *U.S. Statutes at Large 1948, 495-510.* There have been numerous amendments since 1947.

[58] Carnes Lord, "NSC Reform for the Post-Cold War Era," *Orbis,* 44, no. 3 (Summer 2000): 433.

vently divided on how best to accomplish this. Bureaucratic rivalries and turf protection among the military departments were at their zenith, thereby derailing any wide-ranging, collaborative War Department proposals. With the signing of this legislation, President Truman capped off four years of some of the most intensive and protracted public debate about the military institutions in U.S. history.[59] Truman meant to create an intelligence confederation—a small central agency that would coordinate, evaluate, and disseminate intelligence but not collect it. But this intelligence arrangement was anything but a confederation after the passage of the National Security Act of 1947. This arrangement protected all existing intelligence units [military services] by granting each exclusive control over its own sphere of activity and by creating a new, weak central coordinating body called the Central Intelligence Group. Political players, particularly the president, were far more concerned with consolidating the military services than with establishing any kind of peacetime central intelligence agency.[60] Accordingly, these agencies (NSC, JCS, CIA) were creatures of conflict and compromise. They arose from one of the most bureacractic battles in American history. Other than Truman, according to Zegart, "nobody in the executive or legislative branches sat around thinking about ideal or optimal agency organization. The War and Navy departments, the intelligence bureaucracy, and the Congress were all too busy guarding their own interests to worry about national ones."[61]

The National Security Act of 1947 created for the first time in American history a permanent American intelligence service—the CIA. Previously, from the American Revolution up to World War II, intelligence had been primarily a wartime activity. Most intelligence activities were disbanded or at least deemphasized after hostilities had ended. *Time* magazine noted in 1946 that the United States

> is going to join, after all these years, in the game of spying on the neighbors. Harry Truman did not say so, but that is the idea. Other great powers have always maintained espionage systems along with their armies and navies. The U.S., with a mixture of trust and indifference, never has…That historical innocence, which ended with the fiasco at Pearl Harbor is now gone.[62]

Samuel Tower, a New York Times reporter, wrote in August 1947:

> One of the final steps before adjournment, largely overlooked in the avalanche of last-minute legislation, was the stamp of approval Con-

---

[59] Amy B. Zegart, *Flawed by Design: The Evolution of the CIA, JCS, and NSC* (Stanford: Stanford University Press, 1999), 57.

[60] Zegart, 163-165.

[61] Zegart, 10.

[62] "Intelligence," *Time*, 4 February 1946, 24.

gress placed on the creation, for the first time in American history, of an effective world-wide American intelligence service of its own....Now, with America playing a major independent role in world affairs, this country has also embarked on the hidden game of international and national security.[63]

The responsibilities of this new intelligence organization were generally described as follows: coordinating government intelligence activities, advising the NSC on intelligence matters, evaluating and distributing intelligence information, performing services of "common concern" in the intelligence field as determined by the NSC, and "such other functions and duties related to intelligence affecting the national security" as defined by the NSC. The law was explicit that "the Agency shall have no police, subpoena, law enforcement powers or internal security functions."[64] The CIA would be an independent, central agency and as such not part of a policy department. Appendix A of this study—The National Security Act of 1947, as Amended—details the provisions as they relate to the creation of the CIA.[65] On 18 September 1947, the Central Intelligence Agency was officially opened for business; American central intelligence was now operating. By 26 September CIA's Office of Reports and Estimates published its first "intelligence estimate," a "Review of the World Situation as It Relates to Security."[66] A mere five weeks after "opening for business," the Secretary of Defense met with the FBI Director and armed services intelligence chiefs to discuss the "present and widespread belief that our Intelligence Group [sic] is entirely inept."[67] [Author's note: This statement is not further elaborated.]

And what a world it was becoming.

The Bipolar Environment

After World War II, instead of drawing inward as it had after World War I and rejecting a role in leading the new world order, America now embraced its new-found destiny. The Marshall Plan,[68] undertaken in conjunction with the Truman Doctrine,[69] marked the emergence of the United States as a world power bent on

---

[63] Rudgers, 148.

[64] Rudgers, 147.

[65] The National Security Act has been amended numerous times since its enactment. Therefore, any reference to "as amended" signifies legislation passed after 1947.

[66] Rudgers, 149.

[67] Memo for the files by John H. Ohley, 24 October 1947; Department of Defense File—Subject File, 1947: Central Intelligence Agency, Papers of John H. Ohly, HSTL (citation as noted in Rudgers, 150).

[68] The Marshall Plan was a massive economic aid program launched in 1948 designed to help restore Europe's economy.

establishing stability in the international community and willing to expend major resources and adopt an activist role in seeing that U.S. interests abroad were maintained.[70] Most great powers had "risen through the ranks" by means of a long apprenticeship in international involvement and conflict. America, on the other hand, turned to world involvement in the second transition period with all the notions, habits, and practices developed during a national existence focused on separation from that world. Unlike Great Britain or the Soviet Union, the United States became a global superpower almost without training or preparation.[71] The combination of power, commerce and ideology that drove Americans to expand their influence in the world led them to believe that elite views of American principles and national interests were the same thing; further, that the advancement of American power and influence was not only good for America, but also good for the rest of the world.[72]

As the wartime alliance between the United States and the Soviet Union quickly unraveled, opposition to communist expansion became the fundamental principle of American foreign policy. George Kennan outlined a strategic vision focusing on the Soviet Union—"The main element of any U.S. policy toward the Soviet Union must be that of a long-term, patient but firm and vigilant *containment* of Russian expansion tendencies."[73] Kennan emphasized that the threat was not going away because Soviet legitimacy was based on the fiction of an external American menace. As such, in his view the world must give up its idealistic visions of making the world safe for democracy and should focus on creating a balance-of-power world in order to contain the Soviet expansion until citizens throughout the Soviet Union insisted on major domestic reforms, thus moderating Soviet foreign policy.[74] According to Kennan, writing as "X" in his seminal *Foreign Affairs* essay in 1947:

> The main element of any [US] policy …must be that of patient but firm and vigilant containment of Russian expansive tendencies…by the

---

[69] In a 12 March 1947 message to Congress, President Truman stated, "I believe that it must be the policy of the United States to support free people who are resisting attempted subjugation….I believe that we must assist free people to work out their own destinies in their own way" as quoted in Jablonsky, 25. This declaration became known as the Truman Doctrine.

[70] Jordan and others, 69.

[71] Jablonsky, 23.

[72] Robert Kagan, "One Year After: A Grand Strategy for the West"?, *Survival* 44, no.4 (Winter 2002-03): 136.

[73] George Kennan, "The Sources of Soviet Conduct," *Foreign Affairs* 25, no. 4 (1947): 575-576 quoted in Jordan and others, *American National Security*, 5th ed. (Baltimore: The Johns Hopkins University Press, 1999), 67.

[74] Jablonsky, 24.

adroit application of unalterable counterforce at every point where [the Russians] show signs of encroaching upon the interest of a peaceful and stable world...Soviet power bears within it the seeds of its own decay...Russia, as opposed to the Western world is...by far the weaker party...in actuality: the possibilities for American policy are by no means limited to holding the line and hoping for the best...The United States has in its power to promote tendencies which must eventually find their outlet in either the breaking or the gradual mellowing of the Soviet power.[75]

Over the course of the next ten years the doctrine of containment would come to define the U.S. overall national security policy as expressed throughout the remainder of the 20th Century. Berkowitz states,

For the next fifty years no one attending meetings at the White House, Pentagon, or CIA needed to debate first the principles. Everyone knew where the threat lay, and everyone understood the strategy that they United States had adopted to counter it: containment. United States leaders assumed that the most important factor in shaping global affairs was the threat of Soviet expansion.[76]

Thus, not only did this doctrine define the U.S. political landscape as implied by Berkowitz, but it also came to characterize and influence the U.S. industrial base, economy, military composition, international relationships, academic curricula and the like. Zbignew Brzezinski, at the height of the Cold War, speaks of the immensity of effort expended by the U.S. military:

More than a million American troops stationed on some 400 major and almost 300 minor United States military bases scattered all over the globe. . [That there were] more than forty-two nations tied to the United States by security pacts, American military missions training the officers and troops of many other national armies, and the approximately two hundred thousand United States civilian government employees in foreign posts all makes for striking analogies to the great classical imperial systems.[77]

---

[75] X (George Kennan), "The Sources of Soviet Conduct," *Foreign Affairs* 25, no.2 (1947): 582 quoted in Francois Heisbourg, "How the West Could Be Won," in *One Year After: A Grand Strategy for the West? Survival* 44, no.4 (Winter 2002-2003): 146.

[76] Berkowitz, Bruce D. and Allan E. Goodman, *Best Truth: Intelligence in the Information Age* (New Haven: Yale University Press, 2000), 3. Cited hereafter as Berkowitz and Goodman, *Best Truth.*

[77] Jablonsky, 49.

A fundamental intent of the National Security Act of 1947 was to coordinate and to a limited degree centralize, the developing intelligence efforts of the United States as an emergent superpower in the face of a Soviet Union intent upon expanding communism.[78] Most importantly, for the Intelligence Community is that Soviet expansionism provided a consistent and relatively predictable enemy. While the Soviet problem was not the only issue confronting the IC, it was the singular issue of such magnitude that for over five decades it shaped the Community's structure and intelligence collection efforts.

Intelligence Community in the 20th Century

After the end of World War II, American intelligence services had an inauspicious beginning. As reflected in a 1976 Senate Select committee report, "in establishing a peacetime central intelligence body, the United States as one of the great powers came late to defining the need for an intelligence institution as an arm of its foreign policy....The decision to create a separate agency implied recognition of the intelligence function as an integral part of the foreign and military process."[79] While intelligence has always known its importance in war, its significance in times of peace has not long been established. It seems incredible now, almost fifteen years after the end of the Cold War, not to recognize the vital role intelligence plays in supporting American national defense in times of peace or, to use the current military terminology, Military Operations-Other-Than-War[80] (MOOTW); however, in 1945 this was not so apparent. Initially, the outlook for the future in the mid-1940s seemed one of peace and of international cooperation. Therefore, the issuance of Executive Order 9621 in October 1945, to abolish the

---

[78] Richard A. Best, Jr. and Herbert Andrew Boerstling, "Appendix C, IC21: The Intelligence Community in the 21st Century," *CRS Report for Congress* (Washington, D.C.: Congressional Research Service, Library of Congress, 28 February 1996), >*URL:<http://www.access.gpo.gov/congress/house/intel/ic21/ic21018.html>*, accessed 11 May 2004. Cited hereafter as CRS Report, Appendix C, February 1996.

[79] U.S. Senate, Select Committee to Study Government Operations With Respect to Intelligence Activities, *Final Report: Supplementary Detailed Staff Reports on Foreign and Military Intelligence,* book IV, 94th Cong., 2d sess. (Washington, D.C.: USGPO, 1976), 1 (citations as noted in Rudgers, 1).

[80] The Joint Chiefs of Staff (JCS) conceives MOOTW as a "diverse set of activities that includes: arms control, combating terrorism, Department of Defense support to counter-drug operations, enforcement of sanctions/maritime intercept operations, enforcing exclusion zones, ensuring freedom of navigation and overflight, humanitarian assistance, military support to civil authorities, nation assistance/support to counterinsurgency, noncombatant evacuation operations, peace operations, protection of shipping, recovery operations, show of force operations, strikes and raids, and support to insurgency" as cited in Jordan and others, 239. For more detailed information, see Joint Chiefs of Staff, "Joint Doctrine for Military Operations Other Than War" (Joint Publication 3-07), 16 June 1995.

wartime intelligence service, the Office of Strategic Services (OSS), was not anomalous. As one historian notes, "Truman's concern about the possible development of an American police state was the single most important factor in causing him to block early central intelligence agency proposals."[81]

At the end of World War II, the Office of Strategic Services had approximately 3,500 civilian employes, 8,000 army personnel and 800 from the Navy, Marines and Coast Guard attached to it.[82] One OSS veteran affectionately decribed the OSS as:

> sheltered screwballs, crackpots, and adventurers along with professors from Ivy League universities, ex-diplomats, and ex-soldiers, and an unprecedented number of heirs to great fortunes. Every sort of specialized and esoteric skill was represented, from professors of Sanskrit to demolition experts, cryptologists, judo instructors, sharpshooters, and specialists in guerilla warfare.....No scheme was too wild to consider.[83]

Its personnel and secret assets were transferred to the State Department as the Interim Research and Intelligence Service (IRIS)[84] and to the War Department as the Strategic Services Unit.[85]

Nonetheless, the abolishment of the OSS did not signal the end of intelligence support to national security; a centralized postwar intelligence system remained an objective for policymakers. By January 1946, Truman issued his Directive on Coordination of Foreign Intelligence Activities to the secretaries of state, war, and navy. These three and a personal representative of the president were designated the National Intelligence Authority (NIA) and held responsibility for the planning, developing and coordinating of all foreign intelligence activities. Under a presidentially appointed Director of Central Intelligence was the Central Intelligence Group (CIG), subordinate to the NIA, which would draw its funds, facilities, and personnel from the three departments represented on the NIA.[86] The National Intelligence Authority Directive (NIAD) 5,[87] issued on 8 July 1946 by the National Security Council, allowed the DCI to "centralize" research and analysis in "field of national security intelligence that are not presently being performed or are not adequately performed."[88] This directive, NIAD-5, is reputed to

---

[81] Rhodri Jeffreys-Jones, *The CIA and American Democracy* (New Haven, CT: Yale University Press, 1989), 29.

[82] Rudgers, 11.

[83] Rudgers, 10.

[84] Rudgers, 43.

[85] Rudgers, 44.

[86] Rudgers, 90.

have created the real difference between OSS as an operations office with a sophisticated analytical capability and the CIG, a [primeval] national intelligence service authorized to perform strategic intelligence and engage in clandestine activites abroad.[89] Even so, the CIG remained essentially a transitional organization pending the legislative creation of a permanent organization as well as a compromise in the face of government opposition to a centralized organization.[90] Very few seasoned intelligence officers spoke kindly of the CIG. William Colby, former DCI, had a few less-than-complimentary words to say about the CIG:

> the general consensus of professional intelligence people was that the CIG was a disorganized assembly of parts, not a working machine, bigger but not much better than before. What was worse, it even failed to perform that specific function for which it was created. Separate intelligence reports from G-2, ONI, State Department and a host of other agencies still flooded the President's desk. The CIG merely added one more, albeit an iteresting one, to the unstanchable stream.[91]

Another former OSS and CIA analyst, Ray Cline observes that:

> When attempts were made to prepare agreed national estimates on the basis of intelligence available to all, the coordination process was interminable, dissents were the rule rather than the exception, and every policymaking official took his own agency's intelligence appreciations along to the White House to argue his case. The prewar chaos was largely recreated with only a little more lip service to coordination.[92]

And so it was on 18 September 1947 that the "personnel, property, and records of the Central Intelligence Group" transferred to the CIA and "such group [CIG] shall cease to exist,"[93] the CIA opened for business.

---

[87] NIAD 5 was replaced by NSCID 1, titled "Duties and Responsibilities," which established the basic responsibilities of the DCI and interagency workings of the Intelligence Community. All versions of NSCID 1 are declassified and can be viewed at the National Archives and Records Administration, Record Group 263 (CIA), NN3-263-91-004, box , HS/HC-500 (citation as noted in Warner, 7.)

[88] National Intelligence Authority Directive number 5, 8 July 1946, reprinted in FRUS, 391-492 quoted in Michael Warner, *Central Intelligence: Origin and Evolution*, 3.

[89] Michael Warner, *Central Intelligence: Origin and Evolution* (Washington, DC: Center for the Study of Intelligence, 2001), 3.

[90] Rudgers, 129.

[91] William Colby, *Honorable Men* (New York: Simon and Schuster, 1978), 69-70.

[92] Ray Cline, *Secrets, Spies, and Scholars* (Washington, D.C.: Acropolis Books, 1976), 91-92.

[93] Section 102(f), National Security Act of 1947, see Appendix A-National Security Act 1947, as amended, this document for more detail.

At the time the National Security Act of 1947 became law, the IC consisted of the Central Intelligence Agency, the Federal Bureau of Investigation (FBI), the Office of Intelligence Research (Department of State), the Intelligence Division (Army), the Office of Naval Intelligence (ONI), the Diretorate of Intelligence (Air Force), and associated military signals intelligence offices, mainly the Army Security Agency (ASA) and the Navy's OP-20-G. During the Cold War, the number of elements of the United States Government receiving "funds authorized to be appropriated for the conduct of intelligence and intelligence-related activities" grew significantly, reflecting the transforming threat environment. Although the exact annual intelligence budget remains classified, in 1997, the last time it was publicly revealed, the intelligence budget stood at $27 billion.[94] With the inclusion of NIMA (now NGA) in 1996, the IC boasted of the following agencies—CIA, Department of Defense (DOD), Defense Intelligence Agency (DIA), National Security Agency (NSA), National Reconnaissance Office (NRO), Departments of the Army, Air Force, and Navy, Department of State, Department of Treasury, Department of Energy (DOE), Federal Bureau of Investigation (FBI), and Drug Enforcement Administration (DEA).[95] Of national intelligence agencies, only two IC members—CIA and NGA—exist in law. This unique arrangement has guaranteed congressional tweaking of these intelligence organizations whenever Congress sees fit to do so. Until the emplacement of the office of the Director of National Intellligence in February 2005, it also ensured that any tweaking would provoke a response from the Executive Branch (the DCI had been the president's principal intelligence advisor and the NGA is a combat support agency under the Secretary of Defense). NSA, created by NSCID No. 9 in 1952; NRO, created in 1960 by Air Force Order 115.1; and DIA, created in 1961 by DOD Directive 5105.21, could be eliminated by a "stroke of the pen" by the President or the Secretary of Defense.[96]

Cold War Intelligence Reform 1945-89

Efforts to fine-tune the Intelligence Community are as old as the Community itself. While dysfunctional organizations get fixed, disappear or gradually become irrelevant and ignored, the IC seems immovable.[97] By the end of Truman's presidency in 1953, the National Security Council (NSC) had issued fifteen Intelligence Directives (NSCIDs) to clarify further the responsibilities promulgated by the National Security Act. The NSC issued many of these within

---

[94] Berkowitz and Goodman, *Best Truth*, 25.

[95] CRS Report, Appendix C, February 1996.

[96] Dan Elkins, LCDR USN (Ret.), *An Intelligence Resource Manager's Guide*, 5th ed. (Washington, DC: Defense Intelligence Agency, 1997), 6.

[97] Berkowitz and Goodman, *Best Truth*, 27.

months after promulgation of the Act. Foremost was NSCID 1, which set forth the responsibilities of the DCI and the interagency workings of the Intelligence Community.[98] As the Community matured, the criticisms and calls for reform did not abate; they increased. Some thirty-plus years hence, according to press reports, and virtually every year for the past two decades, at least one agency within the IC has been the subject of a scandal or investigation.[99] There have been over 300 initiatives to reform the Community since the passage of the National Security Act of 1947.

Generally, proposals have fallen into two categories—those initiatives to improve efficiency and effectiveness, and to correct abuses such as illegal actions and civil rights infringements. The character of these proposals reflects trends in American foreign policy and the international environment as well as domestic security and governmental accountability concerns at the time of their commencement.[100] As an example, early intelligence reform proposals such as the First Hoover Commission in 1949 were concerned with efficiency and effectiveness. The Soviet Union, a former ally, was becoming an increasing threat and the U.S. concentrated its national defense efforts on this emerging target. Accordingly, many of the reform recommendations reflected the need for improvements in intelligence coordination efforts, U.S. covert actions and counterintelligence capabilities. By the mid-1970s and 80s, intelligence abuses such as the Watergate break-in, human rights abuses and the Iran-Contra Affair dominated the reform agenda; consequently, delimiting intelligence activities instead of efficiency improvements became the primary focus of reform.

Appendix B to this study, Cold War Intelligence Reform 1949-1989, provides summary highlights of selected Cold-War era intelligence reform proposals made by executive branch commissions and major legislative initiatives. This is by no means an exhaustive display of report findings and recommendations. Most of these reports were voluminous. As an example, probably the most notorious commission report during this era, the Senate Select Committee to Study Governmental Operations, affectionately known as the Church Committee Report, weighed in with 183 recommendations in its final report.[101] This committee's study of alleged assassination plots alone consisted of over 8,000 pages of sworn testimony.[102] The present author primarily reviewed the 1996 Congressional Research Service (CRS) Report by Richard A. Best, Jr. and Herbert Andrew Boerstling. This author did not attempt to evaluate the success or failure of any proposed rec-

---

[98] Warner, 7.

[99] Berkowitz and Goodman, *Best Truth*, 27.

[100] CRS Report, Appendix C, February 1996.

[101] CRS Report, Appendix C, February 1996.

[102] Frank J. Smist, Jr., Congress Oversees the United States Intelligence Community, 2nd ed. (Knoxville: The University of Tennessee, 1994), 69.

ommendations as it is beyond the scope of this project. However, repeated short-comings identified year after year, or in many cases, decade after decade, portend serious flaws. The following table shows the author's categorization of the findings/recommendations from selected Cold-War era intelligence reform proposals. This table distills the information in Appendix B.

Cold-War Reform Initiatives 1945-1989
Source: Compiled by author

Year	Title	Admin	DCI Roles/ Respon- sibilities	IC Rela- tions	Analysis	DCI Budget Authority	Centra- lize Intel	CIA Admin	Congress Over- sight	Covert Action
1945	NSCID No.1	Truman	X							
1949	First Hoover Comm	Truman	X	X	X	X	X			
1949	Intell Survey Group	Truman	X		X			X		
1954	Doolittle Comm	Eisenhower						X		
1955	Second Hoover Comm	Eisenhower						X	X	X
1958	NSCID No. 11st Rev	Eisenhower	X	X	X					
1959	Bruce-Lovett	Eisenhower			X					X
1971	Schlesinger Report	Nixon	X		X					
1972	NSCID No. 1 2nd Rev	Nixon	X	X	X	X				
1975	Murphy Comm	Ford			X			X		X
1975	Rockefeller Comm	Ford	X	X	X			X		X

Cold-War Reform Initiatives 1945-1989
(Continued)

Year	Title	Admin	DCI Roles/Responsibilities	IC Relations	Analysis	DCI Budget Authority	Centralize Intel	CIA Admin	Congress Oversight	Covert Action
1975	Church Comm Senate	Ford	X			X		X	X	X
1976	Pike Comm House	Ford	X		X	X		X	X	
1976	Clifford Proposal	Ford	X							
1976	Cline Proposal	Ford	X					X		X
1976	EO 11905	Ford				X		X		
1978	EO 12036	Carter				X				
1978	Draft Nat Intel Reform	Carter	X		X					
1978	FISA/ FISC	Carter		X						
1981	EO 12333	Reagan	X	X	X	X				
1985	Turner Proposal	Reagan	X	X						X
1987	Iran-Contra Investigation	Reagan								X

Measures to Improve Efficiency and Effectiveness

The table above provides a general idea of the intelligence reform issues considered by the White House as well as Congress and their respective recommendations/corrective actions. Certain recurring threads of reform emerge that have consistently been voiced throughout the last half century. Of particular note is the consistent concern over the dual role of the DCI as the central intelligence coordinator and primary IC resource manager. It has long been recognized that effective implementation of these two roles has eluded every DCI since 1947. In addition to particular concern over budget authority for the DCI, there has frequently appeared concern over the quality of analysis in the Community.

The Carter Administration saw the first and last instance of the DCI exerting influence over the entire IC budget. Executive Order 12036 granted the DCI, Stansfield Turner at the time, budget authority over the DIA and Pentagon intelligence arms. However, President Reagan rescinded this EO in 1981.[103] Thus, it remains the case that the DCI's influence is heavily dependent upon his development of a cooperative working relationship with the other agency principals, chiefly the Secretary of Defense as well as the White House.

In 1971, a report suggested creating the position of Director of National Intelligence (DNI). Although this was the first time, it would not be the last instance when reformers proposed the position. The DNI discussion occurred repeatedly throughout the Cold War—for example, in the Draft National Intelligence Reform Act of 1978 and Turner Proposal (1985)—and the DNI discussion carried into the Post-Cold War era as well. In sum, the 1971 report recommended a "strong DCI who could bring intelligence costs under control and intelligence production to an adequate level of quality and responsiveness."[104] In addition, as an innocent omen perhaps, this report noted the Community's "impressive rise in...size and cost" with "apparent inability to achieve a commensurate improvement in the scope and overall quality of intelligence products."[105]

More than a half-century after enactment of the National Security Act, the DCI still did not have the authorities required to discharge efficiently and effectively his Community-wide responsibilities. In 1981, E.O. 12333 designated the DCI as the primary intelligence advisor to the President and NSC on national foreign intelligence. Additionally, it granted the DCI more explicit authority over the development, implementation, and evaluation of the National Foreign Intelligence Program (NFIP).[106] Yet, approximately 80-85 percent of the total intelligence program resources have continued to reside within the Department of Defense. The DCI has not had authority over those funds; the Secretary of Defense has controlled the purse strings.

---

[103] Peter Grier and Faye Bowers, "Can Spy Agencies Ever Work Together?" *Christian Science Monitor,* 21 July 2004, URL *http://www.csmonitor.com/2004/0721/p01s02-uspo.html,* accessed 28 February 2005.

[104] A Review of the Intelligence Community, 10 March 1971, 23-33 (citation as noted in Best, 16). Cited hereafter as Schlesinger Report, CRS Report, Appendix C, IC21 February 1996.

[105] Schlesinger Report, 1; CRS Report, Appendix C, February 1996.

[106] Mark M. Lowenthal, *U.S. Intelligence: Evolution and Anatomy* (Westport, CT: Praeger, 1992), 107.

Cold-War Era Reform Effort in Retrospect

Frequently throughout the Cold War, the question of the role and responsibilities of the Community not only came into question, but also ebbed and flowed with the political environment at the time. In the late 1950s, the CIA was criticized for being "too heavily involved in Third World intrigues while neglecting the hard intelligence on the Soviet Union"[107] whereas a few years earlier Congress had privately applauded the efforts to overthrow the governments of Iran and Guatemala. Yet, by the end of the Cold War, the IC stood accused of focusing too heavily on the Soviet problem and perversely, unable to predict its sudden demise. Ultimately, according to Lowenthal, the Community overestimated the size of the Soviet economy and underestimated the portion of it devoted to defense, which in all probability stood at 40 percent of the annual Soviet GDP (Gross Domestic Product).[108] He noted further that some believed the huge sums spent on defense [intelligence spending implied] in the 1980s had not been necessary because the Soviet Union would have finally collapsed on its own.[109] For some critics, this "intelligence failure," failing to predict the collapse of the Soviet Union, was sufficient reason to demand profound reorganization of the Intelligence Community. Nonetheless, supporters of intelligence pointed to the frequent reporting on internal strife of the Soviet Union and its satellite states as evidence that useful collection and analysis could take place and make a valuable contribution to national security.[110]

In the end, repeated attempts to tweak the CIA and the Community "from the outside" without parallel attention to collection and analysis tradecraft from the inside demonstrate a basic reality—the expectations of the CIA in the National Security Act clearly describe an agency whose mandate has far exceeded its capacity to perform.[111] Innumerable reform recommendations as well as executive orders have sought to strengthen the role of the DCI. Yet, without overall budget authority and overall authorities relating to Community personnel, requirements and intelligence activites, the DCI was not able to become the "great intelligence integrator." According to Zegart, the CIA that emerged from the National Security Act of 1947 satisfied the War and Navy departments [they kept control over their assets]. However, the intelligence-centered organization for national security remained weak by design.[112] Its structural weakness continued throughout the remainder of the last century and into the 21st century.

---

[107]Peter Grose, Gentleman Spy: The Life of Allen Dulles (Boston: Houghton Mifflin, 1994), 445-448 as cited in CRS Report, Appendix C, IC21 February 1996.

[108] Lowenthal, *From Secrets to Policy*, 180.

[109] Gates, 552.

[110] Lowenthal, *From Secrets to Policy*, 181.

[111] Zegart, 188.

[112] Zegart, 174.

Chapter Four

RECENT PAST: STALLED REFORM (1990-2000)

As the free world grows stronger, more united, more attractive to men on both sides on the Iron Curtain—and as the Soviet hopes for easy expansion are blocked—then there will have to come a time of change in the Soviet world. Nobody can say for sure when that is going to be, or exactly how it will come about, whether by revolution or trouble in the satellites, or by a change inside the Kremlin.

Whether the Communist rulers shift the policies of their own free will—or whether change comes about in some other way—I have not a doubt in the world that change will occur.

I have a deep and abiding faith in the destiny of free men. With patience and courage, we shall some day move on into a new era.

—**President Harry S. Truman**
Farewell Address 15 January 1953

I particularly desire that you take the lead in developing a comprehensive and co-ordinated (sic) foreign intelligence program for all Federal agencies concerned with that type of activity. This should be done through the creation of an inter-departmental group, heading up under the State Department, which would formulate plans for my approval. This procedure would permit the planning of complete coverage of the foreign intelligence field and the assigning and controlling of operations in such manner that the needs of both the individual agencies and the Government as a whole will be met with maximum effectiveness.

—**President Harry S. Truman**
Letter to Secretary of State, Transfer of OSS to State 1945

Post-Cold War Environment

Hans Morgenthau, renowned political scientist, referring to the two superpowers, spoke of a "worldwide balance of which the United States and the Soviet Union are the main weights, placed on opposite scales…[other regions] become functions of the new worldwide balance, mere 'theaters' where the power context between two great protagonists is fought."[113] This drama played out with a solemn and dramatic flare for decades between the two great superpowers. Then, almost a half century after the bilateral struggle began, the Cold War between the two great superpowers had ended.

At last, the world change that Truman prophesized in his farewell speech had come about—at the cost to the American taxpayers of almost $2 trillion.[114] This struggle produced an ever more capable and ever more costly worldwide intelligence apparatus—human intelligence agents in distant lands, sophisticated satellites and reconnaissance aircraft, and signal intelligence listening posts aimed at understanding the capabilities of its greatest rival and gravest threat. For decades, the Community spoke of the ominous nuclear and conventional threats of the Soviets and its Eastern European Empire; likewise, the Defense Department procured state-of-the-art weaponry to match and surpass its formidable opponent. Robert Gates as DCI suggested that the greatest contribution of the CIA and the IC during the last half of the Cold War was that there were no strategic surprises—no more bomber or missile gaps that had abruptly startled the nation decades earlier.[115] Relying predominantly on superior satellite capabilities, the Community provided with confidence to U.S. policymakers, Congress, and the international community detailed knowledge of Soviet forces and capabilities.

At the height of the Cold War, approximately 50 percent of the intelligence budget was earmarked for covering the Soviet Union and related issues; everything else was secondary.[116] As a military signals intelligence (SIGINT) officer assigned to the National Security Agency (1986-89), the present author observed firsthand the primacy placed upon the Soviet problem—referred to as A Group. By far, A Group received the largest share of funding, and garnered priority placement of critically skilled personnel. Departmental funding being appropriated based on the concentration of mission requirements, A Group would logically receive the largest share. Just after the Iraqi

---

[113] Hans J. Morgenthau, *Politics Among Nations: The Struggle for Power and Peace*, 4th ed. (New York: Knopf, 1967), 149.

[114] Gates, 532.

[115] Gates, 562.

[116] Lowenthal, *From Secrets to Policy*.

invasion of Kuwait, the author returned to the agency as an army reservist mobilized in support of Operation DESERT SHIELD/DESERT STORM.

With a lack of a recognizable, imminent threat, policymakers, pundits, and private citizens alike began calling for "peace dividends" such as a renewed emphasis on domestic issues, a smaller, more mobile military and naturally, a restructuring of the Intelligence Community. Washington was focused on the peace dividend, according to John MacGaffin, former CIA Deputy Director for Operations, and the Intelligence Community was not able to articulate a Post-Cold War vision. "How do you get out of bed in the morning being mad at a transnational issue?" MacGaffin queried.[117] Francis Fukuyama postulated in his provocative thesis, "The End of History," that the triumph of the Western model of liberal democracy and a market-oriented economic order over socialism and other political-economic systems demonstrates that liberal democracy is the only viable option for modern societies.[118] After all, the national security of the United States no longer confronted an omnipresent peril; socialism had failed, the West had won. The White House and Congress promoted and the public expected reductions in military personnel and equipment; similarly, the Intelligence Community, always a Washington favorite to tinker with, faced its own reductions. Human intelligence operations both in personnel and in funding were seriously depleted during this time. James Pavitt, CIA's Deputy Director for Operations, indicated that the "peace dividend resulted in a 30 percent decline in funding for the CIA's Directorate of Operations—the men and women in the clandestine service who penetrate terrorist networks, recruit spies and steal secrets—and a personnel downsizing of nearly 20 percent."[119]

As an illustration of the fiscal austerity facing the DoD and its resultant effect on the Community, the amount requested in the FY 1998 budget was in real terms 40 percent less than it was in 1985, the peak of the Cold War. Additionally, as a share of the U.S. GDP, outlays fell to the lowest relative level since before World War II, just three percent.[120] Nonetheless, as events would soon demonstrate, the end of the Cold War did not imply a more stable international environment. The Cold War may have ended but a hot peace quickly

---

[117] Gregg Sangillo and Siobhan Gorman, "Smarter Intelligence a Post-9/11 Priority," *National Journal* (22 May 2004): 1575.

[118] Francis Fukuyama and others, "Second Thoughts: The Last Man in the Bottle Responses," *The National Interest* (Summer 1999), accessed via Proquest, 24 November 2003.

[119] James Pavitt, "Change and the CIA," *Washington Post*, 6 August 2004, A19.

[120] Amos A. Jordan and others, *American National Security*, 5th ed. (Baltimore: The Johns Hopkins University Press, 1999), 552.

followed. Paradoxically, although more secure, the United States faced increased challenges from regional instability and disorder that demanded increasing U.S. military and humanitarian support. General Colin Powell, then JCS Chairman, noted:

> The decline of the Soviet threat has fundamentally changed the concept of the threat analysis as a basis for force structure planning. We can still plausibly identify some specific threats—North Korea, a weakened Iraq, perhaps even a hostile Iran. But the real threat is the unknown, the uncertain. In a very real sense, the primary threat to our security is instability and being unprepared to handle a crisis or war that no one expected or predicted.[121]

Strangely enough, as President George H.W. Bush was announcing that a Cold War "peace dividend" would allow a 25 percent reduction in U.S. military forces, Saddam Hussein's forces were invading Kuwait.[122] The first major war of the Post-Cold War era had begun.

While the Cold War between two superpowers meant a long peace and global stability for most of the industrialized world for over fifty years, such was not the case in the Third World.[123] Nearly all of the Third World nations were engaged in one or more of the 127 wars that claimed over 21 million war-related deaths during the same period. The Third World became a profitable market for sophisticated arms produced in the developed world.[124]

Speaking at Harvard University in the Spring 1992, Richard Kerr, at the time Deputy Director of CIA, presented his thoughts on intelligence:

---

[121] General Colin Powell, testimony before the House Committee on Foreign Affairs, 4 March 1992, 3 (citation as noted in Jordan and others, 544).

[122] President George Bush, "Remarks at the Aspen Institute Symposium," 2 August 1990 (Weekly Compilation of Presidential Documents, doc. 1190).

[123] Mahmood Mamdani, *Good Muslim, Bad Muslim* (New York: Pantheon, 2004), review by Emran Qureshi entitled "The Enemy Of My Enemy Is My Enemy," in *Washington Post Book World,* 25 March 2004, 1. Qureshi notes that the struggle against the Soviets made use of the proxy wars in the Third World, which concentrated and privatized violence within non-state actors. While garden-variety terrorists existed before, none had the reach and the desire to refashion Muslim societies globally until after the anti-Soviet jihad in Afghanistan. According to one source Mamdani cited, the financing and arming of the jihadis in Afghanistan was the "largest covert operation in the history of the CIA," amounting to approximately $3 billion in aid. Furthermore, it is estimated that 35,000 mujaheddin from 43 Muslim countries fought and trained in Afghanistan, with more than 100,000 additional Muslim radicals passing through Pakistan and Afghanistan.

[124] David Jablonsky, *Paradigm Lost? Transitions and the Search for a New World Order* (Westport, CT: Praeger, 1995), 56.

Intelligence is in as much a revolution as the former Soviet Union; essentially, we have lost the enemy that the structure was built or designed for; we have lost the simplicity of purpose and cohesion that essentially had driven not only intelligence, but has driven this country for forty plus years....The intelligence system we developed was possible because we had consensus, because there was agreement at nearly every level even across party lines....Very seldom did we argue about the fundamental premise. We argued how best to solve the problem, how to deal with the problem, where best to put the money, but very seldom did we face fundamentally the argument of "I think this is all a phony threat." It just did not happen....these questions are going to become more commonplace because it is not at all certain that there is consensus about the future, about the threat, if there is a threat, and what the nature of the threats are to this country....while there are threats....I think none of those, either individually or collectively, can be seen as life-threatening to this country; they don't jeopardize its very existence.[125]

[125] Richard J. Kerr, "The Evolution of the U.S. Intelligence System in the Post-Soviet Era," Briefing presented at Center for Information Policy Research, Harvard University, Guest Presentations, Spring 1992. Incidental Paper: Seminar on Intelligence, Command and Control, August 1994. URL <http://harvard.edu/pubs_pdf/kerr/kerr-i94-4.pdf>, accessed 1 April 2004.

The success of U.S. military operations during DESERT STORM[126] demonstrated to the world the first prominent example of the potential of the "Revolution in Military Affairs (RMA)," which matched new technologies, particularly information technologies, with new tactics and organizational concepts.[127] A Department of Defense official saw DESERT SHIELD/DESERT STORM as crossing a new frontier in applying modern information technologies to perform C^3I [command, control, communications] functions. He further stated:

> Revolutionary techniques have included the adaptation of new secure telephone units to pass voice, data and pictures, distributed automated command and control systems and the use of large numbers of near instantaneous intelligence systems capable of providing information in picture form to all military echelons. It is the first sustained large-scale joint military operation in the micro-processing era.[128]

Paradoxically, this dazzling success also demonstrated to the world that no other nation-state could compete militarily with the United States in a conventional war scenario. Therefore, rather than engage the U.S. directly, the predominance of U.S. military power almost assuredly disposes adversaries to asymmetrical attack.[129] The same technology that provided U.S. military supremacy would be used to attack its vulnerabilities.

---

[126] Not all talked of successes. Then-DCI James Woolsey testified before the HPSCI in 1994 that General Schwarzkopf's primary criticisms of intelligence support during the Gulf War was the lack of timely imagery support. Woolsey stated, "we must proceed to build the capability to deliver imagery intelligence to battlefield commanders. During DESERT STORM, our commanders found out they had to wait too long for far too few pictures of battlefield areas…and in the field they had to wait longer still…because of antiquated procedures for delivering them." (U.S. Congress, House of Representative, Permanent Select Committee on Intelligence, Hearing, *The Current and Future State of Intelligence.* 103rd Cong., 2nd sess., 24 February 1994. URL: <http://www.fas.org/irp/congress/1994_hr/hpsci022494.pdf>, accessed on 1 June 2004.

[127] Jordan and others, 547. The authors speak of five lessons of DESERT STORM for future U.S. foreign policy. The fourth lesson (cited above) being that the RMA as a new form of conventional warfare holds the potential to change the way policymakers view the military instrument of power in the future. The other lessons include: 1) the world is still a very dangerous place, 2) U.S. has a unique leadership role to play in world affairs as the residual superpower of the Cold War, 3) contributions of allied coalitions are crucial; ad hoc coalitions may be the only feasible way to meet most serious regional challenges in the future; and 5) U.S. military forces were dependent on the logistical support of our allies, particularly for airlift, sealift, and in-theater transportation.

[128] Ronald Elliot, "C3I Warfare Moves into New Era," *Defense News*, 7 January 1991, 20. Citation as noted in Richard A. Best, Jr., "Reforming Defense Intelligence," *CRS Report for Congress*, 91-475 F, Washington, D.C.: Congressional Research Service, Library of Congress, 11 June 1991.

Yet, these technological advancements, readily available in the public domain, did not revolutionize the IC—antiquated, incompatible computer systems were the norm. The explosive telecommunications market, "made it clear to us that we had to recapitalize if we were going to keep up," stated Lt Gen Michael Hayden, Director NSA. "The danger was not that SIGINT would go away, but that it would cease to be an industrial strength of American intelligence."[130]Hayden, recounting a February 2001 "60 Minutes II" interview where he spoke of the technological challenges facing NSA, observed that "al Qa'ida did not need to develop a telecommunications system. All it had to do was harvest the products of a three trillion dollar a year telecommunications industry—an industry that made communications signals varied, global, instantaneous, complex, and encrypted."[131]

The national security agenda of the Post-Cold War remained poorly defined throughout the 1990s. For instance, as 1998 began, CIA's analytical assets were focused on the priorities established with the White House. By year's end, 50 percent of the crises that occurred that year were in "low-priority areas" and other major "developments" such as the global financial crisis, the Kosovo war and India's nuclear test were unanticipated.[132] In another example, before leaving the Pentagon in late 1993, Secretary of Defense Les Aspin asked the Defense Science Board to conduct a study to determine whether the military forces were "ready."

---

[129] As documented a few months after the 11 September 2001 terrorists' attacks against the U.S., in "Bin Laden Lieutenant Admits to September 11 and Explains Al-Qa'ida's Combat Doctrine." *Middle East Media Review of International Relations,* Special Dispatch Series No. 344, 10 February 2002. URL: <http://www.memri.org/bin/articles.cgi, accessed 7 December 2003. Additionally, the author, Abu 'Ubeid Al-Qurashi, a bin Laden lieutenant, explained the Al-Qa'ida combat doctrine. The following excerpts relate to asymmetric warfare:

In 1989[referring to the first Gulf War], some American military experts predicted a fundamental change in the future form of warfare...They predicted that the wars of the 21st century would be dominated by a kind of warfare they called "the fourth generation of wars." Others called it "asymmetric warfare." ...This new type of warfare presents significant difficulties for the Western war machine and it can be expected that [Western] armies will change fundamentally. This forecast did not arise in a vacuum—if only the cowards [among the Muslim clerics] knew that fourth-generation wars have already occurred and that the superiority of the theoretically weaker party has already proven; in many instances, nation-states have been defeated by stateless nations.

Abu 'Ubeid Al-Qurashi further proclaims the Islamic victories within the past twenty years against the best armed, best trained, and most experienced armies in the world (the U.S.S.R. in Afghanistan, the U.S. in Somalia, Russia in Chechnya, and the Zionist entity in southern Lebanon).

[130] LtGen Michael V.Hayden, USAF, "Investigation of Sept 11," 17 October 2002, accessed via LexisNexis, 12 January 2004.

[131] Hayden.

[132] "Time for a Rethink - America's Intelligence Services," *The Economist Newspaper Ltd,* 20 April 2002, accessed via Lexis-Nexis, 28 January 2004.

Aspin had previously declared "readiness" to be his top defense priority. General Edward C. "Shy" Meyer directed this report and his comments reflect a lack of strategic focus in national security. Meyer indicated that it was difficult to evaluate readiness in the absence of policy guidance on what the force was supposed "to be ready to do." [133]

A poorly defined national security strategy created an almost untenable environment for the Intelligence Community. Although the IC had throughout its history a broad understanding of policymaker preferences and the country's most important interests, this understanding does not provide the basis for making a coherent set of plans for investments, collection systems, personnel recruitment and training. [134]

Post-Cold War Intelligence Reform

Reshaping the IC for the 21st Century became the mantra of the 1990s. The Post-Cold-War U.S. political environment demanded a smaller, more cost-efficient intelligence capability. Senator David L. Boren (D-OK), Chairman of the Senate Select Committee on Intelligence, cautioned, "If the Intelligence Community fails to make these changes, [135] it will become an expensive and irrelevant dinosaur just when America most needs information and insight into the complex new challenges that it faces." [136]

Post Cold-War Reform
Source: Compiled by author

Year	Title	Admin	DCI Roles/ Respon- sibilities	IC Relations	Analysis	DCI Budget Authority	Centralize Intel	CIA Admin	Congress Oversight
1992	Boren-McCurdy	Bush 41	X	X	X	X		X	
1992	Intell Reorg Act	Bush 41	X			X			
1995/96	PDD-35	Clinton	X		X	X		X	
1995/96	Brown/ Aspin	Clinton	X					X	X

---

[133] "Framing the Problem of PPBS," *BENS Tail-to-Tooth Commission Report*, January 2000, URL: *http://www.bens.org/images/PPBS2000-Framing.pdf*, accessed 10 November 2004.

[134] Lowenthal, *From Secrets to Policy*, 203.

[135] Refer to Boren-McCurdy Act 1992, this chapter and Appendix C – Post-Cold-War Intelligence Reform (1990-2001) for a list of proposed intelligence reforms.

Year	Title	Admin	DCI Roles/ Respon- sibilities	IC Relations	Analysis	DCI Budget Authority	Centralize Intel	CIA Admin	Congress Oversight
1995/96	C21	Clinton	X					X	
1996	Intel Reform Act of 1996	Clinton						X	

Note: While the Hart-Rudman Commission concluded that the basic structure of the IC did not require changing, it did emphasize an increased recruitment of HUMINT sources on terrorism as one of its three steps toward improvement. Consult Appendix C of this book for more information.

Boren-McCurdy Act 1992

In February 1992, both the Senate Intelligence Committee (Sen. David Boren, Chair) and the House Intelligence Committees (Rep. Dave McCurdy) introduced separate plans for omnibus restructuring of the Intelligence Community to meet the challenges of the Post-Cold War world. Its drafters envisioned this bill to be the Intelligence Community's counterpart to the Department of Defense Reorganization Act of 1986 (Goldwater-Nichols Act). Although there were two versions of the plan, they had many similarities. In fact, most of the recommendations had been proposed previously but had not been addressed legislatively. Both proposals called for:

- Creating a Director of National Intelligence with authority to program and reprogram intelligence funds throughout the IC to include the DOD, and to direct their expenditures; task intelligence agencies and temporarily transfer personnel;
- Creating two Deputy Directors of National Intelligence (DDNIs)— one for analysis and estimates and the other for IC affairs;
- Creating a separate Director, CIA, subordinate to DNI;
- Consolidating analytical and estimative efforts of the IC;
- Creating a National Imagery Agency within DOD to collect, exploit, and analyze imagery. (House version would divide these efforts into two separate agencies)
- Authorizing the Director, DIA to task defense agencies with collection requirements and to shift personnel, funds, functions from one DOD intelligence agency to another.[137]

---

[136] Sen. David L. Boren, (D-OK), "The Intelligence Community: How Crucial?" *Foreign Affairs*, 71, no. 3 (Summer 1992): 53.

The committees believed that replacing the DCI with the new DNI, who would have authority over all U.S. intelligence programs and budgets, would finally end the internecine rivalry for control of the Intelligence Community that had existed for decades between the DCI and the Secretary of Defense.[138] Both bills would have created a National Intelligence Center by consolidating the Community's analysis and estimative efforts in one place, to include stripping the CIA of its analytical capabilities. The CIA would still run covert operations and manage its human intelligence collection. Additionally, this National Intelligence Center would be in charge of all intelligence collection.[139]

Although both the House and the Senate held hearings on their respective bills, there was no expectation that the legislation supporting these sweeping intelligence changes would be enacted in 1992. Senator Boren directed the Senate Intelligence Committee's General Counsel L. Britt Snider to draft an intelligence bill that was "bold and provocative" and that would stimulate the executive branch into thinking imaginatively about intelligence work.[140] The Senate Intelligence Committee noted Title VII of the intelligence authorization bill "provided for the first time in law a comprehensive statement of responsibilities and authorities of the agencies and officials of the U.S. Intelligence Community."[141] The United States intelligence service may have begun its formal operations in 1947 but decades later, the Community still operated without any charter documents formally prescribing what those specific responsibilities entailed. In 1971, the Nixon Administration first considered and then rejected the idea of a Director of National Intelligence. Additionally, during the Carter Administration, the draft National Intelligence Reorganization and Reform Act of 1978 also would have provided statutory charters and created a DNI. However, in the case of the 1978 reform effort, neither the House nor Senate Intelligence Committees reported out the bill.

In a 1992 *Foreign Affairs* article, Ernest R. May argued his position against the Boren-McCurdy legislation while Senator Boren stated his position for its pas-

---

[137] Richard A. Best, Jr., "Proposals for Intelligence Reorganization, 1949-2004," *CRS Report for Congress*, RL32500, Washington, D.C.: Congressional Research Service, Library of Congress, 29 July 2004, CRS-30, >URL: *http://www.fas.org/irp/crs/RL32500.pdf*>>, accessed 25 August 2004. Cited hereafer as CRS Report, July 2004. Note: This is an updated version of a previous compilation entitled, Appendix C, IC21: The Intelligence Community in the 21st Century by Richard A. Best, Jr., and Herbert Andrew Boerstling.

[138] Smist, 286.

[139] Pamela Fessler, "Chairman Boren, McCurdy Urge Leaner, Revamped Operations," *Congressional Quarterly Weekly Report*, 8 February 1992, 316.

[140] Fessler, confidential interview; Smist 286.

[141] Senate Select Committee on Intelligence, *Special Report*, 103rd Cong., 1st sess., 18 March 1993, 3 (citation as noted in Smist, 286).

sage. While May recognized that the world had changed, he believed the Boren-McCurdy bills as drafted would solve the problems of the past, not the future.[142] He took exception with the provisions dealing with the National Security Council, budgets, a revamped CIA and the proposed new analysis agency.[143] Of particular note is May's opposition to putting the entire intelligence budget under the DNI, with the secretary of defense "responsible for ensuring that the policies and resource decisions of the DNI are implemented by elements of DoD." According to May, the intelligence tsar [DNI] could find himself spending money mostly to satisfy requests from the Pentagon.[144]

On the other hand, Senator Boren argued for a closer relationship between military and civilian intelligence. To bring about this closer integration, the leader of the Community must be able to set budgetary and programmatic priorities for the entire community. The DCI or DNI must be able to reprogram funds and rechannel them accordingly from one area or agency to another.[145] Questioning those individuals who contend the United States either does not need intelligence at all or no longer needs a separate Intelligence Community, Boren stressed that change must come in two areas—new priorities and a new structure better suited to those priorities.[146] His arguments for a new Community structure became the foundation of the proposed Boren-McCurdy legislation.

In the end, the legislation did not pass. Had the Boren-McCurdy legislation passed—replacing previous executive directives with statutory mandates—the DCI (or DNI) would have the authority to direct collection and analytical efforts throughout the Intelligence Community.[147] A decade earlier in 1981, President Reagan endeavored to strengthen the role of the DCI through Executive Order (E.O.) 12333. Still, in the absence of explicit legislation, the DCI once again continued to lack authority over all aspects of the IC, predominantly in the areas of budget and personnel.

Although the Boren-McCurdy legislation failed, President Bush signed the last intelligence authorization bill managed under the leadership of Senator Boren into law in October 1992 for FY93. Title VII amended the National Security Act of 1947 and according to Smist, it was one of the most important pieces of intelligence legislation passed since the creation of CIA. It enacted organizational charters for the Intelligence Community and established the foundations for funding

---

[142] Ernest R. May, "Intelligence: Backing into the Future," *Foreign Affairs*, 71, no. 3 (Summer 1992), 63.

[143] May, 64-65.

[144] May, 67.

[145] Boren, 59.

[146] Boren, 54.

[147] CRS Report, 29 July 2004, CRS-31.

intelligence in the Post-Cold War via the annual intelligence authorization acts.[148] If recommendations for charter legislation sound familiar, it should. Charter legislation was one of the Church's Committee's most important recommendations...back in 1976! Also, using the intelligence authorization process, Senator Boren is credited as being the person primarily responsible for creating an independent CIA IG (FY1990), revising the legislation concerning how covert actions would be approved and reported to Congress (FY 1991),[149] and sponsoring the short-lived National Security Education Act of 1991 (FY1992).[150] The Iran-Contra Committee had initially recommended the covert action revisions in 1987.

Smist highlights the passage of the National Security Education Act, designed to train future generations of national security specialists, as the one action that best symbolizes Senator Boren's tenure as Chairman of the Senate Intelligence Committee. Regrettably derailed by congressional politics, the House Committee voted to repeal the Act in 1993.[151] At the same time, however, the ever-magnanimous Committee granted the DCI authority to award fifty-dollar savings bonds at high school science fairs "to recognize the importance of science, mathematics, and engineering to the national security."[152] According to Smist, no better example can be found to illustrate what Richard Cohen calls "the perversity of Congress."[153]

Commission on the Roles and Capabilities of the U.S. Intelligence Community (Brown-Aspin Report)

Another congressional commission established in September 1994 pursuant to the Intelligence Authorization Act for FY1995 (P.L. 103-359) once again sought the holy grail of intelligence—"Given this radically changed global environment, are intelligence capabilities still needed? If so, can their efficiency and effectiveness be improved?"[154]

---

[148] Smist, 285.

[149] Smist, 287.

[150] Smist, 289.

[151] Smist, 310. Smist indicates the program cut was not due to merit but rather a direct political attack by the Glickman (replaced McCurdy in 1993) committee on Senator Boren for not supporting the Clinton budget. The *New York Times* reported: "Today's voice vote had little to do with its merit. This was punishment of a chairman turned political pariah. ("Tribute, a Political Casualty, Is Taken Back," *New York Times*, 19 June 1993 as cited in Smist, 310).

[152] House Permanent Select Committee on Intelligence, *Intelligence Authorization Act for Fiscal Year 1994*, 29 June 1993, 27 (citation as noted in Smist, 310).

[153] Richard Cohen, "Bonne Chance," *Washington Post Magazine*, 11 July 1993, 3.

[154] Report of the Commission on the Roles and Capabilities of the U.S. Intelligence Community. Preparing for the 21st Century: An appraisal of U.S. Intelligence, Washington, DC: GPO, 1996. Hereafter cited as Brown-Aspin Report.

After reviewing resource management procedures within the IC, the Commission concluded that:

> The current program budget structure and diffused responsibilities over basic business areas have resulted in unnecessary duplication, interoperability problems, and other inefficiencies. These problems exist within the NFIP, and among the NFIP, JMIP and TIARA activities, creating a substantial obstacle to the efficient use of intelligence resources.[155]

Because of these inefficiencies, the Commission proposed restructuring of the NFIP budget by creating new discipline-oriented programs for SIGINT, IMINT, MASINT, and HUMINT, each with a single program manager. The Commission also recommended that the total amounts appropriated for intelligence be disclosed. President Clinton implemented this recommendation for FY 1997 and 1998. This is the source for the annual amount of $26 billion plus which has been noted frequently in unclassified correspondence.

Checklist for the Future of Intelligence

Shortly after Congress chartered the Brown-Aspin Commission, Georgetown University's Institute for the Study of Diplomacy (ISD) hosted a series of meetings entitled "American Intelligence for the Twenty-First Century: A Colloquium on the Future of Intelligence After the Cold War."[156] Appendix D - Talking Heads on Intelligence Reform, provides selected highlights from this Checklist. This appendix also highlights additional opinions from various intelligence and national security professionals on reform issues and challenges in the Post-Cold War era.

One ISD colloquium checklist item—to create a joint Committee on Intelligence comprising House and Senate members, appointed by the leadership and supported by a small staff[157]—warrants discussion. Early in the history of the Community (1956), the Senate pushed a joint Senate-House CIA committee to oversee intelligence but this resolution was soundly defeated.[158] Then in the mid-1970s, both the Senate and the House created permanent intelligence committees. Unquestionably, Congress as the overseer of the United States foreign intelligence program has a lawful and important role. However, colloquium participants expressed concern about the extent of congressional oversight and how best

---

[155] Brown-Aspin Report.

[156] John Hedley, ISD Occasional Paper 1, *Checklist for the future of Intelligence* (Gaithersburg, MD: Reproductions, Inc., 1995), v. Cited hereafter as Checklist.

[157] Checklist, 26.

[158] Smist, 8.

to conduct it. A perception exists that the IC works more for Congress than it does for the President. According to John Hollister Hedley, author of the checklist, "Fearing trouble with either appropriations or investigative hearings—so the accusation goes—the Intelligence Community grows more concerned about protecting its congressional flank than serving the executive branch, and is thus more responsive to Capitol Hill."[159] Other concerns centered on the amount of time the DCI spends on Capitol Hill answering congressional inquiries; congressional scrutiny had by the mid-1990s become so detailed as to be unworkable and beyond the scope of ordinary oversight; and finally, intrusive oversight might lead to de facto congressional pre-approval of executive actions instead of performing the expected monitoring and reviewing.[160] The latter concern reflects constitutional separation-of-power principles and issues.

These concerns did not surface just during this colloquium but have been voiced throughout the Community. More than one senior executive has expressed frustration with the amount of time spent responding to congressional inquiries. Quite often, questions asked are similar in nature but have originated from different congressional committees, with each committee requiring a separate response format. As a former senior financial manager for an intelligence agency, the present author has experienced first-hand the excruciating level of detail required in preparing congressional budget justification books (CBJBs). While recognizing the lawful and important role of congressional oversight, it could be conducted more efficiently and effectively by the creation of a joint intelligence committee. However, because there are multiple congressional committees which exercise some level of intelligence oversight—predominantly, Armed Services, Appropriations, SSCI, HPSCI—it is unlikely any of these committees will relinquish their power of the purse to a joint committee.

The Brown-Aspin Committee considered but did not recommend a single joint committee. The Committee explained its non-consideration as follows:

> Creating a single joint committee would not substantially reduce the number in Congress needing access to intelligence, but would reduce the degree of oversight. It would also eliminate the checks and balances inherent in having committees in each body separately consider intelligence funding. A joint committee would no longer handle nominations received by the Senate.[161]

---

[159] Checklist, 25.

[160] Checklist, 26.

[161] Brown-Aspin Report.

IC21: Intelligence Community in the 21st Century

In addition to the Brown-Aspin Commission, the House Intelligence Committee under the Chairmanship of Larry Combest, (R-TX) initiated its own extensive review of intelligence issues. The IC21study was the boldest, most innovative and most radical of the proposals for IC reform.[162] It sought to determine which "intelligence norms"—organizations, products, practices, relationships and ways of doing business that extend throughout the IC—are still relevant in the 21st Century; which need to be either revised or replaced; and what alternatives should be added.[163] The IC2I Overview and Summary declared:

> Everything is on the table. There are no sacred cows in terms of organizations, missions, or functions. Neither are there any preconceptions as to the "right answer" for the future of the IC.[164]

This Committee concluded that a major key to an improved IC is the concept of "corporateness"—the idea that agencies and employees of the IC should behave as part of a more closely integrated enterprise working toward a highly defined common end: the delivery of timely intelligence to civil and military decisionmakers at various levels.[165] To achieve this "corporateness," central management should be strengthened, core competencies (collection, analysis, operations) should be reinforced and infrastructure should be consolidated whenever possible. Furthermore, the DCI should have a stronger voice in the appointment of the directors at NFIP Defense agencies.

Most of the IC21 recommendations were consistent with the Brown-Aspin Report (see Appendix C—Post-Cold War Intelligence Reform for more detail). For example, the IC21 Committee saw no compelling reason to reduce the current, divided oversight system to a joint committee. It concluded, "The current oversight system had been largely effective, and clearly has responded to those problems that prompted the creation of the current committees"[166] [investigations in 1975-76].

---

[162] Abraham H. Miller and Brian Alexander, "Structural Quiescence in the Failure of *IC21* and Intelligence Reform," *International Journal of Intelligence and Counterintelligence,* 14, no. 2 (Summer 2001): 235.

[163] U.S. Congress, House of Representatives, Permanent Select Committee on Intelligence, Staff Study, *IC21: Intelligence Community in the* 21st *Century,* 104th Congress, 9 April 1996, <*http://www.fas.org/irp/congress/1996_rpt/uc21/ic21001.html*>, accessed 21 October 2003. Hereafter cited as IC21.

[164] IC21, Overview and Summary, 2.

[165] IC21, Overview and Summary, 5.

[166] IC21, Section XV. Congressional Oversight, 1.

Nearly all of the panels assembled to look at intelligence reform during this period were in agreement on the advisability of a greater degree of centralization and enhanced authority for the DCI, with the exception of Georgetown political scientist Roy Godson and Harvard historian Ernest May, who found that:

> failure of centralization efforts can be seen as reflecting the reasonable needs of the various components of the national security bureaucracy. In any case, the centralized model was probably better suited to the Cold War, with its emphasis on "national" level intelligence about the Soviet strategic nuclear threat, than to the present period when departmental, regional, and tactical intelligence requirements have exploded and gained new urgency.[167]

Post-Cold War Reform in Context

A common perception held by Congress and the American public was that the Community had lost its focus after the end of the Cold War and needed better guidance and direction.[168] Hence, congressional reform during the 1990s concentrated on measures that sought to improve the efficiency, effectiveness and accountability of the IC. Perhaps the most significant structural change to come out of the countless reform recommendations of the 1990s was the creation of the National Imagery and Mapping Agency (NIMA), now known as the National Geospatial-Intelligence Agency (NGA). The Defense Authorization Act of 1997 (P.L. 104-201) (IAAFY97) established NGA. Recall that the concept of a National Imagery Agency was proposed initially by the Boren-McCurdy legislation in 1992. Yet, the creation of NGA was anything but a smooth process; newspaper articles discussing committee differences referred to the dispute as a three ring "turf battle par excellence."[169] Helen Sullivan, Office of the Deputy General Counsel, DoD and primary drafter of the NIMA legislation, had this to say about the process:

> [i]t has been said that it can be easier to get legislation [to effect intelligence reform] through Congress than the executive branch. NIMA may be proof of that. If we had tried to seek an administration solution to the problem, having the DCI and the Secretary of Defense sign some

---

[167] Michael Warner, *Central Intelligence: Origin and Evolution*, 13.

[168] U.S. Congress, Senate, Select Commission on Intelligence, *Special Report of the Select Committee on Intelligence United States Senate January 4,1995 to October 3, 1996*, 105th Cong., 1st sess., S. Rept.105-1, 22 January 1997. URL: <*www.emergency.com/int03.htm*>, accessed 21 October 2003. Cited hereafter as SSCI Special Report 22 January 1997.

[169] Anne Daugherty Miles, *The Creation of the National Imagery and Mapping Agency: Congress's Role as Overseer*, Occasional Paper Number Nine (Washington, DC: JMIC, 2002), 20.

kind of charter, that would have played into the hands of the bureaucracies, and we would probably still be waiting for approval. Bureaucracies can take a look at senior leadership, recognize the amount of turnover at that level and wait them out.[170]

In her Senate confirmation hearing as the first Deputy DCI for Community Management (Brown-Aspin Commission and IC21 Study recommendation), nominee Joan Dempsey unmistakably pinpoints the most fundamental problem of intelligence organizations—protecting the "turf":

> It's somewhat amusing to me—and I've spent most of my career in the Department of Defense…and when I was in DoD there was always this fear that a very powerful DCI with a full-time emphasis on intelligence and managing the Community would fail to support the DoD the way it needed to be supported with intelligence. Since I've come over to the Central Intelligence Agency side of the Intelligence Community, I've found the same fear, but this time directed at what DoD is going to do to subvert the role of the DCI.[171]

The IC21 Committee may have commanded that "everything is on the table," but the sacred cows were still the guests of honor. Every mother knows that just because everyone got a slice of the chocolate cake, does not mean there will not be arguments over who got the biggest slice!

U.S. Commission on National Security/21st Century (Hart-Rudman Commission)

This Commission, commonly known as the Hart-Rudman Commission) began in mid-1998 but it did not publish its first report until 19 September 1999, two weeks shy of FY2000, the next budgetary period, and three months shy of the next millennium. Two former congressman, Gary Hart, (D-CO) and Warren B. Rudman (R-NH), were Commission Co-Chairs. Its final report was not made available to the public until 15 February 2001. The present author chose to categorize this Commission as belonging to the Post-Cold War period of the 1990s because it has it origins during this decade. Reform issues dis-

---

[170] Helen Sullivan, "Creation of NIMA," 45 (citation as noted in Miles, 22).

[171] U.S. Congress, Senate, Select Committee on Intelligence, Hearing, *Nomination of Joan A. Dempsey to be Deputy Director of Intelligence for Community Management,* 105th Cong., 2n^d sess., Senate Hearing 105-1056, 21-22 May 1998, 1 (citation as noted in Best, CRS Report, July 2004, CRS-36).

cussed in this report occurring in the 21st century proper are annotated as Post-9/11 Reform initiatives.

The U.S. Commission on National Security/21st Century initially began as the National Security Study Group (NSSG). The concept for this Commission arose from a conversation between President William J. Clinton and Congressman Newt Gingrich, (R-GA), Speaker of the House in 1997. According to Rudman, Clinton and Gingrich were discussing some upcoming legislation when Clinton recounted a book he was reading that reminded him of their conversation. Basically, Clinton was referring to what became the National Security Act of 1947, when after World War II "ten to twelve very distinguished Americans got together to look at the whole panoply of the government and what it should look like" for the remaining fifty-three years of the century.[172] Rudman related that Gingrich told Clinton, "You know, Mr. President, we ought to do just that for the twenty-first century, because what we have in place was put there for the Cold War, and isn't necessarily what we ought to have in place for the next fifty years—for the first half of the twenty-first century."[173]

With that pronouncement (and the House and Senate approval), the Commission began its laborious task of examining whether "institutions designed in one way may or may not be appropriate for the future." The Secretary of Defense chartered this Commission in mid-1998 under the provisions of the Federal Advisory Commission Act. There would be three phases to this monumental undertaking: Phase I would describe the world emerging in the first quarter of the century, Phase II would design a national security strategy appropriate to that world, and finally, Phase III would propose necessary changes to the current national security structure to implement Phase II strategy.[174]

This Commission looked at the United States government as a whole with the idea that "fifty years [since 1947] is a long time for any policy structure to endure, particularly during a period of such vast change."[175] The final reports of this Committee encompassed three and one-half years of effort, which culminated in three substantive reports published separately: Phase I (1999), Phase II (2000), and Phase

---

[172] Warren B. Rudman, "Perspectives on National Security in the Twenty-First Century," Briefing presented at Center for Information Policy Research, Harvard University, Guest Presentations, Spring 2002. Incidental Paper: Seminar on Intelligence, Command and Control, June 2003. URL:http://pirp.harvard.edu/pubs_pdf/rudman/rudman.i02.pdf>. Accessed 1 April 2004, 2.

[173] Rudman, 2.

[174] United States Commission on National Security/21st Century, New World Coming: American Security in the 21st Century Major Themes and Implications Phase I Report on the Emerging Global Security Environment for the First Quarter of the 21st Century, 15 September 1999, Preface. URL: *http://www.nssg.gov,* accessed 1 November 2003. Cited hereafter as Hart-Rudman Phase I Report.

[175] Hart-Rudman Phase I Report Foreword, iv.

III (2001). The present review of this expansive effort is to provide a basic under-standing of the major renderings of each of the three reports. After the events of 11 September 2001, the Hart-Rudman Commission received considerable attention, exponentially more so than its initial release months earlier. Consequently, the author chose to provide an annotated version of the Commission's fifty recommendations in APPENDIX C—Post-Cold-War Intelligence Reform (1990-2000).

The Hart-Rudman Commission did not specifically address intelligence reform. However, because "intelligence serves and is subservient to policy and intelligence works best when tied to clearly understood policy goals,"[176] it is prudent to highlight this consummate work; therefore, all three phases are explained briefly. The Commission did delineate "steps" that the Intelligence Community should undertake to ensure successful implementation of the Phase II strategy. These steps are addressed in "Phase III, Road Map for National Security: Imperative for Change," in this chapter.

While the Hart-Rudman Commission did not address the intelligence piece of national security per se, the IC senior leadership had recognized its frailties. At an executive-level Community offsite on 11 September 1998, the IC leadership concluded that "failure to improve operations management, resource allocation, and other key issues within the [IC], including substantial and sweeping changes in the way the nation collects, analyzes, and produces intelligence, will likely result in a catastrophic, systemic intelligence failure."[177]

1999 Phase I Report: Emerging Global Security Environment for the First Quarter of the 21st Century

The Commission articulated twelve beliefs about the United States and its relationship with the rest of the world—the emerging world environment. As should be expected, these beliefs were consistent with the annual renderings of the Post-Cold War environment circulated among the Community, academia, think tanks and focus groups. To summarize these beliefs, the Commission believed the U.S. would remain a primary political, military, and cultural force through 2025; militarily it would remain the principal force in the world. While science and technology would continue to make explosive advancements, its distribution will be uneven; likewise, economic growth will not occur among all segments evenly and widespread poverty will persist. Additionally, increases would

---

[176] Lowenthal, *From Secrets to Policy*, xi.

[177] U.S. Congress, House, Permanent Select Committee on Intelligence, Subcommittee on Terrorism and Homeland Security, *Counterterrorism Intelligence Capabilities and Performance Prior to 9-11*, Report, 107th Cong., 2 sess., 17, July 2002, URL: *http://www.fas.org/irp/congress/2002_rpt/hpsci_ths0702.html*, accessed 21 October 2003.

occur in international business and commerce. Non-governmental organizations (NGOs) would grow in number and importance. Weapons of mass destruction (WMD) and weapons of mass disruption would proliferate.

Two Commission points, Numbers 11 and 12, bear repeating verbatim because in the context of the events that would occur two years hence, in September 2001, these beliefs bore a prophetic truth. These beliefs were:

11. We should expect conflicts in which adversaries, because of cultural affinities different from our own, will resort to forms and levels of violence shocking to our sensibilities.

12. As the United States confronts a variety of complex threats, it will often be dependent on allies; but it will find reliable alliances more difficult to establish and sustain.[178]

Drawing upon such beliefs about the future, the Commission drafted fourteen conclusions that forecast the international security environment for the next twenty-five years.[179] (See Appendix C).

Even though as Casey Stengel lamented, "Forecasting is always difficult, especially about the future,"[180] undoubtedly, these conclusions will come to fruition with varying degrees of effect over the course of the next twenty-five years.

In summary, the Hart-Rudman Commissioners concluded that the Phase I report "points to two contradictory trends ahead: a tide of economic, technological, and intellectual forces that is integrating a global community, amid powerful forces of social and political fragmentation."[181] The Commission regarded this transformation of human society to be of the magnitude of that between the agricultural and industrial epochs but in a drastically reduced time frame.

2000 Phase II Report Seeking a National Strategy: A Concert for Preserving Security and Promoting Freedom

---

[178] Hart-Rudman Phase I Report Our View of the Future, 3.

[179] Hart and Rudman Phase I Report Conclusions, 4-7.

[180] DCI R. James Woolsey invoked Casey Stengel during testimony to the HPSCI on 24 February 1994. U.S. Congress, House of Representative, Permanent Select Committee on Intelligence, Hearing. *The Current and Future State of Intelligence.* 103rd Cong., 2nd sess., 24 February 1994. URL: *http://www.fas.org/irp/congress/1994_hr/hpsci022494.pdf,* accessed on 1 June 2004.

[181] United States Commission on National Security/21st Century, *Seeking a National Strategy : A Concert for Preserving Security and Promoting Freedom Phase II Report on a U.S. National Strategy for the 21st Century,* 15 April 2000, 5. URL: *http://www.nssg.gov,* accessed 1 November 2003. Cited hereafter as Hart-Rudman Phase II Report.

The Phase II Report of the Hart-Rudman Commission suggested strategic precepts that should guide the formulation of U.S. national strategy. American strategy must strike a balance between two key aims, reported the Commission. On one hand, the aim is to embrace a more integrated world as a requisite to expand freedom, security, and prosperity for all Americans and others; while on the other hand, this strategy must lessen the forces of global instability to preserve these benefits.[182]

The Commission indicated that to preserve American liberties and fulfill these goals in a new age, America's priority objectives and key policy objectives must be these:

- To defend the United States and ensure that it is safe from the dangers of a new era.
- To maintain America's social cohesion, economic competitiveness, technological ingenuity, and military strength.
- To assist the integration of key major powers, especially China, Russia, and India, into the mainstream of the emerging international system.
- To promote, with others, the dynamism of the new global economy and improve the effectiveness of international institutions and international law.
- To adapt U.S. alliances and other regional mechanisms to a new era in which America's partners seek greater autonomy and responsibility.[183]

Additionally, the Commission emphasized that the challenges to U.S. policy-making necessitate the need for greater integration between traditional national security agencies such as State, Defense, and the Intelligence Community and other U.S. agencies such as Justice, Commerce, Treasury, and the like. Furthermore, the Commission stressed the need for more effective partnerships with state and local governments. Recognizing that preventive diplomacy and its associated tools (political, economic, other partnerships) may not always work, the Hart-Rudman Commission stipulated the five kinds of military capabilities that the U.S. requires in this new environment:

- Nuclear capabilities to deter and protect the United States and its allies from attack;
- Homeland security capabilities;
- Conventional capabilities necessary to win major wars;

---

[182] Hart and Rudman Phase II Report; Thinking About Strategy, 6.
[183] Hart and Rudman Phase II Report; Key Objectives, 8-12.

- Rapid employable expeditionary/intervention capabilities
- Humanitarian relief and constabulary capabilities.[184]

2001 Phase III Report Road Map for National Security: Imperative for Change

After examining the strategic environment (Phase I) and a strategy to address it, the Commission concluded that significant changes must be made in the structures and processes of the U.S. national security apparatus.[185]

Astonishingly, the Hart-Rudman Commission concluded that the structure of the Intelligence Community did not require change. A few years later, in 2003, Gary Hart, one of the speakers at a World Affairs Council of Northern California symposium on Intelligence Community Reform and at the time, Co-Chair Independent Task Force on Homeland Security Imperitives, stated:

> [The Hart-Rudman Commission] did not undertake to design a Post-Cold War intelligence structure. But we strongly urged the new administration [Bush Administration] to begin that process. Indeed, I think the Clinton Administration should have undertaken a lengthy study of how Post-Cold War intelligence in America should be produced and by whom.[186]

All of the Phase III recommendations in order of their presentation in the United States Commission on National Security/21st Century are listed in Appendix C—Post-Cold War Intelligence Reform.

Hart-Rudman Commission Summary

The U.S. Commission on National Security/21st century is perhaps the most comprehensive attempt to capture the essence of American national security since the efforts encapsulated in the passage of the National Security Act of 1947. Clinton and Gingrich saw their initial historical discussion become an epic vision for 21st-Century government restructuring. Incidentally, when Gingrich introduced this legislation there was a consensus for this Commission. It had Congressional and White House support; the time had come to define a national security policy for the 21st century. According to Rudman, "It went like a rocket

---

[184] Hart and Rudman Phase II Report, Implications for National Security, 14.

[185] Hart-Rudman Phase III Report, viii.

[186] Gary Hart, former Senator (D-CO), speaker at the World Affairs Council of Northern California symposium, "Intelligence Community Reform," San Francisco, CA., 18 November 2003, videotape viewed in the John T.Hughes Library on 1 June 2004. Other speakers included Dale Watson (former FBI), Jane Wales (President, World Affairs Council), John McGaffin (CIA), James Harris (CIA), and John Andrews (Bureau Chief, Economist).

through the House and Senate. Everybody thought it was a great idea. Everybody was behind it."[187]

Unfortunately, once again as in the past, enthusiasm and ultimately, support for government reform waned. This Herculean effort to restructure the government for the 21st Century, mandated by Congress to be provided to the incoming President in January 2001, became just another shelved commission report. Despite elaborate public relations attempts to get the word out on the Hart-Rudman Commission Reports, these efforts fell short of the expected responses. According to Rudman, although representatives from every major media outlet and every network attended the February 2001 Senate roll-out of this Commission report, only one of the three major networks, ABC, devoted time to it during its broadcast—a total of eight seconds. Furthermore, only two newspapers, *The Washington Post* and *The Los Angeles Times,* provided decent coverage of the event. Rudman noted that a *New York Times* reporter walked out of the February press conference halfway through. When the Commission Executive Director (Charles G. Boyd) called the reporter to inquire why he left, the reporter replied, "Hell, that's not the kind of story the *Times* reports. That's just one of these government reports that pile up and get thrown in the dustbin." Ironically, the first time anyone in America, according to Rudman, knew that there was a National Security Study Group (NSSG) in the pages of the newspaper of record of the United States, *The New York Times*, was on 12 September 2001.[188]

As most of America knows by now, the U.S. Commission on National Security/21st century, pointed out that in its first report dated September 1999, as its first conclusion—America will become increasingly vulnerable to hostile attack on our homeland, and our military superiority will not entirely protect us. The last sentence of this conclusion that now seems tragically prescient warns, "Americans will likely die on American soil, possibly in large numbers."[189]

After the tragic events of 11 September 2001, some of the Hart-Rudman Commission Report recommendations were finally implemented, although not as originally suggested. After much debate, a reluctant White House allowed the creation of the Department of Homeland Security. The next chapter will address two of the major investigations, known as the Joint Inquiry and the 9/11 Commission, that were undertaken in response to the terrorist attacks on the United States. Strangely, Gary Hart, the co-chair of the most comprehensive review of U.S. national security since 1947, was not called to testify before the 9/11 Com-

---

[187] Rudman, 2-3.
[188] Rudman, 5.
[189] Hart-Rudman Report Conclusions, 4.

mission. In early April 2004, as the 9/11 Commission was drawing to a close and preparing its final report, Hart questioned why he and others had not been called to testify:

> I am increasingly asked what information our earlier commission, the U.S. Commission on National Security/21st Century, has provided the 9/11 Commission and why that information has not been made public. When told that the 9/11 Commission has not asked for any public testimony from us, most people are incredulous. If the 9/11 Commission is really trying to find out what was known and when it was known, they ask, why would your national security commission's warnings and recommendations not be of direct relevance and urgent interest?...The simple answer to all these questions is: I don't know why we have not been called to testify.[190]

Why indeed?

---

[190] Gary Hart, "Gary Hart: A Paul Revere No One Wants to Hear From," salon.com, 6 April 2004.

Chapter Five

PRESENT: POST 9/11 STRATEGIES FOR REFORM

I don't think anybody could have predicted that these same people would take an airplane and slam it into the World Trade Center, taken another one and slam it into the Pentagon; that they would try to use an airplane as a missile, a hijacked airplane as a missile. All of this reporting about hijacking was about traditional hijacking. You take a plane—people were worried they might blow one up, but they were worried that they might take a plane and use it for the release of the blind Sheikh or some of their own people.

National Security Advisor Condoleezza Rice
May 2002 Press Briefing

The Joint Inquiry confirmed that, before September 11, the Intelligence Community produced at least twelve reports over a seven-year period suggesting terrorists might use planes as weapons.

Joint Inquiry Report
December 2002

The 9/11 Surprise?

This point must be underscored. Without a doubt, *terrorists were responsible for the 11 September 2001 murder* of 2,749 innocents in New York, 184 innocents in Washington, and 40 innocents in Pennsylvania. As tragic as the events of 11 September 2001 were, 9/11 was not a surprise attack. It may have been an attack that surprised us beyond our worst nightmares but it was not a surprise attack. While this statement may appear self-contradictory, it is not. A surprise attack would imply that the United States had no forewarning of an attack. After three plus years of agonizing questions, investigations, and examinations, we know this is not the case. There were warnings not heeded and warnings missed, information not shared and information not processed. "The 9/11 attacks were a shock," the 9/11 panel concluded, "but they should not have come as a surprise."[191] For the present author, a brief review of selected statements presented to the Senate Intelligence Committee Hearing on the Investigation of 11 September (as part of the Joint Inquiry) a year after the attacks demonstrated that portents had been building for years.

On an emotional level, the September 11 attacks have been compared to the attack on Pearl Harbor sixty years prior. While both the 9/11 and Pearl Harbor attacks were abashedly intelligence failures, they are dissimilar. Frank L. Borch, in "Comparing Pearl Harbor and "9/11": Intelligence Failure? American Unpreparedness? Military Responsibility? *Journal of Military History*, 67, no. 3 (July 2003), accessed via Proquest 4 December 2003, compares the attacks of 9/11 to the Japanese attacks on Pearl Harbor and points to dissimilarities in the nature of the failure, level of readiness, and military responsibilities. He acknowledges that it is possible to compare the two as intelligence failures providing there is recognition that the nature of the two intelligence failures is dissimilar. Borch states, "those in command in Hawaii had sufficient intelligence to justify a higher state of vigilance (and prepare a better defense)," and he further asserts, "no information had been collected (or probably could have been) that would have caused the FBI or FAA to respond differently on 9/11."

The present author strongly disagrees with his premise concerning 9/11 that no information had been collected which would have warranted a different response. Information had been collected but it was not properly disseminated nor was its importance properly recognized. As Eleanor Hill, Staff Director of the Joint Inquiry Commission, explained:

> While the specifics of the September 11 attacks were not known in advance, relevant information was available in the summer of 2001. The collective significance of that information was not, however, recognized. Perhaps as a result, the information was not fully shared, in a timely and effective manner, both within the Intelligence Community and with other federal agencies

Historically, we know from an aviation perspective, as reiterated in the Statement of Karen Breitweiser, Co-Chairperson, September 11th Advocates, that crashing an airplane into a building was not unimaginable. In fact, there had been multiple attempts to do so:

- In 1993, a draft document depicting a scenario where an airplane bombs national landmarks was circulated throughout the Pentagon, the Justice Department and to the Federal Emergency Management Agency (FEMA).

---

[191] David Von Drehle, "Analysis: the Findings-America's Failings, in Depressing Detail:" *Washington Post*, 23 July 2004, A20.

- In 1994, a disgruntled FEDEX employee invaded the cockpit of a company aircraft with the intent to crash it into a company building in Memphis.
- In 1994, a lone pilot crashed a small plane onto the White House grounds.
- In 1994, an Air France flight was hijacked by members of the Armed Islamic Group, intending to crash the plane into the Eiffel Tower.
- In 1995, Philippine authorities uncovered a plot, Project Bojinka, to blow up 11 airlines over the Pacific and in the alternate plot; several planes were to be flown into civilian targets in the U.S. The targets selected included: CIA Headquarters, The World Trade Center, the Sears Tower, and the White House.[192]

Historically, we know from a national security and intelligence perspective, as presented in the Statement of George Tenet, DCI, that asymmetric attacks against U.S. interests were a logical response to U.S. military superiority:

- In the 1995 National Intelligence Estimate we warned, "As an open and free democracy, the United States is particularly vulnerable to various types of intelligence attacks. Several kinds of targets are especially at risk: National symbols such as the White House and the Capitol, and symbols of U.S. capitalism such as Wall Street; power grids...places where large numbers of people congregate, such as large office buildings,...and airports and other large transportation terminals. Civil aviation will figure prominently among possible terrorist targets in the United States."
- In 1999, during open session testimony, "I told you there is not the slightest doubt that Usama Bin Ladin, his worldwide allies, and his sympathizers are planning further attacks against us." I said, "He will strike wherever in the world he thinks we are vulnerable" and we were concerned that one or more of Bin Laden's attacks could occur at any time.
- In 2000, during open session testimony, I told you, "Everything we have learned recently confirms our conviction that (UBL) wants to strike further blows against America" and that he could strike "without additional warning."[193]

Eleanor Hill, Joint Inquiry Staff Director, imparted these pre-9/11 key facts with respect to the Usama Bin Ladin that confronted the Intelligence Community:

---

[192] Karen Breitweiser, "Investigation of Sept 11,"18 September 2002, accessed via LexisNexis, 12 January 2004.

[193] George Tenet, "Investigation of Sept 11,"17 October 2002, accessed via LexisNexis, 12 January 2004.

- In 1998, Bin Laden issued his public fatwa authorizing attacks against American civilian and military personnel worldwide.
- During a three-year period, the IC acquired information indicating Bin Laden's intent to carry out attacks inside the United States.
- In 1998, the DCI's statement "we are at war" with Bin Laden (after the East Africa embassy bombings) and that no resources should be spared by the IC in that regard.
- Over a seven-year period, the IC accumulated information indicating international terrorists were considering using airplanes as weapons.
- Spring/Summer of 2001, numerous indicators detected by the IC of a major impending terrorist attack which would have dramatic consequences for governments and cause mass casualties.[194]

The controversial 6 August 2001 Presidential Daily Brief (PDB),[195] (see tonebox on next page) entitled, "Bin Laden Determined to Strike in US," offered yet another example that the terrorist attacks upon the U.S. were in fact not surprise attacks. Several times during the spring and summer of 2001, President Bush asked his briefers if any of the threats pointed to the United States. According to the 9/11 Commission Report, the CIA decided to write a briefing communicating their view that the threat of a Bin Laden attack in the United States remained both current and serious. This became the 36th PDB briefed thus far that year (2001) concerning Bin Ladin or al Qaeda, and the first PDB indicating the possibility of an attack in the United States. President Bush told the Commissioners that the 6 August 2001 PDB was historical in nature and he did not recall discussing it with the Attorney General or whether the National Security Advisor had done so. The President said that if his advisors had told him there was a cell in the United States, they would have moved to take care of it. That never happened.[196]

[194] Eleanor Hill, "Investigation of Sept 11, 17 October 2002, accessed via Lexis-Nexis, 12 January 2004.

[195] After much castigation from the National Commission on Terrorist Attacks Upon the United States Commission (9/11 Commission), the White House acquiesced and declassified the PDB and approved it for release on 10 April 2004. The following text was printed in the 9/11 Commission Report: The Final Report of the National Commission on Terrorist Attacks Upon the United States (New York: W.W. Norton & Company, 2004), 261-262. Cited hereafter as the 9/11 Report. The text presentation includes italics and bold as it appeared in the 9/11 Commission report. Brackets indicate redacted material.

[196] 9/11 Report, 260.

Bin Laden Determined to Strike the U.S.

Clandestine, foreign government, and media reports indicate Bin Laden since 1997 has wanted to conduct terrorist attacks in the US. Bin Laden implied in US television interviews in 1997 and 1998 that his followers would follow the example of World Trade Center bomber Ramzi Yousef and "bring the fighting to America."

After US missile strikes on his base in Afghanistan in 1998, Bin Ladin told followers he wanted to retaliate in Washington, according to a [—] service. An Egyptian Islamic Jihad (EIJ) operative told an [—] service at the same time that Bin Laden was planning to exploit the operative's access to the US to mount a terrorist strike.

The millennium plotting in Canada in 1999 may have been part of Bin Laden's first serious attempt to implement a terrorist strike in the US. Convicted plotter Ahmed Ressam has told the FBI that he conceived the idea to attack Los Angeles International Airport himself, but that Bin Laden lieutenant Abu Zabaydah encouraged him and helped facilitate the operation. Ressam also said that in 1998 Abu Zabaydah was planning his own US attack.

Ressam says Bin Laden was aware of the Los Angeles operation.

Although Bin Laden has not succeeded, his attacks against the US Embassies in Kenya and Tanzania in 1998 demonstrate that he prepares operations years in advance and is not deterred by setbacks. Bin Laden associates surveilled our Embassies in Nairobi and Dar es Salaam as early as 1993, and some members of the Nairobi cell planning the bombings were arrested and deported in 1997.

Al-Qa`ida members, including some who are US citizens—have resided in or traveled to the US for years, and the group apparently maintains a support structure that could aid attacks. Two al-Qa'ida members found guilty in the conspiracy to bomb our embassies in East Africa were US citizens, and a senior EIJ member lived in California in the mid-1990s.

A Clandestine source said in 1998 that a Bin Laden cell in New York was recruiting Muslim-American youth for attacks.

We have not been able to corroborate some of the more sensational threat reporting, such as that from a [--] service in 1998 saying that Bin Laden wanted to hijack a US aircraft to gain the release of "Blind Saykh" 'Umar 'Abd al-Rahman and other US-held extremists.

Nevertheless, FBI information since that time indicates patterns of suspicious activity in this country consistent with preparations for hijackings or other types of attacks, including recent surveillance of federal buildings in New York.

The FBI is conducting approximately 70 full field investigations throughout the US that it considers Bin Ladin-related. CIA and the FBI are investigating a call to our Embassy in UAE in May saying that a group of Bin Laden supporters was in the US planning to attack with explosives.

In defending the actions of the NSC regarding the 6 August 2001 PDB, National Security Advisor Condoleezza Rice, in her testimony to the 9/11 Commission, testified, "It did not warn of attacks inside the United States. It was historical information based on old reporting. There was no new threat information. And it did not, in fact, warn of any coming attacks inside the United States."[197]

Additionally, Lt Gen Hayden in his testimony before the Joint Inquiry, when responding to 'What did NSA know prior to September 11?' testified:

> Sadly, NSA had no SIGINT suggesting that al-Qa'ida was specifically targeting New York and Washington, D.C., or even that it was planning an attack on U.S. soil. Indeed, NSA had no knowledge before September 11th that any of the attackers were in the United States...To put it into some perspective, throughout the summer of 2001 we had more than 30 warnings that something was imminent. We dutifully reported these, yet none of these subsequently correlated with terrorist attacks. The concept of "imminent" to our adversaries is relative; it can mean soon or simply sometime in the future." [198]

While the United States may not have known the precise date, place and time of these catastrophic attacks on 11 September 2001, they are, nonetheless, a very tragic example of predictable surprise. Predictable surprises are events, according to two Harvard professors—see tone box on next page—that could have been anticipated and prepared for. In many cases, the warning signs were present for years. Watkins and Bazerman acknowledge that many surprises are truly out-of-the-blue unpredictable and in those cases leaders should not be blamed for lack of foresight especially when all reasonable preventative measures have been taken. Viewed in this context, 11 September 2001 was not one of these. It was not a surprise attack but rather an attack that indelibly surprised the government of the United States. "If only Osama had faxed an X-mark-the-spot map to the Crawford ranch showing the Pentagon, the Capitol, the twin towers and the word "BOOM!" scrawled in Arabic, wrote Maureen Dowd, a New York Times Op-Ed columnist, "That might have sparked sluggish imaginations. Or maybe not."[199]

---

[197]Condoleezza Rice, National Security Advisor, "Transcript: Rice's Testimony on 9/11," *Washington Post FDCH E-Media*, online ed., *http://www.washingtonpost.com/ac2/wp-dyn/A61252-2004Apr8*, accessed 14 April 2004.

[198] Hayden.

[199] Maureen Dowd, "Head Spook Sputter," *The New York Times*, online ed., 15 April 2004, URL: <*http://www.nytimes.com/2004/04/15/opinion/15DOWD.html?th=&page wanted=print& pos...*>, accessed 19 April 2004.

Predictable Surprise

Two Harvard University professors, Michael D. Watkins and Max H. Bazerman, "Predictable Surprises: The Disasters You Should Have Seen Coming, *Harvard Business Review*, March 2003: 72-80, refer to predictable surprises as disastrous events that could have been anticipated and prepared for. Predictable surprises arise out of failures of recognition, prioritization, or mobilization. They studied predictable surprises that occurred in business and government and they ascertained that an organization's inability to prepare itself can be traced to three kinds of barriers: psychological, organizational, and political. While a leader might not be able to eliminate these barriers entirely, they can be minimized.

They cited the case of the Royal Dutch /Shell Company and Greenpeace protesters who occupied an obsolete oil-storage platform called the Brent Spar as a classic example of predictable surprise. In 1995, Shell decided to junk the Spar. But environmental protesters boarded the site to prevent its demolition. It became a public relations nightmare as Shell blasted the protesters with water cannons. Soon protests and boycotts of Shell products mounted throughout Europe. Shortly thereafter, Shell abandoned its plans. Shell had the information it needed to predict what would transpire but even with all the warning signs, Shell never foresaw the looming calamity.

In a brief examination of 9/11, Watkins and Bazerman infer that the failure to anticipate and take precautionary measures can be traced to lapses in recognition, prioritization, and mobilization. They stipulated that:

Information that might have been pieced together to highlight the precise contours of the threat remained fragmented among the FBI, CIA, and other governmental agencies. No one gave priority to plugging the security holes in the aviation system because, psychologically, the substantial and certain short-term costs of fixing the problems loomed far larger than the uncertain long-term costs of inaction. And the organizations responsible for airline security, the airlines, had the wrong incentives, desiring faster, lower-cost screening to boost profitability. Inevitably, plans to fix the system fell afoul of concerted political lobbying by the airline industry.

Senator Richard C. Shelby, (R-AL), Vice-Chairman and former Chairman of the SSCI, expressed no inhibitions in his criticism of Community leadership or lack thereof, when he adamantly stated:

Long before the September 11 attacks, I made no secret of my feelings of disappointment in the U.S. Intelligence Community for its performance in a string of smaller-scale intelligence failures during the last decade. Since September 11 I have similarly hid from no one my belief that the Intelligence Community does not have the decisive and innovative leadership it needs to reform itself and to adapt to the formidable challenges of the 21st Century...The failures of September 11 were generally not ones of reckless commission but rather of nervous omission. They were failures to take the necessary steps to rise above petty parochial interests and concerns in the service of the common good...I advocate no crusade to hold low-level employees accountable for the failures of September 11...The IC's rank-and-file deserve no discredit for resource decisions and for creating these policies...Responsibility must lie with the leaders who took so little action for so long, to address problems so well known.[200]

James R. Thompson, (R-IL), former governor and member of the 9/11 Commission, commented that, "Blame, if there's blame, has to be spread across the board. Even the public could be said to have failed, because the American people never demanded more or better." *The Washington Post* further reported that though quick, the historical judgment [of 9/11 attacks] seems conclusive: That American leadership failed across the board.[201]

At least 100 families of the victims of 11 September 2001 are demanding more. They decided to sue the airlines and government agencies after rejecting the federal government's compensation offer—$250,000 minimum for deaths, though awards could top $1 million. The lawsuit charges that the airlines and government agencies knew in 2001 that terrorist groups were targeting airlines and airports and failed to respond accordingly with sufficient steps to forestall the attacks. The reasons for rejecting the compensation offer are varied but some families hoped the lawsuit would uncover information about government and corporate missteps while others disliked the idea that taxpayers would be footing the bill for the federal compensation. Nonetheless, the majority of the families have accepted the federal compensation offer—2,924 of the total eligible of 2,976.[202]

Two major investigations were launched to look into the events of 9/11.[203] The first, the Joint Inquiry into Intelligence Community Activities Before and After the Terrorist Attacks of September 11, 2001 (Joint Inquiry)[204] under the direction of Staff Director Eleanor Hill, began in February 2002 and completed its investigation in December 2002. The unclassified version was published mid-2003. The

[200] Sen. Richard C. Shelby (R-AL), "September 11 and the Imperative of Reform in the U.S. Intelligence Community: Additional Views of Senator Richard C. Shelby," 10 December 2002, URL: <http://intelligence.senate.gov/Shelby.pdf>, accessed 21 October 2003. Cited hereafter as Shelby on 9/11 and IC Reform.

[201] Von Drehle, A20.

[202] Michelle Garcia, "Nearly 100 Families are Suing Over 9/11: Federal Compensation is Forsaken," *Washington Post*, 23 January 2004, A9.

second investigation, The National Commission on Terrorists Attacks Upon the United States (9/11 Commission) was established by the Intelligence Authorization Act for FY2003 (P.L. 107-306). Thomas H. Kean presided as Chair and Lee H. Hamiliton was the Vice-Chair. The 9/11 Commission published its report in July 2004. Committee staff members as well as a complete listing of recommendations by both committees are provided in Appendix D—Talking Heads Intelligence Reform, and Appendix E—Post-9/11 Intelligence Reform, respectively. Recommendations specifically addressing IC functions and capabilities are discussed later in this chapter.

These investigations grew not from executive leadership but from the grassroots efforts of family members of victims lost to the tragedy of September 11. Robin Wiener, a board member of the Families of September 11 said, "We need to understand the role that each of these agencies and cabinet offices played and whether or not they were doing their jobs—and if not find out why. We don't want any other family to suffer the way we suffered."[205]

Before discussing these two investigations surrounding the events of 9/11, it is important to acquaint the reader with another report on intelligence reorganization completed more than three years ago but which still has not been released to Congress. In May 2001, President Bush established National Security Presidential Directive-5 (NSPD), which established a Commission on Intelligence Reform

---

[203] Four inquiries into the U.S. Intelligence Community have been initiated since 9/11. The two not discussed further in this project relate to WMD. The Senate Intelligence Committee investigation, led bySenators Pat Roberts (R-KS) and John D. Rockefeller IV, (D-WV), in its findings reported in *Washington Post*, 23 July 2004, A20: "Either the IC overstated evidence that Iraq possessed chemical and biological weapons and was actively reconstituting its nuclear program or the claims were not supported by underlying evidence." The other investigation, the President's Commission, was led by former Senator Charles S. Robb (R-VA) and federal judge Laurence H. Silberman. They were to report their findings to the president by 31 March 2005. This committee was to report on how the United States collects, analyzes and disseminates intelligence related to weapons of mass destruction. This inquiry also was to determine what information the White House had on Iraq prior to the U.S. invasion of that country.

[204] The Senate Intelligence Committee (section 5(a)(1) of Senate Resolution 400, 94th Congress, Rule 6 of the Rules of Procedure of the SSCI) and the House Intelligence Committee (Rule XI (1)(b) of the rules of the House of Representatives and Rule 9 of the Rules of Procedures of the HPSCI) authorized an investigation to be conducted as a Joint Inquiry.

Cited as: U.S. Congress, Senate, Select Committee on Intelligence and House, Permanent Select Committee on Intelligence, *Joint Inquiry into Intelligence Community Activities Before and After the Terrorist Attacks of September 11, 2001,* 107th Cong., 2nd sess., S.Rept. 107-351 and H. Rept. 107-792, December 2002, Preamble, 1. Cited hereafter as Joint Inquiry Report, (Section).

[205] Scot J. Paltrow, "White House Hurdles Delay 9/11 Commission Investigation: Documents and Interviews are Subject of Tense Talks as Tight Deadline Looms," *Wall Street Journal,* online ed., 8 July 2003, <http: // online.wsj.com/public/us>, accessed 9 July 2003.

to review the intelligence community. This review was underway when the terror-ist attacks occurred on 11 September 2001. Very little is known publicly about this Commission, or the Scowcroft Panel, as it is commonly known. It was headed by Lt Gen Brent Scowcroft (USAF Ret), Chairman of the President's For-eign Intelligence Advisory Board (PFIAB) and former national security advisor. The final report remains classified and only brief accounts have been published openly. An NGA senior executive who participated in this panel informed the present author that most participants immediately returned to their respective agencies after the 9/11 attacks. At that point, he had no further involvement. He did comment that by 11 September 2001, the panel had completed their task; all that remained was drafting the cover letter to accompany the panel's report.

In November 2001, according to published reports in the *CQ Weekly*, the Scowcroft panel recommended a major realignment of the intelligence system. This realignment would include moving the National Security Agency (NSA), National Reconnaissance Office (NRO) and the National Imagery and Mapping Agency (NIMA now known as the National Geospatial-Intelligence Agency (NGA)) from the control of the Pentagon to that of the Director, Central Intelli-gence (DCI).[206] The New York Times reported that the Scowcroft panel called for the management of the 15 intelligence agencies and their budgets to be placed under the direction of a single person. However, it is uncertain whether this single intelligence chief would also have been the director of central intelligence or whether that function would be separated.[207]

Apparently, these recommendations received a less than enthusiastic recep-tion from the Defense Department. According to one senior intelligence offi-cial, "The Scowcroft report was stopped dead in its tracks by [Secretary of Defense] Rumsfeld. The Department of Defense didn't want to lose control over its intelligence agencies."[208]

Interestingly, in September 2002, speaking before the Joint House and Senate Intelligence Committee, Scowcroft was asked to comment on the DoD proposal for an Undersecretary of Defense for Intelligence. He replied:

---

[206] Chuck McCutcheon, "Push for Intelligence Overhaul Losing Momentum on the Hill," *CQ Weekly*, 27 April 2002, 1109.

[207] Philip Shenon, "9/11 Panel is Said to Urge New Post for Intelligence," *New York Times*, online ed., 17 July 2004, URL: *http://www.nytimes.com/2004/17/politics/17panel.htm*, accessed 19 July 2004.

[208] Shaun Waterman, "Intelligence Community Reform Stalls," *United Press International*, 11 December 2003, accessed via LexisNexis, 28 January 2004.

Well, let me just say that while the things I have read about it make it look like a housekeeping measure within the Defense Department, I really think that it ought to be viewed in the light of the structural discussions that are going on, whether it's the report of my group—and there are many other things going on—because it will have profound implications for the intelligence community as a whole. And, it seems to me to make a one single step unassociated with all the other things that your committees are now deliberating would be a mistake because then you either predetermine the direction of the structure or you have to change it to go back again. So I would urge, as a first step, that no decision be made on anything which ipso facto will affect the entire community.[209]

The talk around town was that Rumsfeld trumped the Scowcroft panel by publicly announcing the Defense Department's intention to create the USDI position, knowing full-well the recommendations of the Scowcroft panel. On 11 March 2003, Stephen Cambone was sworn in as the first U.S. Undersecretary of Defense for Intelligence (USDI). His 100-person office guides the policies, programs and budgets of the defense intelligence agencies (NSA, NRO, NGA, DIA) and oversees the military services' intelligence, surveillance, reconnaissance and space programs.[210]

As *Time* reported in April 2004:

The report [Scowcroft] was so sensitive that Bush has yet to provide a copy to Congress, and Scowcroft was not allowed to give the 9/11 Commission a detailed brief on it findings. The plan went into a coma in large part because Secretary of Defense Donald Rumsfeld opposed any dilution of Pentagon authority over the spy networks." [211]

Shortly after the release of the 9/11 Commission Report, Senate Minority Leader Thomas A. Daschle (D-SD) sent a letter to President Bush requesting he

---

[209] U.S. Congress, Joint House and Senate Intelligence Committee, "September 19, 2002 Committee Hearing: Brent Scowcroft and Samuel R. Berger," URL: *http://www.complete911* timeline.org/2002/Congressionalinquiry091902b.html>, accessed 21 October 2003.

[210] Glenn W. Goodman, Jr., "Interview with Stephen Cambone," Defense News, online ed., 8 December 2003, URL: http://www.defensenews.com/story, accessed 9 December 2004.

[211] Michael Duffy, "How to Fix Our Intelligence: The CIA and FBI Desperately Need to be Reformed to Deter the Next 9/11. But are They and the Administration Willing to Change?" *Time*, 26 April 2004, online ed., URL: <http://www.time.com/time/magazine/prinout/0,8816,1101040426-612372.html>, accessed 27 April 2004. Cited hereafter as How to Fix Our Intelligence.

provide Congress with a copy of the Scowcroft report. Daschle said that the report would assist Congress in its current review.[212] As of December 2004, the Scowcroft Report still has not been released to anyone outside the White House.

Joint Inquiry Commission

Although U.S. citizens have come to expect thoughtful reflection and when necessary, stalwart examination of perceived government failings or misconduct, reconstructing the government's activities leading up to and surrounding 11 September 2001 proved difficult because of executive-branch-imposed barriers. In its report accompanying the fiscal guidance for the FY 2002 intelligence authorization bill (a few weeks after 9/11), the House Intelligence Committee declared, "There is a fundamental need for both a cultural revolution within the intelligence community as well as significant structural changes.[213] However, if there was a revolution, the revolutionaries were not invited. Before the first anniversary of 9/11, it seemed the call for a cultural revolution had been replaced by the bureaucratic waltz—well-orchestrated procedures to avoid the task at hand, that is, investigate the events leading up to the tragic events of 11 September 2001. "The impetus for getting structural changes in place seems to have been wasted. Hopefully something will come out of this [joint congressional inquiry], but I'm not all that optimistic,"[214] admitted Vincent Cannistraro, a former CIA chief of counterterrorism operations.

Almost a year and a half later (February 2002), the Senate and House Intelligence Committee agreed to conduct a Joint Inquiry into the activities of the Intelligence Community. This joint action was unprecedented in congressional history; never before had two permanent committees joined together to conduct a single, unified inquiry. This Committee had one year to complete its goals:

- Conducting a factual review of what the IC knew or should have known prior to 11 September 2001, regarding the international terrorist threat to the United States, to include the scope and nature of any possible international terrorist attacks against the United States and its interests;
- Identifying and examining any systemic problems that may have impeded the Intelligence Community in learning of or preventing these attacks in advance, and

---

[212] Dan Eggen and Walter Pincus, "Key Idea of 9/11 Panel is Faulted: Commission Seeks Intelligence Chief in White House," *Washington Post*, 31 July 2004, A10. Cited hereafter as Key 9/11 Idea Faulted.

[213] McCutcheon, 1109.

[214] McCutcheon, 1109.

- Making recommendations to improve the Intelligence Community's ability to identify and prevent future international terrorist attacks.[215]

Should not this unprecedented, distinguished group of individuals, who have been entrusted to provide oversight as authorized by the U.S. Constitution have had an edge in obtaining requested information from the U.S. government? They did not. Even as major intelligence agencies in the Inquiry—CIA, FBI, NSA—provided substantial support and allowed access to large volumes of information, the Joint Inquiry encountered access limitations that by the Joint Inquiry's own account, "limited the scope of the Inquiry's work." [216] Numerous executive branch agencies to include the White House, denied the Joint Inquiry access to pertinent information as the following examples attest:

- **PDB** – White House determined and DCI and CIA agreed to no PDB access. Eventually, this denial even extended to prohibiting CIA personnel from being interviewed about the PDB process.
- **Foreign Liaison Relationships** – DCI refused to allow access to Counterterrorism Center (CTC) reports relating to the CIA's liaison relationship with numerous foreign governments. Hence, the Joint Inquiry could not ascertain the level of cooperation/information sharing with the U.S. in countering Bin Laden and al-Qa'ida prior to September 11.
- **Budget** – Lack of resources had been highlighted repeatedly by the IC. A logical exercise would have been to compare the agencies request for monies with the treatment of those requests from within the originating agencies, within the Administration, and by Congress. While agencies and Congress provided some information, the White House and Office of Management and Budget (OMB) refused to share information regarding agency budget requests submitted to OMB and the actions OMB undertook to increase or decrease these requests.
- **NSC-Level Information** – Denied access to most NSC-level discussions. Also, denied access to, or a briefing concerning, the findings and conclusions of the report of the National Security Presidential Directive-5 (NSPD) Commission on Intelligence Reform (Scowcroft Commission).
- **DCI Interview** – Interview with DCI was delayed then made conditional on further discussions with DCI staff. DCI George Tenet eventually testified in an open and closed session and the interview was later denied on that basis.

---

[215] Joint Inquiry Report, Part One—Findings and Conclusions, I. The Joint Inquiry, 1.

[216] Joint Inquiry Report, Access Limitation Encountered by the Joint Inquiry, 1.

- **Military Options** – Requested to review 13 military options that had been reportedly prepared by the Joint Chiefs of Staff (JCS). The Inquiry had wanted to determine the relationship between CIA and the military involving counterterrorism operations prior to 9/11. There were allegations of military reluctance to become involved in the effort against Bin Ladin prior to September 11. The JCS Legal Counsel, supported by DoD General Counsel and the NSC, denied this request as outside the scope of the Joint Inquiry's authority. Later, the Inquiry received a summary briefing of the options.[217]

Furthermore, many of the Intelligence Community agencies restricted the Joint Inquiry's access to information by insisting that legal or congressional affairs personnel be present to monitor all interviews of their personnel. Many interviewees had been pre-briefed by their respective agency as to what the agency position was on certain matters or urged them not to range too broadly in their responses. Additionally, the Community imposed information delays by requiring that any information from one agency found in another agency's file had to be approved by the originating agency before the information could be released; redacting certain information; and refusing to provide electronic access to information, thereby requiring paper copies to be duplicated before release.[218]

Nevertheless, despite attempts to thwart the investigative process, the Joint Inquiry investigation was completed. The complete list of findings is annotated in their entirety in Appendix E—Post-9/11 Intelligence Reform. The Joint Inquiry's Conclusion—Factual Findings—are presented below:

> In short, the Intelligence Community failed to capitalize on both the individual and collective significance of available information that appears relevant to the events of September 11. As a result, the Community missed opportunities to disrupt the September 11 plot by denying entry to or detaining would-be hijackers; to at least try to unravel the plot through surveillance and other investigative work within the United States; and finally, to generate a heightened state of alert and thus harden the homeland against attack.
>
> No one will ever know what might have happened had more connections been drawn between these disparate pieces of information. We will never definitively know to what extent the Community would have been able and willing to exploit fully all the opportunities that may have emerged. The important point is *that the Intelligence Community, for a*

---

[217] Joint Inquiry Report, Access Limitation Encountered by the Joint Inquiry, 1-5.

[218] Joint Inquiry Report, Access Limitation Encountered by the Joint Inquiry, 5-7.

variety of reasons, did not bring together and fully appreciate a range of information that could have greatly enhanced its chances of uncovering and preventing Usama Bin Laden's plan to attack the United States on September 11, 2001.[219] (Italics added by present author).

The National Commission on Terrorist Attacks Upon the United States (9/11 Commission)

The 9/11 Commission also had a less than auspicious beginning. Instead of launching a presidential inquiry into the events surrounding 9/11, as President Roosevelt had done shortly after the Japanese attack on Pearl Harbor, Congress waited almost a year before it formed the panel and then the White House fought its creation, its budget and its duration.[220] Speaking publicly, President Bush said an independent investigation would distract leaders from his newly-declared war on terrorism.[221] Senator Jon Kyl, (R-AZ), senior member of the SSCI, stated, "We're in the middle of a war right now, and everybody's engaged in that. I don't think that most of us want to direct attention from the first priority here."[222] However, not everyone agreed with this excuse for the delays. After all, the United States was involved in a world war when Roosevelt commissioned the Roberts Commission in the early 1940s. Vincent Cannistraro stressed, "The arguments that we're at war and that since we're in the middle of it, we don't have time to do any reflection—I don't buy it because theoretically, this is going to be continuing for a long, long time.[223] Nonetheless, after the Joint Inquiry exposed information sharing issues relating to the September 11 hijackers, congressional support for an independent commission mushroomed, in the words of a *Wall Street Journal* reporter. Consequently, one year later, the White House reversed itself and announced "strong support" for the 9/11 Commission.[224]

In the words of the National Commission on Terrorist Acts Upon the United States, "Our mandate was sweeping." The law directed us to investigate "facts and circumstances relating to the terrorist attacks of September 11, 2001," including those relating to intelligence agencies, law enforcement agencies, diplomacy, immigration issues and border control, the flow of assets to terrorist organiza-

---

[219] Joint Inquiry Report, B. Conclusion-Factual Findings, 33.

[220] *How to Fix Our Intelligence.*

[221] At the time, in 2002, when President Bush made this statement, the United States had actively engaged in a war against the Taliban in Afghanistan in retaliation for harboring Bin Ladin and Al Qa'ida. The United States had not yet ousted the regime of Saddam Hussein in Iraq.

[222] McCutcheon, 1110.

[223] McCutcheon, 1110.

[224] 9/11 Commission Delays.

tions, commercial aviation, the role of congressional oversight and resource allocation, and other areas as determined relevant by the Commission.[225] Yet, the eventual White House endorsement was not enough to allow the Commission to undertake this review. What they needed was a "strong arm of persuasion." Senator Charles Schumer (D-NY) held a news conference on 9 July 2003, a day after the bipartisan 9/11 Commission issued its first interim report, blasting the lack of cooperation from federal agencies. He observed,

> Here's what the stonewalling included: no response from the Defense Department to repeated commission requests for information related to the operations of NORAD, the Joint Chiefs, and the DoD's historical office; continuing delays in sharing of documents in the possession of the Department of Justice, despite repeated DOJ promises to produce the material; a disturbing insistence by DOJ that any interview the commission conducts with a DOJ official can only be undertaken in the presence of a DOJ representative.

> Less than full cooperation from the CIA and Department of Homeland Security, which have been slow to produce documents outlining the use of counterterror resources and immigration practices.[226]

Furthermore, the avowed White House "strong support" proved to be considerably less than advertised. The 9/11 Commission issued three subpoenas for White House documents and twice threatened to do the same for presidential briefing records prepared by the CIA. Eventually, the White House granted limited document access to a select number of Commissioners but provided only a 17-page summary of the CIA-prepared briefings to the remaining members.[227] Finally, in April 2004, almost a year after the existence of the 6 August 2001 PDB became known publicly; the PDB was declassified and released. Other executive impediments, such as refusing the request for a 60-day extension to complete the 9/11 report, setting a one-hour time limit for the President to address the Commissioners and the refusal to allow National Security Advisor Condoleezza Rice to testify in public were eventually resolved. President Bush agreed to a 60-day extension and Congress approved it. Bush and Vice-President Cheney finally spoke to the 9/11 Commission—they spoke together in private to a select number of Commissioners for a limited amount of time. Rice did testify publicly before the Commis-

---

[225] 9/11 Report, Preface, xv.

[226] Sen. Charles Schumer (D-NY), "U.S. Senator Charles Schumer (D-NY) Holds News Conference on 9/11,"9 July 2003, via LexisNexis, accessed 12 January 2004.

[227] Mike Allen and Dan Eggen, "Bush Backs off Limit on 9/11 Questioning: Talk to Panel Leaders to be Open-Ended," *Washington Post,* 10 March 2004, A3. Cited hereafter as Bush Backs off Limit.

sion on 8 April 2004. On the flip side, Scott McClellan, White House press secretary, maintained that the White House had been cooperative by "providing more than two million pages of documents, more than 60 compact disks, more than 800 audiocassette tapes, more than 100 briefings, and more than 560 interviews.[228] Stephen Hess, a senior fellow at the Brookings Institution, reflected on the interplay between the White House and the 9/11 Commission:

> The jockeying between the two sides [White House and the 9/11 Commission] has seemed almost scripted. This seems to me to be the pattern of most controversial commissions. It's sort of a back-and-forth that's almost traditional....They always want more than the president or the executive branch wants to give them, and the executive branch initially objects before giving in on some things.[229]

After a review of more than 2.5 million pages of documents; after interviews with more than 1,200 individuals in ten countries, which encompassed nearly every senior official from the current and previous administrations who had responsibility for the mandated topics; and following 19 days of public hearings with testimony from 160 witnesses,[230] the word processors fell silent and the presses roared. The 9/11 Commission had completed its work and released the final report on 22 July 2004.

The present author, speaking to a former senior executive intelligence specialist, expressed her sense of frustration over the countless reform recommendations made by scores of talented individuals and how these repeated recommendations were shelved time and time again without action or minimal action being undertaken. After casually mentioning the galvanizing effects of the public protests of the 1960s (civil rights movement, Vietnam War activists) had on influencing the government to take action, this colleague asked jokingly, "What, you expect people to "take to the streets" over intelligence reform. Hell, the general public doesn't know the first thing about the Intelligence Community." However, on 22 July 2004, the public began educating itself on the Intelligence Community. Less than a week later, 600,000 copies of the initial press run had been sold and 200,000 more copies were being printed. Additionally, the Commission's web site, which includes free access to the report, recorded more than 50 million hits.[231] By 12 September 2004, the 567-page, *9/11 Commission Final Report of*

---

[228] Bush Backs off Limit, A3.

[229] Dan Eggen, "For the Record: While House vs. 9/11 Panel: Resistance, Resolution," *Washington Post*, 9 March 2004, A2.

[230] 9/11 Report, Preface, xv.

[231] Mike Allen and Dan Eggen, "Bush May Move Soon on 9/11 Report: President Close to Announcing Plans for Revamping Intelligence System," *Washington Post*, A6.

the *National Commission on Terrorist Attacks Upon the United States* had remained the Washington area's Number 1 Nonfiction bestseller for seven weeks and counting.[232] Lest one think that the interest in the 9/11 report is only "inside the Beltway," it also a garnered the top spot on The *New York Times* bestseller list as well. It hit No.1 in sales on the Amazon.com website. The New York *Daily News* positioned the 9/11 Report cover emblazoned in a red box with the words, "Act Now!" on its 23 July 2004 cover.[233] As of 10 October 2004, 1.5 million copies are in print and it has been named as a finalist for a National Book Award by the National Book Foundation.[234] The *New York Times* reported plans by Imagine Entertainment to make the 9/11 Commission Report into an eight-hour mini-series on NBC![235]

"Let's Get Ready to Rumble"[236] – Discussion of Joint Inquiry/ 9/11 Commission Recommendations

"Since the plotters were flexible and resourceful, we cannot know whether any single step or series of steps would have defeated them," 9/11 Commission Chairman Thomas H. Kean admitted at a news conference the day the Commission released its report. "What we can say with a good deal of confidence is that none of the measures adopted by the United States government before 9/11 disturbed or even delayed the progress of the al Qaeda plot…The government failed to protect the American people. The United States government was simply not active enough in combating the terrorist threat before 9/11."[237] "This was a failure of policy, management, capability, and above all a failure of imagination."[238] Although the Commission could not determine whether the attacks could have been prevented, it did identify ten "Operational Opportunities" that were missed in detecting the plot to attack the United States (see tonebox below).

---

[232] Book World, "Washington Area Bestsellers," *Washington Post,* 12 September 2004, 11.

[233] Philip Kennicott, "Remembering: A Novel Approach," *Washington Post,* 1 August 2004, B4.

[234] Jeff Baenen, "9/11 Report Is Up for National Book Award," *Washington Post,* 14 October 2004, C4.

[235] "9/11 Report to Be TV Mini-Series," *New York Times*, 15 November 2004, B2.

[236] Michael Buffer, announcer for professional boxing events.

[237] Dan Eggen, "9/11 Panel Chronicles U.S. Failures: Final Report Faults Two Administrations and Calls for Broad Reform," *Washington Post,* 23 July 2004, A18.

[238] E.J. Dionne, Jr., "A Lesson From 9/11: Openness," *Washington Post,* 23 July 2004, A29.

10 Missed Opportunities — 9/11 Report

1. January 2000: CIA does not watchlist Khalid al Mihdhar or notify FBI when it learned Mihdhar possessed a valid U.S. visa.

2. January 2000: CIA does not develop a transnational plan for tracking Mihdhar and his associates so that they could be followed to Bangkok and onward, including the United States.

3. March 2000: CIA does not watchlist Nawaf al Hazmi or notify the FBI when it learned that he possessed a U.S. visa and had flown to Los Angeles on 15 January 2000.

4. January 2001: CIA does not inform the FBI that a source had identified Khallad, or Tawfiq bin Attash, a major figure in the October 2000 bombing of the USS *Cole*, as having attended the meeting in Kuala Lumpur with Khalid al Mihdhar.

5. May 2001: CIA official does not notify the FBI about Mihdhar's U.S. visa, Hazmi's U.S. travel, or Khallad's having attended the Kuala Lumpur meeting (identified when he reviewed all of the relevant traffic because of the high level of threats).

6. June 2001: FBI and CIA officials do not ensure all relevant information regarding the Kuala Lumpur meeting was shared with the *Cole* investigators at the June 11 meeting.

7. August 2001: FBI does not recognize the significance of the information regarding Mihdhar and Hazmi's possible arrival in the United States and thus does not take adequate action to share information, assign resources, and give sufficient priority to the search.

8. August 2001: FBI headquarters does not recognize the significance of the information regarding Moussaoui's training and beliefs and thus does not take adequate action to share information, involve higher-level officials across agencies, obtain information regarding Moussaoui's ties to al Qaeda, and give sufficient priority to determining what Moussaoui might be planning.

9. August 2001: CIA does not focus on information that Khalkd Sheikh Mohammed is a key al Qaeda lieutenant or connect information identifying KSM as the "Mukhtar" mentioned in other reports to the analysis that could have linked "Mukhtar" with Ramzi Binalshibh and Moussaoui.

10. August 2001: CIA and FBI do not connect the presence of Mihdhar, Hazmi, and Moussaoui to the general threat reporting about imminent attacks.

The Commission identified 28 major recommendations in the Report's section titled "What to Do? A Global Strategy." As the title suggests, these recommendations provide the fundamental underpinnings of what this U.S. national strategy should be. These recommendations are listed in Appendix E—Post 9-11 Intelligence Reform. As they do not relate specifically, but rather generally to the IC, these recommendations are not discussed further in this report.

The 9/11 Commission asserted that, "As presently configured, the national security institutions of the U.S. government are still the institutions constructed to win the Cold War."[239] Although the United States has the people and the resources, the Commission underscored the need for the government to combine them more effectively, achieving "unity of effort." The Commission proposed five major recommendations to realize this unity of effort. (For more precise recommendations proposed by the Commission, see Appendix E.)

- Unifying strategic intelligence and operational planning against Islamist terrorists across the foreign-domestic divide with a National Counterterrorism Center (NCTC)
- Unifying the Intelligence Community with a new National Intelligence Director
- Unifying the many participants in the counterterrorism effort and their knowledge in a network-based information-sharing system that transcends traditional governmental boundaries
- Unifying and strengthening congressional oversight to improve quality and accountability
- Strengthening the FBI's homeland defense capabilities.[240]

Of all the recommendations put forth by the Commission, creating the National Counterterrorism Center, the National Intelligence Director and the subsequent intelligence centers, and letting the Pentagon have lead responsibility for covert paramilitary operations have become the most controversial and will be addressed further below. According to Philip D. Zelikow, executive director of the 9/11 Commission, the Intelligence Community structure proposed by the Commission is modeled on the reform of the U.S. military under the Goldwater-Nichols Act of 1986—unifying the military under a single, unified command to ensure coordination. Zelikow remarked in a recent interview, "Ours is not a panacea. We may not have all the right answers, but we looked at other options. If someone can come up with a better way, they should....[our proposals were] designed to make a difference in the real world for real problems and were not just academic fixes.[241]

The 9/11 Commission recommended that the NCTC be built on the foundation of the existing Terrorist Threat Integration Center (TTIC).[242] The TTIC would

---

[239] 9/11 Report, 400.

[240] 9/11 Report, 400-401.

[241] Walter Pincus, "9/11 Panel's Plan Would Reduce Influence of CIA: Experts Predict Realignment of Roles," *Washington Post,* 29 July 2004, A6. Cited hereafter as Pincus 9/11 Panel Reduces CIA Influence.

become the center for *joint operational planning and joint intelligence.* Additionally, the head of the NCTC, appointed by the president with rank commensurate to a deputy head of cabinet, would have authority to evaluate the performance of the people assigned to the Center. The Commission stresses the importance of joint *action* for three primary reasons—the virtue of joint planning; the advantage of having someone in charge to ensure a unified effort; and, finally the shortage of critical skill sets. The NCTC would perform joint planning with operational responsibilities assigned to lead agencies such as State, CIA, FBI, Defense and the combatant commands. However, the NCTC would not execute these plans. The director of the NCTC would report directly to the national intelligence director and indirectly to the president. The NCTC would lead strategic analysis and provide net assessments—comparing enemy capabilities and intentions against U.S. defenses and countermeasures. In this strategic role, the NCTC would absorb most all of the CIA's Counterterrorism Center and DIA's Joint Intelligence Task Force (JITF-CT).[243]

The Commission recognized that this arrangement might result in a concentration of "too much power" in one place. Nonetheless, law or executive order would define the parameters of this organization. The National Security Council would still arbitrate interagency policy disputes.[244]

After their lengthy investigation, the 9/11 Commission recognized that the need to restructure the Intelligence Community can be attributed to six problems that were apparent before and after 9/11. These problems constitute evidence that the current IC structure is not compatible with the challenges facing the Community in the 21st Century:

1. Structural barriers to performing joint intelligence work. National intelligence continues to be stove-piped through specific collection disciplines.
2. Lack of common standards and practices across the foreign-domestic divide. A common set of standards encompassing both arenas for both information processing and personnel must be set in place.
3. Divided management of national intelligence capabilities. Following the end

---

[242] As noted in 9/11 Report, 401, the TTIC created in 2003 is based at the CIA headquarters but is staffed with various agency representatives. However, the CIA also has a fusion center—the Counterterrorist Center. Then there is the Defense Intelligence Agency with its counterterrorism center-the Joint Intelligence Task Force (JITF-CT), Homeland Security concentrates on homeland vulnerabilities. The FBI created the Terrorist Screening Center and is building its analytic capability. The U.S. Government cannot afford all this duplication—there is not enough experience to go around.

[243] 9/11 Report, 401-405.

[244] 9/11 Report, 406.

of the Cold War, the DCI has been less able to influence the use of imagery and signal intelligence capabilities of the NSA, NGA, and NRO, resulting in a comparatively greater demand made by the Defense Department on these technical systems.

4. Weak capacity to set priorities and move resources. The priorities for collection are national; however, agencies are organized around what they collect or the way they collect it.

5. Too many jobs. The DCI has too many jobs—run the CIA, manage the IC, brief the president—all tasks that are complex and secret. Over the decades the Community has encompassed many agencies, and the Community has grown more arcane. The DCI lacks the authority to control the purse strings, hire or fire senior managers and the ability to set standards for information infrastructure and personnel.[245]

The suggestion that there be a single director of national intelligence is certainly not a new recommendation: the Joint Inquiry proposed creating a DNI, as did the unreleased, classified Scowcroft study. Historically, the Boren-McCurdy Act in 1992 called for creating a Director of National Intelligence, and the Schlesinger Report in 1971 criticized "unproductive duplicative" collection systems and the failure in forward planning to coordinate the allocation of resources. That report considered the creation of a DNI to correct these problems.[246] However, Schlesinger's recommendation was not included in the final report which instead recommended a "strong DCI who could bring intelligence costs under control and intelligence production to an adequate level of quality and responsiveness." Before that, in 1955, the Second Hoover Commission recommended that the DCI concentrate on intelligence issues facing the entire community.[247]

Nevertheless, while the specifics of all these recommendations have been and will continue to be debated, intelligence professionals, scholars, national security specialists and others have carried forward a debate in the open press. It has been said that anyone who have ever stood before a microphone has an opinion about intelligence reform. This is certainly the case in the aftermath of the publication

---

[245] 9/11 Report, 407-409.

[246] A Review of the Intelligence Community, 10 March 1991, 1 (citation as noted in: Richard A. Best, Jr. and Herbert Andrew Boertling, "Appendix C, IC21: The Intelligence Community in the 21st Century," *CRS Report for Congress* (Washington, D.C.: Congressional Research Service, Library of Congress, 28 February 1996), 16. >*URL:<http://www.access.gpo.gov/congress/house/intel/ic21/ic21018.html>*, accessed 11 May 2004. Cited hereafter as CRS Report, Appendix C, February 1996.

[247] U.S. Congress, Senate, Select Committee to Study Governmental Operations with Respect to Intelligence Activities Intelligence, Final Report, Book I, 94th Cong., 2nd sess., 1976, 1 (citation as noted in CRS Report, Appendix C, February 1996).

of the Joint Inquiry and particularly, the 9/11 Commission Report. Some have urged caution in moving too quickly with intelligence reform as indicated by the following views:

> We must not allow false urgency dictated by the political calendar to overtake the need for serious reform…There is no debate about the need to reform our 20th Century intelligence infrastructure. While inaction is unacceptable, serious consequences will come with reform. Policymakers owe it to the American people to understand these consequences before they act.[248]

> —Senator Chuck Hagel, (R-NE)

> It is important that we move with all deliberate speed; however, moving too quickly risks enormous error. And we are considering important matters while at war. If you more unwisely and get it wrong, the penalty will be great.[249]

> —Donald Rumsfeld
> *Secretary of Defense*

> I sincerely urge those who, with the best intentions, seek to heal the nation's intentions, seek to heal the nation's wounds and improve the intelligence community, to adopt the ancient medical dictum of "first, do no harm." If we rush to implement sweeping change, especially at the time when threats to America are as great or greater than they have been at any time since September 11, we may do more harm than good.[250]

> —James L. Pavitt
> *former CIA Deputy Director for Operations*

Whether the pace of reform is slow or swift, the intelligence reform alarm now sounds across the nation. Shortly after the Commission released its report, National Security Advisor Condoleezza Rice observed, "I don't think it's a matter of whether there will be intelligence reform. I think there will be further intelligence reform. It's a matter of how and precisely what will be done."[251]

---

[248]Sen Chuck Hagel (R-NE), "Intelligence Reform and False Urgency," *Washington Post,* 3 August 2004, A17.

[249]Donald Rumsfeld, Secretary of Defense, "Rumsfeld: Use Caution in Intelligence Reform," *Washington Post,* 18 August 2004, A10.

[250] Pavitt, A19.

[251] Dan Eggen, "9/11 Panel Chronicles U.S. Failures: Final Report Faults Two Administrations and Calls for Broad Reform," *Washington Post,* 23 July 2004, A18.

Luminaries Respond to 9/11 Committee Recommendations

- Lt Gen James R. Clapper, (USAF Ret), Director, NGA:

I do not believe that we [national agencies—NGA, NSA, NRO] have to be administratively embedded in the Department of Defense—or, for that matter, any cabinet department—in order to sustain such support. As things stand now, our major customers get to determine whether, and to what extent, we provide support to our other cabinet departments, who also have legitimate and growing demands for our products, services, and solutions.

The underlying basis for the current configuration of the Intelligence Community is Cold-War inspired…That is no longer the operative paradigm. We have a much different threat and we need, accordingly, to adjust organizationally.

Like the President, I agree with the 9/11 Commission recommendation that we need an empowered National Intelligence Director. I believe the NID should manage at least three agencies—CIA, NSA, NGA and, perhaps NRO….This does not mean that our support to military operations would in any way be compromised. In fact, I would assert it would be even better than it is today. Our direct support to military operations—required by law in the case of NGA—would continue to the nine Combatant Commands and, increasingly, to levels far below the traditional boundary of these Commands, or even their subordinate Joint Task Forces.[252]

- Colin L. Powell, Secretary of State:

[creating a new national intelligence director could guard against faulty intelligence like that behind] some of the sourcing that was used to give me the basis upon which to bring forward that judgment [Iraq had WMD] to the United Nations [and that] were flawed, were wrong….with an important, empowered national intelligence director, you are less likely to have those kinds of mistakes.[253]

---

[252] Lt Gen James R. Clapper, USAF (Ret), Director, National Geospatial-Intelligence Agency, D/NGA Testimony Before HPSCI on 9/11 Commission Report," 19 August 2004.

[253] Walter Pincus, "Support for Intelligence Plan: Powell, Ridge Back One Director But Defer to Bush on Specifics," *Washington Post*, 14 September 2004, A4.

● Robert C. McFarlane, national security advisor (1983-1985):

Over the past 30 years, through abuse, neglect and poor leadership, the CIA has slowly ground to a virtual halt. More broadly, the so-called intelligence "community"—structurally dysfunctional and lacking effective oversight—essentially failed in its analyses of the two salient threats of the late 20th Century: the Soviet Union and radical Islam.

In addition, as it [restructuring] would be unfettered by agency loyalty and bias, the new staff could have a dramatic impact on what I call "inertial budgeting"—the practice of funding systems and programs this year because we did it last year—and instead could make it possible to focus resources on new priorities or to exploit new technologies in a timely way.

The military's unified command structure…is a sound model for the new director's office…Giving the new director a fixed term that overlaps administration, as suggested by some in Congress, is the right way to avoid the post's becoming politicized.[254]

● William E. Odom, former director NSA (1985-1988):

No organizational design will compensate for incompetent incumbents, but some designs prevent competent incumbents from performing well. The 9/11 commission's design for a new national intelligence director (NID) is sure to accomplish the latter. There is already a layer of bureaucracy above the CIA, NSA, DIA and other intelligence agencies, and it consists of the Community Management Staff and the National Intelligence Council. It simply has not been used effectively because the director of central intelligence is double-hatted….Creating a NID with three deputies…would make things much worse. It would assure turf battles and prevent effective budget management

[fixed term for NID] It's a bad idea….There is no way to depoliticize the role of the president's intelligence chief. It is a desirable aspiration, but intelligence is just as political as policymaking and military operations. The popular notion that apolitical intelligence will prevent bad policies is an illusion. Intelligence chiefs can be no more effective than their political leaders or military commanders will allow them to be or demand that they be. The intelligence failures surrounding the 9/11 attacks and in Iraq are primarily political failures. Effective leaders do

---

[254] Robert C. McFarlane, "Restructuring From the Top…," *Washington Post*, 1 August 2004, B4.

not tolerate inadequate intelligence performance or leave it to commissions to fix intelligence problems.[255]

● William S. Cohen, former secretary of defense (1997-2001):

Creating an effective joint staff will be no easy task. Traditions and old habits die hard.... One of my principal concerns about the commission's recommendations is making sure that the NID office, however it is structured, [should be] prohibited from having any advocacy role on operational matters...Those charged with collecting, collating and distilling intelligence should not indulge in policy debates.

Congress must be vigorous in the exercise of its oversight responsibilities. And as Congress examines deficiencies within the executive branch, it should give equal weight to the need to reform its own budgetary and oversight processes.

If we are serious about real reform, we have to contemplate both the intended and unintended consequences of any changes that are made....But virtually every reorganization of an institution aimed at improving efficiency and decision-making will eventually reveal weaknesses or produce dislocations that will, in turn, need to be reengineered.[256]

● Gary Hart, former senator (D-CO) and Vice-Chair, Hart-Rudman Commission:

It would be a disaster [if NID went into the Cabinet or White House staff]. You have to have a clear organizational separation between those responsible for generating intelligence and those policymakers who are consumers. You mix them and you will inevitably get political pressures affecting the quality of the information....Unless the new man has control over the whole intelligence budget of government, you simply have added a new layer of bureaucracy and set it up to fail....Every past proposal...has foundered on the refusal of the Pentagon to give up an inch of control of its own intelligence budget.[257]

---

[255] William E. Odom, "Restructuring From the Top...," *Washington Post,* 1 August 2004, B5.

[256] William S. Cohen, "Restructuring From the Top...," *Washington Post,* 1 August 2004, B4.

[257] Gary Hart, "Heeding the 9/11 Panel," interview by David S. Broder, in *Washington Post,* 8 August 2004, B07.

- Phyllis Oakley, former assistant secretary of state for intelligence and research:

With the intelligence czar and a unified intelligence center, the system would lose the competitiveness that's been an important element of its successes until now....It seems to me that whatever structure is set up, the principle of competitive analysis, as well as a system in which people can argue and disagree, needs to be preserved. And those people need to be heard by the national security advisor or the president....

It may seem paradoxical, but the only thing we need as much as competitiveness among agencies is coordination, especially if we go along with the commission plan to maintain separate agencies....Having a joint coordination center might have helped [lack of coordination post 9/11], but having an overarching czar wouldn't have solved that problem....the real coordination isn't going to come from the top—it has to be encouraged at a lower level, among analysts.

But there ought to be real discussion about how any reconfigured intelligence structure would work. The thought that the president is just going to adopt all these things [commission recommendations]—especially in an election year—is just wacky. You have to look at the total intelligence structure before you can say yea or nay.[258]

- Senator Pat Roberts (R-KS), Chairman of the Senate Intelligence Committee and eight other Republicans called for more extensive changes in intelligence organizations than proposed by the 9/11 Commission. Their plan would have removed the CIA's three main directorates—operations, analysis and technology and turned them into separate entities reporting to separate directors; NSA and NGA would be put under the DNI; and the human intelligence (HUMINT) component within DIA would be removed from the Pentagon. Roberts defended his proposal saying,

  We didn't pay attention to turf or agencies or boxes. I'm trying to build a consensus around something that's different and very bold...No one agency, no matter how distinguished its history, is more important than national security.[259]

[258] Phyllis Oakley, "Restructuring From the Top...," *Washington Post,* 1 August 2004, B5.

[259] Dan Eggen, "GOP Plan Calls for Revamping Intelligence: Pentagon, CIA Would Give Up Many Duties," Washington Post, 23 August 2004, A7.

Although Robert's proposal was not seriously considered by the Senate as a whole, it did provoke discussion among Washington's professionals. George Tenet, former DCI, was especially critical of Robert's plan, saying the proposal:

> Would gut the CIA...is a dangerous misunderstanding of the business of intelligence...Senator Robert's proposal is yet another episode in the mad rush to rearrange wiring diagrams in an attempt to be seen as doing something. It is time for someone to slam the brakes on before the politics of the moment drives the security of the American people off a cliff.[260]

Julius Kobyakov Major General SVR (Retired), former KGB officer, posted this interesting musing, reflecting on Senator Pat Roberts (R-KS) intelligence reform proposal:

> Distinguished members:

> Back in the heyday of Cold War some of my KGB colleagues toyed with an idea of breaking up the C.I.A. by setting it off against the F.B.I. and both of them against the Pentagon. Most were harebrained schemes but none had been as sweeping as the one proposed by Senator Pat Roberts of Kansas. (This is not to imply that present setup is perfect.)

> But as a KGB/SVR veteran, who lived through quite a few sweeping organizations of the Soviet/Russian era I can share my general experience.

> It usually looks swell on charts with all the bells and whistles but when you try to implement it the place stops working, then it falls apart with some of the best people running sway [away]. And then the ones, who for this or that reason stayed behind are faced with an enormous Sisyphean labor of trying to jump start the new bastard, or parts of what once was a functioning system. This may take years.[261]

---

[260]Dan Eggen and Charles Barrington, "Many are Cool to Intelligence Plan: Bush Expresses Reservation; Tenet Says GOP Proposal would 'Gut the CIA," Washington Post, 24 August 2004, A3.

[261] Major General Julius Kobyakov, Ret., email to Intelligence Forum listserv, subject: "U.S. Intelligence Reform," 23 August 2004.

Reform Effects of Presidential Executive Order

After weeks of speculation as to what the White House would propose in response to the 9/11 Commission recommendations, President Bush issued four Executive Orders on 27 August 2004. They:

- Directed the Strengthened Management of the Intelligence Community
- Established the National Counterterrorism Center
- Strenghened the Sharing of Terrorism Information to Protect Americans
- Established the President's Board on Safeguarding Americans' Civil Liberties

These EOs are presented in more detail in Appendix E.

The first EO, Directing the Strengthened Management of the Intelligence Community, amended EO 12333, which had been the guiding but often ineffective IC directive for decades. The DCI, until the NID[262] is created by Congress, will discharge the responsibilities outlined in this EO. In the opinion of this author, this EO did nothing more than perhaps tighten the gloves of the DCI (NID) to enable a more capable punch but the heavyweight champion is still the Defense Department in the fight for intelligence dollars. Much of the language of this Executive Order expanded on authority the DCI already had with respect to coordinating activities across the Community, as granted by EO 12333. One senior congressional aide reported that the orders seem to have the quality of, "This time, we really mean it."[263] Without full budget authority, the authority to decide how funds should be appropriated among the agencies, to include the Pentagon, the NID will remain weak. Although Bush stated, "We believe that there ought to be a national intelligence director who has full budgetary authority," this authority only pertained to the NFIP—that 70 percent of the intelligence budget

---

[262] Two of these EOs—strengthening the management of the IC and the creation of the NCTC—were meant to be interim measures until such time as Congress passed legislation. After much discussion, the House approved its compromised version on 8 December and the Senate on 9 December 2004. President Bush signed the Intelligence Reform and Terrorist Prevention Act of 2004 into law on 17 December 2004. One of the main provisions of this legislation was the separation of the Director of Central Intelligence position from the Director of Central Intelligence Agency position. No longer would the head of the IC be dual-hatted. The National Intelligence Director (NID), also known as the Director of National Intelligence (DNI), is the new head of the IC. The executive orders issued by President Bush were co-opted by the enactment of this legislation. The Intelligence Reform and Terrorist Prevention Act of 2004 will be discussed briefly in a subsequent chapter.

[263] Walter Pincus, "Analysis: Bush's Intelligence Moves Don't Attain Scope Urged by 9/11 Panel," *Washington Post,* 2 September 2004, A4.

that is not related solely to military operations. However, most of the NFIP money goes to support defense organizations such as NSA, NGA and DIA. The only organization the DCI truly manages is the CIA. The other 30 percent remains under the control of the Defense Department and is dispersed among the Joint Military Intelligence Program (JMIP) and Tactical Intelligence and Related Activities (TIARA) programs. According to the White House, its plan would "avoid the disruption of war effort that a more far-reaching restructuring could create."[264] Describing the President's NID proposal as it exists now, Robert M. Gates said, "it's creating a new layer of bureaucracy in the Intelligence Community....The NID position, without direct control of a single line agency or organization, will eventually have its authorities eroded, eventually becoming not an intelligence czar, but eunuch."[265]

It is difficult to understand how the current "war efforts" in Iraq and Afghanistan argue against restructuring as these cannot even be considered comparable to the war effort during World War II when the U.S. industrial, societal and intelligence organizations underwent a massive restructuring. Within a relatively short time frame during WWII, the United States revamped its economy to create an enormous industrial base to supply U.S. and Allied forces; inducted millions of its citizens to fight globally dispersed enemies and simultaneously defeated the Axis Powers of Germany, Italy and Japan. Moreover, within months of the end of WWII, the United States steadied itself to face the emergence of communism and the evolving Soviet Union. At the same time, the U.S. restructured not only its armed services by abolishing the Army Air Corps and creating the Air Force but created the CIA, NCS and JCS with the passage of the National Security Act of 1947.

The EO creating the National Counterterrorism Center restricted its counterterrorism activities. The NCTC would not have the authority to direct covert counterterrorism operations abroad or at home, and though it would be involved in planning of operations, it would not execute them. Operations execution remained with the FBI, CIA, and Pentagon depending on the activity. John E. McLaughlin, Acting DCI, in referring to the NCTC, which was created by the second executive order, said, "[NCTC] would be a kind of clearinghouse of what needs to be done, and then the doing would be passed on to those who must do it."[266]

---

[264] Walter Pincus and Dana Milbank, "Bush Plan Draws on Advice of 9/11 Panel: New Proposal Gives Intelligence Chief More Budget Power," *Washington Post*, 9 September 2004, A1.

[265] Walter Pincus, "Bush's Plan Limits Intelligence Chief: Other Would Carry Out Operations," *Washington Post*, 11 September 2004, *Washington Post* A4. Cited hereafter as Bush's Plan Limits Intel Chief.

[266] Bush Plan Limits Intel Chief, A4.

The third EO directed all Executive Branch agencies to do the obvious—promptly share information relating to terrorism with other agencies with counterterrorism functions. It required a Presidential Directive in essence, to proclaim to the senior managers of one intelligence agency that they should be sharing their secret information with other senior managers of other intelligence agencies within the Intelligence Community. Policy decisions worked to prevent this exchange of information prior to 11 September 2001. These policies were written long ago, before their current implications could be envisioned.

The "information sharing" EO ordered the DCI to establish common standards across the Intelligence Community and to establish an Information Systems Council that will plan and oversee an interoperable terrorism-information-sharing environment. Amazingly, sixty years after the enactment of the National Security Act of 1947, it is finally agreed that Intelligence Community members should be able to communicate with other Intelligence Community members. Any historian may have supposed that at the very least, EO 12333, which in part "Granted the DCI full responsibility for the production and dissemination of national foreign intelligence"[267] would have ensured such communication. Again, we can see the weakness of executive orders, in comparison to the edicts of legislation.

The fourth EO, enacted on the heels of the 9/11 Commission Report, creates a President's Board on Safeguarding Americans' Civil Liberties. As the title suggests, the President created this board to ensure the safeguard of legal rights of all Americans. The Deputy Attorney General is the Chair and the Under Secretary for Border and Transportation Security of the Department of Homeland Security is the Vice-Chair. Other members are senior officials across the federal government.

Perhaps no other organization, public or private, has been scrutinized more thoroughly than the Intelligence Community. The time for thoughtful reflection has now passed, however. Clearly, 9/11 demonstrated the weaknesses of an almost 60-year old intelligence service. With the constraints of the Cold War removed, globalization is once again the prime mover in the world environment, requiring the Community to employ new business processes and procedures to understand effectively this rapidly changing environment.

As an example, Imam Samudra represents the new face of the enemy in the globalized 21st Century. Samudra, who was charged in the deadly Bali bombings in 2002 that left 202 people dead—mostly foreign (Western) tourists—recently authored a book entitled "Me Against the Terrorist." A chapter of particular inter-

---

[267]Section 1.5 (a,d,e,h,k), Executive Order 12333, 4 December 1981, United States Intelligence Activities (citation as noted in Best and Boerstling, 27).

est is "Hacking, Why Not?" While U.S. computers have always been a favorite target of would-be hackers (and often an easy target due to lax computer security), Samudra explains how to commit credit card fraud, complete with accompanying web links for specific instructions. According to *The Washington Post*, Samudra is among the most technologically savvy members of the underground Islamic movement in Southeast Asia, the Jemaah Islamiah. He sought to finance the Bali bombings through credit card fraud but it is not known if he was successful in this arrangement. Evan F. Kohlmann, a U.S. consultant on international terrorism, indicated that online credit fraud is an increasingly attractive source of funding for al Qa'ida operatives in several parts of the world.[268] The next chapter will illustrate compelling examples of challenges/threats facing the Community in the 21st Century. As Senator Bob Graham (D-FL) maintains, the situation is basic Darwinism: "If you don't understand changes in your habitat, you will die."[269]

---

[268] Alan Sipress, "An Indonesian's Prison Memoir Takes Holy War Into Cyberspace: In Sign of New Threat, Militant Offers Tips on Credit Card Fraud," *Washington Post,* 14 December 2004, A19.

[269] "Time to Rethink – America's Intelligence Services," *The Economist Newspaper Ltd.,* 20 April 2002, accessed via Lexis-Nexis, 28 January 2004.

Chapter Six

INTELLIGENCE IN THE POST-9/11 WORLD

In the Post-9/11 world, threats are defined more by the fault lines within societies than by the territorial boundaries between them. From terrorism to global disease or environmental degradation, the challenges have become transnational rather than international. That is the defining quality of world politics in the twenty-first century.

—The 9/11 Commission Report
22 July 2004

Globalization and the Intelligence Community

One cannot discuss the role of the Intelligence Community in the 21st Century and the need to reform or transform its current structure without discussing the context in which it operates—that being a globalized environment. Globalization, the quintessence of interconnectedness, is not a new phenomenon[270] nor is it strictly a function of Westernization; it is a function of the economic integration of nearly the entire world. "Over thousands of years, globalization has progressed through travel, trade, migration, spread of cultural influences and dissemination of knowledge and understanding (including of science and technology),"[271] maintains Cambridge University Nobel Laureate Amartya Sen. In fact, the period of globalization preceding World War I was quite similar to the era the world is experiencing now, with the difference being that Great Britain was the dominant global power like the United States today. Comparing the volumes of trade and capital flows across borders and the flows of labor across the borders, relative to the GNPs and the populations respectively, the similarities are apparent. Falling transportation costs—sea lanes, railways, automobiles, airplanes defined the first era of globalization in the 20th century and contrib-

---

[270] Richard N. Haass, "Policy Makers and the Intelligence Community: Supporting US Foreign Policy in the Post-911 World," *Studies in Intelligence*, 46, no. 3 cites multinational corporations, transnational religious movements, substantial international capital flows, global pandemics, the emergence of global networks of commerce, and non-governmental organizations and private foundations as examples that globalization is **not** a new phenomenon. These examples of globalization predate not just the end of the Cold War, but the World Wars as well.

[271] Amartya Sen, "If It's Fair, It's Good: 10 Truths About Globalization," *Canadian Dimension*, 14 July 2001, accessed via LexisNexis, 30 September 2004.

uted immeasurably to the migration of things and people. World events such as WWI, the Russian Revolution and the Great Depression interrupted 20th Century globalization, as did WWII and the protracted Cold War. The Cold War was an international system, which, according to Thomas Friedman, was replaced by another system—a new era of globalization. "It turns out that the roughly seventy-five-year period from the start of World War I to the end of the Cold War," says Friedman, "was just a long time-out between one era of globalization and another.[272] Falling telecommunications and PC costs would come to define the second era of globalization of the 20th century that would rapidly accelerate and extend its reach.

The growth in international trade has been touted as a source of increased productivity for all participants. Most economic evidence supports this claim. While wages of workers in overseas locations such as China, Bangladesh and Central America are not comparable to those in the United States, in most cases, the existing wage structure has raised the standard of living for those workers. A recent Columbia University study showed that in some developing companies, multinational corporations pay their workers more than 10 percent above the going wage in their own factories (subcontractors may pay only the prevailing wage). Additionally, wage differentials against women have decreased faster in industries that compete internationally.[273] Economists maintain that trade is not a zero-sum game but rather a positive-sum game whereby there is an opportunity for increased diversity of products, increased specialization, transmission of information and technology, and the like.[274] As transportation costs decreased and more transportation options became available, international trade mushroomed during the 20th Century. In 1990, daily foreign exchange trading was measured in millions of dollars. By 1992, it was recorded at $820 billion and astonishingly, six years later, the daily foreign exchange trading had exploded to $1.5 trillion daily and climbing. Private capital cash flows from developed countries to developing countries measured in the millions in the early 1900s but by 2000, it was in the hundreds of billions of dollars.[275]

A second truth about globalization espoused by Amartya Sen is that globalization in itself is not a folly: It has enriched the world scientifically and cul-

---

[272] Thomas Friedman, *The Lexus and the Olive Tree* (New York: Farrar, Straus and Giroux, 1999), xvi.

[273] Fagdish Bhagwati, "Coping with Antiglobalization: A Triology of Discontents," *Foreign Affairs,* (January/February 2002): 5.

[274] Jeffrey D. Sachs, *The Geography of Economic Development* (Newport: National War College, 2000), 2. URL: <http://www.nwc.navy.mil/press/review/2000/Autumn/art6%2DA00. Htm>, accessed 29 June 2003.

[275] Friedman, xvii.

turally and benefited many people economically. No doubt, modern technology and economic interrelations have reduced poverty.[276] However, while it might not be a zero-sum game, globalization has not affected nations equally. A crucial fact, according to Jeffrey D. Sachs, professor of International Trade at Harvard University and director of the Center for International Development, is that "globalization is taking place in a world of astounding inequality—the greatest inequality in world history."[277] Robert K. Kaplan writes, "We are entering a bifurcated world. Part of the globe is inhabited by Hegel"s and Fukuyama's Last Man—healthy, well fed, and pampered by technology. The other, larger part is inhabited by Hobbes's First Man, condemned to a life that is poor, nasty, brutish, and short."[278]Today, one-half of all humanity—three billion people—live under the $2-a-day line.[279]

Historically, these inequalities did not always exist at the level of today. Throughout world history, most countries were poor with not much variance in wealth up through 1800. However, shortly thereafter, fostered by industrialization and mechanized technology, Western European (particularly Britain) and North Atlantic nations (particularly the United States) prospered. In 1820, the richest part of the world was Western Europe, with a per capita income around $1,200 and the poorest was Sub-Saharan Africa, with a per capita income around $400. The gap between wealthy and poor nations was approximately 3:1. During the next 180 years, the rich nations got richer and most poor nations got poorer. Western European and U.S. income grew twentyfold while in Sub-Saharan Africa it grew a miserly threefold. However, what is more shocking still is that by 2000, the Sub-Saharan Africa region had only reached a per capita level comparable to Britain in the 1820s! In other words, *economically* in 180 years, this region had only advanced 20 years. Looking at the dispersion between the very richest countries and the very poorest countries,[280] the ratio becomes 40:1, 50:1, and even 60:1.[281]

Regionally speaking, the oil-rich Middle East countries have not fared much better economically. In the past 25 years, the Middle Eastern economies have averaged only 2.8 percent GDP growth, slightly more than Sub-Saharan Africa.[282] In 1980, the Middle East accounted for 13 percent of global exports; by 2004 that percentage dropped to 3 percent, with an overwhelming share being in oil and natural gas. A generation ago,

---

[276] Sen.

[277]Sachs.

[278] Robert K. Kaplan, "The Coming Anarchy: How Scarcity, Crime, Overpopulation, Tribalism, and Disease are Rapidly Destroying the Social Fabric of Our Planet," *The Atlantic,* online ed., February 1994, URL: *http://www.theatlantic.com/politics/foreign/anarchy.htm*>, accessed 22 June 2004.

[279] Sebastian Mallaby, "The World Bank's Force of Nature," *Washington Post,* 27 September 2004, A19.

the Middle East attracted 5 percent of foreign direct investment; today, 1.5 percent. "Simply put," contends Thomas P.M. Barnett, "the Middle East exports oil and terrorism and virtually nothing else of significance to the global economy."[283]

Location, location, location. The three most important factors in real estate (geography) are also crucial in the distribution of the world's wealth. Sachs identified two major barriers to international development—a climatic and a geographical, or physical transport, barrier. Virtually all of the rich countries are outside of the tropics and almost all of the poor countries are located within them with the exception being Singapore and Hong Kong. The largest portion—some 90 percent of world trade when measured in weight and volume[284]—is transported by sea and therefore, proximity to markets is vital for successful international trade. The poorest seven countries in the world—Chad, Mali, Niger, Central Africa Republic, Rwanda, Burundi, and Bolivia are in the tropical zone and all are landlocked. Additionally, tropical and geographically disadvantaged countries have experienced greater humanitarian crises and social disaster.[285]

While there may be countless discussions as to the reasons for economic failures and stagnation in these regions, the underlying reasons are the same today as they were when Adam Smith identified them in 1776—closing doors means losing access to world knowledge. Sachs reported, "Open economies grew 1.2 percentage points per year faster than closed economies, controlling for everything else, because the more open you are, the more integrated you are into today's world network of ideas, markets, technologies and management innovations.[286] *Global Trends 2015* forecasts that the

---

[280] Joseph Nye in "Globalisation and Discontent," *The World Today*, 57, no. 8/9 (Aug/Sep 2001), accessed via ProQuest, 14 January 2004. He pointed out that, according to the United Nations Development Program, the ratio of incomes of the 20 percent of the people in the world living in the richest countries, compared to 20 percent living in the poorest countries, had increased from 30:1 in 1960 to 74:1 in 1997. In comparison, the inequality only increased from 7:1 in 1870 to 11:1 in 1913. Equally striking according to Nye was the uneven distribution of benefits to individuals within and across countries. For example, in Brazil in 1995, the richest tenth of the population received almost half on the national income, and the richest fifth had 64 percent, while the poorest fifth had only 2.5 percent and the poorest tenth had less than one percent.

[281] Sachs.

[282] George Tenet, "Testimony on World-Wide Threats," 7 February 2001, accessed via Lexis Nexis, 5 February 2004.

[283] Thomas P.M. Barnett, *The Pentagon's New Map* (New York: G.P. Putnam's Sons, 2004), 218.

[284] *Globalization and Maritime Power*, Ed. Sam J. Tangredi (Washington, D.C.: National University Press, 2002), xxvi.

[285] Sachs, 8.

[286] Friedman, 219.

economies in Sub-Saharan Africa and the Middle East and some in Latin America will continue to fall behind economically due to endemic internal and/or regional conflicts and failure to diversify their economies. Additionally, a large segment of the Eurasian landmass extending from Central Asia through the Caucasus to parts of southeastern Europe faces dim economic prospects.[287]

Measures of Globalization

Undoubtedly, the main face of globalization is in economics; nonetheless, a basic reality is that globalization is also changing the very nature of international relations. Richard Haass,[288] former U.S. Ambassador and Director of the Policy Planning Staff at Department of State and now President of the Council on Foreign Relations, stressed that globalization should be viewed more broadly, beyond merely economic exchange. "Globalization is the totality and velocity of connections and interactions—be they economic, political, social, cultural, that are sometimes beyond the control or even knowledge of governments and other authorities....It is a multifaceted, transnational phenomenon.[289] The following paragraphs represent three recent viewpoints on the complexities of globalization. The first view, offered by the Heritage Foundation and *The Wall Street Journal*, assesses a country's level of economic openness over a range of factors from level of trade to property rights. The second view, offered by A.T. Kearney and *Foreign Policy,* assesses a country's level of change across four components of global integration—economic integration, personal contact, technological connectivity, and political engagement. Finally, the third view, offered by Thomas P.M. Barnett, professor of warfare analysis and consultant to the Pentagon, categorizes the world into areas where globalization has taken root—the Functioning Core, or simply the Core, and where globalization has not—the Non-Integrating Gap, or the Gap. Barnett posits a new security paradigm that is shaping the 21st century, namely, *Disconnectedness defines danger.*[290]

---

[287] Central Intelligence Agency, "Global Trends 2015: A Dialogue About the Future with Non-government Experts, NIC2000-02, December 2000, <http://www.cia.gov/cia/reports/globaltrends2015/index.html.

[288] Richard Haass, in Haass, 2, cautions that U.S. foreign policy should be based on the fundamental dynamics shaping the international environment and not just the events of the past twelve months (referring to 9/11 attacks), no matter how significant they may be; otherwise, U.S. foreign policy risks becoming tactical and temporary rather than strategic and sustainable. Haass believes there are five fundamental factors shaping the future of international relations: globalization, the fate of democratic governance, the changing nature of security, the evolution of our alliances and relations with other major powers, and the future of the American power.

[289] Haass, 2.

[290] Thomas P.M. Barnett, "The Pentagon's New Map: It Explains Why We're Going to War, And Why We'll Keep Going to War," *Esquire,* 1 March 2003, accessed via ProQuest, 11 May 2004. Cited as Pentagon's New Map (Esquire).

The Heritage Foundation and *The Wall Street Journal*'s 2004 Index of Economic Freedom views globalization through a kaleidoscopic lens. Their tenth annual country-by-country report on openness of economies worldwide illustrates that "the road to growth is paved with liberty." This recurring study measures how well 155 countries have scored against 50 variables divided into ten factors—trade policy, fiscal burden of government, government intervention in the economy, monetary policy, capital flows and foreign investment, banking and finance, wages and prices, property rights, regulation and informal (or black) market activity. The editors did not include Angola, Burundi, Congo, Sudan and Iraq due to civil unrest or anarchy and did not include Serbia and Montenegro due to data unreliability. Lower scores are the most desirable, higher scores indicate less economic freedom. The bottom line of this study is straightforward and should not be surprising—countries with the most economic freedoms also have higher rates of long-term economic growth and are more prosperous than are those with less economic freedom. Not surprisingly, none of the 18 countries comprising the North Africa/Middle East region was classified "free." For the tenth year running, North Korea has the dubious honor of being the least economically free country with the worst possible score on all ten factors.[291] This study defines economic freedom as the absence of government coercion or constraint on the production, distribution, or consumption of goods and services beyond the extent necessary for citizens to protect and maintain liberty itself.[292] The top ten and the bottom ten ranked countries are highlighted in the tables on the facing page.

---

[291] Marc A. Miles, Edwin J. Feulner, and Mary Anastasia O'Grady, *2004 Index of Economic Freedom* (Washington, D.C.: The Heritage Foundation, 2004 and New York: Wall Street Journal, 2004), URL: <http://www.heritage.org/research/features/index/countries.html>, accessed 14 January 2004. Cited hereafter as 2004 Economic Freedom Index.

[292] 2004 Economic Freedom Index, Chapter 5, 49.

Top Ten Economically Free Countries

Rank	More Free Country	Score	Trade Policy	Fiscal Burden	Govt Intervention	$$ Policy	Foreign Invest	Banking/Finance	Wages/Prices	Property Rights	Regulation	Informal Market Rank
1	Hong Kong	1.34	1.0	1.9	2.0	1.0	1.0	1.0	2.0	1.0	1.0	1.5
2	Singapore	1.61	1.0	2.6	3.5	1.0	1.0	2.0	2.0	1.0	1.0	1.0
3	New Zealand	1.70	2.0	4.0	2.0	1.0	1.0	1.0	2.0	1.0	2.0	1.0
4	Luxembourg	1.71	2.0	4.1	2.0	1.0	1.0	1.0	2.0	1.0	2.0	1.0
5	Ireland	1.74	2.0	2.4	2.0	2.0	1.0	1.0	2.0	1.0	2.0	2.0
6	Estonia	1.76	1.0	2.1	2.0	2.0	1.0	1.0	2.0	2.0	2.0	2.5
7	United Kingdom	1.79	2.0	3.9	2.0	1.0	2.0	1.0	2.0	1.0	2.0	1.0
8	Denmark	1.80	2.0	4.0	3.0	1.0	2.0	1.0	2.0	1.0	1.0	1.0
9	Switzerland	1.84	2.0	3.4	2.0	1.0	2.0	1.0	2.0	1.0	3.0	1.0
10	United States	1.85	2.0	4.0	2.0	1.0	2.0	1.0	2.0	1.0	2.0	1.5

Bottom 10 Least Free Economically Countries

Least Free Rank	Country	Trade Policy Score	Fiscal Burden Rank	Govt Intervention	$$ Policy	Foreign	Invest	Banking/Finance	Wages/Prices	Property Rights	Regulation	Informal Market
146	Tajikistan	4.15	4.10	4.09	4.11	4.21	4.15	4.30	n/a	n/a	n/a
147	Venezuela	4.18	3.71	3.88	3.78	3.43	3.48	3.43	3.58	3.63	3.28
148	Iran	4.26	4.30	4.63	4.84	4.69	4.56	4.76	4.80	4.79	n/a
149	Uzbekistan	4.29	4.29	4.39	4.61	4.56	4.64	4.68	n/a	n/a	n/a
150	Turkmenistan	4.31	4.21	4.39	4.39	4.40	4.39	4.50	n/a	n/a	n/a
151	Burma	4.45	4.35	4.33	4.45	4.28	4.15	4.31	4.38	4.45	n/a
152	Laos	4.45	4.73	4.81	4.75	4.80	4.75	4.63	4.70	4.51	n/a
153	Zimbabwe	4.54	4.63	4.39	4.21	4.04	3.89	4.16	3.89	3.79	4.09
154	Libya	4.55	4.48	4.60	4.90	4.85	4.95	4.95	4.95	4.95	n/a
155	North Korea	5.0	5.0	5.0	5.0	5.0	5.0	5.0	5.0	5.0	5.0

Another recent study is the A.T. Kearney/Foreign Policy 2004 Globalization Index that tracked and assessed changes in four key components of global integration. The first component, economic integration, looked at trade, foreign direct investment (FDI) and portfolio capital flows in addition to investment income payments and receipts. The personal contact component assessed international travel and tourism, international telephone traffic and cross-border remittances and personnel transfers. The third component, technological connectivity, considered the number of Internet users, the number of Internet hosts, and the number of secure servers within a country. Finally, the fourth component, political engagement, was tracked through a country's membership in international organizations, personnel and financial contributions to United Nations (UN) Security Council missions, ratification of selected multilateral international treaties, and the amount of government transfer payments and receipts.[293] Although only 62 countries are represented in the 2004 index, these 62 ranked countries represent 96 percent of the world's gross domestic product and 84 percent of the world's population.[294]

This index was designed to measure the extent of globalizing forces of trade, travel, telecommunications and the like in selected countries and makes no judgment as to whether the net effect of globalization is "good" or bad." It does not measure competitiveness. Nevertheless, previously the index results have shown that the most global nations are also those with the "strongest records of equality, the most robust protection for natural resources, the most inclusive political systems, the lowest corruption," and are countries "where residents live the longest, healthiest lives and where women enjoy the strongest social, educational, and economic progress."[295] Leading the ranks for Internet hosts and secure servers per capita, the United States finally broke into the Top 10. Nonetheless, the U.S.'s not being a signatory on many key international treaties during the past decade such as the International Criminal Court (ICC) and Anti-Personnel Landmine Treaty, assured the U.S. a 60th place in rankings in terms of signing international agreements.[296]

---

[293] "Measuring Globalization: Economic Reversals, Forward Momentum," *Foreign Policy*, March/April 2004, 58. Cited hereafter as A.T. Kearney Index/FP.

[294] Data collected for the 2004 index was obtained from a variety of sources such as the World Bank's World Development Indicators 2003, International Monetary Fund's (IMF) International Financial Statistics Yearbook 2003 and Balance of Payment Statistics, Telecommunications Union's International Telecommunications Union Yearbook of Statistics 2003, World Tourism Organization's Compendium of Tourism, Netcraft's Secure Server Survey 2003, and CIA's World Factbook 2003 as cited in FP/A.T.Kearney/FOREIGN POLICY Globalization Index. The data, in Excel spreadsheets, are available online at *www.foreignpolicy.com* and *www.atkearney.com*.

[295] A.T. Kearney/FP, 68.

[296] A.T. Kearney/FP, 63.

2004 A.T. Kearney/Foreign Policy Magazine Globalization Index[297]

Rank	Country	Rank	Country
1	Ireland	32	South Korea
2	Singapore	33	Philippines
3	Switzerland	34	Argentina
4	Netherlands	35	Tunisia
5	Finland	36	Taiwan
6	Canada	37	Chile
7	United States	38	Uganda
8	New Zealand	39	Romania
9	Austria	40	Senegal
10	Denmark	41	Saudi Arabia
11	Sweden	42	Nigeria
12	United Kingdom	43	Ukraine
13	Australia	44	Russian Federation
14	Czech Republic	45	Mexico
15	France	46	Pakistan
16	Portugal	47	Morocco
17	Norway	48	Thailand
18	Germany	49	South Africa
19	Slovenia	50	Columbia
20	Malaysia	51	Sri Lanka
21	Slovak Republic	52	Peru
22	Israel	53	Brazil
23	Croatia	54	Kenya
24	Spain	55	Turkey
25	Italy	56	Bangladesh
26	Hungary	57	China
27	Panama	58	Venezuela
28	Greece	59	Indonesia
29	Japan	60	Egypt
30	Botswana	61	India
31	Poland	62	Iran

---

[297] Foreign Policy, A.T. Kearney, "Measuring Globalization: Economic Reversals, Forward Momentum," *Foreign Policy*, online ed., February 2004, *http://www.foreignpolicy.com/* issue_marapr-2004/countrydetail.php, accessed 26 February 2004.

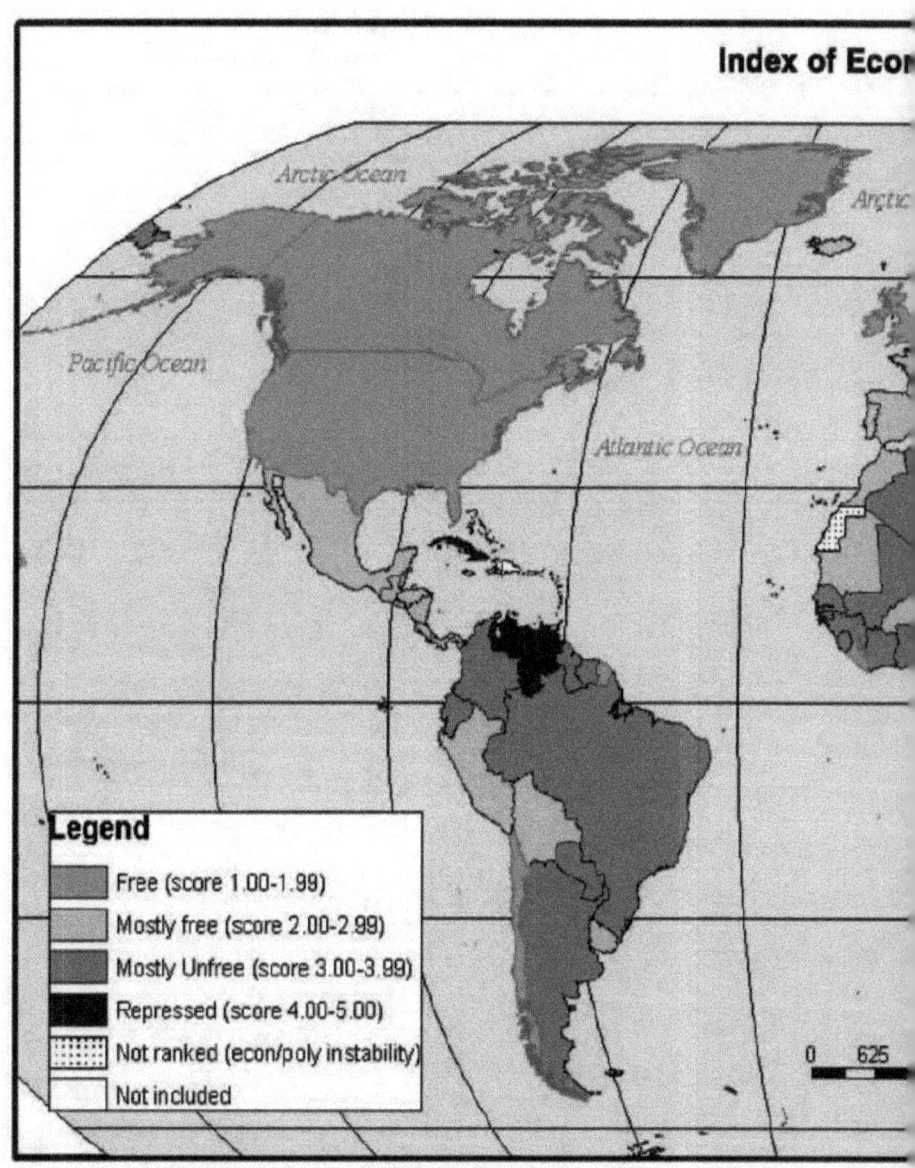

Index of Econ

Legend

	Free (score 1.00-1.99)
	Mostly free (score 2.00-2.99)
	Mostly Unfree (score 3.00-3.99)
	Repressed (score 4.00-5.00)
	Not ranked (econ/poly instability)
	Not included

Source: Modified by author and produced by an Analyst at the National Geospatial-Intelligence
Agency, 22 March 2005, from Marc A. Miles, and others, 2004 EIndex of Economic Freedom

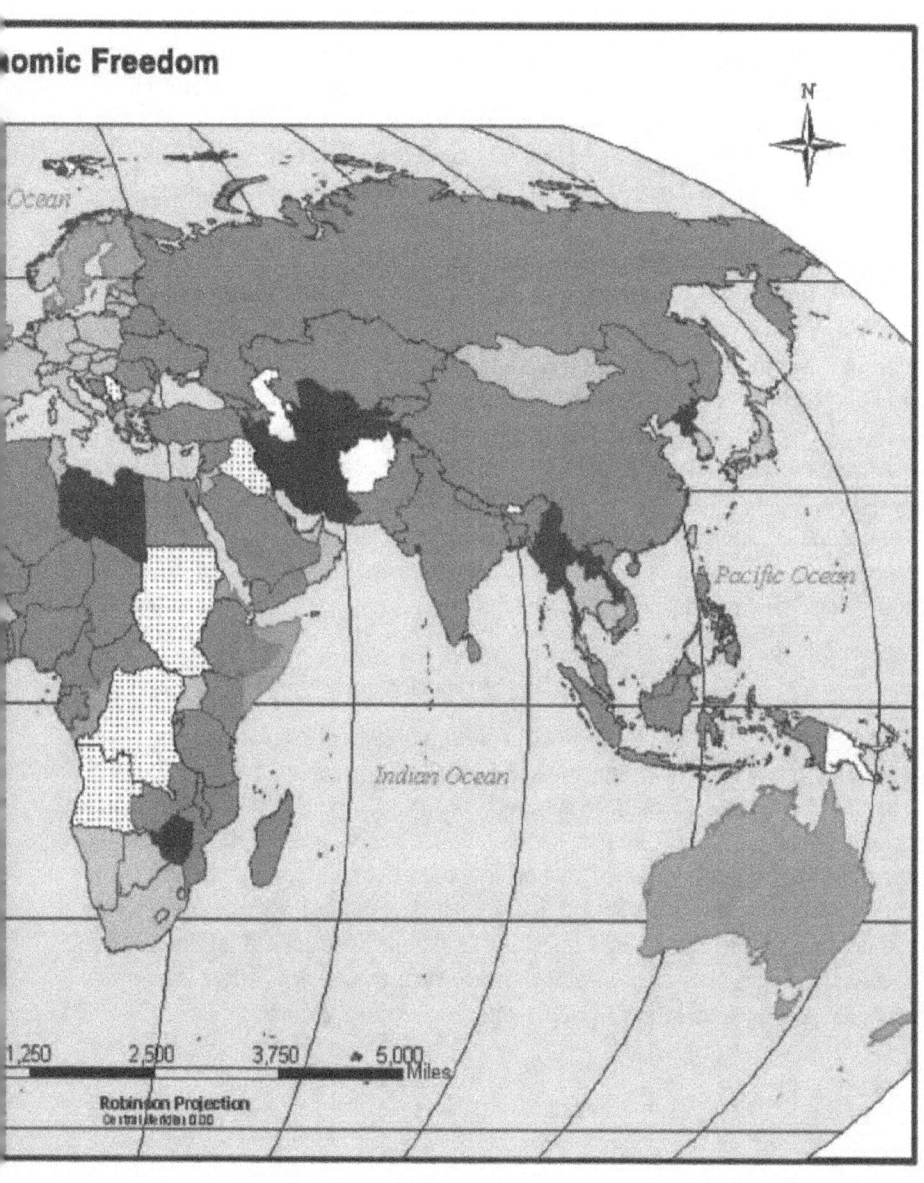

(Washington, DC: The Heritage Foundation, 2004) and Wall Street Journal, 2004.

As he provides the third measure of globalization, Barnett observes that "The problem with globalization is that too many experts treat it as a binary outcome: Either it is great and sweeping the planet, or it is horrid and failing humanity everywhere. Neither works…. [The] new world must be defined by where globalization has truly taken root, the Functioning Core and where it has not, the Non-Integrating Gap."[298] Expansive network connectivity, financial transactions, liberal media flows, and collective security are highlights of the Functioning Core. These areas are North America and much of South America, the European Union, Putin's Russia, Japan and Asia (India and China[299]), Australia and South Africa, and they are linked by trade, migration and capital flows. The Core areas constitute 4 billion of the 6 billion total for world population. The remaining two billion people are concentrated within the Gap—countries where globalization is "lite" or absent and where countries are saddled with repressive political regimes, widespread poverty and disease. The Gap area includes the Caribbean Rim, virtually all of Africa, the Balkans, the Caucasus, Central Asia, the Middle East, and much of Southwest Asia. An old Pentagon hand, Vice Admiral (Ret.) Arthur Cebrowski, Director of the Pentagon's Office of Force Transformation, notes that "The Gap is a petri dish of grief, repression, terrorism and disease…and 9/11 shows we can't wall ourselves off from it." [300]

Emerging Threats

Since the end of the Cold War, globalization has spread dramatically and with it, two major changes have come to the international security environment. The first, the source of mass violence, has migrated from the state to the individual. Unfortunately, the United States witnessed the most spectacular display of "Super-empowered individuals"[301] when nineteen ticketed passengers commandeered four airplanes on 9/11. The U.S. response was against a Super-empowered individual, Osama bin Laden, and his supporters, and was not a retaliatory strike against Afghanistan. The U.S., a nation-state of unparallel political, economic and military power, is at war with Super-empowered *individuals*.

---

[298] "Pentagon's New Map" (Esquire).

[299] China as part of the Functioning Core? Yes. The line between the Core and Gap, according to Barnett, is constantly shifting but he suggests that the direction of change is more critical than degree. Barnett, Pentagon's new map, 129.

[300] As quoted in Greg Jaffe, "At the Pentagon, Quirky Powerpoint Carries Big Punch: In a World of 'Gap' States, Mr. Barnett Urges Generals to Split Force in Two; Austin Powers on Soundtrack," *The Wall Street Journal,* 11 May 2004, A1.

[301] Thomas Friedman coined this term in his book *The Lexus and the Olive Tree* (New York: Farrar, Straus and Giroux, 1999), 13-14.

During the Cold War, the U.S. defined its national security objectives in terms of protection from attacks from a like-nation state. It followed that if the U.S. was prepared militarily to defend against a like nation-state, any smaller threats would be easily countered. Unfortunately, the United States was and is woefully unprepared for attacks from non-state actors. Warren Rudman, commenting on the 9/11 Commission Report stated:

> The report itself addressed that we have an asymmetric threat here that is absolutely stunning when you look at the amount of money we spend on the armed forces. We have an incredible Navy, a great Air Force, a wonderful Army, smart weapons, and great technology, which are worthless in the defensive sense against terrorism. They don't work. You can't deploy an Army division against a cell of Al Qaeda in Rochester, New York, that you don't know is there.[302]

The second major change to the international security environment is that nation-states still "compete" but now "friends" and "enemies" alike are turned into "competitors."[303] Yet, the recurring and in many cases, sustained violence in the unglobalized, disconnected world—or as Barnett calls this area—the Gap, demonstrates that competition for many remains more of guns and bullets than of dollars and cents. According to RAND, the number of violent conflicts declined throughout the 1990s in every part of the world with the exception of Sub-Saharan Africa. Not surprisingly, the Middle East is the world's most militarized region with an average of 10.3 soldiers for every 1,000 people; whereas Europe has 6.4, North America 4.5, South America 2.8 and South Asia 1.6.[304] Mapping out the U.S. military responses since the end of the Cold War indicates an overwhelming concentration of activity in the regions that are excluded from globalization's growing Core.[305]

---

[302] Warren B. Rudman, "Perspectives on National Security in the Twenty-First Century," Briefing presented at Center for Information Policy Research, Harvard University, Guest Presentations, Spring 2002. Incidental Paper: Seminar on Intelligence, Command and Control, June 2003, 4. URL: <http://www/pirp.harvard.edu/pubs_pdf/rudman/rudman.i02.pdf>, accessed 1 April 2004.

[303] Friedman, 12.

[304] "Headlines Over the Horizon: Analysts at the RAND Corporation Lay Out Ten International-Security Developments that Aren't Getting the Attention They Deserve," Atlantic, 292 no. 1 (July/August 2003): 89. Cited hereafter as RAND.

[305] "Pentagon's New Map" (Esquire).

The Dark Side of Globalization: Why Transnational Issues Matter

As early as 1997, the Defense Department recognized that in the immediate future the United States would likely face threats that were non-state-centric. While the potential existed for major theater war in the Middle East or on the Korean peninsula, in its *Quadrennial Defense Review* (QDR), DoD indicated that the absence over the next ten to fifteen years of a "global peer competitor" meant that most of the threats facing the United States would involve failed states, transnational dangers, and asymmetric challenges.[306] A Specialist in International Terrorism with the Congressional Research Service at the Library of Congress speculates that if there is a trend emerging in the latest phase of terrorism, the jihad era, it is the existence of a two-level challenge. The challenge facing the United States and others is the hyperreligious medley of small groups of terrorists and, according to Cronin, the much broader enabling environment of bad governance, nonexistent social services, and poverty[307] that defines much of the developing world.[308]

> **Terrorism** – Prior to the events of 11 September 2001, a trend involving terrorist attacks on U.S. targets had become disturbingly alarming. Attacks increased from a low of 66 in 1994 to a high of 200 in 2000. International attacks against U.S. targets or persons increased from 20 percent of the world total in 1993-1995 to almost 50 percent by 2000.[309] Globally, in 2003, there were 625 terrorism deaths, the largest number since 1998. Additionally, terrorists injured 3,646 people, the largest increase in six years.[310]

> **Illegal Drugs** – Efforts to curtail opium-growing and heroin laboratories in Afghanistan appear to have failed miserably. "Drug trafficking from

---

[306] Amos A. Jordan and others, *American National Security*, 5th ed. (Baltimore: The Johns Hopkins University Press, 1999) 248.

[307] Michael Mousseau in "Market Civilization and Its Clash with Terror," *International Security* 27, no. 3 (Winter 2002/03): 6, reminds his readers that the direct, casual linkages between poverty and terror are more elusive than scholars suggest. Mousseau is not aware of any comprehensive explanations in print for how poverty causes terrorism nor has there been any correlation between the two. Consequently, Mousseau believes that the call for increased foreign aid to fight terrorism is misplaced and he doubts if it will have any significant positive effect in combating terrorism. In fact, it may increase the terrorist threat by making their relative, material deprivation known to, especially, young, vengeful men, who become willing recruits to terrorist operations.

[308] Audrey Kurth Cronin, "Behind the Curve: Globalization and International Terrorism," *International Security* 27, no. 3 (Winter 2002/03): 38.

[309] Cronin, 43.

Afghanistan is the main source of support for international terrorism now," said Avaz Yuldashov of the Tajikistan Drug Control Agency. "Drugs, weapons, ammunition, terrorism, more drugs, more terrorism—it's a closed circle," said Col. Alexander Kondratiyev, a senior Russian officer who served with Tajikistan border guards. The U.S. Drug Enforcement Agency (DEA) had two agents to cover all of Afghanistan; there are no DEA agents in Tajikistan or neighboring Kyrgyzstan.[311] Altogether, 28 of Afghanistan's 32 provinces are involved in opium production, employing more than 1.7 million people. Opium production accounted for 3,600 tons—three-quarters of the world's production.[312]

Guatemala has become the hottest destination for Colombian cocaine destined for the United States. The trafficking is bringing with it more violence and instability. The U.S. Ambassador there describes the sensational mob-style killings as "like something from the Godfather." The majority of Guatemala's 12 million live in poverty, 30 percent cannot read or write, and half of Guatemala's population is under 18, most without job prospects. Hugo Beteta, a Guatemalan planning official said, "Poor idle youths see two choices: migrate to the United States or get involved in the drug trade."[313]

Weapons Proliferation – It is estimated that Abdul Qadeer Khan, the Pakistani nuclear scientist, netted $100 million dollars for the nuclear technology he sold to Libya alone. In addition to dealing with Libya, Khan's network sold nuclear equipment to Iran and North Korea. Commenting on Libya's efforts, Robert Joseph, who heads National Security Council's counterproliferation efforts, said, "The program was much more advanced that we assessed. It was much larger that we assessed."[314]

---

[310] Peter Slevin, "New 2003 Data: 625 Terrorism, not 307," *Washington Post,* 23 June 2004, A1.
Note: As cited in Slevin, the State Department initially reported 307 deaths based on information supplied by the CIA. Based on this information, Deputy Secretary of State Richard Armitage stated that it "provided clear evidence that we are prevailing in the fight." CIA employee John O. Brennan blamed antiquated computers and personnel shortages for the errors and dismissed suggestions that the administration purposely fabricated the figures.

[311] Mark McDonald, "As Heroin Flourishes, So Could Terror," *Philadelphia Inquirer,* 10 May 2004, A1.

[312] Michele Alliot-Marie, "Afghanistan's Drug Boom: The Opium Problem Could Undo Everything That's Being Done to Help the Afghan People," *Washington Post,* 6 October 2004, A27.

[313] Mary Jordan, "Pit Stop on the Cocaine Highway: Guatemala Becomes Favored Link for U.S.-Bound Drugs," *Washington Post,* 6 October 2004, A20.

Iran's former president, Alk Akbar Hashemi Rafsanjani, declared, "Now we have the power to launch a missile with a 2,000-kilometer range. Iran is determined to improve its military capabilities. If the Americans attack Iran, the world will change….They will not dare to make such a mistake." The range of this missile would put parts of Europe within reach for the first time. State Department spokesman, J. Adam Ereli stated, "We view Iran's efforts to further develop its missile capabilities as a threat to the region and to the United States interests, and all the more so in light of its ongoing nuclear program."[315]

Infectious Disease – HIV/AIDS, tuberculosis, and malaria collectively have caused 25 percent of all deaths worldwide. An estimated 40 million people are already infected with HIV/AIDS and it is expanding rapidly. The rate of HIV/AIDS infection has increased 1300 percent in the last five years in Eastern Europe.[316] The AIDS pandemic, particularly in Africa, is notorious. The United Nations reported that 28 million people in Sub-Saharan have HIV/AIDS, and in some countries 40 percent of the adult population are infected with HIV. During 2001, some 900,000 southern Africans died from AIDS, leaving more than three million children without one or both parents.[317] The National Intelligence Council publication, *Global Trends 2015: A Dialog About the Future With Nongovernment Experts*, stated that AIDS will reduce the average lifespan in some African countries by as much as 30 to 40 years, thereby, generating more than 40 million orphans and contributing to poverty, crime and instability.[318] Equally disturbing is the fact that AIDS is decimating the ranks of the African armed forces. A recent RAND study reported these staggering data on the militaries hit hardest by HIV/AIDS infection: Zimbabwe (50 percent), Angola (40-60 percent), Tanzania (15-25 percent), Congo-Brazzaville (10-25 percent), Cote d'Ivoire (10-20 percent), the Democratic Republic of the Congo (40-60 percent), Eritrea (10 percent) and Nigeria (10-20 percent). The rate of infection in the South African National Defense Force is an *amazing* 90 percent in some units.[319]

---

[314] David E. Sanger and William J. Broad, "Pakistani's Nuclear Earnings: $100 Million," *The New York Times*, online ed., 16 March 2004, URL: <http: //www/nytimes.com/2004/03/16/international/asia/16NUKE.html?>, accessed 17 March 2004.

[315] "Iran's Missles Can Now Hit Europe, Ex-Official Says," *Reuters, Washington Post,* 6 October 2004, A21.

[316] Haass, 4.

[317] RAND, 86.

[318] Global Trends 2015.

In raw numbers. people living with HIV/AIDS, excluding Africa: North America 950,000; Caribbean 430,000; Latin America 1.6 million; Western Europe 580,000; Eastern Europe and Central Asia 1.3 million; East Asia 900,000; South and Southeast Asia 6.5illion; and Oceania 32,000.[320]

Counterfeit Goods-"Interpol believes there is a significant link between counterfeiting and terrorism in locations where there are entrenched terrorist groups," stated Ronald Noble, the international police network's secretary general. Interpol has linked terrorism and counterfeiting in the Middle East, Europe and Latin Area. The Brussels-based World Customs Organization estimated more than $500 billion in counterfeit products last year, 6 percent of global trade. Confiscated counterfeit goods thus far have included auto parts, music CDs, cigarettes, shampoo and toiletries. Noble commented that it was inevitable that terrorists would follow organized crime into the counterfeiting business.[321]

Terrorist Sanctuary in West Africa – U.S. General Charles Wald, deputy commander of European Command, expressed his concern that al Qaeda-affiliated groups are active in Mauritania, Mali, Chad and Niger. Terrorists are continuing to trade in diamonds in spite of international efforts. "The terrorist activity is not going to go away in this area....If we don't do something about it, we are going to have a real problem on our hands."[322]

Conurbations – Ninety-five percent of population increase in the coming years will take place in developing countries. The prospects of jobs will continue to draw people from rural, interior regions to already overcrowded metropolitan areas that will further strain the state infrastructure and services.[323] Examples of conurbations include Washington-to-Boston (35-40 million people), Sao Paulo, Brazil (30 million plus), and Baghdad (4.3 million).[324] By 2007, for the first time in human history, a majority of the world's population will live in cities.[325]

---

[319] RAND, 86.

[320] Ellen Nakashima, "U.N. Cites Record in HIV Cases, Faults Prevention as Inadequate," *Washington Post,* 7 July 2004, A14.

[321] News Reports, "Terrorist Profiting in Illicit Goods: Interpol Chief Warns About Counterfeiting," *International Herald Tribune,* 26 May 2004.

[322] Douglas Farah and Richard Shultz, "Al Qaeda's Growing Sanctuary," *Washington Post,* 14 July 2004, A19.

[323] Haass, 4.

Information Warfare – South Korea's Defense Ministry claims North Korea may have trained as many as 600 computer hackers to launch cyber-attacks against the United States and South Korea. Although computers are a rarity and Internet access in North Korea is almost non-existent, the Defense Ministry maintains North Korea information warfare capabilities had reached the level of advanced countries.[326]

These issues require a more agile, streamlined, fluid, cooperative and collaborative Intelligence Community, in other words, the IC needs to operate as effectively as its adversaries do. As an example of what needs to change within the IC to engage effectively against the threats of the 21st century, Douglas Farah and Richard Schultz refer to the activities of al Qaeda and Hezbollah in West Africa as lessons for the current intelligence reform debate. Farah is currently a senior fellow at the Consortium for the Study of Intelligence while on leave from the Washington Post and Schultz is the director of security studies at Tufts University. They contend that despite General Wald's reporting of al Qaeda's regional activities and diamond trafficking in this area, the Intelligence Community, and particularly the CIA, has dismissed these reports as inaccurate or irrelevant. They attributed this attitude to the state-centric culture within the IC as a holdover from the Cold War era. This culture must be changed to reflect the national security threats posed by armed groups, operating beyond state control, as de facto rulers in large parts of Sub-Saharan Africa, Asia and Latin America. Farah and Shultz presented four guides to intelligence reform that can be drawn from the activities of al Qaeda and Hezbollah in West Africa:

- Terrorists and other armed groups are sophisticated in their exploitation of "gray areas" where governments are weak, corruption is rampant and the rule of law is nonexistent.

- Terrorists are adaptable and learn from each other and their own mistakes.

- Terrorist networks and criminal networks can take over failed states such as Liberia and Afghanistan and turn them into multifaceted international threats.

- The Intelligence Community reacts poorly to information that was not on its radar screen.[327]

---

[324] Patrick M. Hughes, "Future Conditions: The Character and Conduct of War, 2010 and 2020," briefing presented at Center for Information Policy Research, Harvard University, Guest Presentations, Spring 2003. Incidental Paper: Seminar on Intelligence, Command and Control, July 2003. URL: *http://pirp.harvard.edu/Pubs-pdf/Hughes/Hughes-i03-1.pdf*, accessed 1 April 2004.

[325] Hutchings.

[326] World in Brief, *Washington Post,* 6 October 2004, A22.

These are mere samples of the challenges confronting the IC today.

Barnett maintains that America can only increase its security when it extends connectivity or expands globalization's reach, by expanding the Core but also shrinking the Gap. In the Post-9/11 world, Barnett envisions a split-level military, in a way unlike any previous recommendations. The first military force, the "Leviathan," would be hard-hitting, ready to take on conventional foes much like the current military structure and the other, the "System Administrators," would focus on bringing dysfunctional states into the mainstream through nation-build-ing operations.[328] Theoretically, the predominant U.S. military operations in March 2003 against Iraq and the subsequent follow-on operations should have been a classic application of Barnett's proposed force structure. Using Barnett's model, the Leviathan (U.S. military and Coalition Forces) neutralized the enemy during the period March-May 2003 through overwhelming force. Since that time, the System Administrators (military forces, international agencies, businesses, local populace, and the like) have begun nation-building activities. Unfortunately, while military strength (personnel and equipment superiority) were sufficient for the Leviathan phase, successes of System Administrators phase have been few. The nation-building efforts have been thwarted by violent and deadly insurgent operations. This has forced the military to sustain large numbers of combat troops to protect the combat support and combat service support troops and civilian con-tract personnel involved in reconstruction efforts. In many parts of the country, insurgent violence has escalated to the point where all military have become combat troops and all civilians combat casualties; there is no distinction between the two. The U.S. Department of State reported in its "Post Reports," a compre-hensive guide to Iraq:

> the security situation throughout Iraq remains unstable and the insur-gent elements continue to be extremely active, and they continue to tar-get not only Coalition Forces but civilians who are viewed "as helping the United States." The total number of attacks in August [2004]…was nearly 2,800…the high-water mark in terms of sheer numbers of attacks. The road that runs from [the airport to the International Zone] continues to be the scene of improvised explosive devices, small arms fires, and RPG attacks, despite concerted efforts by the military to secure the route."[329]

---

[327] Farah and Shultz, A19.

[328] Jaffe.

[329] Al Kamen, "In the Loop: There's No Place Like Zone," *Washington Post,* 8 October 2004, A23.

Furthermore, the Center for Strategic and International Studies reported that of the $7.1 billion obligated for Iraq reconstruction projects, almost one third of this amount has been spent on security. The breakdown of dollars for Iraq identifies as few as 27 cents of every dollar spent on Iraq's reconstruction benefiting the Iraqis directly—30 percent Security; 15 percent Corruption, fraud, mismanagement; 10 percent Coalition Provisional Authority and U.S. Embassy overhead; 6 percent Contractor profits, Other (insurance/salaries of non-Iraqi workers 12 percent; Intended reconstruction projects 27 percent.[330]

The current nation-building obstacles in Iraq would not be surprising to retired Army Lieutentent General, Patrick M. Hughes, former Director DIA and currently DHS Assistant Secretary for Information Analysis. Speaking at the Center for Information Policy Research at Harvard University in early 2003, Hughes stated:

> Peacekeeping operations is an activity that the U.S. military, and frankly, most of the security and intelligence elements of the United States, are not well trained for. They're not equipped for it, and they're not really focused well for it, although they've had to do it for many years. I think I can characterize the Department of Defense's view about peacekeeping like this: We'll do it because we have to, but we don't want to do it. We don't like to do it. We are trained, equipped, and meant for the conduct of war. Peacekeeping is somebody else's problem.

> [Commenting on the on-going Iraq operations, Hughes continued]: More specifically, what it means is that we're going to be there in some guise—and I use that word advisedly—for quite a while. It might be under the umbrella of the United Nations, but it will be a guise. It's us, folks, the United States of America, and nobody else is going to remain in the aftermath of conflict and shepherd Iraq into the future, whatever that means. Once again, there might be a big sign somewhere painted blue and white that says "United Nations," but let's face it, it's mainly a facade.[331]

How prevalent have peacekeeping operations become in the 21st Century? According to A.T. Kearney/Foreign Policy Globalization Index, [excludes the current military coalition operations in Iraq] although the financial and personnel contributions to U.N. Security Council missions declined slightly in 2002, it was still four times higher than in 1998. Eighty-nine countries supported 15 active global missions with 39,000 personnel. The developing countries of Bangladesh,

---

[330] Jonathan Weisman and Robin Wright, "Funds to Rebuild Iraq are Drifting Away from Target: State Department to Rethink U.S. Effort," *Washington Post*, 6 October 2004, A18.

[331] Hughes, 2-4.

Pakistan and Nigeria were among the top personnel contributors.[332] A tragic irony concerning peacekeeping operations is the example of mutinous Guinea-Bissau soldiers who seized key buildings and killed Gen Verissimo Seabra Correia, the commander of Guinea-Bissau's armed forces, in October 2004. Corrieia ousted Kumba Yalla in a previous coup in 2003 of this West African nation. The soldiers were demanding payment for past peacekeeping duty abroad.[333]

What Does this Mean for the IC?

As George Tenet succinctly informed the Senate Armed Services Committee during the DCI's Worldwide Threat Briefing, the IC faces unique challenges:

> America stood out as an object for admiration, envy, and blame. This created a kind of cultural asymmetry. To us, Afghanistan seemed very far away. To members of al-Qa'ida, America seemed very close. In a sense, they were more globalized than we were.[334]

> Mr. Chairman, what I want to say to you now may be the most important thing I tell you today. The steady spread of Usama bin Ladin's anti-U.S. sentiment—through the wider Sunni extremist movement and through the broad dissemination of al-Qa'ida's destructive expertise—ensures that a serious threat will remain for the foreseeable future…with or without al-Qa'ida in the picture….For the growing number of jihadists interested in attacking the United States, a spectacular attack on the U.S. Homeland is the "brass ring" that many strive for—with or without encouragement by al-Qa'ida's central leadership.[335]

Cronin likewise does not foresee any immediate abatement of international terrorism:

> The coincidence between evolving changes of globalization, the inherent weaknesses of the Arab region, and the inadequate American response to both ensures that terrorism will continue to be the most serious threat to the U.S. and Western interests in the twenty-first century…The current wave of international terrorism, characterized by

---

[332] A.T. Kearney/FP, 58.

[333] "World in Brief," *Washington Post*, 7 October 2004, A26.

[334] *The 9/11 Commission Report: The Final Report of the National Commission on Terrorist Attacks Upon the United States* (New York: W.W. Norton & Company, 2004), 261-262. Cited hereafter as 9/11 Report.

[335] George Tenet, "DCI's Worldwide Threat Briefing: The Worldwide Threat 2004: Challenges in a Changing Global Context," Presented to Senate Armed Services Committee, 9 March 2004.

unpredictable and unprecedented threats from non-state actors, not only is a reaction to globalization but is facilitated by it; the U.S. response to this reality has been reactive and anachronistic.[336]

Globalization—the good, the bad, and the ugly—will continue to present security challenges for all nations. However, because the United States is associated with globalization and blamed for its ill effects, particularly by the disadvantaged and alienated populations of developing countries, the effects of globalization present significant security challenges for the United States and subsequently, for the Intelligence Community. According to Cronin, globalization represents an onslaught by oppressive forces against the less privileged people in conservative cultures who are repelled by the fundamental changes these forces are bringing or angered by the distortions and uneven distributions of benefits that result. Whether unintentional or not, the United States is projecting uncoordinated economic, social, and political power even more so than its military power.[337]

"Globalization—including its darker potential—is a fact, not a policy option for the United States or anyone else," states Haass. "How we respond to it, though, is a matter of policy….The future of international relations will be shaped to a large extent by how the bright and dark sides of globalization interact and how nations and peoples respond."[338] U.S. national intelligence exists to respond to specific policy requirements and to inform policymakers. IC capabilities will need to reflect the capabilities of its adversaries much as "containment" during the Cold War era defined the collection requirements and capabilities of the Community. The Community has witnessed the gradual decline of the nation-states' geopolitical power and the accelerated rise in the power of transnational threats particularly since the collapse of the former Soviet Union, yet the Community has not realigned its resources accordingly. "In recent years, the escalation of transnational threats and demands for peacekeeping around the world has increased the imperative to strengthen the management and organization of US intelligence writ large," states Larry C. Kindsvater, Executive Director for Intelligence Community Affairs. "The Community is not managed and organized to directly address national security missions and threats." [339] The DCI's "Community authorities" have been oriented toward the CIA and not the Community as a whole.

---

[336] Cronin, 30.

[337] Cronin, 45.

[338] Haass, 5.

[339] Larry C. Kindsvater, "A Senior Officer's Perspective: The Need to Reorganize the Intelligence Community," Studies in Intelligence 47, no. 1 (2003), 34.

Without a doubt, the attacks on 9/11 demonstrated the frailties and shortcomings in the U.S. intelligence apparatus in the 21st Century, most notably in intelligence sharing. At the time of the 9/11 attacks, despite the increased al-Qa'ida chatter and recognition of an increased threat, the IC analytical focus on al-Qa'ida was nothing short of pitiful. For example, at the CIA's Counterterrorism Center (CTC), with worldwide responsibilities for all terrorist threats, there were five analysts assigned to work on al-Qa'ida between 2000 and 11 September 2001. This was an increase over the numbers who worked this problem full-time between 1998 and 2000—only three analysts worked it then.[340] Keep in mind this was after DCI George Tenet issued a 4 December 1998 directive to several CIA officials and his deputy for community management, stating, "We are at war. I want no resources or people spared in this effort, either inside CIA or the Community."[341] Tenet declared war against al-Qa'ida in the aftermath of the East Africa embassy bombings and because terrorist attacks against U.S. persons and U.S. interests had been steadily rising. Including part-time analysts working elsewhere in CIA, the total number of analysts dedicated to this imminent threat was fewer than 40.

The remainder of the Community did not fare much better. The FBI had fewer than ten tactical analysts and only one strategic analyst assigned to al-Qa'ida. NSA had only a limited number of Arabic linguists dedicated full-time to al-Qa'ida and these same linguists were used to support other high-priority targets and translation activities as well. DIA and the Department of State's Bureau of Intelligence Research (INR) were primarily interested in anti-terrorism and force protection issues overseas. State had one analyst dedicated to al-Qa'ida and DIA had 30 analysts devoted to Sunni extremists and on any given day, they might or might not be involved with al-Qa'ida-related issues.[342] In late 2000, Cofer Black, then Chief of the CTC, concerned about protecting sources and methods, declined FAA's offer of nearly two-dozen analysts to address transportation security issues in exchange for broader information sharing.[343] These examples plainly illustrate the lack of authority the DCI possessed over the Community—even as Director of Central Intelligence, he could not effectively influence the direction and priorities of the Community. The DCI may have declared war, but few enlisted to the cause.

---

[340] U.S. Congress, Senate, Select Committee on Intelligence and House, Permanent Select Committee on Intelligence, *Joint Inquiry into Intelligence Community Activities Before and After the Terrorist Attacks of September 11, 2001,* 107th Cong., 2nd sess., S.Rept. 107-351 and H. Rept. 107-792, December 2002, C. Systemic Findings, 59. Cited hereafter as Joint Inquiry Report

[341] 9/11 Report, 356.

[342] Joint Inquiry Report, Part 1 Findings and Conclusions, 59

[343] Joint Inquiry Report, C. Systemic Findings, 60.

For decades, the DCI functioned as the "great coordinator" rather than the "great integrator" of intelligence as envisioned by framers of the National Security Act of 1947. Subsequent authorities such as the National Security Council Intelligence Directives (NSIDs) during the Truman Administration, according to Warner, were more explicit in outlining prohibitions than they were in clarifying the permissions of the DCI. Consequently, every DCI exercised a looser rather than tighter oversight of common IC issues.[344] The DCI's authorities have not improved remarkably since then despite numerous executive orders to strengthen them.

Most recently, the 9/11 Commission noted the limitations of the DCI's authority over the direction and priority of the IC, especially its elements within the Department of Defense. According to the Commission:

> The DCI has to direct agencies without controlling them. He does not receive an appropriation for their activities, and therefore does not control their purse strings. He has little insight into how they spend their resources. Congress attempted to strengthen the DCI's authority in 1996 by creating the deputy DCI for Community Management and Assistant DCIs for Collection, Analysis and Production, and Administration. But the authority of these positions is limited and the vision of central management clearly has not been realized.[345]

The recently passed Intelligence Reform and Terrorist Prevention Act of 2004 in theory remedies this situation by establishing a Senate-confirmed Director of National Intelligence (DNI) who shall not serve as the Director of the CIA or the head of any other element in the Intelligence Community. This separation of powers is the most significant change to the IC structure.

This act grants the DNI specific budgetary and personnel realignment authorities. The Director of OMB apportions National Intelligence Program (NIP) funds, formerly called NFIP, at the "exclusive direction" of the DNI for allocation to IC elements. The DNI manages NIP appropriations by "directing the allotment or allocation" of these appropriations through IC agency heads. Additionally, the DNI may transfer or reprogram NIP funds from any IC element with some stipulations—the total amount to be moved out in any fiscal year cannot exceed $150 million, is less than 5 percent of the impacted agency's NIP budget and does not terminate an acquisition program. However, the DNI *cannot* exercise this authority unilaterally as the OMB and the affected agency must approve this movement

---

[344] Michael Warner, *Central Intelligence: Origins and Evolution*, 7.
[345] 9/11 Report, 357.

of funds. These limitations may be waived with the concurrence of the affected department head.[346]

Regarding IC personnel transfers, within twelve months of establishing the newly authorized intelligence centers, the DNI may transfer not more than 100 IC people to these centers. This action *is contingent* upon approval of OMB and congressional consultation. Also, the DNI can transfer unlimited numbers of personnel from one IC element to another for not more than two years. However, transfers of this nature are allowed only if personnel are being "transferred to a higher priority intelligence activity, and the transfer supports an emergent need, improves program effectiveness, or increases efficiency." Respective congressional committees *must be notified* of such transfers.[347]

Information Revolution and the Intelligence Community

If there were a Moore's Law[348] for transportation, such as air travel, a modern commercial aircraft would cost $500, circle the earth in twenty minutes, and use only five gallons of fuel. However, it might only be the size of a shoebox.

—Gordon Moore

Without question, information and communications technologies have been prime global integrators, changing the way we communicate and how we receive our information. "Printing made us all readers," said former NBC News president Lawrence Grossman. "Xeroxing made us all publishers. Television made us all viewers. Digitalization makes us all broadcasters."[349] The

---

[346] United States Congress, Senate, Committee on Governmental Affairs, *Summary of Intelligence Reform and Terrorist Prevention Act of 2004*, 108th Cong. 2nd sess., 6 December 2004. Cited hereafter as GAC Summary.

[347] GAC Summary.

[348] In 1965, Gordon Moore, co-founder of Intel (semiconductor microchip company), observed that the density of transistors on a semiconductor microchip doubles roughly every 18 months. In other words, the processing power of a computer doubles. This has been constant for the past four decades. Moore's Law has been the driver for the explosive rise in PC and Internet use and the rapid rate of technological change in communications, medical equipment and electronics sectors. W.S. Bainbridge, in a speech presented at 2003 Nanotechnology Conference and Trade Show, "Converging Technologies, San Francisco, CA, 23-27 February 2003, URL: < *http://mysite.verizon.net//william.bainbridge/dl/nbic.htm*>, accessed 13 October 2004, notes that Moore's law could be "repealed" within a decade because transistors on conventional chips are nearing their physical size limits. If so, the U.S. semiconductor industry could evaporate. Therefore, there is a lot of interest, from American government and industry, in nanotechnology that could extend Moore's Law another decade or two.

[349] Friedman, 49.

"CNN factor" has made world events instantaneous. Reflecting on Tiananmen Square protests, former Secretary of State James Baker said that live coverage "signaled a powerful new phenomenon: the ability of the global communications revolution to drive policy...[to] create a powerful new imperative for prompt action that was not present in less frenetic times."[350] The U.S. government used media coverage of live events initially to its advantage by allowing reporters to embed with the front line troops leading up to and including the assault on Baghdad during Operation IRAQI FREEDOM. Censorship was enforced sparingly and when enforced, done so for operational security. Currently, Iraqi insurgents under the presumed leadership of Jordanian Militant Abu Musab al-Zarqawi are using the powers of the Internet, print, and news media to broadcast their cause. A recent *Washington Post* article reported that Zarqawi is using his role as leader of the insurgents to become a major figure in the broader Islamic jihad movement. Anthony H. Cordesman, senior fellow at the Center for Strategic and International Studies, indicated that Zarqawi has shown sophistication in using the media, taking responsibility publicly for bombings and appearing in a series of videos of beheadings [via postings on the Internet].[351]

To get an idea of how just how connected the world has become, Lucent, the leading U.S. telecommunications-equipment company, in an annual report to its stockholders stated:

- Every minute, 5 million email messages are sent out.
- Every hour, 35 million voice mail messages are left.
- Every day 50,000 people sign up for wireless phone service.
- Every day 37 million people log onto the Internet.
- Every week 630,000 phone lines are installed.
- Every 100 days Internet traffic doubles.[352]

Additionally, a *2000* University of California-Berkeley study indicated more than 610 billion email messages were delivered that year. The Web consisted of 2.1 billion static pages and was projected to double in 2001. All the

---

[350] David A. Radi, "Intelligence Inside the White House: The Influence of Executive Style and Technology," Briefing presented at Center for Information Policy Research, Harvard University, Guest Presentations, March 1997. Incidental Paper, <URL:*http://pirp.harvard.edu/pubs_pdf/radi/radi-i97-3.pdf*>, accessed 1 April 2004.

[351] Walter Pincus, "Iraq Called 'Springboard' for Insurgency Figure: Intelligence Experts Say Jordanian Militant Zarqawi Wants Broader Role in Jihad Movement," *Washington Post,* 21 October 2004, A25.

[352] Bruce Berkowitz, *The New Face of War: How War Will Be Fought in the 21st Century* (New York: The Free Press, 2003), 199.

information created around the world—email, snail mail, the Web, books, TV, photographs, databases—totaled two exabytes in 2000--an exabyte is 10 to the 18th power. Confused yet? EMC, a computer storage maker, states that *if every word ever spoken by every human being on the planet throughout recorded history were added together, it would equal five exabytes of information.* Within two years time, by 2002, information storage would come to exceed five exabytes.[353]

Declining telecommunications costs, as well as reductions in personal computer and telephony equipment costs, have propelled the information explosion. Much of this decrease could be attributed to the deregulation brought on by the Telecommunications Act of 1996 when companies spent billions laying new long-distance lines nationally and around the globe. Less than four percent of the long-distance lines in the ground are being used now, so costs savings and increased capabilities are likely. As an example of plummeting telecommunications costs, the cost of a link capable of carrying 2,000 calls simultaneously has decreased from $155,000 a month in January 2000 to $6,200 a month by August 2004. In 1920, a 10-minute call between Los Angeles and New York cost $26.17—the equivalent of almost $250 in 2004 dollars; the costs in 1998 for the same 10-minute call was 50 cents.[354] International telephone traffic has continued its rapid ascent for a total of 135 billion minutes in 2002. This amount equated to 21 minutes per person for **every** person on the planet—all six billion plus of us!

Many of the largest countries showed the largest connectivity increases. For example, the A.T. Kearney Globalization Index indicates that in China, the number of Internet users increased 75 percent in 2002, in Brazil, 78.5 percent; and in India, 136 percent. Meanwhile, the Middle East as a whole remains one of the world's least connected areas, although even here the number of Internet users was up by 116 percent.[355] Wireless communications (mobile telephone service) proliferated in developing countries, allowing countries such as Botswana, Hungary, Indonesia, and South Africa to be more connected than ever. For the first time, in 2002 the number of mobile telephones per capita worldwide exceeded

---

[353] Russ Mitchell, "The Ghosts in the Machine: Can Technology Find Terrorists?" *The American Spectator,* Nov/Dec 2001, accessed via ProQuest, 4 December 2003.

[354] Christopher Stern, "So Long to Long Distance? Calling Packages, Internet Phoning Swiftly Ending a High-Cost Category,"*Washington Post,* 5 August 2004, E4.

[355]Note: According to A.T. Kearney/FP Globalization Index, 59, the digital divide between users may be narrowing but the infrastructure divide remained constant. The 2002 data reflected the world's total number of Internet hosts (computers permanently tied to the Internet). Even with 3.3 million new hosts added globally, developing countries still had less than 10 percent of the total.

that of main telephone lines (landlines)—18.9 mobile subscribers per 100 inhabitants to 17.95 for landlines.[356]

Regardless of the measurements used to gauge the world's communications patterns, electronic communications have become as ubiquitous as fastfood—they're everywhere, and represent a $3 trillion-per-year communications industry![357] The question for the Intelligence Community is, "How has this information explosion affected the Community's ability to collect, process, analyze and disseminate intelligence?" Lt. Gen. Michael V. Hayden, Director, National Security Agency/Chief, Central Security Service, answered this question in part with his testimony before the Joint Intelligence Community of the events of 11 September 2001, on 17 October 2004. He stated:

> The volume, variety and velocity of human communications make our mission more difficult each day. A SIGINT agency has to look like its target. We have to master whatever technology the target is using....We had competed successfully against a resource-poor, oligarchic, technologically inferior, and overly bureaucratic nation state. Now we had to keep pace with a global telecommunication revolution, probably the most dramatic revolution in human communications since Gutenberg's invention of the movable type.[358]

The peace dividends of the 1990s had devastating effects on the modernization efforts of the community in terms of personnel and recapitalization. DCI George Tenet remarked that NSA was hiring no new technologists during the greatest information technology change in our lifetime.[359] During the 1990s, NSA downsized its workforce by one-third and reduced its budget proportionately. "The Agency [NSA] accomplished the downsizing that was imposed on it in the easiest and most humane way possible," said Hayden, "it shut the front door." However, according to Hayden, during this same period, telecommunications surged ahead. Mobile cell phones increased from 16 million to 741 million—an increase of nearly 50 times. Internet users went from 4 million to 261 million—an increase of over 90 times. Half as many landlines were laid in the last six years of the 1990s as had been laid in the previ-

---

[356] A.T. Kearney/FP, 60.

[357] 9/11 Report, 88.

[358] Hayden.

[359] George Tenet, "Investigation of Sept 11," 17 October 2002, accessed via LexisNexis, 12 January 2004.

ous history of the world. International telephone traffic increased from 38 billion minutes to over 100 billion.[360]

Undeniably, the Intelligence Community is awash in digital information, which is affecting every aspect of the intelligence process. Instead of collecting against Cold-War era military command and control targets that were hierarchal, familiar and often predictable, the Community must now endeavor to collect against loosely affiliated, networked adversaries using commercial off-the-shelf communications equipment and encryption devices.Unequivocally, operations required to penetrate an opponent's information system, literally touching the system in most cases, are extremely sensitive and perishable. These types of operations require human intelligence (HUMINT).[361] "A setback of inestimable consequences in the war against terrorism occurred when Usama bin Laden and his key lieutenants stopped using a phone following 1998 press reports of our [NSA] intercepts,"[362] Hayden told the Joint Inquiry Commission.

To appreciate the challenges posed to the Community, particularly to the NSA, by these new transmission media, consider these sobering facts and analogies as noted in a July 2004 *Washington Post* article:

- A single strand of fiber-optic cable exceeds the capacity of all the telecommunications satellites orbiting the globe. Email, in 2004 alone, is expected to be the equivalent of 40 copies of the fully digitized holdings of the Library of Congress.

---

[360] Hayden.

[361] Much discussion during the past decade has centered on the decimation of HUMINT ranks due to lack of funding and the purging of DO during Stansfield Turner's short reign as DCI in the late 70s and the recruitment restrictions imposed by another DCI, John Deutch. Berkowitz, in Bruce Berkowitz, *The New Face of War: How War Will Be Fought in the 21st Century* (New York: The Free Press, 2003), 201, dismisses these assertions. Regarding Turner's reign, Berkowitz reminds his readers that since Turner ran the CIA—four presidents, twelve Congresses, and six directors of CIA have come and gone. Therefore, if the U.S. wanted to make changes to HUMINT operations, there have been many opportunities. In regard to Deutch's reign as DCI, most members of Congress as well as top CIA officers on the "scene" today supported the restrictions on controversial HUMINT sources, the intelligence budget cuts and the intelligence priorities that supposedly slighted HUMINT.

More recently, in George Tenet, "Investigation of September 11,"17 October 2004, accessed via LexisNexis, 12 January 2004, Tenet stated: "It will take us another five years to have the kind of clandestine service our country needs. There is a creative, innovative strategy to get us there that requires sustained commitment, leadership and funding." Berkowitz debunks Tenet's timetable. Berkowitz states that the oft-repeated line that "HUMINT sources take decades to rebuild," is simply not true. He adds that William Casey put together a network of HUMINT agents during World War II in just eighteen months.

[362] Hayden.

- Instant messaging is now estimated to generate 530 billion messages per day.
- Telephone calls can now be sent over the Internet, using a protocol called Voice-over-Internet (VOIP) or voice-over-IP as it is commonly called. By 2005, enough fiber-optic cable to support VOIP will have been laid to carry the equivalent of one Library of Congress every 14.4 seconds.[363]

Disconnected Intelligence Community

Nonetheless, as the outside world became more connected, the Community became less so. Speaking before the 9/11 Commission in April 2004, Tenet admitted that during the mid-1990s, the Community was not able to keep pace with technological change as the Community "lost close to 25 percent of our people and billions of dollars in capital investment."[364] The consequences of forced deferment of intelligence systems and infrastructure due to reduced funding are many. Perhaps one of the most vivid is from January 2000 when catastrophic failure struck NSA's powerful computers (officially described as a software anomaly in the communications infrastructure), which were not able to process information for three days.[365] Another is the creation of NIMA in 1995 but without the requisite funds ("enormous shortfalls" according to Tenet) to adequately merge and modernize its geospatial and imagery functions. Another casualty of deferred investment is the Community's aging satellite constellation.[366]

Technological change, when it occurred, remained for the most part an isolated endeavor. Community agencies sought improvements to existing systems that supported their respective specializations. These improvements tended to be straight-line. Minimal, if any, consideration was given to integration of systems. John F. Lehman, 9/11 Commissioner and former Secretary of the Navy, while commenting on the importance of information sharing, expressed this frustration with the Community: "There are no protocols [standards] for the Intelligence Community for sharing. This is an IT problem. It's a deep, embedded, functional problem throughout the Community for common protocols for information."[367]

---

[363] Michael A. Wertheimer, "Crippling Innovation—And Intelligence," *Washington Post*, 21 July 2004, A19.

[364] George Tenet, "Transcript: 9/11 Commission Hearing on Intelligence," *Washington Post*, online ed., 14 April 2004, URL: http://www.washingtonpost.com/ac2/wp-dyn/A11115-2004Apr14?>, accessed 15 April 2004. Cited hereafter as Tenet, 9/11 Commission, 14 April 2004.

[365] "A Special Relationship? The US and UK Spying Alliance Is Put Under the Spotlight," *London Financial Times*, 6 July 2004.

[366] Tenet, Investigation of Sept 11.

[367] Tenet, 9/11 Commission, 14 April 2004

Hayden spoke of NSA's efforts to modernize amidst budget shortfalls by taking $200 million dollars away from current, still-active, still-producing activities and investing those dollars in future capabilities. "$200 million per year was far short of what we needed, and in fact, I could only make about one-third of that number stick as our program went through the Executive Branch and the Congress."[368] This "Rob Peter to Pay Paul" scenario played out throughout the Community as agency directors sought to recapitalize their information systems and infrastructure by reallocating monies from other areas. Older systems due to be decommissioned within a few years became, in essence, bill-payers for any modernization effort not currently funded. In many cases, this pickpocket approach to program management fell short of its intended goal. Consequently, due to a host of reasons, systems that were to be decommissioned continued operation beyond their "expiration dates" thereby bringing additional expenditures for both the recapitalization efforts as well as for continuation of the bill-payer system(s).

Decades ago, T. S. Eliot noted, "Where is the knowledge we have lost in information?" The Community has outstripped its ability to process, exploit, and analyze the information it collects. Tragically, even as the Joint Inquiry reported:

> This inquiry uncovered no intelligence information in the possession of the Intelligence Community prior to the attacks of September 11 that, if fully considered, would have provided specific, advance warning of the details of those attacks. But it also noted,

> Within the huge volume of intelligence reporting that was available prior to September 11, there were various threads and pieces of information that, at least in retrospect, are both relevant and significant."[369]

The Community, in particular the CIA and FBI, missed numerous operational opportunities to detect the 9/11 plot (as noted on page 75). The "threads and pieces of information" could not be woven into a coherent pattern because this information resided in segmented databases that could not be accessed easily within an agency let alone between Community agencies; resided in hand-written notes known only to the writer; and resided in the thoughts of seasoned analysts who chose to keep these

---

[368] Hayden.

Note: NSA has two major modernization efforts underway—Project GROUNDBREAKER and TRAILBLAZER. GROUNDBREAKER is an outsourced IT activity and TRAILBLAZER is an effort to revolutionize how to produce SIGINT in a digital age. Hayden related that a future project is to jointly (NSA/private corporation) develop a data mining system. Nevertheless, according to the Joint Inquiry Report, 55, "NSA's highly publicized TRAILBLAZER program was often cited by NSA officials as the solution to many of these problems [lack of current analytical tools to identify critical intelligence amidst large volumes of information], but the implementation of those solutions is three to five years away and confusion still exists at NSA as to what will actually be provided by that program."

[369] Joint Inquiry Report, III. Findings and Conclusions, 7.

thoughts silent. This information remained protected by cultural-based attitudes and biases and misunderstood legal statutes that prevented collaboration among analysts.

John C. Ashcroft, U.S. Attorney General, testifying before the 9/11 Commission, reported on the terrible shape of the FBI's computer technology and information management:

> The Bureau essentially had 42 separate information systems, none of which were connected. Agents lacked access to even the most basic Internet technology. These problems didn't just hamper interagency communication, they hindered information sharing in the Justice Department, the Intelligence Community, and communication with state and local law enforcement. It's no wonder, given the state of this technology, that the Phoenix memo warning the terrorists may be training in commercial aviation was lost in the antique computers at the Washington headquarters.[370]

James R. Thompson, 9/11 Commissioner, read parts of Janet Reno's (Attorney General during the Clinton Administration) prepared testimony before the same 9/11 Commission which disputed the existence of the "wall," (see tonebox below). He quoted her as remarking:

> There are simply no walls or restrictions on sharing the vast majority of counterterrorism information. There are no legal restrictions at all on the ability of the members of the Intelligence Community to share intelligence information with each other. With respect to sharing between intelligence investigators and criminal investigators, information learned as a result of a physical surveillance or from a confidential source can legally be shared without restriction. While there are restrictions on information gathered by grand jury investigations or Title III wiretaps, in practice they did not prove to be a serious impediment since there was very little significant information that could not be shared.[371]

---

[370] John C. Ashcroft, "Transcript: 9/11 Commission Hearing," *Washington Post*, online ed., 13 April 2004, URL: http://www.washingtonpost.com/ac2/wp-dyn/A9088-2004Apr13?, accessed 14 April 2004.

[371] Janet Reno, "Transcript: 9/11 Commission Hearing," *Washington Post*, online ed., 13 April 2004, 58, URL: http://www.washingtonpost.com/ac2/wp-dyn/A9088-2004Apr13?, accessed 14 April 2004. Cited hereafter as Reno /11 Commission Hearing 13 April 2004, 58. Note: Thompson read from Reno's prepared testimony page number 5 but the exchange between Thompson and Reno was cited as listed.

The Wall

John C. Ashcroft surprised the 9/11 Commission during his testimony in John C. Ashcroft, "Transcript: 9/11 Commission Hearing," *Washington Post,* online ed., 13 April 2004,URL http://www.washingtonpost.com/ac2/wp-dyn/A9088-2004Apr13?, accessed 14 April 2004 165-166, when after noting that the single greatest structural cause for the September 11th problem was the "wall" that segregated or separated criminal investigators and intelligence agents, he announced that Jamie Gorelick was the author of the 1995 memo that, in his words, was the basic architecture for the wall, and she was a member of the 9/11 Commission. The day following Ashcroft's testimony, Representative F. James Sensenbrenner, Jr. (R-WI), Chairman of the House Judiciary Committee in Dan Eggen and Walter Pincus, "House Member Seeks Gorelick's Resignation," *Washington Post,* 15 April 2004, A12, called on Gorelick, former deputy attorney general during the Clinton administration and the 9/11 Commissioner in question, to resign, arguing she has "an inherent conflict of interest" because of the memo she drafted nine years ago.

Gorelick, responded to this charge in "The Truth About 'the Wall,'" *Washington Post,* 18 April 2004, B7. Gorelick stated: "This is simply not true," and listed the following five reasons:

1) I did not invent the "wall," which is not a wall but a set of procedures implementing the 1978 statue (the Foreign Intelligenc e Surveillance Act) and federal court decision interpreting it. The law said that intelligence investigators could conduct electronic surveillance in the United States against foreign targets under a more lenient standard than is required in ordinary criminal cases, but only if the "primary purpose" of the surveillance were foreign intelligence rather than a criminal prosecution.

Thompson then asked Reno, "If you were to have used those words in a legal opinion directed to the members of the Intelligence Community and specifically to members of the FBI and CIA...the members of the Intelligence Community would be astounded. Or am I wrong about that?" Reno responded:

> I think some would have been astounded. I think it's again very important to understand—and I think I learned from this how important it is when you announce a policy, when you try to do something, that you make sure you train, you get feedback from people. And I think one of the things I failed to do was to get feedback from them to understand exactly what their problems were with it, try to accommodate those interests and proceed to ensure a full exchange of information.[372]

The following are just a few of the examples cited in the Joint Inquiry Report highlighting technological roadblocks to information sharing within the Intelligence Community.

- FBI—Over the years, the FBI has failed to develop sufficient capacity to collect, store, search, retrieve, analyze, and share information within its own agency and with other agencies. As of 26 September

---

[372] Reno, 9/11 Commission Hearing 13 April 2004, 58.

2002, there were still 68,000 outstanding unassigned leads directed to the Counterterrorism Division, dating back to 1995. One FBI Chief stated that "Communications coming into our building from NSA, from CIA, cannot be integrated into our existing databases....It is a setup for failure in terms of keeping a strategic picture of what we are up against."[373]

- NSA—Language analysts still conduct the bulk of their work with pencil and paper and create their own personal "database" on index cards. Obviously, the information on the index cards cannot be readily made available to other Community analysts.[374]

- NSA/CIA—While working-level relationships and cooperation between NSA and CIA employees were good, mid- and upper management-level relationships were strained. CIA thought NSA wanted to control technology use and development and NSA thought CIA was engaged in operations that were in NSA's purview. No less than seven executive-level memoranda were necessary to reach agreement on authorities on one counterterrorism effort.[375]

Information-Sharing a Policy Issue

Bruce Berkowitz, noted author and former CIA officer, spent 2001-2002 as a Scholar-in-Residence at the CIA's Sherman Kent Center for Intelligence Analysis. During this period he looked at how the Directorate of Intelligence (DI) used information technology and how it might use IT more effectively. While the quality of DI analysts impressed Berkowitz, he expressed concern about the analysts' lack of awareness of and access to new information technology and services that could benefit them in their work.[376]

- Despite supporting improvements in communications capabilities with external IC agencies, the email interface requires unfamiliar addressing protocols and offers no searchable directory, undermining the speed and convenience of electronic communication.

- CIA analysts cannot easily communicate with DoD using the secret-level SIPRNET system. SIPRNET is the standard means of communication throughout DoD.

---

[373] Joint Inquiry Report, Part One Findings and Conclusions, 58.

[374] Joint Inquiry Report, Part One Findings and Conclusions, 58.

[375] Joint Inquiry Report, Part One Findings and Conclusions, 57.

[376] Bruce Berkowitz, "The DI and "IT:" Failing to Keep Up With the Information Revolution," Studies in Intelligence 47, no.1 (2003), 67. Cited hereafter as Berkowtiz DI and "IT."

- CIA does not post many of its classified reports on Intelink[377] because CIA cannot control further dissemination once the document has been posted. CIA prefers to list its products on CIASource—an Agency-maintained website that requires CIA access certification and the requisite equipment to view its site.[378]

- The most used analytical database is CIRAS (Corporate Information Retrieval and Storage). While an improvement over past systems, CIRAS is extremely primitive when compared to what is currently available commercially. [379]

These limitations make it difficult for CIA analysts to communicate with other IC analysts in a classified environment. Berkowitz maintains that the current IT security environment sends an implicit message to CIA analysts: "that technology is a threat, not a benefit; that the CIA does not put a high priority on analysts using IT easily or creatively; and worst of all, that data outside the CIA's own network are secondary to the intelligence mission."[380] In his judgment, lack of resources, while a constraint, is not the primary obstacle to improved IT effectiveness. Even if more money were available, the CIA (DI) would not be able to use technology more effectively unless it changed its operating procedures and culture.[381]

The aforementioned limitations annotated by Berkowitz as well as those mentioned in the Joint Inquiry Report reflect that circumstances, while technological in context, are not constrained by technology; they are constrained by policy. Technological solutions exist. Inherent CIA and subsequent Community policy decisions have imposed limitations and obstacles to sharing information within the Community and outside the Community. Although Berkowitz examined only the CIA's IT environment, similar scenarios of limited connectivity and data access restrictions are prevalent throughout the Community. When the author spoke with Michelle Westlander, Deputy Technical Executive for the National Geospatial-Intelligence Agency about Community interoperability issues, she maintained that Community information-sharing obstacles were solvable and had been for some time…Multi-level security options, currently available, could enable the Community to communicate more easily and more efficiently than the

---

[377] In Dan Verton, "Rice Grilled on Information-Sharing Shortfalls," *ComputerWorld,* online ed. 8 April 2004, URL: <http://www.computerworld.com, accessed 14 April 2004, Intelink, first deployed in 1994 as the first IC intranet for classified information, has grown to more than 2.4 million web pages. This massive growth, according to Verton, has led some in the IC to liken conducting an Intelink search to "shooting craps."

[378] Berkowitz DI and "IT,"68.

[379] Berkowtiz DI and "IT," 69.

[380] Berkowtiz DI and "IT," 68.

[381] Berkowtiz DI and "IT," 69.

current arrangement. Technology is not the limiting factor toward greater interoperability and collaboration within the Community—Agencies' cultures and policies are.[382] The 9/11 Commission Report recognized this salient fact: "Even the best information technology will not improve information sharing so long as the intelligence agencies' personnel and security systems reward protecting information rather than disseminating it....Technology produces its best results when an organization has the doctrine, structure, and incentives to exploit it." Unfortunately, the Community is wanting in all three areas.

Fewer than ten years ago, Joseph S. Nye, Jr., Chairman of the National Intelligence Council and then Dean of the John F. Kennedy School of Government at Harvard University, and Admiral William A. Owens, USN (Ret) former Vice Chairman of the Joints Chief of Staff, stated, "Knowledge, more than ever before, is power. The one country that can best lead the information revolution will be more powerful than any other. For the foreseeable future, that country is the United States." We understand that America possesses military and economic strength but its more subtle comparative advantage, according to the authors, is its ability to collect, process, act upon and disseminate information. America's information edge is equally as important a force multiplier of American diplomacy as other elements of soft power—democracy and free markets.[383] Although their premise that information is a form of national power appears sound, the U.S. lead in the information revolution in 2004 and beyond cannot be taken for granted any longer.

"Technology is no longer a U.S. monopoly," stated Aris A. Pappas and James M. Simon, Jr., senior Community Management Staff (CMS) officers. "We are now facing the same reality that confronted the Soviets: technology is, and has

---

[382] Effective 4 June 2004, the DCI released a new Community-wide directive, DCID 8/1—Intelligence Community Policy on Intelligence Information Sharing. One aspect of this directive requires IC components to utilize a specific infrastructure and common policies, services and standards for all new IC systems to foster secure sharing of information. In theory, DCID 8/1 indicates a step in the right direction to ensure Community-wide standardization of IT systems. However, the test will be successful implementation.

[383] Joseph S. Nye, Jr., and William A. Owens, "America's Information Edge," *Foreign Affairs*, 75, no. 2 (Mar/Apr 1996), 20.

Nye defines soft power as the ability to achieve a desired outcome in international affairs through attraction rather than coercion. It works by convincing others to follow, or getting them to agree to, norms and institutions that produce the desired behavior. Soft power can rest on the appeal of one's ideas or the ability to set the agenda in ways that shape the preference of others. If a state can make its power legitimate in the perception of others and establish international institutions that encourage them to channel or limit their activities, it may not need to expend as many of its costly traditional economic or military resources. See Joseph S. Nye, Jr., *Bound to Lead: The Changing Nature of American Power* (New York: Basic Books, 1990) for more information.

always been, ideologically neutral. It benefits anyone with access and means. This simple fact now represents an enormous challenge to US intelligence."[384] Two Cold-War era collection capabilities—Satellite imagery and signal and communications intercepts—provided the U.S. an unparalleled "information edge." However, in the 21st Century these capabilities may no longer provide the edge they once did. Many of the IC's collection capabilities have been publicly disclosed, alerting our adversaries to our techniques. For example, the relaxation of the previous Cold-War restrictions on satellite imaging technologies as well as advances in satellite and optical sensor technologies, spurred the development of imaging satellites that were smaller, cheaper, and more agile than the relatively large and expensive Landsat and other commercial satellites. Furthermore, the reduction of technical and cost barriers such as increased computer processing capability, user-friendly software, Internet accessibility, and decreased storage costs created a broader range of customers and usage for satellite imagery.[385]

Satellite imagery is commercially available to any potential buyer—friend or foe. As an example, during the 2001 Operation ENDURING FREEDOM campaign, Space Imaging was the only U.S. company with commercial imagery on orbit at the time for the areas of interest to the U.S. government. The U.S. had an option with Space Imaging, and with other companies as well, to buy all of the time on orbit over a particular place. Consequently, to ensure that the U.S. had "full and complete access to all of that imagery collection...without competition," according to Roberta E. Lenczowski, then-NGA technical executive, NGA purchased all commercial imagery over Afghanistan and Pakistan for a period of two months. Lenczowski also stated, "What Space Imaging would be more than happy to point out is that if somebody else had come to them with a contract to buy all the time, they would have sat in negotiation with them."[386] DigitalGlobe, another commercial remote sensing imaging company, can provide image resolution of six-tenths of a meter. The only restriction is that under Department of Commerce guidelines, any commercial imagery with less than approximately eight-tenths of a meter or more must have a twenty-four hour delay in distribution. A twenty-four hour delay would prevent the potential disclosure of any real-time high-resolution tactical operation.[387]

---

[384] Aris A. Pappas and James M. Simon, Jr., "Daunting Challenges, Hard Decisions: The Intelligence Community—2001-2015," *Studies in Intelligence*, 46, no. 1 (2002), 42.

[385] John C. Baker, Ray A. Williamson, and Kevin M. O'Connell, "Introduction," in *Commercial Observation Satellites: At the Leading Edge of Global Transparency*, eds. John C. Baker, Ray A. Williamson, and Kevin M. O'Connell (Arlington, VA: RAND, 2001), 5.

A second technological area where the U.S. "information edge" is eroding is in the area of signals and communications intercept. Intercepts have been degraded by the use of digital communications, encryption devices, and fiber optic transmissions while at the same time, the ever-decreasing costs of these devices ensures that secure communications is available to all—Auntie Em and al-Qa'ida too. Pappas and Simon project that any U.S. advantage in intelligence collection systems will diminish as the rest of the world acquires technology via advanced, commercial, off-the-shelf tools. The current and future security environment of a more-level technological playing field presupposes that "the IC will encounter surprises from both the use of known technology in unexpected ways and the innovative application of a combination of new technologies.[388]

---

[386] Roberta E. Lenczowski, "NIMA and the Intelligence Community," briefing presented at Center for Information Policy Research, Harvard University, Guest Presentations, Spring 2003. Incidental Paper: Seminar on Intelligence, Command and Control, July 2003, 15, URL: *http:// pirp.harvard. edu/pubs_pdf/lenczow-i03-1.pdf>*, accessed 1 April 2004. In the briefing, Lenczowski stressed, "Never has shutter control been invoked. Never." She then explained that shutter control is part of the U.S. government licensing conditions with the U.S. commercial remote sensing industry. These conditions are applied through the Department of Commerce. These commercial imagery providers in turn inform any international customers of these constraints. According to Lenczowski, the spirit behind shutter control as an option the government can exercise is the shortest period of time, and the smallest footprint, so that the remainder of the commercial activity is not inhibited.

[387] Lenczowski, 21.

[388] Pappas and others, 43.

Chapter Seven

21ST CENTURY: THE ROCKY ROAD AHEAD

> We have a huge American problem, and it starts in the National Security Act of 1947. It divided the Intelligence Community into two parts, foreign intelligence and domestic intelligence....It didn't matter too much during the Cold War, because most of the problems were overseas....Then comes terrorism....The terrorists don't care about national borders.
>
> **—Anonymous Participant,**
> **Center for the Study of Intelligence (CSI)**
> *"Intelligence for a New Era in American Foreign Policy"*
> *Conference, September 2003*
>
> We recommend significant changes in the organization of the government. We know that the quality of the people is more important than the quality of the wiring diagrams. Some of the saddest aspects of the 9/11 story are the outstanding efforts of so many individual officials straining, often without success, against the boundaries of the possible. Good people can overcome bad structures. They should not have to.
>
> **The 9/11 Commission Report**
> *22 July 2004*

A Changed Community Since 9/11?

Mark Lowenthal, Assistant Director of Intelligence for Analysis and Production, speaking before the House Permanent Select Committee on Intelligence, questioned whether the 9/11 Commission Report recommendations considered the many changes made since the attack. Lowenthal asked, "Do the recommendations speak to the Community that exists today or the Community that the Commission was investigating that existed that morning on 9/11? Another vocal critic of the 9/11 recommendations, John Hamre, former Deputy Defense Secretary [Clinton Administration], remarked,

The agencies are working together better than any time in my professional recollection…but if you were to listen to our public discourse, it'd sound like we've done nothing, and it sounds like we're just naked and vulnerable today as we were on September 10, 2001, the day before the attacks.[389]

Inherent in their comments is the implication that if the 9/11 Commission recommendations speak for the Community as it existed Pre-9/11 and not Post-9/11, then further change may not be warranted. George Tenet, DCI for seven years, knew well the bureaucratic inertia that plagues the Community. Richard K. Betts, noted Columbia University professor, reports that shortly after 9/11, in a directive leaked to the press, Tenet declared it was time to end business as usual, to cut through red tape and "give people the authority to do things they might not ordinarily be allowed to do….If there is some bureaucratic hurdle, leap it….We don't have time to have meetings about how to fix problems, just fix them." Betts maintains that reform in a bureaucracy means reorganization; reorganization means changing relationships of authority; and that means altering checks and balances.[390] Has the Community reformed *itself* in the Post-9/11 era as Lowenthal and Hamre imply, something the Community had not been able to accomplish in its five and one-half decades of existence?

Undoubtedly, there has been a flurry of movement within the Intelligence Community since the events of 11 September 2001, and any action to improve often-strained Community relationships, regardless of the scope, would be beneficial. However, have these changes been undertaken under the guise of just "doing something" for the sake of public recognition that *something* is being done? As an example, we can look at the issue of recruitment. The Community has long waited for increased hiring authority to fill its ranks after years of zero or minimal hiring. All of the major IC agencies have major recruitment efforts ongoing: NSA boasts of receiving 100,000 resumes since 9/11;[391] the FBI has had over 57,000 people apply for jobs as intelligence analysts;[392] and the CIA receives 2200 resumes weekly.[393] Yet, even with the many aspirants, Community personnel demands exceed supply of qualified applicants, and without

---

[389] As quoted in Walter Pincus, "September 11 Commission Critics Question Panel's Study of New Measures: Report Said to Overlook Changes," *Washington Post,* 10 August 2004, A3.

[390] Richard K. Betts, "Fixing Intelligence," *Foreign Affairs,* 81, no 1 (January/February 2002): 52.

[391] Stephen Barr, "NSA Makes No Secret of Stepped-Up Recruitment Effort," *Washington Post,* 26 April 2004, C2. Cited hereafter as Barr, NSA Recruitment.

[392] Stephen Barr, "Talk of 9/11 Report Centers on Importance of People, Rather Than Structure," *Washington Post,* 15 September 2004, B2.

Community-wide prioritization of personnel hires, each agency in effect not only competes with each other for critical personnel such as qualified Middle Eastern and South Asian linguists; they compete with each other for the adjudication of security clearances.[394] The Information Analysis and Infrastructure Protection (IAIP) Directorate of DHS had only filled 36 percent of its personnel authorization as of January 2004.[395] With hundreds of thousands of new as well as old hires backlogged in the security pipeline, this competition for the same resources is detrimental to all concerned. Yes, it is good that the Community can hire, but without a prioritization of critical skills across the Community and a centralized hiring program to support this prioritization, has the increased hiring solved this shortage or exacerbated it? Additionally, how many of these people will still be available after waiting more than a year for a security clearance before they can draw their first federal paycheck?

One high-demand skill is foreign language fluency. The national agencies as well as the military services are critically short of linguists. The Army is DoD's Executive Agent for the Defense Language Institute and Foreign Language Center (DLIFLC), which trains over 3,500 linguists annually in 23 languages at the Monterey (CA) campus and 85 languages through the Washington office. Yet, according to LTG Keith B. Alexander, Deputy Chief of Staff for Intelligence (DCSINT), the thousands of additional requirements in Arabic,[396] Kurdish, Pashto, Urdu, Dari and other languages have exhausted the Army's linguist base in the Active and Reserve Components, which provide trained linguists in support of DoD and national agencies. As a result, the Army has outsourced more than 6,000 linguist requirements in support of GWOT. The costs in FY2004 for Army contract linguists exceeded $250 million. "Given the number of linguists required

---

[393] "Foreign Policy Association: DDO's Remarks, 24 June 2004, URL: *http://www.americanintelligence.us/modules.php?name=News&file=article&sid=18*>, accessed 26 June 2004.

[394] The 9/11 Commission recommended the creation of a single federal security agency to improve the government's security clearance process. This will be no easy task. In the GAO's *Human Capital Considerations Critical to 9/11 Commission's Proposed Reforms* (Washington, DC: GPO, 14 September 2004), it is noted that the already-taxed system is confronted with existing impediments such as the lack of a government-wide database of clearance information, a large clearance workload, and too few investigators, all hindering efforts to provide timely, high-quality clearance determinations. The increase in security clearance requests since 9/11 ensures that this situation will not improve in the short term. According to the report, it takes 16 times the investigative effort and 6 times the adjudicative effort to conduct a Top Secret investigation than for a Secret-level investigation (17). The number of requests for Top Secret clearances for industry personnel increased from 17 to 27 percent from 1996 through fiscal year 2003.

[395] U.S. Congress, House, (Democratic Members) House Select Committee on Homeland Security, *America at Risk: The State of Homeland Security Initial Findings,* 108th Cong., 2 sess., January 2004, 3. Cited hereafter as Democratic Members Homeland Security Report.

by Commanders across the battlespace, contracted linguists will remain a necessity for the foreseeable future," Alexander noted.[397]

Furthermore, as another overarching example, consider the amount spent on information technology (IT). By the end of FY2004, the Defense Department was to have spent almost $27 billion on IT and consulting services; the IC itself $9.2 billion. These amounts are small in comparison to the total the Pentagon will have spent in 2004, $460 billion.[398] As an example, one military program, the Army's Future Combat System, recently had its modernization program restructured. This increased the cost by between $20 billion or $25 billion and was necessary because the originally structured program had only a 28 percent chance of success.[399] In fact, the Intelligence Community spends less money on annual IT expenditures than the government loses in one year—$20.7 billion in estimated *annual* erroneous payments made by the federal government.[400] Nonetheless, this amount is sufficient to have improved Community members' ability to communicate with each other. But has communication improved?

Christine Healey, a 9/11 Commissioner, reported during Committee testimony that basic connectivity is still a problem for some FBI field offices. A Washington field office employee informed the Commission that as of August 2003, he still could not email anyone at the Department of Justice from his desk. Further, the Washington field office, the second largest field office in the nation, still has only one Internet terminal on each floor.[401] The DHS Chief Information Officer told a

---

[396] Incidentally, the shortage of Arabic linguists is not a recent deficiency. As reported by Glenn R. Simpson, "Language Lessons for Pentagon: Lack of Arabic Speakers Hinders Commanders in Battle for Iraq," *Wall Street Journal*, 3 December 2003, A4, prior to 9/11, the Army had filled only half of its 84 budgeted positions for Arabic translators and interpreters, according to a GAO report, which was by far its biggest shortfall in language specialists. In 2000, DLIFLC graduated 409 Arabic linguists but by 2003 this number dropped to 354 graduates. However, DLIFLIC officials predict the number to rise because of the number of students in the pipeline.

[397] U.S. Congress, Senate, Committee on Armed Services, *Fiscal Year 2005 Joint Military Intelligence Program (JMIP) and Army Tactical Intelligence and Related Activities (TIARA)*, Hearings, 108th Cong., 2nd sess., 7 April 2004, 13. Cited hereafter as Alexander, SAS Testimony.

[398] Anitha Reddy, "Local Firms Respond to a Changing U.S. Military," *Washington Post*, online ed., 26 April 2004, URL: *http://www.washingtonpost.com/ac2/wp-dyn/A40181-2004Apr25?language=printer>*, accessed 29 April 2004.

[399] Renae Merle, "Army Raises Cost of Combat Modernization: Futuristic Project Includes Drones, Unmanned Vehicles, "Smart' Munitions," *Washington Post*, 23 July 2004, A23.

[400] General Accountability Office, *Major Management Challenges and Program Risks: A Government Perspective* (Washington, DC: GPO, January 2003), 26. Also, available online URL: *www.gao.gov/cgi-bin/getrpt?GAO-03-95.*

[401] "Transcript: 9/11 Commission Hearing on Law Enforcement, Counterterrorism," *Washington Post*, online ed., 14 Apil 2004. *<URL: www.washingtonpost.com/ac2wp-dyn/ A12238-2004Apr14?*, accessed 15 April 2004.

group of technology executives that for DHS to fight terrorism effectively, its divisions and their disparate information technology systems are going to have to start operating cohesively. "If we can't send classified emails from one undersecretary to another undersecretary, or undersecretary to [the department] secretary, I'd argue we've got a bit of a problem," he declared.[402] LTG William S. Wallace, Commanding General, Combined Arms Center U.S. Army Training and Doctrine Command (TRADOC), commenting on Operation IRAQI FREEDOM (OFI) "command, control, communications, computers, intelligence" (C4I) at the tactical level, noted:

> No matter how perfect a future network and CP (command post) we build, it won't do much good until we fix the overarching problem of bandwidth management. Limited bandwidth was a major issue during OIF. While fixed command and control installations reliably use high bandwidth communications, the communications architecture for mobile or semi-mobile CPs at the tactical level is too fragile and not robust enough to support our needs. It affected collaboration, information sharing and in some cases, the Commander's ability to command.[403]

The following paragraphs are representative of the current (2004) issues challenging the Intelligence Community as identified in the open press. Initially, it may not be intuitive that some of these examples are specifically addressing challenges facing the IC; however, they may affect the IC indirectly. As a case in point, border/airport security is not a function of the IC but rather the Border Patrol; the Community does not check credentials at U.S. borders or U.S. airports. Nonetheless, the Community (FBI, CIA, NSA, State, DHS) is responsible for contributing to the compilation of terrorist watch lists and related materials that are used to check passenger identification. Another example concerns federal fiscal programs. Strong fiscal management policies and procedures are necessary to assure continued funding for current programs but perhaps most importantly, for future program development.

John E. McLaughlin, as Acting DCI, boasted that the Community was undergoing a "real revolution in intelligence"—from recruiting and technology to interagency cooperation and morale." McLaughlin made this comment in response to criticisms of the Intelligence Community's performance as character-

[402] Ellen McCarthy, "Homeland Security Wants Better Integration," *Washington Post,* 25 March 2004, E4.

[403] U.S. Congress, House, Armed Services Committee, Terrorism, Unconventional Threats and Capabilities Subcommittee, *C4I Interoperability: New Challenges in 21st Century Warfare,* 108th Cong., 2nd sess., 21 October 2004.

ized in the Joint Inquiry and 9/11 Commission Reports. These criticisms of the Community were current as of mid-2004. Do these issues reflect a revolution within the Community—a reflection that the Community has really changed? Or do they reflect the continued inefficiencies of business as usual?

Post-9/11 Community-Wide Issues

Information-Sharing/Technology/ Policy

Disparate Watch Lists Still Abound — Eighteen months after 9/11, the General Accountability Office (GAO) reported nine federal agencies maintained twelve separate lists with different names,[404] and described them as "diffuse and nonstandard," creating a dangerous enforcement gap. In September 2003, the President issued a directive to merge the multiple, disparate terrorist watch lists. The new database and multi-agency Terrorist Screening Center (TSC) were to be operational by 1 December 2003. However, by then it only contained some 11,250 names culled from the State Department's TIPOFF watch list and the FBI's National Crime Information Center; it is expected to contain over 60,000 names. FBI Director Robert Mueller used the analogy of lining up the colors on a Rubik's cube in describing the challenge of organizing the mismatched data from the various agency watchlists— CIA, Justice, State, Defense, DHS. "Each of the agencies has different information and different fields and different records and also a different set of criteria for making their lists," said Mueller. "These tools exist [to merge all the data]," said Roy Hite, GAO's Information Technology Director.[405]

Erroneous "Do Not Fly" Lists Snag Congressmen — Representative John Lewis (D-GA) and Senator Edward M. Kennedy (D-MA) are two of the many travelers who have been flagged at airports as a result of having appeared on the government's terrorist watch lists. The no-fly list is a collection of names from the FBI and intelligence agencies that is managed by the TSA and provided to the airlines. However, each airline has its own system for matching the names. According to security experts, the reasons for the false matches is because the lists are based on antiquated technology and are unevenly administered by airline per-

---

[404] Frank Davies, "Grahman, 2 Allies Introduce Overhaul of U.S. Intelligence," *Miami Herald,* 1 August 2003, 17A.
[405] Samatha Levine, "Spinning Terror's Rolodex: Creating a Master List of Bad Guys is Turning Out to be a Tall Order," *U.S. News & World Report,* 2 February 2004, 31.

sonnel instead of security personnel. In July 2004, 258 passengers alone filed to have their names removed from the no-fly list.[406] The American Civil Liberties Union (ACLU) filed suit in U.S. District Court for western Washington on behalf of John Shaw, a 75 year-old retired minister and eight others. They had been repeatedly detained and interrogated at airports.[407]

FBI Relying on 1980s Technology — Many FBI officials reported that they do not know what information is in its files. The FBI's Automated Case Support system, a 1980s-era technology, "user-unfriendly" system, cannot be used to store or transmit top secret or sensitive compartmented information. In his testimony before the 9/11 Commission, James L. Pavitt, former CIA Deputy Director for Operations, reported that for a variety of reasons, significant information collected by the FBI never gets uploaded into the Automated Case Support system or gets uploaded long after it is available. A December 2003 Department of Justice (DOJ) IG report stated that the FBI still had not established adequate policies and procedures for sharing intelligence. "We are kidding ourselves if we think that there is a seamless integration among all of the agencies," said Michael Rolince, the acting Director of the Office of Intelligence. John Brennan, Director of TTIC, reported seeing a "cacophony of activities" within the IC but no strategy and planning. According to Pavitt, there is no national strategy for sharing information to counter terrorism.[408]

FBI's Modernization Effort is Folly — After the 9/11 attacks, the FBI embarked on a $600 million computer modernization program named Trilogy. A centerpiece of this massive effort was the Virtual Case File (VCF), a modern database for storing and indexing all case information by agents that was to be completed by late 2003. This effort would allow agents to share files electronically. Nevertheless, in January 2005, after spending $170 million on the Virtual Case File system, the FBI abandoned its efforts due to serious system deficiencies. An independent research report by the National Research Council indicated that the sys-

---

[406] Sara Kehaulani Goo, "Hundreds Report Watch-List Trials: Some Ended Hassles at Airports by Making Slight Change to Name," *Washington Post,* 21 August 2004, A8.

[407] "Nation in Brief," *Washington Post,* 5 November 2004, A4.

[408] James L. Pavitt, "Testimony of James L. Pavitt Before the National Commission on Terrorist Attacks Upon the United States, 14 April 2004, URL: <http: //www.9-11commission.gov/hearings/hearing8/staff_statement_5.pdf>, accessed 20 April 2004. Cited as Pavitt, 9/11 Commission Testimony, 14 April 2004.

tem would not assist anti-terrorism investigations because "it was designed with criminal investigation requirements in mind." Senator Patrick J. Leahy (D-VT) observed: "The FBI's long-anticipated Virtual Case File has been a train wreck in slow motion. As recently as last May, the FBI was still claiming that VCF would be completed by the end of 2004, and that it would at last give the FBI the 'cutting-edge technology' it needs. Now we learn that the FBI began to explore new options last August, because it feared that VCF was going to fail...The FBI needs to stop hiding its problems and begin confronting them early on."[409]

Foreign Relations Affected by Lack of Information-Sharing — Sharing of information among countries is still problematic. The "third-country rule" prohibits the country receiving the tip from passing it on to anyone else. The United States, France, Britain, Russia and others all observe this rule. Vince Cannistraro, a former CIA counterterrorism chief, thinks the third-party rule "makes it impossible to have a European CIA" and it should be discarded in the war on terrorism. "When you're talking about transnational groups there is no excuse for keeping the old rules. They need to devise a system to share that kind of information, they need to do it multilaterally, and they need to do it right away." [410]

NSA's Technological Edge Less So — *The Washington Post* reported that Harry D. Gatanas, NSA's senior acquisition executive, is blunt about what happened at NSA over the past fifteen years: The code-breaking organization lost its technological edge. NSA lost its edge when the Internet ushered in commercial innovation that outpaced NSA's advancements. "All these companies are out there building things and the adversaries have access to that technology," said Gatanas. "We don't want to have blinders on: We want to look at these new technologies." Approximately 85 percent of all NSA's procurements are technology-related. In 2003 NSA spent more than $2 billion buying goods and services from companies in Maryland.[411] Unfortunately, Congress severely crippled NSA's momentum to modernize when it passed the FY 2004 National Defense Authorization Act

---

[409] Jonathan Krim, "FBI Rejects Its New Case File Software: Database Project Has Cost Nearly $170 Million," *Washington Post,* 14 January 2005, A5.

[410] Dafna Linzer, "Rules Still Hinder Intelligence Sharing," *Associated Press,* online ed., 28 March 2004, URL: *http://www.mercurynews.com,* accessed 29 March 2004.

[411] Ellen McCarthy, "NSA is Making No Secret of Its Technology Intent," *Washington Post,* 24 June 2004, E1.

revoking NSA's "milestone decision authority." Revoking this authority effectively stripped NSA of its ability to manage directly its own modernization program. This action has restricted NSA's ability to invest broadly in unproven but highly promising technologies. The Undersecretary of Defense for Acquisition, Technology, and Logistics now holds this authority.[412]

Wartime Intelligence Constrained by Policy — LTG Keith B. Alexander, DCSINT, reported that quick access to useful intelligence remained a major battlefield problem [in Iraq]. "Intelligence access is constrained by policies that restricted dissemination and use, especially at the tactical level," said Alexander. The Army pinpointed 127 intelligence areas that require "fixing." Alexander stated, "We must develop technology to permit rapid data exploitation by users who need it most urgently." We haven't figured out a way to share information "horizontally" and still ensure that it remains secret." Stephen Cambone, Undersecretary of Defense for Intelligence (USDI), in written testimony, indicated that intelligence gathering remains "burdened by legacy policies and stovepiped activities that are…not integrated either within the Defense Department or between the Defense Department and the Intelligence Community."[413]

Who's In Charge of Domestic Threats? — Two senators, Carl Levin (D-MI) and Susan Collins (R-ME) of the Senate Armed Services Committee, questioned why they still have no answer to their question of which federal agency is ultimately responsible for the analysis of foreign and domestic intelligence on threats to the United States. Is it the Defense Department, Homeland Security Department, or the CIA? Collins said, "I am told the reason we haven't received an answer to our letters is the DHS, DoD and CIA can't agree on an answer, which implies to me that the lines of authority are not clear and that the answer is still being devised."[414] In June 2004 a series of conflicting news releases, press conferences and television appearances by Attorney General Ashcroft, FBI Director Mueller, and Homeland Chief

---

[412] Michael A. Wertheimer, "Crippling Innovation—And Intelligence," *Washington Post,* 21 July 2004, A19.

[413] William Matthews, "U.S. Army Cites Deficiencies With Data Collection," *Defense News,* online ed., 12 April 2004, URL: <http://www.defensenews.com/story.Phy?F =280391&C=America>, accessed 10 November 2004.

[414] Chris Strohm, "Senators Ask Who's in Charge of Homeland Intelligence," *GovExec.com,* 25 March 2004, URL: http://www.govexec.com/news/index.cfm?, accessed 29 March 2004.

Ridge concerning terrorist threat warnings questioned once again who was in charge. Roger Cressey, terrorism expert, criticized the joint DOJ/DHS statement hastily issued to assuage previous uncoordinated announcements saying, "The fact that two and a half-years after 9/11 we have to have a press release from the Justice Department to say that DOJ and DHS are working well together, are working in coordination – [that] should not give the American people a whole lot of comfort."[415]

Security Clearance/Personnel

Security Clearance Backlog Keeps Growing — DoD's backlog of security clearance investigations and adjudications reached 360,000 by September 2003. Additionally, the number of top-secret clearance requests by 2003 totaled 27 percent of all clearance requests, compared to 17 percent in 1995. A February 2004 GAO report indicated that 8,000 investigators would be required to eliminate the backlog. Yet, as of December 2003, the Office of Personnel Management (OPM) and DoD have only a combined total of 4,200 investigators of which 1,300 are federal employees; the remaining investigators are private contractors.[416] Another report indicated the estimated backlog for overdue reinvestigations for clearances grew from 300,000 in 1986 to over 500,000 in 2000. Now, on average, it takes 375 days to grant a security clearance to industry personnel, up 56 days since 2001.[417]

The IC Wants You — In the biggest recruitment drive in decades, NSA plans to hire 7,500 people from 2004 through 2008, particularly applicants who possess foreign language skills (Arabic and Chinese are a plus), and those in the fields of engineering, mathematics, computer science and procurement as well as non-technical fields. Approximately 4,500 of these new hires will replace NSA employees who leave, mostly through retirement, and the remainder are new positions. It takes three to five years to train most employees and seven years to bring a new language specialist up to speed.[418] Under a new Pentagon policy, DoD can hire as many as 2,500 experts with state-of-the-art knowledge

---

[415] Justin Rood, "Ashcroft, Mueller and Ridge En Route to Hill Spotlights," *CQ Homeland Security – Intelligence,* 1 June 2004 via *http://homeland.cq.com/hs/news.do,* accessed 2 June 2004.

[416] Ellen McCarthy, "Dealing With Clearance Insecurity," *Washington Post,* 15 April 2004, E6.

[417] Carolyn Duffy Marsan, "Management Strategies—Worth the Wait: Security Clearances Take More Than a Year to Obtain, But Federal IT Work Pays Well," *Network World,* 7 June 2004, 65.

[418] Stephen Barr, "Pentagon Can Hire 2,500 Experts for National Security," *Washington Post,* 26 March 2004, B2.Stephen Barr, "Pentagon Can Hire 2,500 Experts for National Security," *Washington Post,* 26 March 2004, B2.

in fields related to national security for appointments of five years with a one-year extension possible. Policy advocates maintain that this approach will help the government attract the talent it needs to modernize technology and revamp internal organizations.[419] Similar recruitment efforts are underway at other IC agencies.

Language Shortages Impede Translation Efforts — The Justice Department's Inspector General found that the FBI as of April still had not translated more than 123,000 hours of recordings "in languages primarily related to counterterrorism activities and more than 370,000 hours of recordings in languages connected to counterintelligence probes." These figures represent a 30 percent backlog of audio recordings in these categories. The IG report indicated despite the hiring of 620 additional linguists since 9/11, "nearly 24 percent of ongoing counterintelligence and counterterrorism intercepts are not being monitored." [420] The language shortages are in Arabic, Urdu, Farsi, and Pashto. The IG also reported that the FBI's lack of computer storage capacity is impeding translation operations. In some cases, this limitation means that surveillance recordings may be deleted before they are reviewed and even though the deletions can be restored from archives, translators have no idea in advance if something was deleted. The FBI now spends $70 million annually on language services compared to $21 million in FY2001.

Little is Known About Radical Islam — Michael Rolince, then-Acting Director of the Washington field office, reported that although the FBI knows "ten times" more now about the radical Islamic community than before 9/11, its knowledge is at about 20 on a scale of 1 to 100.[421]

Federal Government Top Heavy with Bureaucrats — A Brookings Institution study released in July 2003 by government scholar Paul C. Light indicated that the federal government is top-heavy with more layers of high-ranking bureaucrats than ever before, a situation that is

---

[419] Barr, B2.

[420] Dan Eggen, "FBI Backlogged in Translation of Counterterrorism Wiretaps," *Washington Post,* 28 September 2004, A25. Note: The surveillance recordings backlog no doubt is the result of increased FISA warrants. In 2003, the number of secret surveillance warrants issued in federal terrorism and espionage cases under FISA exceeded the total number of wiretaps issued in criminal cases as noted in Dan Eggen and Susan Schmidt, "Data Show Different Spy Game Since 9/11," *Washington Post,* 1 May 2004, A1. The number of FISA warrants approved in 2003 (more than 1,700) was an 85 percent increase over 2001 total (934).

[421] Pavitt, 9/11 Commission Testimony, 14 April 2004.

impeding the flow of information and clouding the accountability of officials who run the Intelligence Community agencies. The number of senior federal executives rose to 64 in 2004 compared with just 17 in 1960 and 51 in 1998. "It [the increase] explains why information flows are sometimes so sluggish and it also explains why we can't hold anybody accountable for what goes right or wrong," said Light. "There are just so many places that decisions get made, or not made, that you can't really figure out who is responsible." The trend in the private sector is to reduce the corporate layers. "Many companies began a long march to streamline and flatten," said Michael Useem, a Professor of Management at the Wharton School at the University of Pennsylvania. "Everybody with any management sense whatsoever says it is a good idea, not only for information coming up, but to ensure actions get taken and not snarled in endless approval and red tape."[422]

Analysis

- **State Publishes Inaccurate Terrorist Attack Data** — The State Department's report, *Patterns of Global Terrorism*, in indicating that the number of global terrorist attacks was at the lowest ebb in the past thirty-four years, was simply wrong. At the request of the State Department, the Terrorist Threat and Integration Center (TTIC) revised its statistics for 2003. Larry C. Johnson, former CIA analyst and former State Deputy Director for Counterterrorism, urged the correction. He stated, "When you read the report, TTIC did not add [the data] properly. Even a third-grader could have found this. The body counts in 2002 and 2003 were at the highest levels in history.[423] The TTIC, formed in the aftermath of 9/11 to address the failure of the intelligence agencies to "connect the dots," has personnel from CIA, FBI, DoD, State and Homeland Security. It maintains a database of known and suspected terrorists with more than 100,000 names in it and a Top Secret web site available to 2,600 users with a search capability covering 3.5 million documents. John Brennan, TTIC Director, stated, "The good news is now we in the TTIC for the first time have this access which is unparalleled in the U.S. government. The bad news is that we have all these different systems." Brennan had six different computer systems under his desk. TTIC analysts cannot yet

---

[422] Christopher Lee, "Agencies Getting Heavier on Top: 17 Executive Titles Created Since 1960," *Washington Post*, 23 July 2004, A27.

[423] R. Jeffrey Smith, "State Dept. Concedes Errors in Terror Data," *Washington Post*, 10 June 2004, A17.

conduct one search that will span across the agencies. Another IC issue affecting the TTIC is how much of a respective contributing agency's guarded information is willingly given to the Center.[424]

- **IC Wrong on Iraqi WMD** — The Senate Intelligence Committee's Commission on Iraq's WMD Program reported that the Intelligence Community "overstated" the evidence that Iraq possessed chemical and biological weapons and was actively reconstituting its nuclear program, in short, that the claims were "not supported by the underlying intelligence."[425] The Commission's report indicated that a DIA official warned CIA about questionable reliability of an Iraqi defector who was the chief source of allegations regarding Iraq's mobile biological facilities. After seeing a draft of Secretary of State Colin L. Powell's scheduled 5 February 2003 address to the United Nations, the DIA employee, assigned to CIA, questioned the "validity of the information." According to the DIA employee, this information "warranted further inquiry before we use the information as the backbone of one of our major findings for the existence of a continuing Iraqi BW program!" The employee also emailed the deputy chief of the CIA's Iraq Task Force. The deputy chief later told the Senate Intelligence Committee he reassured the employee that the war [Operation IRAQI FREEDOM] was not going to hinge on what the source [Curveball—a discredited Iraqi defector] said.[426]

- **CIA Analysts to Receive Source Information** — In evaluating its prewar assessment of Iraqi's WMD program, an internal CIA review revealed several occasions where CIA analysts mistakenly thought the source had been corroborated by multiple sources when in actuality, it only came from one source. In light of this finding, Tenet, the DCI at the time, ordered an end to the long-standing practice of withholding source information from the analysts. This practice, while designed to protect agents' identities, also maintained the bureaucratic divide between the Directorate of Operations (DO) and the Directorate of Intelligence (DI). According to Jami A. Miscik, CIA's Deputy Director for Intelligence, the internal review also identified another problem: reliance on "inherited assumptions" or failing to retest past intelli-

---

[424] "Terrorism Center Wrestles Technology, Secrecy," *Reuters,* 28 April 2004.

[425] Dana Priest and Dafna Linzer, "Panel Condems Iraq Prewar Intelligence: Senate Report Faults 2002 Estimate Sent to Hill, Accuses the CIA of "Group-Think," *Washington Post,* 10 July 2004, A1.

[426] Walter Pincus, "Skepticism About Defector's Weapons Allegations Ignored," *Washington Post,* 13 July 2004, A12.

gence conclusions as time went on. This is "the single most important aspect of our tradecraft that needs to be examined," said Miscik. "How do we ensure we are not passing along assumptions that haven't been sufficiently questioned or reexamined?"[427]

- **Threat Assessment Will Take DHS Five Years to Complete** — Congress created the Information Analysis and Infrastructure Protection Directorate (DHS) to analyze intelligence related to the terrorist threat and to match threats to specific homeland vulnerabilities. Robert Liscouski, DHS Assistant Secretary for Infrastructure Protection, indicated that a comprehensive terrorist threat and vulnerability assessment is unlikely to be completed within the next five years.[428] The IAIP remains a skeletal organization with only 60 employees in its information-analysis wing of 300 employees total. These IAIP personnel represent less than two-tenths of 1 percent of all DHS employees. Tom Ridge, Secretary of DHS, stated, "We accept the notion that we're not where we need to be. I'm not sure I accept the criticism that we could do it faster."[429]

Classification

- **Too Many Secrets** — The Information Security Oversight Office (ISOO), part of the National Archives, reported that the federal government "discovered" more than 14 million new secrets in 2003, a 25 percent increase from the previous year. For the year prior to 11 September 2001, the number was 8 million.[430] Representative Christopher Shays (R-CN), Chairman, House Government Reform Committee's National Security Panel, stated "There are too many secrets....No one knows how much is classified and the system often does not distinguish between the critically important and the comically irrelevant [example—terrorist plot to kidnap Santa Claus and inserted into classified traffic]." Carol A. Haave, Deputy Undersecretary of Defense for Counterintelligence and Security, indicated that most misclassification was unintentional, resulting perhaps from misunderstandings or failure to declassify no longer sensitive data. "Collectors of information can never know how it could best be used. We have to move to a user-driven environment," stated Haave. Haave also indicated this is a weakness, particularly for anti-terrorism efforts.[431]

---

[427] As quoted in Walter Pincus, "CIA Alters Policy After Iraq Lapses," *Washington Post*, 12 February 2004, A1.

[428] Democratic House Members Homeland Security Report, 3.

[429] Siobhan Gorman, "On Guard, But How Well?" *National Journal*, 3 May 2004, 696-703.

[430] Al Kamen, "In the Loop: Millions of Secrets," *Washington Post*, 4 May 2004, A23.

Airport/Border Security

- **Airport Screeners Continue to Perform Poorly** — A Department of Homeland Security Inspector General report indicated that covert testing in 15 airports in November 2003 revealed screeners performed as poorly as they had prior to the 11 September terrorist attacks.[432] Since its inception in November 2001 until January 2004, the Transportation Security Administration (TSA) has spent more than $10 billion on passenger and baggage screening. [433]

- **Border Fingerprinting at Least Five Years Away** — The Justice Department Inspector General determined it will probably take at least four more years (until 2008) for the FBI and Border Patrol systems to be combined to quickly check fingerprints for the more than one million illegal immigrants[434] who are caught each year. The FBI fingerprint database contains 10-digit fingerprints, which are superior because often a crime scene may only have one fingerprint. However, the Border Patrol's separate system contains approximately six million 2-digit fingerprints while a second database contains an undisclosed number of 10-digit fingerprints.[435] Incidentally, although DHS announced that there were 1,000 agents along the 5,525 mile border with Canada, this was accomplished by removing several hundred border agents from the 1,989 mile border with Mexico.[436]

---

[431] Michael J. Sniffen, "Secrets Perplex Panel: Classified Data Growing to Include "Comically Irrelevant," *Washington Post,* 3 September 2004, A17.

[432] "Airport Security Still Lacking," *Washington Post,* 23 September 2004, E2.

[433] Democratic House Members Homeland Security Report, 5.

[434] Illegal immigration into the United States is predominantly a post-1965 and Mexican occurrence according to Samuel P. Huntington, distinguished Yale University scholar. In Samuel P. Huntington, "The Hispanic Challenge," *FP Foreign Policy,* March/April 2004, he reports that for almost a century after adoption of the U.S. Constitution, there were no national laws restricting or prohibiting immigration, and only a few states imposed modest limits. During the next 90 years, illegal immigration was minimal. However, that changed with the 1965 immigration law, increased transportation, and Mexican emigration policies. The U.S. must now contend with massive illegal immigration (apprehension rate was 1.6 million in the 1960s but by the 1990s this increased to 14.7 million) across a porous 2,000 mile border. Huntington remarks that the U.S/Mexico border situation is unique: "No other First World country has such an extensive land frontier with a Third World country." It is apparent the face of immigration has changed. In the 1960s the principal sources of foreign-born population was relatively evenly spread amongst Poland, U.K., Canada, Germany, and Italy. However, in the 1990s this distribution changed—to Cuba, India, Philippines, China, and Mexico, with the Mexican numbers being very large.

[435] "Records Gap Leaves Borders Vulnerable: Report Says U.S. Border Patrol Won't Get Complete FBI Fingerprint Files for Years," *Washington Post,* 3 March 2004, A11.

[436] Democratic House Members Homeland Security Report.7.

- **Ninety-five Percent of all Cargo is Not Inspected** — Six million cargo containers entered through the U.S.'s 361 ports in 2003 and of these six million, 5.4 percent were inspected—nearly double the percentage from 2002.[437] It is noteworthy that the number of inspected ports has increased; however, the flip side is that 95.6 percent of the cargo containers were NOT inspected at all.

Financial Issues

- **Government's Fiscal Ills** — David M. Walker, Comptroller General and Head of the General Accountability Office, indicated that the vast majority of federal fiscal programs and policies were put in place decades ago but have not undergone a fundamental review in years. "The simple truth is that the base of government is not okay....It's time to streamline and simplify the federal government's organizational structure to make it more economical, efficient, effective, flexible, responsive and accountable. During a December 2003 Press Club speech, Walker stated, "The bottom line is that, in my view, the federal government's current financial statements and annual reports do not give policymakers and the American people an adequate picture of our government's overall performance and true financial condition. This is a serious issue."[438] Furthermore, GAO auditors for the eighth year in a row could not provide a definitive opinion on the quality of the federal government's consolidated financial statements (fiscal years 2003, 2004). They could not determine whether the federal books met generally accepted accounting principles. At least 10 of 23 major agencies and departments restated their 2003 statements to correct financial errors.[439]

- **Poor DoD Fiscal Management Procedures** — A recent GAO study stated, "Overhauling DoD's financial management represents a major challenge that goes far beyond financial accounting to the very fiber of the department's range of business operations and management culture." GAO reported that of the 25 government-wide "high risk" list, six belong to DoD and DoD shares three other high-risk areas. GAO identified four underlying causes of DoD's inability to solve its fiscal

---

[437] "Terrorism Expert Calls Seaports Vulnerable," *Washington Post,* 28 January 2004.

[438] Stephen Barr, "GAO Chief Refuses to Stop Doing the Math," *Washington Post,* 18 January 2004, C2.

[439] Christopher Lee, "GAO Again Finds Fault With the Federal Books: Auditors Say That Government's Records Are So Inadequate They Cannot be Evaluated, but Bush Official Cites Progress," *Washington Post,* 21 December 2004, A23.

problems: 1) a lack of sustained top-level leadership and management accountability for correcting problems; 2) deeply embedded cultural resistance to change, including military parochialism and stovepiped operations; a lack of results-oriented goals and performance measures and monitoring; and inadequate incentives for seeking change.[440] These underlying causes are applicable to any number of IC agencies as well.

Are these examples evidence of a Revolution already underway in Intelligence? This author thinks not. These are examples of continuing lack of prioritization, lack of authorities, lack of accountability, poor fiscal management, duplication of services, and the like. Improvements have been recognized throughout the Community, such as the new analytical fusion initiatives between NGA and NSA, increased Community personnel assignments/duties at other agency headquarters as well as deployment forward with military commands, and joint operation efforts; however, these improvements should not be viewed as reasons for arbitrarily dismissing the vocal critics of the IC. Most improvements have been marginal, small scale, mostly cosmetic overtures. The aforementioned examples affirm that despite large infusions of money (lack of resources having been blamed for past inadequacies) and assurances that the Community has changed its practices, business within the IC continues as it has since 9/11 (with a few notable exceptions), since the end of the Cold War, and for the most part, since 1947.

With the cornucopia of commercially available technology, it is shameful that vast parts of the IC operate not only independently of each other but do so with outdated computers and analytical tools. The Community's communication and connectivity problems are technological in nature, but technology is not responsible for these divisions. Community policies prohibiting or limiting collaboration are responsible. Scot McNealy, Sun Microsystems President and CEO, coined the phrase: "The network is the computer." This was not a cheap marketing ploy of the mid-1990s to increase Sun's bottom line, but rather was the fundamental understanding that an individual computer is merely a communication device. The computer's real value is in its ability to link to other computers and not its own individual processing power. On the other hand, the network is the platform upon which knowledge can be "shared, amplified, and recreated" in innovative forms. It is these networked pieces of information which added together become more than the sum of their parts. [441] This concept is the antithesis of the IC's tradition of maintaining information flows in stovepipes.

---

[440] General Accountability Office, *Department of Defense: Status of Financial Management Weaknesses and Progress Towards Reform* (Washington, DC: GPO, 25 June 2003), cover page.

A few weeks after 9/11, this author, an Army Reserve Military Intelligence Officer, was recalled to active duty and assigned to the 1st Information Operations Command (known then as the Land Information Warfare Activity, LIWA) at Fort Belvoir, VA, working a special terrorism-related project. We struggled frequently in our attempts to gain access to NSA data. The requirement for special access briefings, system training, and message release authority were but a few of the policy roadblocks in our way. All concerned parties could easily have worked together to meet these requirements but there was little NSA effort to expedite the processes. While the situation has changed somewhat, there is still a reluctance to share information as noted in a recent conversation with one of my former team members. He is a fully cleared intelligence analyst who requested specific raw data from NSA. Unfortunately, NSA's response to this analyst's inquiry was all too typical, "If we gave you access to the database, you might do something with the information."[442] This response illustrated the continuing hold of the old Cold-War, restrictive "need to know" principle, rather than the new "need to share" imperative.

The Way Ahead: The Networked Community

Kevin O'Connell, RAND Intelligence Policy Center Director and Robert R. Tomes, NGA New Concepts Office Deputy Chief, advocate rethinking U.S. security controls and policies. "The underlying logic of information compartments loses its appeal in an era where much is uncertain, where we grapple with mysteries rather than the collective pieces of a known puzzle and where we want human abstraction and cognitive capabilities to intuit otherwise hidden relationship."[443] A year after 9/11, Paul Wolfowitz, Deputy Secretary for Defense, testifying before the Joint Inquiry, expressed his thoughts on sharing information:

> A culture of excessive compartmentation will hinder our ability to defeat new threats.... There is much more that we can do to exploit the full benefits of new information technologies such as data mining and change detection....Partly because of the inescapable need for security of information, the Intelligence Community lags behind the private sector in its ability to tag and store massive amounts of data, and to mine that information to determine patterns. Again, a culture that discourages collaboration and the sharing of information forfeits these new technological advantages....We need to break down information so those who need it, get access to it.[444]

---

[441] Russ Mitchell, "The Ghosts in the Machine: Can Technology Find Terrorists?"*The American Spectator* (Nov/Dec 2001), accessed via ProQuest, 4 December 2003.

[442] Jeff Mitchell, intelligence analyst at 1st IO Command, interview by the author, 1 March 2004.

[443] Kevin O'Connell and Robert R. Tomes, "Keeping the Information Edge," *Policy Review,* no. 122 (Dec 2003/Jan 2004), accessed via ProQuest, 14 June 2004.

Since the attack on Pearl Harbor over sixty years ago, the Intelligence Community has continued to perfect its ability to deliver strategic warning based on "indicators" of a surprise attack. The 9/11 Commission in its final report listed four elements common to the "rigorous analytical methods" developed over the ensuing years. These elements are: 1) think about how surprise attacks might be launched; 2) identify telltale indicators connected to the most dangerous possibilities; 3) where feasible, collect intelligence on these indicators; and 4) adopt defenses to deflect the most dangerous possibilities or at least trigger an earlier warning.[445] The 9/11 Commission further reported that these analytical methods "did not fail; instead, they were not really tried."[446] However, in the 21st Century national security landscape, there are no tripwires, no single bit of information that will provide the U.S. strategic warning. These analytical methods were perfected throughout the Cold War against an enemy (the Soviet Union) who itself changed incrementally. Consequently, the traditional bureaucratic model of intelligence was befitting for an organization that monitored the Soviet threat because the Soviet Union itself was such an incorrigibly bureaucratic system.[447]

Since the end of the Cold War, there has been a growing consensus about how best to provide intelligence in the Post-Cold War, information-age environment. Chapter 4 has highlighted the significant reform initiatives during the 1990s, which sought to better align Community resources. For the most part, these reform initiatives were unsuccessful. According to Bruce Berkowitz, this consensus centered on five ideas that are necessary to provide the best intelligence. First, the Community needs to have a wide field of vision to survey the ever-changing threat landscape. Second, it must have organizational agility and flexibility. Third, it must be flexible in focus. Fourth, it needs multiple lines of communication connecting people who have information with the people who need it. Finally, an intelligence organization needs to have direct interaction and transparency between intelligence producers and consumers.[448] These generally accepted ideas are the characteristics of a networked organization and not the traditional bureaucratic organization represented by the defining characteristics of division of labor, a hierarchical structure and chain of command. A

---

[444] U.S. Congress, Senate, Select Committee on Intelligence and House, Permanent Select Committee on Intelligence, *Joint Inquiry on Counterterrorist Center Customer Perspective,* 19 September 2002, accessed via LexisNexis, 12 January 2004.

[445] *The 9/11 Commission Report: The Final Report of the National Commission on Terrorist Attacks Upon the United States* (New York: W.W. Norton & Company, 2004), 346. Cited hereafter as 9/11 Report.

[446] 9/11 Report, 348.

[447] Bruce Berkowitz, "Better Ways to Fix Intelligence," *Orbis,* 45, no. 4 (Fall 2001): 614. Cited hereafter as Berkowitz, Better Ways.

[448] Berkowitz, Better Ways 609-610.

recent appraisal of intelligence support during a 21st Century conflict, Operation ENDURING FREEDOM (Afghanistan operation), was presented to the Senate Armed Services Committee in June 2004. General John P. Abizaid, then U.S. Central Command nominee, told the Committee, "Intelligence was the most accurate that I've ever seen on the tactical level, probably the best I've ever seen on the operational level, and perplexingly incomplete on the strategic level with regard to weapons of mass destruction."[449] Many intelligence professionals maintain that analysts have become so intensely absorbed in current intelligence that in-depth strategic analysis is wanting. Obviously, this is a trend which does not foster "best" intelligence.

Understanding the type of organization needed in the 21st Century is one thing but changing the organization to reflect this need is a difficult task indeed. The new model of intelligence, the networked and adaptable organization, according to Berkowitz, is not compatible with the long-held beliefs about how intelligence organizations are supposed to operate. Berkowitz advises:

> A traditional bureaucracy is ill suited for using modern information technology, especially networked communications. In an open-architecture, networked organization, the number of opportunities for providing, supplying, or sharing information—and, thus, the power of the network–increases exponentially as each new member joins.[450] Yet a bureaucracy's traditional chain of command, lines of authority, and mission responsibilities are all aimed at channeling and limiting the opportunities of organization members to interact with each other and with outsiders. A bureaucratic intelligence agency erects its own barriers to the information revolution.[451]

However, the networked organization is precisely the type of organizational structure necessary for optimal functioning of the Intelligence Community in the 21st Century. It would be naïve and terribly misguided to suppose that what's good for the global marketplace and readily available—the latest "gizmos"—is

---

[449] Gregory F. Treverton, "Intelligence: The Achilles Heel of the Bush Doctrine," *Arms Control Today,* 33, no. 6, (Jul/Aug 2003), accessed via Proquest, 6 November 2003.

[450] This concept is referred to as Metcalfe's Law. Metcalfe's Law is expressed as 1) the number of possible cross-connections in a network grows as the square of the number of computers in the network and 2) the community value of a network grows as the square of the number of its users. Robert Metcalfe is the founder of the Ethernet protocol for computer networks. This information was obtained from URL: http://searchnetworking.techtarget.com/sDefinition/0,sid7_gci214115,00.html, accessed on 15 November 2005.

[451] Berkowitz, Better Ways, 615.

not also good for our adversaries. Technology is an equal opportunity enabler. As noted in *Global Trends 2015,*

> IT-driven globalization will significantly increase interaction among terrorists, narcotraffickers, weapons proliferators, and organized criminals, who in a networked world will have greater access to information, to technology, to finances, to sophisticated deception-and-denial techniques and to each other. Such asymmetric approaches—whether undertaken by states or nonstate actors—will become the dominant characteristics of most threats to the U.S. homeland.[452]

The Joint Inquiry and the 9/11 Commission demonstrated the overwhelming failure of the Community to communicate both vertically within its organizations and horizontally across them. This failure to communicate not only implies the lack of technical capability but the inability of personal communications as well. The Joint Inquiry, in criticizing the IC, noted, "the Community too often failed to focus on that information and consider and appreciate its collective significance...the Community failed to capitalize fully on available, and potentially important, information."[453] In its recommendations, the 9/11 Commission proposed that,

> Information be shared horizontally, across new networks that transcend individual agencies....An outstanding conceptual framework for this kind of "trusted information network" has been developed by a task force of leading professionals in national security, information technology, and law assembled by the Markle Foundation (see "Markle Foundation" tonebox on next page).[454]

Without the ability to communicate effectively, the Community becomes not a knowledge-based network, but what Russ Mitchell would describe as "an archipelago."[455] The Community—its analysts and its databases—remains isolated on digital islands. The Community must break down its self-perpetuating stovepipes.

---

[452] Central Intelligence Agency, *Global Trends 2015: A Dialogue About the Future with a Nongovernment Expert,* NIC2000-02, December 2000, URL: <http: //www.cia.gov/cia/reports/globaltrends2015 >, accessed 29 September 2004.

[453] U.S. Congress, Senate, Select Committee on Intelligence and House, Permanent Select Committee on Intelligence, *Joint Inquiry into Intelligence Community Activities Before and After the Terrorist Attacks of September 11, 2001,* 107th Cong., 2nd sess., S. Rept. 107-351 and H. Rept. 107-792, 20 December 2002, 10-11.

[454] 9/11 Report, 418.

[455] Mitchell, "Ghosts in the Machine."

"If you don't like change, you're going to like irrelevance even less," proclaimed General Eric Shinseki, then Chief of Staff, U.S. Army. While this author does not believe the business of intelligence will ever become unimportant, let alone irrelevant, she does believe that the Intelligence Community, in order to improve itself, like those companies described by Tom Peters—can do so by "self-destructing"—tearing down the bureaucratic barriers to continually reinvent itself (see "Subduing Stovepipes"). "Ultimately, reform is not about intelligence in the classic sense of intelligence cycles and consumer-producer relationships," O'Connell and Tomes allege. "It is about information and knowledge, wisdom and foresight, agility and flexibility, leadership and vision."[456]

Markle Foundation

The Markle Foundation is a private philanthropic organization. Zoë Baird, a former Justice Department and White House Attorney (Clinton Administration) directed the Task Force on National Security in the Information Age with James Barkdale, co-founder of Netscape Communications. Its first report, *Protecting America's Freedom in the Information Age: The First Report of the Markle Foundation Task Force*, issued in 7 October 2002, stressed the importance of creating a decentralized network of information sharing and analysis to address the challenge of homeland security. *Creating a Trusted Network for Homeland Security: Second Report of the Markle Foundation Task Force*, released 2 December 2003, reaffirmed the principles for capitalizing on the U.S. strengths in information and technology and how the government should create networks; it proposed building an information network called the Systemwide Homeland Analysis and Response Exchange (SHARE). Incidentally, the Second Task Force Report indicated that "sharing of terrorist-related information between relevant agencies at different levels of government has been only marginally improved in the past year [2003]....sharing remains haphazard and still overly dependent on...personal relations among known colleagues." For more information consult: *http://www.markletaskforce.org*.

In a criticism of the first Task Force Report, in Marcia Savage, "No Rave Reviews," CRN, no. 1016, 14 October 2002, accessed via ProQuest, 28 January 2004, Steve Crutchley, Chief Security Officer for a security-consulting firm, said the task force recommendations would have little impact. "There is a place for a task force like this, but they are ineffective because they are not lobbying for the government to pass laws to hold people accountable for security in business and for service providers that provide security services. Government should set the example: The coming together of bureaus and the sharing of information between the FBI, CIA and whoever else will never happen unless it is mandated."

---

[456] O'Connell and Tomes.

Horizontal Integration and the IC

Community-wide integration, at least at the systems level, is the essence of the concept of horizontal integration (see Principles of Horizontal Integration tonebox). Recognizing the need for a more integrated Intelligence Community, the Defense Department (USDI) and the Intelligence Community (ADCI-C) initiated a multi-agency effort (Horizontal Integration Senior Steering Group ((HISSG[457])) to explore and formulate a vision for the national security community (DoD, IC and Homeland Security Community). This effort resulted in a focus on "processes and capabilities

---

[457] In addition to the HISSG reviewing major issues relating to system integration, the Community also has the National Intelligence Collection Board, chaired by Charlie Allen and the National Intelligence Analytic and Production Board, chaired by Mark Lowenthal, Vice-Chairman of the National Intelligence Council and Assistant Director of Central Intelligence for Analysis, to ensure that systems focus on national needs and priorities. The Mission Requirements Board, Co-Chaired by Allen and Lowenthal, works with the Community to develop the long-range requirements for systems acquisition five to fifteen years ahead.

Principles of Horizontal Integration

The concept of horizontal integration is not new nor is it strictly a government-owned initiative. In the 1990s, the term horizontal organization began appearing in management circles. A horizontal organization is a flatter organization structure whereby cross-functional, end-to-end work flows link internal processes with the needs of both suppliers and customers. Frank Ostroff, a management consultant, in *The Horizontal Organization: What the Organization of the Future Actually Looks Like and How It Delivers Value to Customers* (New York: Oxford University Press, Inc., 1999), 10-11, describes applicable principles:

1. Organize around cross-functional core processes, not tasks or functions.

2. Make teams, not individuals, the cornerstone of organizational design and performance.

3. Decrease hierarchy by eliminating non-value-added work and by giving team members who are not necessarily senior management the authority to make decisions directly related to their activities within the process flow.

4. Use information technology (IT) to help people reach performance objectives and deliver the value proposition to the customer.

5. Emphasize multiple competencies and train people to handle issues and work productively in cross-functional areas within the new organization.

6. Promote multiskilling, the ability to think creatively and respond flexibly to new challenges that arise in the work that teams do.

7. Build a corporate culture of openness, cooperation, and collaboration, a culture that focuses on continuous performance improvement and values employee empowerment, responsibility, and well-being.

Ostroff stresses that companies adopting these principles also must have in place a demanding, aspirations-driven senior leadership, a focus on key customers and markets, a strong performance ethic, world-class capabilities in at least one dimension critical to delivering the value proposition, and other fundamentals, such as an effective balance sheet and capital structure management and adequate investment in research and development (Ostroff, 67).

to acquire, synchronize, correlate, and deliver National Security Community data with responsiveness to ensure success across all policy and operational missions."[458] Inherently, the concept of horizontal integration is all about the data—getting the right data to the right user at the right time. To accomplish this, as indicated in the process graphic, requires transforming the Producer-Centric Model (TPED) intelligence process that defines the Community today into the Consumer-Centric Model (APEC) Model of the future. Data previously restricted

---

[458] Keith E. Herrington, "Inside DIA: Horizontal Integration—The Transformation Roadmap for U.S. Intelligence and the National Security Community," *Communique* [DIA news bulletin], August 2004, 10-11.

by closed architectures and "owned" by stovepiped organizations becomes more usable due to network-centric standards and more available at the earliest point of consumability. This all-encompassing concept requires the end-to-end management and integration of all enterprise information and intelligence functions—requirements, tasking, collection, operations, content management, correlation, exploitation, fusion and analysis. [459]

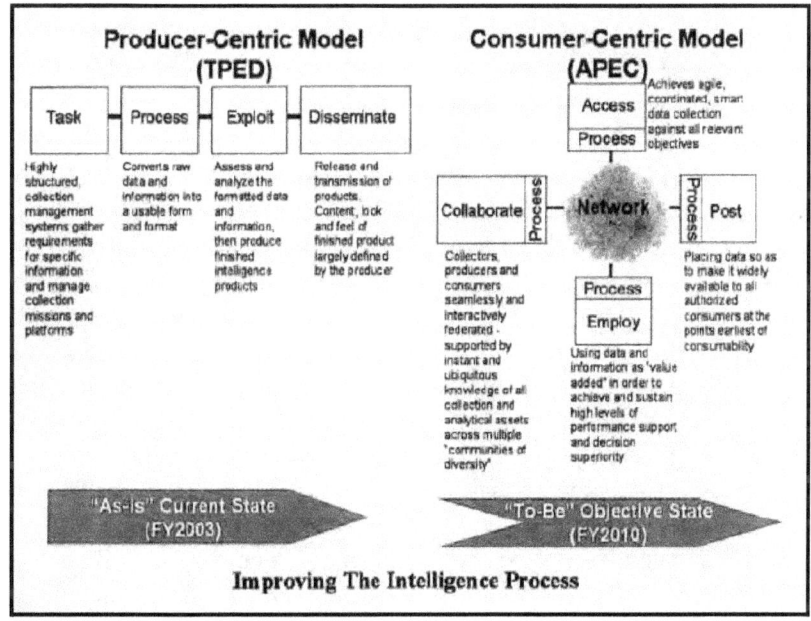

Source: Herrington, 10.

"The need for horizontal integration is very urgent," stated Charles E. "Charlie" Allen, Assistant Director of Central Intelligence for Collection:

> I believe not only that the threat to this country over the next decade and beyond requires us to do this—to become a more effective and efficient intelligence community—but also that we are going to be advised by the Congress that it expects this community to become more integrated and more collaborative. [460]

---

[459] The earliest point of consumability, as defined in Herrington 11, refers to processing data only as much as required to render it useful and usable to consumers. Timeliness of delivery is ensured because minimal handling occurs between the sensor/collector and the consumer. These data are available securely to the consumer without regard to collection methods. The earliest point of consumability will vary between consumers.

[460] Robert K. Ackerman, "Horizontal Integration Challenges Intelligence Planners," *Signal*, 58, no. 2 (October 2003), accessed via ProQuest, 22 January 2004.

Allen acknowledged that as the Community began to build more advanced, technical systems, it became aware that the complexity of today's threats required a more integrated approach—cross-discipline action, cross-cueing, multiple-source access, and the like. "In the past, we built one system at a time...we did not sit down and say, 'How should that system be integrated with the others?' Today, we cannot do that any longer and that's good," remarked Allen. "If we had thought this way [horizontal integration] when we had embarked on the Future Imagery Architecture (FIA),[461] we probably would have had less difficulty and had a much better system."[462]

Undoubtedly, horizontal integration of intelligence systems is the way ahead for vast improvements in Community-wide information sharing and collaboration. Descriptively speaking, according to Ackerman, the IC is in a race against international adversaries, and to win, the IC must link disparate data systems and information processes to learn enemy intentions and plans. This race toward HI encompasses both data exchange at the collection level and information exchange at various levels of command and throughout civil government decisionmaking.[463] Yet, this race is one that will not be won quickly, easily, or without detours. Any future DoD and Community system developmental efforts will incorporate HI at the onset of system design. Understandably, it is less complex and costly at the initial build to design systems with the requisite security and integration features. However, the fielding of these new systems is not forthcoming; these horizontally integrated systems will not be deployed for as long as *ten* years. In the interim, for the multitudes of existing intelligence systems, costly and often cumbersome work-arounds or stopgap fixes will be required for Community-wide data exchange.

An example currently underway to improve communication between disparate systems is the Horizontal Fusion Portfolio. The Office of the Assistant Secretary of Defense for Networks and Information Integration in January 2003 created the Portfolio to accelerate the fielding of DoD's net-centric warfighting vision. The IC, DoD and other federal agencies will invest funds to enhance the technology initiatives comprising the Portfolio. These applications will eventually be integrated into a "col-

---

[461] As reported in Dougles Jehl, "Boeing Lags in Building Spy Satellites," *The New York Times,* 4 December 2003, C1 the next generation of reconnaissance satellites initially had a budget of $6 billion, but the NRO Director acknowledged that the project was "underfunded" and "underscoped" and would require an additional $4 billion. The Senate Intelligence Committee earlier had blamed both the contractor, Boeing and the FIA program office for "mismanagement and poor planning." Even with NRO's scaled-backed expectations of what Boeing had promised it could deliver, several anonymous senior officials estimated only a 50-50 chance Boeing would meet the 2006 initial launch date.

[462] Ackerman.

[463] Ackerman.

lateral space," which rides on DoD's Secret Internet Protocol Router Network (SIPR-NET). In the Horizontal Fusion-NSA initiative, individual NSA analysts will be able to access some DoD information deemed at or below their individual security classification using a virtual private network (VPN) tunnel. While NSA analysts will have unprecedented access into military databases, it is not a two-way street; DoD will not have access to NSA computers. The Horizontal Fusion Portfolio Manager understands the IC's hesitancy about posting potentially sensitive information on a computer network:"The technology is available…that will prevent [users] from seeing the information [they] are not allowed to see." The Horizontal Fusion office had $150 million in its FY 2004 budget for its programs.[464]

Another example is the collaboration between NGA and NSA analysts. The *Los Angeles Times* reports that Project Geocell has provided real-time tips and warning to field operatives and the White House and NGA-NSA teams were posted together in Iraq. "The NGA and NSA are acting closer together now than any intelligence organizations in history," said Joan Dempsey, Executive Director of the President's Foreign Intelligence Advisory Board.[465]

The Intelligence Reform and Terrorism Prevention Act of 2004 "requires the President to establish an Information Sharing Environment (ISE) to facilitate the sharing of terrorism information among all appropriate Federal, State, local, tribal and private sector entities through the use of policy guidelines and technologies."[466] This type of network was proposed initially by the Markle Foundation Task Force and later adopted as one of the 9/11 Commission Report recommendations. Zoë Baird, Task Force Director, said that although the government needs to use the information to prevent terrorism, "The challenge of this will be writing the policy rules. That will be more challenging than the technology."[467]

As expected with any "new" initiative, there has been opposition. O'Connell and Tomes identified six long-standing impediments to Community-wide integration efforts. The view of this author is that these are Community self-imposed impediments. To address them requires a commitment by the Community senior leadership to rectify. Their six points are: First, the Community limits the develop-

[464] "Intelligence Agency to 'Tunnel' Into Pentagon Information Databases," *Inside the Pentagon,* 29 January 2004.

[465] Bob Drogin, "THE NATION: Two Agencies Melding Minds on Intelligence-National Security and National Geospatial-Intelligence are Sharing Intercepted Messages, Satellite Data and More to Provide Real-Time Tips,"*Los Angeles Times,* 31 December 2004, accessed via Proquest, 7 January 2005.

[466] United States Congress, Senate, Committee on Governmental Affairs, *Summary of Intelligence Reform and Terrorist Prevention Act of 2004,* 108th Cong. 2nd sess., 6 December 2004.

[467] As quoted in Robert O'Harrow, Jr., "Senate Bill Proposes Anti-Terror Database: Civil Liberties Groups Express Concern, *Washington Post,* 28 September 2004, A4.

ment of new collaboration and information-sharing methods by the strict divisions of intelligence disciplines and the security and legal restrictions on data exchange. Second, where one sits with regard to intelligence determines where one stands on reform issues. Third, the lack of tangible intelligence reform results from the lack of support from middle and senior managers to aggressively support innovation.[468] The fourth point refers to the continued reform debate with only minimal change—the pathos of "studying without action." The fifth impediment is the current fiscal management system with its intelligence-planning processes that entails essentially "formalized systems to tend fiscal rice bowls." They assert that by compartmentalizing the planning and funding of information and knowledge sharing, compartmentalization practices are reinforced. Finally, too often, "change" discussions become stuck on marginal issues.[469]

Yet, by far the biggest obstacle facing horizontal integration is not technology. Not surprisingly, it is Community policies and cultural issues. As Charles Allen observes,

> I believe that policies, processes, culture and so-called turf issues will be some of the more difficult and frustrating aspects of making this [HI] happen....There have been self-imposed barriers employed by many elements of the Intelligence Community—problems of sharing, problems of collaboration, problems of security. Some agencies find it difficult to share intelligence with others.[470]

---

[468]Michael Wertheimer, former NSA Senior Technical Director wrote in "Crippling Innovation—and Intelligence," *Washington Post,* 21 July 2004, A19, that given a dollar to spend on intelligence, the most profitable near-term return continues to come from existing systems. This is particularly true now that the current transnational and terrorist threats have encouraged intelligence consumers toward intelligence on demand. Unfortunately, this inverted cycle of demand and supply comes at the expense of laying the groundwork for future capabilities. Wertheimer maintains that the U.S. is not heeding the disruptive shift that is occurring with the growing dominance of the Internet. "History and best business practices obligate us to encourage "disruptive innovators" to create new sources and methods for intelligence....to succeed we must demand far less near-term intelligence product from the Signals Intelligence Community, give it [NSA] control of its resources and allow it to plan for a disruptive future."

An insightful book dealing with the failure of initially successful companies to continue to thrive is Clayton M. Christensen, The Innovator's Dilemma: When New Technologies Cause Great Firms to Fail (Boston: Harvard Business School Press, 1997). He describes how good business practices such as focusing on the most profitable products that are in high demand can actually weaken a great firm. Christensen shows how mainstream customers initially reject truly breakthrough innovations or "disruptive technologies" because they cannot use them initially. A follow-on book is Clayton M. Christensen and Michael E. Raynor, *The Innovator's Solution: Creating and Sustaining Successful Growth* (Boston: Harvard Business School Press, 2003).

[469] O'Connell and Tomes.

[470] Ackerman.

Nevertheless, technology is not the only enabler to effective information sharing and collaboration. The most important aspect is *people*. Evon Jones, a Senior Vice President and Chief Information Officer (CIO) of the Dial Corporation, a computer company, speaking at *Computerworld's* Premier 100 IT Leaders Conference, agrees that there is too much focus on IT as technology and not enough on people: "Before you get to tools, you need to invest in human capital to generate the ideas the tools will enable."[471] Captain Robert L. Hubbard, former Deputy Chief, Transnational Warfare Group (DIA) believes that the Intelligence Community's current analytical deficiencies have evolved largely because of years of budget-based-vice-requirements-based intelligence force planning and acquisition strategies. Hubbard argues:

> In its efforts to respond to pressures to streamline and reduce costs following the Cold War, the Intelligence Community has created a corps of resource planners, programmers, and budgeters with insufficient knowledge of national security requirements and a corps of intelligence substantive experts lacking in the ability to express precisely and quantitatively the intelligence resources they need to support national security objectives.[472]

He maintains that the Community at large has yet to demonstrate that its work force reengineering strategies in response to the threat environment have been integrative and coherent.

Strategic capital management is the ideal centerpiece of any serious change management initiative. According to a 2004 GAO report, "successful major change management initiatives in large public and private sector organizations can take *5 to 7* years to create the accountability needed to ensure this success. As a result, committed and sustained leadership is indispensable to making lasting changes in the Intelligence Community.[473] J. Christopher Mihm, GAO Managing Director for Strategic Issues, testifying before the Subcommittee on Oversight of Government Management, the Federal Workforce, and the District of Columbia, Committee on Governmental Affairs, stated in September 2004:

---

[471] Kathleen Melymuka, "Premier 100 Panel Weighs Infrastructure Hype, Reality: Changes Are Coming, But Not as Fast as Vendors Like to Think," *Computerworld,* online ed., 9 March 2004, URL: *http://www.computerworld.com/printthis/2004/0,4814,90931,00.html,* accessed 11 March 2004.

[472] Robert L. Hubbard, "Another Response to Terrorism: Reconstituting Intelligence Analysis for 21st Century Requirements," *Defense Intelligence Journal,* 1 no.1 (2002), 72.

[473] Government Accountability Office, *Human Capital Considerations Critical to 9/11 Commission's Proposed Reforms* (Washington, D.C: GPO, 14 September 2004), cover page. Cited hereafter as GAO Human Capital Report.

Federal human capital strategies are not yet appropriately constituted to meet current and emerging challenges or to drive the needed transformation across the federal government. The basic problem has been the longstanding lack of a consistent approach to marshaling, managing, and maintaining the human capital needed to maximize government performance and ensure accountability because people define the organization's culture, drive its performance, and embody its knowledge base.[474]

Committed, sustained, highly qualified, and inspired leadership, and persistent attention by all key parties in the successful implementation of organizational transformation are indispensable to making lasting changes in the Intelligence Community.[475]

Mihm further commented that the experiences of leading organizations suggest that a performance management system will be helpful to the Community as it moves from a "need to know" to a "need to share" culture. "An effective performance management system is a vital tool for aligning the organization with desired results and creating a 'line of sight' showing how the team, unit, individual performance can contribute to overall organizational results."[476] Appendix F provides GAO's suggested key practices for mergers and transformations and for effective performance measurement. The Community could employ these as guiding principles.

Congressional Oversight and the IC

Congress plays a significant role in reforming the Intelligence Community. Without congressional support, reform initiatives and transformational initiatives will not receive the priority they deserve because Community leaders will continue to be hindered by inadequate authorities and resources. "Intelligence is an inherent function, whether performed ill or well, of every state; the governing authority must provide itself with intelligence in order to be effective and to protect itself."[477] The recent 9/11 Commission Report recognized the critical role Congress plays in securing our nation against its enemies.

The 9/11 Commission Report emphasized that strengthening congressional oversight is both difficult and important:

---

[474] GAO Human Capital Report, 2.

[475] GAO Human Capital Report, 6.

[476] GAO Human Capital Report, 8.

[477] Jordan and others, *American National Security,* 5th ed., (Baltimore: The Johns Hopkins University Press, 1999), 144 .

Few things are more difficult to change in Washington than congressional committee jurisdiction and prerogatives....Tinkering with the existing structure is not sufficient. Either Congress should create a joint committee for intelligence using the Joint Atomic Energy Committee as its model, or it should create House and Senate committees with combined authorizing and appropriations powers....The other reforms we have suggested—for a National Counterterrorism Center and a National Intelligence Director—will not work if congressional oversight does not change too. Unity of effort in executive management can be lost if it is fractured by divided congressional oversight.[478]

This recommendation would bring major change to congressional business as usual. Presently, both current and new intelligence programs and their respective spending levels are discussed in both the House and Senate Intelligence Committees. However, the House (HAC) and Senate Appropriations Committee (SAC) set the intelligence spending levels. The recommendation to grant one congressional committee the powers to set intelligence priorities and approve its expenditures is radical, as it would force the most powerful committees, the Appropriations, Armed Services and Foreign Relations committees, to relinquish some of their powers. Lee H. Hamilton noted that "Structural change is essential, because you must have budget authority to have effective oversight. What you have now is not working...There's a lot more interest in Congress in reforming the executive branch than in reforming themselves." Senator Ted Stevens (R-AK), Chairman of the Senate Appropriations Committee, commented matter-of-factly, "I don't think it will fly." A GOP House aide, speaking on background, was more succinct stating the recommendation "doesn't have a snowball's chance in hell." Interestingly, Representative John P. Murtha (D-PA), member of the House Appropriations Committee, indicated that public indifference to this debate makes it easy for Congress to resist changing its "arcane, tradition-bound structures." "I haven't had one person at home ask me about this stuff. It's a Washington thing."[479] Senator John McCain (R-AZ) accused the appropriators of "trying to protect their turf," adding, "If we do not give this new permanent intelligence committee the appropriating authority that they need, then there will be no reform and a vital part of the 9/11 commission recommendations will be neutered."[480] Former Senator Bob Kerrey (D-NE), a 9/11 Commissioner, called Congress's refusal to take up congressional oversight "Outrageous. The American people should be angry." He indicated that it would have been better to drop the executive-branch changes [from the 9/11 Commission recommenda-

---

[478] 9/11 Commission Report, 420.

[479] Quotations from Charles Babington, "Hill Wary of Intelligence Oversight Changes, Lawmakers from Both Parties Resist Recommendations of 9/11 Commission," *Washington Post*, 12 September 2004, A5.

[480] Dewar, Senate New Oversight Structure. Note: Congress failed to address this issue in the *Intelligence Reform and Terrorism Prevention Act of 2004*.

tions] if Congress was not going to reform itself. "These are secret agencies," he said, "Unless you put in strong oversight, it isn't going to work."[481]

Why is appropriation authority so important? Think of the simple Washington golden rule of economics: "He who has the gold, rules." The Intelligence Community as well as its major contractors quite frequently can safely ignore the pressures of the intelligence committees because the "power of the purse" resides with the appropriators. According to McCain, "the appropriators rule here—the fix is in." So how "special" are the appropriations committees? McCain compiled a study indicating that in the past 10 years in which the Republicans have controlled Congress, the number of "earmarked" pork-barrel spending projects moving through the appropriations committees has risen from 4,126 a session to 14,040. The Senate defense appropriations subcommittee alone gets more than 3,000 requests for special projects and during the session [108 Cong. 2 sess. (2004)], the House Appropriations Committee received more than 33,000 requests.[482]

The sheer number of congressional committees monitoring intelligence and security—83 as reported by the Hart-Rudman Commission—alone attests to the need to improve congressional oversight. The Department of Homeland Security responds to 88 congressional committees and subcommittees.[483] The staggering amount of resources required to prepare for congressional appearances or responses to congressional queries could be better spent elsewhere. This is not to say that congressional oversight is not necessary but rather a large proportion of congressional curiosity could be better served by its own Congressional Research Service.

The budgetary process is in need of reform. Only *twice* in the last 50 years have all appropriations bills been enacted by the beginning of the fiscal year! Accordingly, since Congress must enact these bills each year, Congress cannot devote the time necessary to provide effective program oversight. The Congressional Budget Office (CBO) estimated that each year there is about $90-$120 billion in unauthorized appropriations. Changing to a biennial budget would allow Congress more time for review. Additionally, government agencies would enjoy more stable funding. This would be a big plus for the IC, which during the past few years has had to rely on annual supplemental funding for many of its operations.[484]

---

[481] David Ignatius, "Hypocrisy on Spy Reform," *Washington Post,* 8 October 2004, A35.

[482] Ignatius, A35.

[483] Dan Morgan, "Overhaul of Congressional Panels Urged: Report Finds Responsibility, Accountability Lacking," *Washington Post,* 23 July 2004, A21.

[484] "Budget of the United States Government, Fiscal Year 2005 Budget Reform Proposals," *Government Printing Office,* URL: <*http://frwebgate4.access.gpo.gov/cgi-bin/wais-gate.cgi?WAISdocID=08729814703+41+0+...*>, accessed 21 August 2004.

The DoD's Planning, Programming, and Budgeting System (PPBS)[485] has generally served DoD well as a strategic planning process since its inception in the 1960s. However, according to the first Business Executives for National Security (BENS) Tail-to-Tooth Commission Report, because of internal practices and external demands over the subsequent years, PPBS has become bureaucratized to the point of being insufficiently agile to perform its intended purposes. Its original purposes were forecasting and describing the most likely strategic environment and defining the military capabilities it requires; allocating resources to meet identified missions according to established priorities; integrating the military service programs; and formulating the annual defense budget.[486] Forty years later, however, PPBS has become a "broken accounting system with more than 5,000 program elements (PE) that generates a glut of budgetary trivia."[487]Henry Kissinger once referred to the government planning efforts in this way: "What passes for planning is frequently the projection of the familiar into the future."[488] The United States spends more on national security than any other nation; likewise, we should expect more for our investment.

In today's environment, PPBS (and the Capabilities Programming and Budgeting System—CPBS) no longer constitute an effective strategic planning process. Its inflexibility has become readily apparent since 9/11. The Intelligence Community, besieged with burgeoning requirements, has had to rely on yearly supplemental funds to sustain continuing operations. The central recommendation to the Senate Intelligence Committee suggested by Cofer Black, former Director of the CIA's Counterterrorist Center, aiming to improve the IC's counterterrorism efforts, was succinct:

> My central recommendation is to support the war with people and money and appropriate operational authorities. We can't win the war on the cheap. Lurching from supplemental funding to supplemental funding is not a very effective way to support a global counterterrorist intelligence war. Provide multiyear funds so that we can manage and plan our programs effectively. Resources won't solve all of our problems— but resources will solve the majority of them.[489]

---

[485] The Intelligence Community has a similar program called Capabilities Programming and Budgeting System (CPBS). NFIP program managers use this system to propose and justify budget requests and by the DCI to control the allocation of NFIP resources. It too is in need of an overhaul.

[486] "Framing the Problem of PPBS," *BENS Tail-to-Tooth Commission Report*, January 2000, URL: *http://www.bens.org/images/PPBS2000-Framing.pdf*, accessed 10 November 2004. Cited hereafter as BENS.

[487] "Intelligence Resource Management," *Potomac Strategies & Analysis, Inc.,* December 2003, 64.

[488] BENS.

[489] Cofer Black, "Investigation of Sept 11 Intelligence Failures," 26 September 2002, accessed via LexisNexis, 12 January 2004.

James L. Pavitt indicated that although Congress and the White House have given CIA [and the Community] healthy increases, too much of the new money, to stay within deficit ceilings, is given in yearly supplemental bills. Without a sustained financial commitment to pay for increased recruiting and training programs, managers cannot put the requisite clandestine service and other valuable Community-wide intelligence programs in place. "It's a hell of a way to run a railroad, by the way," Pavitt recounted. "We've got money now to deal with the crisis of the moment and the crisis of the moment is Iraq and terrorism. There's some money but nowhere near the kind of investment that's necessary."[490]

In brief, to provide for an effective, reformed Intelligence Community, Congress can best put its own House (and Senate) in order. In the following chapter, the author assesses the reform potential of hurriedly enacted intelligence legislation in the fall of 2004. In view of the inability of the Intelligence Community to reform itself thoroughly, Congressional action appears to offer the ultimate impetus for correcting the deficiencies noted in the present chapter.

---

[490] Dana Priest, "Retired Official Defends the CIA's Performance," *Washington Post*, 5 November 2004, A23.

Chapter Eight

POST 9/11 INTELLIGENCE REFORM

> There's no use trying, said Alice. One cannot believe impossible things.
>
> I daresay you haven't had much practice, said the Queen.
>
> When I was your age, I always did it for half an hour a day.
>
> Why sometimes I've believed as many as six impossible things before breakfast.
>
> —**Lewis Carroll**
> *Alice's Adventures in Wonderland*

Protecting the Turf

The usually staid Washington-in-August was anything but that in the summer of 2004 after the release of the long-awaited 9/11 Commission report. The events of 9/11 created an "opportunity," remarked Richard K. Betts, "to override entrenched and outdated interests, to crack heads and force the sorts of consolidation and cooperation that have been inhibited by bureaucratic constipation."[491] It seemed that anyone who knew anything about the Intelligence Community and national security was *someone* with *something* to say. Suggestions emerged to bring Congress back *early* from its recess to discuss the 9/11 Commission recommendations and propose legislation prior to the November 2004 election! That did not happen, but Thomas Kean, Co-Chair of the 9/11 Commission, warned that Congress was moving too slowly to negotiate a comprehensive intelligence reform package. "If we lose the momentum, we may lose the whole thing," said Kean. "We need a bill, and we need it soon."[492] James L. Pavitt disagreed that creating a National Intelligence Director (NID) would necessarily fix the IC problems:

---

[491] Richard K. Betts, "Fixing Intelligence," *Foreign Affairs* 81, no. 1 (January/ February 2002): 52.

[492] Dan Eggen and Helen Dewar, "Intelligence Reforms May be Stalled: 9/11 Panel Chief Fears Momentum Loss; Victims' Kin Critical," *Washington Post,* 15 October 2004, A13.

To suggest that if we don't act [to create a national intelligence director that terrorist strikes against the U.S. are more likely] is simply not right. There are no easy fixes. Terrorism is not going to be gone a few years from now. My children, your children are going to have to worry about this a long time from now. If that's true, we're not going to just make it all better, make the nation safer overnight by making a new bureaucratic structure.[493]

For the fourth election year in a row, Congress had to return to a lame-duck session[494] after the November election to take up unfinished business of the 108th Congress. A chief question was whether Congress would pass a comprehensive intelligence reform bill prior to its adjournment. One basic issue[495] on which the House and Senate had difficulty in reaching agreement was the recurrent turf battle over control of intelligence spending. The Senate version called for funding of the NSA, NRO, and NGA to be declassified and consolidated under the new National Intelligence Director; whereas, under the House version, intelligence funding would remain classified, hidden within the Pentagon's overall budget. A surprising vote against two of the Senate's most powerful and senior members, Senators Ted Stevens, Chairman Appropriations Committee and Robert C. Byrd (D-WV), this committee's ranking minority member, occurred as the Senate hammered out its intelligence reform proposal. The Senate voted against Steven's proposal, 55 to 37, to drop the recommendation to declassify the intelligence budget and voted against Byrd's proposal, 62 to 29, to eliminate the budgetary powers of the NID.[496]

With two days in December 2004 remaining for Congress to pass the intelligence reform bill, the prospects looked dim. In late November, House Speaker J. Dennis Hastert (R-IL) had pulled the bill from floor consideration after two com-

---

[493] As quoted in Dana Priest, "Retired Official Defends the CIA's Performance," *Washington Post*, 5 November 2004, A23.

[494] Note: The 20th Amendment to the Constitution in 1933 changed the presidential inauguration and congressional calendars in the hopes of eliminating the need for post-election sessions. Nonetheless, as noted by the Senate Historical Society and reproduced in Helen Dewar, "Another Congress to Return for Another Lame-Duck Stint: Post-Election Meetings to Finish Work Set for Mid-November," Washington Post, 27 October 2004, A23, Congress's affinity for lame-duck sessions is becoming prevalent.

[495] For an assessment of the major similarities and differences between the two bills as passed by the House initially on 8 October 2004 and the Senate initially on 6 October 2004, consult *H.R. 10 (9/11 Recommendations Implementation Act)* and *S.2845 (National Intelligence Reform Act of 2004): A Comparative Analysis* by the Congressional Research Service, updated 21 October 2004.

[496] Helen Dewar, "Senators Offer New Oversight Structure: Intelligence Panels Would be Reworked," *Washington Post*, 5 October 2004, A4. Cited hereafter as New Senate Oversight Structure.

mittee chairs strongly objected to the provisions worked out among House and Senate negotiators who had been deadlocked since October trying to reconcile the separate reform bills. House Armed Services Committee Chairman Duncan Hunter (R-CA) objected to provisions he believed would give the new intelligence director (NID) authority over Pentagon intelligence collection agencies, and House Judiciary Committee Chairman F. James Sensenbrenner Jr. (R-WI) sought provisions to make it easier to deport immigrant suspects and to deny a driver's license to undocumented immigrants.[497] Both had expressed their stalwart determination not to change their positions but later relented after intense and persistent negotiations. Senator Susan Collins (R-ME) referred to these two provisions as a "poison pill" that could have prevented any passage of legislative reform in 2004.[498]

Hunter, backed by Chairman of the Joint Chiefs of Staff (JCS) General Richard Myers and the rest of the JCS, expressed two major arguments against giving up some of the Pentagon's control (see tonebox on next page). The first argument maintained that the proposed NID budget powers would affect future technologies, possibly at the expense of combat troops. The chief complaint was that sharing power with a civilian czar [NID] could undermine the ability to get intelligence to the front lines. "If the military is stripped of their ability to control their own intelligence lines, it can prove to be a deadly mistake," Hunter declared.[499]

Sensenbrenner, angered by the House's removal of previously approved key immigration changes, charged that "This bill [amended House bill] fails to include the strong provision in the House bill because my Senate colleagues found them 'too controversial.' That's unfortunate, because their refusal to consider these security provisions on their merits will keep Americans unnecessarily at risk." Sensenbrenner also objected that the bill did not include a provision that would have prevented the release of suspected terrorists who seek political asylum.[500]

"There's been a lot of opposition to this from the first. Some of it is from the Pentagon. Some of it, quite frankly from the White House, despite what the president has said," acknowledged Senate Intelligence Committee Chairman Senator Pat Roberts (R-KS) on a weekly news talk show. Roberts further commented, "I

---

[497] Walter Pincus, "No Intelligence Compromise Seen: Lawmakers See Slim Chance for Passage in December Session," *Washington Post*, 23 November 2004, A9. Cited hereafter as No Intelligence Compromise.

[498] Brian DeBose, "Senate Approves Intelligence Bill," *The Washington Times*, 9 December 2004, A1. Cited hereafter as Senate Approves Bill.

[499] Diamond, 6.

[500] Brian DeBose, "House OKs Intelligence Reform Bill," *The Washington Times*, 8 December 2004, A1.

just don't see it [intelligence reform bill] passing."[501]   Others in Congress expressed a somewhat more guarded optimism. Senator Mitch McConnell (R-KY) commented, "The bill may be on life support, but I think it's still breathing."[502]   Senate Governmental Affairs Committee Chairman (sic) Susan Collins (R-ME) said, "I don't see reopening of the issue in conference. We've compromised as much as we can...The bill is not dead, but is in trouble...only a small chance it could pass in December."[503]

Operational Intelligence Funding

As noted in John Diamond, "Intelligence Impasse Mainly a Question of Control: But Civilians, Military Share Power Already," *USA Today,* 29 November 2004, 6, many intelligence professionals disagreed with Hunter's criticism and viewed his actions as a matter of control, noting that the military (field commanders) generally get top priority. "What you see here is the forces of the status quo protecting their turf in the Congress and in the bureaucracy," said Susan Collins, (ME-D), Chair of the Governmental Affairs Committee. David Burpee, NGA spokesman, noted that rarely do disputes over satellite coverage priorities require arbitration at the DCI level. "It works pretty smoothly...When lives are at risk, the interests of the combat commander and those in political power coincide," Burpee stated. Gregory Treverton, head of the intelligence policy center at the RAND Corporation, agreed stating, "If people are fighting a war, they're going to get first claim no matter what." Treverton further noted, "When you ask, 'Why do we have so little intelligence on the weapons of mass destruction target in Iraq?' the answer was sometimes that we were so busy with force protection." Walter Pincus, "Turf War Stalls Intelligence Bill: Pentagon Allies at Odds with Advocates of New Director," *Washington Post,* 27 October 2004, A4, reported that some skeptical legislators and staff members viewed the turf war over control of intelligence spending as a ploy by those opposed to the creation of the NID or concerned that their committees will lose clout. Others noted that previous budget disputes between former CIA Director George Tenet and Secretary of Defense Rumsfeld were settled easily. One former CIA colleague stated, "Tenet never wanted to take on money issues...the problem was more in theory than in practice." A senior Rumsfeld aide stated, "Everyone wants actionable intelligence fast and unfiltered, and sometimes there is professional disagreement on how. But I can't think of a disagreement over funds and have been told we worked closer [with the CIA] than at any time in history."

---

[501] Walter Pincus, "Passage of Intelligence Bill Called Doubtful: Lawmakers Say Bush, Cheney Need to Lobby," *Washington Post,* 22 November 2004, A3. Cited hereafter as Intelligence Bill Passage Doubtful.

[502] Intelligence Bill Passage Doubtful, A3.

[503] No Intelligence Compromise, A9.

Passage of Intelligence Reform and Terrorism Prevention Act of 2004

After much debate, round-the-clock negotiations, and last-minute White House appeals for support,[504] the House approved legislation on 8 December to restructure the Intelligence Community in a vote of 336 to 75.[505] The Senate followed suit on 9 December in a vote of 89 to 2. Senators Robert C. Byrd (D-WV) and James M. Inhofe (R-OK) voted against the measure. Byrd believed the measure was prepared too hastily and voiced his opposition when the Senate version was introduced initially in August 2004. "No legislation alone can forestall a terrorist attack on our nation," Byrd said after Senate approval of the bill.[506] Inhofe, echoing Byrd's criticism of the bill's "rush to judgment," stated "I also think this needs more time...without exception every time we've rushed to do something and then accepted promises that we would get it fixed in three weeks or next year, it never seems to happen."[507]

On 17 December 2004, President Bush signed the Intelligence Reform and Terrorism Prevention Act of 2004—a 563-page bill that has been cited as the "largest overhaul of U.S. intelligence-gathering since the passage of the National Security Act of 1947." Bush stated during the Act's signing ceremony, "A key lesson of September the 11th, 2001 is that intelligence agencies must work together as a single, unified enterprise."[508] The IC has long been regarded not as

---

[504] As reported in Philip Shenon and Carl Hulse, "House Leadership Blocks Vote on Intelligence Bill," *The New York Times,* 21 November 2004, A1 when negotiations stalled and further compromise appeared uncertain, House Speaker J. Dennis Hastert (R-IL) decided to block the vote on the proposed intelligence bill. Hastert said, "It's hard to reform; it's hard to make change. We are going to keep working on this." Later both President Bush and Vice-President Cheney telephoned the leading opponents of the intelligence reform bill in attempts to persuade them to reconsider and garner their support for the measure. In the days leading up to the eventual passage of the bill, House, Senate and even White House officials met in a conference committee to hammer out the differences. As reported in Dana Priest and Walter Pincus, "Analysis: Director's Control is a Concern," *Washington Post,* 8 December 2004, A1, "The president and the vice president's interventions with House members were absolutely key in moving this bill forward," said Susan Collins (R-ME).

[505] Brian DeBose, "House OKs Intelligence Reform Bill," *The Washington Times,* 8 December 2004, 1, reported that of the 336 supporters of the bill—152 were Republicans, 183 Democrats and one Independent while 67 Republicans and eight Democrats voted against the bill. Twenty-two members did not record a vote.

[506] Walter Pincus, "Intelligence Bill Clears Congress: Bush Expected to Approve Post 9/11 Reforms Next Week," *Washington Post,* 9 December 2004, A4. Cited hereafter as Intelligence Bill Clears Congress.

[507] Senate Approves Bill, A1.

[508] Peter Baker and Walter Pincus, "Bush Signs Intelligence Reform Bill: President Now Must Find an Experienced Hand to Guide 15 Agencies," *Washington Post,* 18 December 2004, A1. Cited hereafter as Bush Signs Reform Bill.

a "community" but rather a federation of independent fiefdoms. James Woolsey, a former DCI, once remarked that his predecessor, Robert Gates, had warned him that his position as DCI was like that of the kings in medieval France: the nobles all swear fealty to you, but do not fear you. [509] Unquestionably, this act holds one Community person responsible to the president, Congress and the American public—the Director of National Intelligence. However, only implementation and further evaluation of this Act will determine if the authorities granted to the DNI truly facilitate a "single, unified enterprise" with the DNI at its helm or whether this Act, like so many reform initiatives before it, brings only marginal changes because its provisions had been compromised to the least common denominator to ensure its passage.

Appendix G highlights intelligence reform provisions as extracted from the United States Senate Committee on Governmental Affairs *Summary of Intelligence Reform and Terrorism Prevention Act of 2004.* The majority of this Act addresses agency and department provisions that are non-IC related—they are predominantly law enforcement (LE)-related and are not discussed further in this report. Furthermore, Appendix G identifies these non-IC related provisions by their respective titles only. Two examples of LE initiatives stipulated by this Act include 1) the FBI is given the authority to raise the mandatory retirement age to 65 for 50 FBI employees per fiscal year through 30 September 2007[510] and 2) the Secretary of Homeland Security, in each fiscal year 2006 through 2010, is authorized to increase the number of border patrol agents by not less to 2,000, subject to available appropriations.[511] For more detailed information on these provisions as well as the intelligence provisions, consult the online version of the Intelligence Reform and Terrorism Prevention Act of 2004 at *http://www.gpoaccess.gov/ serialset/creports/intel_reform.html.* The provisions briefly discussed herein are: national intelligence definition, the DNI and its budget and personnel authorities, and the creation of national centers; other intelligence-related provisions are noted in the appendix.

National Intelligence Definition

The Act redefined "national intelligence" as including all information gathered in the U.S. or abroad that pertains to more than one agency and involves threats to

---

[509] "Time to Rethink – America's Intelligence Services," *The Economist Newspaper Ltd.,* 20 April 2002, accessed via Lexis-Nexis, 28 January 2004.

[510] United States Congress, Senate, Committee on Governmental Affairs, *Summary of Intelligence Reform and Terrorist Prevention Act of 2004,* 108th Cong. 2nd sess., 6 December 2004, 10. Cited hereafter as GAC Summary.

[511] GAC Summary, 12.

the U.S., its people, property, or interests; the development, proliferation, or use of weapons of mass destruction; or any other matter bearing on national or homeland security.[512] This new definition emphasizes "WMD" as a separate category of information related to U.S. national security issues.

Director of National Intelligence

The Senate-confirmed Director of National Intelligence is restricted from serving as the Director of CIA or the head of any other IC element.[513] For now, the Office of the DNI will remain at CIA headquarters but has only until 1 October 2008 to find new quarters—the DNI may not be collocated with any other IC element after that time. The DNI will become the President's principal intelligence advisor, a role formerly assigned to the DCI by EO 12333.

For decades, intelligence reform initiatives have attempted to aid the DCI in the execution of his dual-hatted role and responsibilities as DCI and Director, CIA, by creating assistant DCI positions and a large Community Management Staff (CMS), all with limited success. The 9/11 Commission Report noted that the DCI had "too many jobs" and "no recent DCI has been able to do all three [DCI, Director of CIA and Principal Intelligence Advisor to the President] effectively. Usually what loses out is management of the Intelligence Community...."[514] The congressional solution granted the DNI authority for 500 new personnel billets within the Office of the DNI, plus an additional transfer of 150 Community personnel to assist in the management of IC responsibilities.[515] The present author questions whether these 650 Community personnel will be any more successful in managing the Community than were the approximately 300 personnel in past years. She suggests that a lack of personnel was not the primary reason for continual Community management issues but rather it was the lack of substantive authorities to make "things happen." As the following paragraphs illustrate, the recently legislated but not yet implemented authorities of the DNI may centralize more "power" than that enjoyed by the DCI, but it is unclear whether they are powerful enough to run the Community as a single, unified enterprise.

---

[512] GAC Summary, 5.

[513] GAC Summary, 1.

[514]*The 9/11 Commission Report: The Final Report of the National Commission on Terrorist Attacks Upon the United States* (New York: W.W. Norton & Company, 2004), 409. Cited hereafter as 9/11 Report.

[515] GAC Summary, 2.

Budget and Personnel Authorities

Under the new provisions the DNI shall "develop and determine" the National Intelligence Program (NIP) budget based on proposals submitted by other IC agencies; "ensure the effective execution" of the annual budget; and "monitor the implementation and execution of the NIP." At present, it is uncertain if these provisions are more "powerful" than the authority in EO 12333 (signed in 1981) that granted the DCI "more explicit authority over the development, implementation, and evaluation of the NFIP."[516] One aspect of the Act that promises to strengthen the DNI's budget authorities is that the Director of OMB must apportion NIP funds at the "exclusive direction" of the DNI for allocation to the IC elements. The DNI, in turn, manages these NIP appropriations by "directing the allotment or allocation" through the IC department heads.[517]

Although the DNI was granted authority to transfer and reprogram funds, the Act imposed three stipulations on such actions. All transfers or reprogrammings must 1) be for a higher priority intelligence activity; 2) must support an emergent need, improve program effectiveness, or increase efficiency; and 3) may not involve funds from the CIA Reserve for Contingencies or a DNI Reserve for Contingencies. These stipulations are not without merit. However, the DNI can only move funds after OMB and affected agency approval and only if the amount in a single fiscal year is less than $150 million, is less than 5 percent of the IC element's NIP funds, and does not terminate an acquisition program. If the affected element concurs, then these limits do not apply.[518] These monetary amounts are small—"decimal dust" according to one critic[519]—when one considers the IC's reported budget of $40 billion.

With approval of OMB, the DNI may transfer 150 Community-funded personnel to the Office of the DNI. Once the national intelligence center is created, the DNI may transfer an additional 100 personnel but to do so, the DNI must obtain approval from Director of OMB and notify appropriate Congressional committees. The DNI may also transfer an unlimited number of personnel to another IC element if the same three stipulations required above to transfer or reprogram NIP funds are met. Once again, approval must be granted by the OMB and appropriate Congressional committees must be notified.[520]

---

[516] Mark M. Lowenthal, *U.S. Intelligence: Evolution and Anatomy* (Westport, CT: Praeger, 1992), 107.

[517] GAC Summary, 1.

[518] GAC Summary, 2.

[519] David E. Kaplan and Kevin Whitelaw, "Intelligence Reform—At Last," *U.S. News and World Report,* 20 December 2004, 31.

[520] GAC Summary, 2.

The 9/11 Report sought to give the DNI the "full range of management, budgetary and personnel responsibilities needed to make the entire U.S. intelligence Community operate as a coherent whole."[521] These provisions grant considerably less authority than recommended by the 9/11 Commission and are indicative of compromised provisions. Lt. Gen. Michael Hayden, Director of NSA, during a closed House hearing in August 2004, spoke of the need for greater DNI authority when he stated, "More is better than less; total is better than part…The worst of all possible worlds would be to close out today's DCI and replace him with a feckless [DNI]."[522] "You're still not in charge," commented James Simon, former Assistant DCI. "Without control of budget and personnel, all you have is the authority to use tact and goodwill."[523]

Creation of National Centers

National Counterterrorism Center

The Act gave Congressional authority and support for the National Counterterrorism Center (NCTC), originally created in September 2004 by executive order. The NCTC will serve as the primary organization in the U.S. Government for analyzing and integrating terrorism and counterterrorism information, excepting that concerning purely domestic counterterrorism, which is under the purview of the FBI.[524] The Director of the NCTC (D/NCTC) is a Senate-confirmed position and its director may not simultaneously serve in any other capacity in the executive branch. The D/NCTC reports to the DNI on budget and intelligence matters, but to the President on the planning and progress of joint counterterrorism operations. The NCTC is charged with conducting "strategic operational planning," which covers missions, the objectives to be achieved, the tasks to be performed, interagency coordination of operational activities, and the assignment of roles and responsibilities.[525]

National Counterproliferation Center

Although the President may create a national counterproliferation center within 18 months after the promulgation of the Intelligence Reform and Terrorist Prevention Act of 2004, he may ignore this requirement if he determines its cre-

---

[521] 9/11 Report, 411-414.

[522] Kaplan and Whitelaw, 31.

[523] Kaplan and Whitelaw, 31.

[524] U.S. President, "Executive Order National Counterterrorism Center,"27 August 2004, URL: *www.whitehouse.gov/news/releases/2004/08/20040827-5.html*, accessed 2 September 2004.

[525] GAC Summary, 8.

ation does not materially improve the government's ability to halt the proliferation of weapons of mass destruction. His waiver must be in writing and submitted to Congress.[526]

National Intelligence Centers

This Act authorizes the DNI to establish other National Intelligence Centers to address intelligence priorities. Within their areas of intelligence responsibility, these centers will have primary responsibility for providing all-source analysis and for identifying and proposing to the DNI intelligence collection and production requirements.[527]

The Reform Act's Potential Weaknesses

There are high expectations in some quarters that the Intelligence Reform and Terrorist Prevention Act of 2004 is just what America needs for greater defense of its homeland. When signing the legislation President Bush stated, "Our vast intelligence enterprise will become more unified, coordinated, and effective. It will enable us to better do our duty, which is to protect the American people."[528] Additionally, he said, "The many reforms of this act have a single goal: to ensure that the people in government responsible for defending America have the best possible information to make the best possible decisions."[529]

While many of the Act's provisions will move the Intelligence Community, Federal Government, and in some cases, State and local governments toward a more secure environment and improve the sharing of information among these entities, it would be naïve to see this Act as a panacea for all that ails the Community. Its passage has ended the debate on the question "Should There Be a DNI?" The answer is "Yes." However, the ambiguity of many provisions as well as the question of whether this Act engenders intelligence reform, has created new debates for intelligence professionals, the American public and the press alike to ponder. The following paragraphs are reflective of a few of those ongoing issues.

---

[526] GAC Summary, 8.

[527] GAC Summary, 8.

[528] Bryan Bender, "US Intelligence Shake-Up Meets Growing Criticism," *Boston Globe*, 2 January 2004, A1.

[529] Jennifer Loven, "President Signs Measure Overhauling Intelligence: Aiming to Improve Spy Network in Wake of 9/11 Attacks, Bill Creates Counterterror Center, New Director,"*Associated Press*, 17 December 2004, accessed via *http://www.baltimoresun.com/news/custom/attack/bal-bush1217,0,6868674.story.*

Congressional Oversight

One of the most glaring deficiencies in the Intelligence Reform and Terrorist Prevention Act of 2004 is the failure of Congress to reform itself. The failure of Congress, once again, to get its own House (and Senate) in order is disgraceful. Two of Congress' own—Representative Christopher Shays (R-CN) and Representative Carolyn Maloney (D-NY) expressed their displeasure with their colleagues:

> During the monumental struggle to pass much-needed intelligence reforms, one absolute truth about Washington was reinforced: The hardest thing to do in this town is to take someone's power away. It does not matter if pending legislation is vital to our national security or even if it is three years overdue; it's only human to protect one's turf.[530]

More than three years after the creation of the Department of Homeland Security (DHS), Congress had failed to create one permanent authorizing committee in each chamber tasked with conducting oversight of DHS. The 9/11 Commission Report stressed that the two "other reform measures—National Intelligence Director and the National Counterterrorism Center—will not work if congressional oversight does not change too. Unity of effort in executive management can be lost if it is fractured by divided congressional oversight." The Commission called congressional oversight for intelligence and counterterrorism "dysfunctional."[531] Just how fractured is the oversight of DHS? The number of committees with oversight of DHS decreased slightly from 88 to 79 in the 108th Congress—DHS now responds to requests for information from 79 committees. Every single senator and at least 412 of the 435 representatives have some level of responsibility for homeland security operations. Compare this with the Department of Defense, with its budget 10 times that of DHS and hundreds of thousands more personnel, reporting to "*only*" 36 committees and subcommittees. In 2004, then Director of DHS Tom Ridge and other top DHS officials testified **145 times** before various committees and subcommittees.[532] This is congressional oversight run amok.

Let us examine a Community management issue likely to cross the DNI's desk, to illustrate the intelligence oversight nightmare that Congress failed to address. Retired Army Lieutenant General Pat Hughes, DHS Deputy Director for Information Analysis and Infrastructure Protection, commented during an inter-

---

[530] Reps.Christopher Shays (R-CN) and Carolyn Maloney (D-NY), "Congress, Reorganize Thyself," *Washington Post,* 22 December 2004, A27.

[531] 9/11 Report, 420.

[532] "Homeland Security Oversight," editorial, *Washington Post,* 28 December 2004, A18.

view that DHS has too few intelligence analysts. "If you had a hundred, we'd take them. We have to look, search, test, assess. You don't just get analysts off a tree…We need people, but we need good people."[533] For the sake of discussion, let us assume that the DNI, as authorized by the Act, has completed the necessary requirements to transfer Community personnel. The Office of the DNI has already completed the arduous process of determining that DHS is engaged in *high priority intelligence activities* and that the transfer of Community personnel to assist DHS in these activities will *support an emergent need, improve program effectiveness, or increase efficiency.* Now, the only remaining requirement for the Director of National Intelligence—the CEO of U.S. intelligence—to get DHS the personnel it needs in a timely manner is to *notify the appropriate congressional committees of such transfers*—all SEVENTY-NINE of them!

Shays and Maloney have introduced changes to the Rules of the House of Representatives for the 109th Congress to consider. Their proposal would:

- Create a permanent standing committee on homeland security with exclusive jurisdiction.
- Create a permanent standing committee on intelligence with exclusive jurisdiction over intelligence and counterterrorism.
- Create a 14th Appropriations subcommittee to deal with intelligence.[534]

They admit these proposals will not be easy to enact, but they maintain they are a no-brainer from a national security perspective.

Senator John McCain (R-AZ) remarked that the Senate Intelligence Committee "tinkered with oversight responsibilities" but brought nothing "substantial." "We will have a status quo intelligence committee without the combined authorization and appropriations power." The Senate Intelligence Committee's "tinkering" consisted of decreasing its own membership by two, but at the same time it increased the size of the staff for each of its 15 members by one—Loss 2, Gain 15. Purportedly, this increase of staff would be necessary because the Senate intended to combine its authorization and appropriations activities as recommended by the 9/11 Commission. However, after adding the additional employees, the Senate Intelligence Committee decided to continue authorizing intelligence programs but created a new intelligence subcommittee within the Senate Appropriations Committee to handle the money.[535]

---

[533] Katherine Pfleger Shrader, "Analysts Are in Great Demand: Intelligence Agencies Scramble for Talent," *Washington Post,* 30 December 2004, A24.

[534] Shays and Maloney, A27.

[535] Walter Pincus, "Senate Realigns Intelligence Procedures; New Reform Statute Calls for Some Changes," *Washington Post,* 23 December 2004, A21.

In October 2004, the Senate added "Homeland Security" to the name of the Governmental Affairs Committee, chaired by Senator Susan Collins (R-ME). However, it then only authorized the committee oversight of 38 percent of the Department of Homeland Security's budget and only eight (8) percent of its 175,000 employees. As reported in the *Washington Post,* Collins became so frustrated as DHS agencies were taken away from her panel that she remarked, "We are just going to end up with jurisdiction over [then-Secretary] Tom Ridge's personal staff. That is about what is going to be left."[536]

During floor debate in the 105th Congress, McCain, then Chairman of the Commerce, Science and Transportation Committee, after losing a motion to take jurisdiction for the Transportation Security Administration (TSA) away from his panel and give it to Collins' panel, expressed his frustrations by calling it a "joke" that the Coast Guard remained in his committee. McCain stated, "Why don't we just stop, why don't we call it a night and say the heck with this farce? This is crazy. This is stupid."[537] Reforming the existing congressional oversight committees remains a necessary Congressional action.

DNI and Community Relationships

Mark Lowenthal has recognized the importance of Community relationships, noting that:

> All "wiring" diagrams, no matter how sophisticated, are deceptive. They portray where agencies sit in relation to one another, but they cannot portray how they interact and which relationships matter and why. Moreover, although we are loath to admit it, personalities do matter. However much we like to think of government as one of laws and institutions, the personalities and relationships of the people filling these important positions also affect agency working relations.[538]

Without question, the DNI's relationship with Congress as well as that office's relationship with other IC agency heads is pivotal for success. However, the one relationship that matters most in defining its role and relative power, is the relationship the DNI has with the chief executive. "The director of national intelligence is not going to be able to do this job if the President has any doubts at all,"

---

[536] Walter Pincus, "Congress Resists Key Recommendation of 9/11 Panel: Without Consolidation, Homeland Security Department Officials Report to 88 Panels on Capitol Hill," *Washington Post,* 1 January 2005, A4. Cited hereafter as Congress Resists Key Recommendation.

[537] Congress Resists Key Recommendation, A4.

[538] Mark M. Lowenthal, *Intelligence: From Secrets to Policy* (CQ Press: Washington, DC, 2003), 30.

stated Thomas H. Kean, Co-Chair of the 9/11 Commission. "This person must have the real confidence of the president."[539] "Whether we have a drug czar or a truly effective manager will depend on the president," in the words of former DCI Stansfield Turner. "These other people—the secretary of defense, the attorney general—are cabinet officers with huge departments and congressional delegations behind them."[540] "If the president doesn't back this person up in the first battle with Rumsfeld [Secretary of Defense], then the position is effectively neutered," said Roger Cressey, a former White House counterterrorism adviser during the Clinton administration.[541] William Webster, former DCI and Director of the FBI, noted the DNI must have a strong relationship with the president. "That's one of the most important things—his ability to work with members of the Community and to work cooperatively with Congress in its oversight responsibilities and the president to whom he will report."[542]

President Bush, responding to a reporter's question on his pick for the DNI,[543] presented his own list of DNI qualifications when he replied, "I'm going to find somebody who knows something about intelligence and capable and honest and ready to do the job—and I'll let you know at the appropriate time when I find such a person."[544] Paul C. Light, a government reform professor at New York University and a senior fellow at the Brookings Institution, considers the selection of the DNI to be the most important appointment President Bush will make in the executive branch. "You need someone who knows something about organi-

[539] Phillip Shenon, "Next Round is Set in Push to Reorganize Intelligence," *New York Times,* 20 December 2004, A19.

[540] Kaplan and Whitelaw, 31.

[541] David S. Cloud, "Huge Challenge Awaits Intelligence Chief," *Wall Street Journal,* 21 December 2004, A4.

[542] Faye Bowers, "The New Top in Redrawn US Intelligence," *Christian Science Monitor,* 15 December 2004, 2.

[543] Many names were bandied about as to who might be considered for the DNI position. While current CIA Director Porter Goss had early on been considered a likely candidate, his housecleaning of senior CIA employees had not endeared him to many in Congress and as such his confirmation appeared unlikely. The following list of possible DNI's was reported in Bowers, 2: Lt. Gen. Michael Hayden—current Director, NSA; Thomas Kean—Co-Chair of 9/11 Commission; Lee Hamilton—Co-chair of 9/11 Commission; Representative Peter Hoesktra (R-MI)—Chairman of House Intelligence Committee; Representative Jane Harman (D-CA)—Ranking Democrat of House Intelligence Committee; and Former Senator Sam Nunn (D-GA)-Former Chairman of the Armed Services Committee. Possibilities for active or retired military as mentioned in Walter Pincus, "President Gets to Fill Ranks of New Intelligence Superstructure: Reform Legislation is Set to Be Signed into Law on Friday," *Washington Post,* 16 December 2004, A35, include: Retired General Tommy R. Franks—Former commander in Afghanistan and Iraq and Retired Admiral William O. Studeman—Former CIA deputy director.

[544] Cloud, A4.

zational life and intelligence."[545] Contemplating the President's comments, this author is drawn to Diogenes' own futile search for an "honest" man and trusts the President's search will be more successful. Senator John D. Rockefeller IV (D-WV), Vice-chair of the Senate Select Intelligence Committee, admitted the recently passed intelligence reform legislation left the role of the DNI fraught with uncertainties but "it was better to be a little vague" in writing such a law: "The person chosen to be DNI should be one of the five most powerful people in government and his or her actions will eliminate the vagueness."[546]

Analysis

Some former intelligence professionals have expressed concern that the Intelligence Reform and Terrorist Prevention Act of 2004 with its organizational changes could be overshadowing more serious "down-in-the-weeds" national security issues that must be addressed and resolved. Former NSA Director Retired Army General William Odom and other intelligence professionals spoke critically of the Act as failing to address the lack of accurate intelligence coming in from the field and the shortage of analysts. As evidenced by their strident comments, the Act does not appear to "fix" intelligence shortcomings.

> I feel sorry for these 9/11 families who thought passing this intelligence bill will improve things. They have been swindled. The more I think about it, the more awful it is. It's tragic."[547]

Retired Army General William Odom
Former Director of NSA

> It does little to address analytic and collection capabilities. I'm not optimistic the so-called reforms are going to lead to quality intelligence. It does nothing to remedy the poor source information we have.[548]

Vincent Cannistraro
Former head of CIA's Counterterrorism Center

It's a sham. I don't think it changes anything.[549]

---

[545] As quoted in Martin Kady II and John Donnelly, "Many Decisions Ahead after Intelligence Bill Clears," *CQ TODAY*, 7 December 2004, 2938.

[546] Walter Pincus, "National Intelligence Director Proves to be Difficult Post to Fill: Uncertainties Over Role, Authority are Blames for Delay," *Washington Post*, 31 January 2005, A4.

[547] Bender, A1.

[548] Bender, A1.

[549] Bender, A1.

Melvin Goodman

Former CIA Analyst

They add an extra layer. But the problem is not a structural one. [Because the 9/11 Commission declined to blame individuals for the intelligence failure, it had to find fault somewhere] the Commission concluded, therefore, that "it must have been the system, it must be something with how we organized ourselves." That is 90 percent wrong. It is the people, stupid.[550]

Ray McGovern

Former CIA (clandestine service) Officer

I suppose the American people look to their leaders for safety and security, and the new national intelligence director will give the impression of there being somebody in control of the whole intelligence community. But I don't think there is much to it in substance.[551]

Michael Scheuer

Former head of CIA's Bin Laden Unit

It's half a reform bill. They've done some positive things, but they haven't dealt with the analytical side. We need what some call a Chinese wall. This is necessary so that the analysts are totally independent from and without any loyalty to any [intelligence collector]....I don't believe you will solve a lot of the problems we've seen either in the run-up to 9/11 or the run-up to Iraq until you separate collection from analysis....This bill doesn't address that.[552]

---

[550] Bender, A1.

[551] Mark Huband, "Ex-CIA Officer Dismisses Reforms," *London Financial Times,* 12 December 2004, A6.

[552] A.L. Bardach, "Interrogation: Listen to the Admiral," *Slate,* online ed., 16 December 2004, URL: *<http://slate.msn.com>*, accessed 17 December 2004. Note: Mark Lowenthal in *Intelligence: From Secrets to Policy* (Washington, DC: CQ Press, 2003), 45, briefly discusses this "interesting phenomenon" among analysts: Different analytical groups have a preference for different types of intelligence. He indicates that a CIA analyst may put more emphasis in human intelligence sources (HUMINT) because it is a product of his own agency's activities whereas an all-source analyst in the Defense Department may not. Inman often refers to this misplaced kinship toward one collection source over another in his comments.

The following is an example of why Inman and others insist on separating analysts from collectors. Although a DIA official warned CIA about the questionable reliability of an Iraqi defector, for example, the erroneous CIA-source information remained in a 5 February 2003 speech delivered by Secretary of State Powell to the United Nations concerning weapons of mass destruction in Iraq.

Retired Admiral Bobby Ray Inman

Former Director of NSA
Former Vice Director of DIA
Former Director of Naval Intelligence
Former Deputy Director CIA

Assorted Ambiguities and Unsettling Provisions

Throughout the Intelligence Reform and Terrorist Prevention Act of 2004, there are instances where provisions forthrightly contradict one another, or at the very least, are confusing. For example, in Title 1 (intelligence section), the DNI is charged with establishing "uniform security standards and procedures." However, a later section, Title III (security clearances section) states that the "President designates a single entity [not further defined] to oversee the security clearance process and develop uniform standards and policies for access to classified information."[553]

Representative David Obey (D-W), ranking minority member on the House Appropriations Committee, notes that "One of the bill's most glaring shortcomings is that it does not guarantee that dissenting or alternative views will ever be clearly stated to the President. That was a major problem in the decision to go to war in Iraq."[554] The Act does stipulate however, that within 180 days after the effective date of the Act, the DNI will establish a process to conduct alternative analysis and within 270 days will notify the Congressional intelligence committees of its implementation.[555]

One of the reasons some of the Act's provision are confusing is that the Senate had less than twenty-four hours to read the final version of the legislation. The House completed its vote on Monday, 8 December 2004 and it went immediately to the Senate for approval. However, Senator Robert Byrd (D-WV), one of the two senators who voted against this legislation, offers another reason for its passage. According to *The Nation*, Byrd suggests that in the Post-9/11 era most members of Congress do not have the stomach for an honest debate about fighting terrorism or defending liberty. Byrd, speaking of the Senate, remarked, "Like pygmies on the battlefield of history, we cower like whipped dogs in the face of political pressure when it comes to issues like intelligence reform."[556]

---

[553] Intelligence Bill Clears Congress, A4.

[554] John Nichols, "Flawed Intelligence Bill," *The Nation,* 3 January 2004, 6.

[555] GAC Summary.7.

[556] Nichols, 6.

Regardless of the period—2004, the 1990s, the 1970s or even shortly after the passage of the 1947 National Security Act, serious reform has eluded the Intelligence Community for decades. In the continuing absence of dramatic intelligence reform legislation, it appears likely that this trend will continue. Michael Warner, of the CIA History Staff at the Center for the Study of Intelligence, surmises that the ambiguity [about intelligence] is likely to endure for the same reasons it arose in the first place: no one can agree on what should replace it. These same obstacles faced Truman in 1945.

Everyone has a notion of what intelligence should be or how reform should be implemented, but everyone also has a specific list of changes they will not tolerate. The mix of preferences and objections produces a veto to almost every proposal, until the one that survives is the one policymakers and legislators dislike the least.[557]

---

[557] Michael Warner, *Central Intelligence: Origin and Evolution* (Washington, DC: Center for the Study of Intelligence, 2001), 17.

Chapter Nine

CONCLUSION

> Alice soon came to the conclusion that it was a very difficult game indeed.
>
> —**Lewis Carroll**
> *Alice's Adventures in Wonderland*

Although Deputy Commerce Secretary Samuel W. Bodman, in the passage below, was responding to a comment on the government's vision for manufacturing, his comments are indicative of the way Washington works.

> I will tell you, it is very hard for this government to have a vision on anything. We are totally stovepiped, and we live within these compartments. This is not by the way of a complaint. This is not by the way of an excuse. It is by way of a fact. Congress likes it this way, and making organizational changes in the federal government is, as many of you know, a massive undertaking, a several-year job. It is not a several-month job. It is a several-year job, and so you don't do it very often, because it's certainly not worth it.[558]

Perhaps the image in the past decade of an Intelligence Community "drifting—unsure of what it does and for whom,"[559] is reaching its zenith. Deborah G. Barger, a recent RAND Intelligence Community Fellow, described eight trends that suggest the IC has reached a strategic inflection point,[560] a time when an organization must change, become irrelevant, or cease to exist. Change is needed for survival not so much because of past mistakes but because the external environment has itself become so different. Trends illustrating this altered environment include:

- The nature of the threat to U.S. security
- The nature of warfare and military strategy

---

[558] Johnathan Weisman, "Bush Economic Aide Says Government Lacks Vision," *Washington Post,* 13 December 2003, A1.

[559] Gregory F. Treverton, *Reshaping National Intelligence in an Age of Information* (Cambridge: Cambridge University Press, 2001), 1.

[560] Andrew Grove, *Only the Paranoid Survive: How to Exploit the Crisis Points that Challenge Every Company and Career* (New York: Doubleday, 1996), 3-6.

- The nature of peace
- The U.S. national security strategy for addressing these changes
- The quality and quantity of information in general and the speed with which it can be shared
- Technology, which is outpacing the ability of large organizations to adapt organizationally and operationally
- The expectations of intelligence consumers
- The expectations of the American public[561]

Through exploration of the trends cited above, the present research has laid the foundation for appropriate modifications in the intelligence process, or "reform from within." Without question, the Intelligence Community is a vastly bureaucratic beast; however, the Community should be capable of change. As Barger noted, successful transformation efforts appear to have three things in common. First, there is a period of strategic reflection about the "business" before any attempts to change it. Second, change agents stay with the organization long enough to see their ideas or efforts come to fruition. Lastly, a mechanism exists to evaluate how well the change proposal serves strategic objectives.[562] The Community has repeatedly fallen short on all three of these criteria.

Consider the FBI, an example of an organization whose attempt to transform itself has been fraught with institutional failure. In December 2004, the FBI named its sixth counterterrorism director since 9/11 and further disclosed that all of the senior positions in that office have turned over at least once since then.[563] Two weeks later, the FBI abandoned its newly developed $170 million computer system before it was fully launched due to severe system deficiencies.[564]

Former DCI George Tenet knows too well the difficulties inherent in the tasks that lie ahead in changing an organization. Testifying before the 9/11 Commission in April 2004, he responded to a question from Commissioner John Lehman, former Secretary of the Navy, who asked, "How do you do a revolution without losing sight of the business you're in?"

---

[561] Deborah G. Barger, "It is Time to Transform, Not Reform, U.S. Intelligence," *SAIS Review*, vol. 24, no. 1 (Winter-Spring 2004), 28.

[562] Barger, 29.

[563] Dan Eggen, "FBI Names 6th Counterterrorism Chief Since 9/11," *Washington Post*, 29 December 2004, A17.

[564] Jonathan Krim, "FBI Rejects Its New Case File Software: Database Project Has Cost Nearly $170 Million," *Washington Post*, 14 January 2005, A5.

Frankly, my personal view is that you really do need an outside group engagement, recommendations to come forward. I think it's—people like me and John [McLaughlin] and people working in the business can certainly inform....I think it's hard when you're sitting—I mean, the day I retire, I'll be a great person to sit on one of these things, and I'd love to do it. [Tenet retired as DCI a few months later in July 2004]

But I think that the important thing is, it's very hard for people when they're sitting in the in-box on the crisis of the day to be reflective....I think you've got to separate the current group to allow—we can give you the data, give you our experience and talk to you about it. But I think you almost need a separate group of people who have been around this.

But you also need people who have revolutionary ideas about technology and how it works and a new mindset, because the people you're recruiting aren't 30-year veterans anymore. You're attracting a whole new labor force that doesn't remember the Cold War, and they expect a structure that's going to be more agile and mobile and more technologically proficient.

And once people lose sight of where the country needs to be, the starts and fits in cycles that this Community has gone through has to stop. Let's get budgeting on a two-or three-year cycle. Let's allow us to build programs in depth. Let's really look at basic expenditures over the course of time. Let's put the metrics in place. But I'll tell you, you can't build this Community in fits and starts. It won't happen and the country will suffer. And you know, this, I think, is a debate that has to be joined quite publicly.[565]

There is no denying that reform of the monolithic Intelligence Community, entrenched by decades of parochialism, nurtured by lackadaisical congressional and executive oversight, burdened by a bureaucratized strategic planning system and excused from public scrutiny, is going to be hard in reality, really hard. Nevertheless, as Barger concluded in her review of intelligence reform:

The Intelligence Community must transform itself when faced with a constant barrage of new realities; its management culture and ethos

---

[565] George Tenet, "Transcript: 9/11 Commission Hearing on Intelligence," *Washington Post,* online ed., 14 April 2004, URL: *http://www.washingtonpost.com/ac2/wp-dyn/A11115-2004Apr14,* accessed 15 April 2004.

must embrace critical self-examination, as well as constant reassessment of the external environment. Intelligence management must help the workforce prepare for and adapt to not one, but a continuing series of revolutionary changes.[566]

Change will require not only the "three-way partnership among external catalysts who bring new ideas to the table, legislative overseers who support new ideas through funding and legislation, and internal supporters who evaluate and then implement change,"[567] but will also require the American media establishment to report on these efforts as guardians of the public watch. The immediate task for the external catalysts, the legislative overseers, external supporters, and the press is to restore public confidence in the competence and integrity of the nation's intelligence system. The late historian Richard Hofstadter said, "the reformist impulse often wanders over the border between reality and impossibility."[568] Preserving at least some of the utopian expectations of intelligence reform without inevitable disappointment may be tricky. While it is true that the Intelligence Community will never bat 1.000, this does not mean that the Community cannot improve its batting average! Nonetheless, Richard K. Betts cautions,

> at the end of the day, the strongest defense against intelligence mistakes will come less from any structural or procedural tweak than from the good sense, good character, and good mental habits of senior officials. How to assure a steady supply of those, unfortunately, has never been clear.[569]

Only time will tell whether intelligence "reform" envisioned with the passage of the Intelligence Reform and Terrorist Prevention Act of 2004 will be realized; whether this Act, like the countless reform initiatives of the past that aimed to alter the IC's business-as-usual processes and procedures, merely amounted to the re-arrangement of deck chairs or even whether these measures distracted from other more pressing national security needs as some intelligence professionals suggest. As a born and raised Missourian from the "Show Me" State, this author requires more convincing than just a signed piece of paper (or all 563 pages) that "change" is forthcoming. Analyzing the

---

[566] Barger, 30.

[567] Barger, 30.

[568] As cited by Robert J. Samuelson, "Seduced by 'Reform," *Washington Post*, 2 June 2004, A25.

[569] Richard K. Betts, "The New Politics of Intelligence: Will Reforms Work This Time?" *Foreign Affairs*, 83, no. 3 (May/June 2004), accessed via ProQuest, 21 August 2004.

implementation of this Act will be an important undertaking for future scholars, the American public, and the press.

Nonetheless, this author believes that for now the significance of the Intelligence Reform and Terrorist Prevention Act of 2004 lies not in its being dissected to determine whether it calls forth the myriad changes necessary to facilitate a more secure national security environment in a globalized era: It certainly does not. Rather, this Act and its ensuing changes—whether momentous or marginal—must be seen as the start of Community reform in the 21st Century, not the endgame.

Joan Dempsey, Executive Director of the President's Foreign Intelligence Advisory Board, warned in an October 2004 speech that "We are at the beginning of intelligence reform, not the end. We are making our first tentative steps toward changing the way we do intelligence in this country, and we are decades away from completing it."[570] This author disagrees with Ms Dempsey's point— in an ever-changing environment, where adaptability ensures survival—intelligence reform will never be complete. Reform must be construed as a Community-wide, never-ending series of process improvement tasks. Processes and procedures that guarantee success against our opponent today will be ill-advised as we face tomorrow's enemy. The Community must maintain a constant watch against complacency.

Pendleton Herring, chief intellectual architect of the National Security Act of 1947 and Paul Nitze, architect of NSC 68—the blueprint for American strategy in the Cold War, served their country long and well. Nevertheless, in August and October 2004 respectively, the inevitable occurred. Mr. Henning and Mr. Nitze died. It would be fitting for us now to lay to rest those Cold War vestiges that are embedded in the organizational, procedural, and also, the managerial processes of the Intelligence Community. The Cold War era has long passed. Old ideas have served this country long and well, but now new processes established on the foundation of "need to share," not "need to know" must guide the Community in this globalized world. The challenges of today demand the solutions of tomorrow, not the perfection of the past. The Intelligence Community must change itself, and with some rapidity. This process will be facilitated by the Community's becoming an integrated whole, rather than remaining the archipelago that it is. In the fashion of the enduring words of President Abraham Lincoln's 1862 Congressional Address, the Community too must rise to the occasion:

---

[570] David E. Kaplan, "Intelligence Reform—at Last," *U.S. News & World Report*, 20 December 2004, 32.

The dogmas of the quiet past are inadequate to the stormy present. The occasion is piled high with difficulty, and we must rise with the occasion. As our case is new, so we think anew and act anew.

Appendix A — National Security Act of 1947, as amended

Title 1—Coordination for National Security

National Security Council

SECTION 101. (a) There is established a council to be known as the National Security (hereinafter in this section referred to as the "Council").[571]

The President of the United States shall preside over meetings of the Council: *Provided,* That in his absence he may designate a member of the Council to preside in his place.

The function of the Council shall be to advise the President with respect to the integration of domestic, foreign, and military policies relating to the national security so as to enable the military services and the other departments and agencies of the Government to cooperate more effectively in matters involving the national security.

The Council shall be composed of—

1   the President;
2.   the Vice President;
3.   the Secretary of State;
4.   the Secretary of Defense;
5.   the Director for Mutual Security [now abolished];
6.   the Chairman of the National Security Resources Board [now abolished];
7.   the Secretaries and Under Secretaries of other executive departments and of the military departments, the Chairman of the Munitions Board [now abolished]; and the Chairman of the Research and Development Board [now abolished]; when appointed by the President by and with the advice and consent of the Senate, to serve at his pleasure.

---

[571] National Security Act of 1947, as amended, *http://www.history-matters.com/archive/church/rockcomm/html/Rockefeller_0144a.htm,* accessed 3 August 2004.

Central Intelligence Agency

SECTION 102.

(a) There is established under the National Security Council a Central Intelligence Agency with a Director of Central Intelligence who shall be the head thereof, and with a Deputy Director of Central Intelligence who shall act for, and exercise the powers of the Director during his absence or disability. The Director and the Deputy Director shall be appointed by the President, by and with the advice and consent of the Senate, from among the commissioned officers of the armed services, whether in an active or retired status, or from among individuals in civilian life: *Provided, however,* That at no time shall the two positions of the Director and Deputy Director be occupied simultaneously by commissioned officers of the armed services, whether in an active or retired status.

(b) (1) If a commissioned officer of the armed services is appointed as Director, or Deputy Director, then—

(A) in the performance of his duties as Director, or Deputy Director, he shall be subject to no supervision, control, restriction, or prohibition (military or otherwise) other than would be operative with respect to him if he were a civilian in no way connected with the Department of the Army, the Department of the Navy, the Department of the Air Force, or the armed services or any component thereof; and

(B) he shall not possess or exercise any supervision, control, powers or functions (other than such as he possesses, or is authorized or directed to exercise, as Director or Deputy Director) with respect to the armed services or any component thereof, the Department of the Army, the Department of the Navy, or the Department of the Air Force, or any branch, bureau, unit or division thereof, or with respect to any of the personnel (military or civilian) of any of the foregoing.

(2) Except as provided in paragraph (1) of this subsection, the appointment of the office of the Director, or Deputy Director, of a commissioned officer of the armed services, and his acceptance of and service is such office, shall in no way affect any status, office, rank, or grade he may occupy or hold in the armed services, or any emolument, perquisite, right privilege, or benefit incident to or arising out of any such status, office, rank, or grade. Any such commissioned officer shall, while serving in the office of Director or Deputy Director, continue to hold rank and grade not lower than that in which serving at the time of his appointment and to receive the military pay and allowances (active

or retired, as the case may be, including personal money allowance) payable to a commissioned officer of his grade and length of service for which the appropriate department shall be reimbursed from any funds available to defray the expenses of the Central Intelligence Agency. He shall also be paid by the Central Intelligence Agency from such funds an annual compensation at the rate equal to the amount by which the compensation established for such position exceeds the amount of his annual military pay and allowances.

(3) The rank or grade of any such commissioned officer shall, during the period in which such commissioned officer occupies the office of Director of Central Intelligence, or Deputy Director of Central Intelligence, be in addition to the numbers and percentages otherwise authorized and appropriated for the armed services of which he is a member.

(c) Notwithstanding the provisions of section 652 [now 7501] of Title 5, or the provisions of any other law, the Director of Central Intelligence may, in his discretion, terminate the employment of any officer or employee of the Agency whenever he shall deem such termination necessary or advisable in the interests of the United States, but such termination shall not affect the right of such officer or employee to seek or accept employment in any other department or agency of the Government if declared eligible for such employment by the Unites States Civil Service Commission.

(d) For the purpose of coordinating the intelligence activities of the several Government departments and agencies in the interest of national security, it shall be the duty of the Agency, under the direction of the National Security Council—

(1) to advise the National Security Council in matters concerning such intelligence activities of the Government departments and agencies as relate to national security;

(2) to make recommendations to the National Security Council for the coordination of such intelligence activities of the departments and agencies of the Government as relate to the national security;

(3) to correlate and evaluate intelligence relating to the national security, and provide for the appropriate dissemination of such intelligence within the Government using where appropriate existing agencies and facilities: *Provided*, That the Agency shall have no police, subpoena, law-enforcement powers, or internal security functions: *Provided further*, That the departments and other agencies of the Government shall continue to collect, evaluate, correlate and disseminate departmental intelligence: *And provided further*, that the Director of Central Intelli-

gence shall be responsible for protecting intelligence sources and methods from unauthorized disclosure;

(4) to perform, for the benefit of the existing intelligence agencies, such additional services of common concern as the National Security Council determines can be more efficiently accomplished centrally;

(5) to perform such other functions and duties related to intelligence affecting the national security as the National Security Council may from time to time direct.

(e) To the extent recommended by the National Security Council and approved by the President, such intelligence of the departments and agencies of the Government, except as hereinafter provided, relating to the national security shall be open to the inspection of the Director of Central Intelligence, and such intelligence as relates to the national security and is possessed by such departments and other agencies of the Government, except as hereinafter provided, shall be made available to the Director of Central Intelligence for correlation, evaluation, and dissemination: *Provided, however,* That upon the written request of the Director of Central Intelligence, the Director of the Federal Bureau of Investigation shall make available to the Director of Central Intelligence such information for correlation, evaluation, and dissemination as may be essential to the national security.

(f) Effective when the Director first appointed under subsection (a) of this section has taken office—

(1) the National Intelligence Authority (11 Fed. Reg. 1337, 1339, February 5, 1946 shall cease to exist; and

(2) the personnel, property, and records of the Central Intelligence Group are transferred to the Central Intelligence Agency, and such group shall cease to exist. Any unexpected balances of appropriations, allocations, or other such funds available or authorized to be made available for such Group shall be available and shall be authorized to be made available in like manner for expenditure by the Agency.

Appendix B — Cold-War Intelligence Reform 1945-1989[572]

Truman Administration 1945-1953

- NSCIDs Nos. 1-15 were promulgated by the end of Truman's administration. NSCID No. 1, "Duties and Responsibilities," replaced NIAD-5.[573] NSCID No. 9 created the National Security Agency.[574]

1949   First Hoover Commission (Eberstadt Report)

Selected Major Findings/Comments:

- National Security Organization, established by National Security Act of 1947, [to be] soundly constructed, but not yet working well.[575]

- Principal concern was the adversarial relationship and lack of coordination between the CIA, the military and the State Department resulting in unnecessary duplication and the issuance of departmental intelligence reports that have often been subjective and biased.[576]

- Particular concern noted in professionalism of military intelligence and inadequacies of medical and scientific research.[577]

---

[572]Richard A. Best, Jr. and Herbert Andrew Boerstling, "Appendix C, IC21: The Intelligence Community in the 21st Century," *CRS Report for Congress* (Washington, D.C.: Congressional Research Service, Library of Congress, 28 February 1996), *URL:<http://www.access.gpo.gov/congress/house/intel/ic21/ic21018.html>*, accessed 11 May 2004. Cited hereafter as CRS Report, Appendix C, IC21 February 1996. If this source document indicated the number of recommendations noted in the original reports then this author indicated the number in parentheses. The CRS authors provided a summary review and this author further delineated their efforts for the purpose of her report.

[573]Michael Warner, *Central Intelligence: Origin and Evolution* (Washington, DC: Center for the Study of Intelligence, 2001), 7.

[574]According to author James Bamford, *The Puzzle Palace: A Report on America's Most Secret Agency* (Boston: Houghton Mifflin Company, 1982), 55, President Truman mandated in a classified 24 October 1952 memorandum, that NSA be established effective 4 November of that year. Truman officially acknowledged the creation of the agency when he signed NSCID No. 9 on 29 December 1952 (citation as in Elkins, 20).

[575]The Commission on Organization of the Executive Branch of the Government, Task Force Report on National Security Organization, Appendix G, January 1949, 3 (citation as noted in Best and Boerstling, 6). Cited hereafter as the Eberstadt Report, CRS Report, Appendix C, IC21 February 1996.

[576] Eberstadt Report, 76, CRS Report, Appendix C, IC21 February 1996.

[577] Eberstadt Report, 77, CRS Report, Appendix C, IC21 February 1996.

Selected Recommendations:

- Positive efforts [must] be made to foster relations of mutual confidence between [CIA] and the several departments and agencies it serves.[578]

- Stressed that the "CIA must be the central organization of the national intelligence system"[579] and favored a civilian DCI with a long term in office.[580]

- Supported establishing a legal framework for budgetary procedures and authority and in maintaining the CIA budget secret to provide "administrative flexibility and anonymity that are essential to satisfactory intelligence.[581]

- U.S. needs a central authority to collect, collate, and evaluate scientific and medical intelligence.[582]

1949   Intelligence Survey Group (Dulles-Jackson-Correa Report)

Major Findings/Comments:

- Many recommendations highly critical of the CIA and DCI.[583]
- Criticized the quality of national intelligence estimates and DCI's failure to take charge of the estimate production.[584]
- CIA's current trend in secret intelligence should be reversed in favor of its mandated role as coordinator of intelligence.[585]

Recommendations (56):

- Proposed large-scale reorganization of the CIA to end overlapping and duplication of functions.

- Incorporate covert operations and clandestine intelligence into one office[586] as well as replacing existing CIA offices with four

---

[578] Eberstadt Report, 16, CRS Report, Appendix C, IC21 February 1996.

[579] Arthur B. Darling, *The Central Intelligence Agency: An Instrument of Government to 1950* (University Park, PA: Pennsylvania State University Press, 1990), 293 (citation as noted in Best and Boerstling, 7).

[580] Darling, Arthur B., Introduction to Chapter VIII (citation as noted in Best and Boerstling, 7).

[581] Darling, Arthur B, 18 (citation as noted in Best and Boerstling, 7).

[582] Eberstadt Report, 289, CRS Report, Appendix C, IC21 February 1996.

[583] "The Central Intelligence Agency and National Organization for Intelligence: A Report to the National Security Council, "1 January 1949 (citation as noted in Best and Boerstling, 8). Cited hereafter as the Dulles-Jackson-Correa Report, CRS Report, Appendix C, IC21 February 1996.

[584] Dulles-Jackson-Correa Report 5, 11, CRS Report, Appendix C, IC21 February 1996.

[585] Dulles-Jackson-Correa Report 39, CRS Report, Appendix C, IC21 February 1996.

new divisions—coordination, estimates, research and reports, and operations.[587]

- Increased coordination between DCI and Director, FBI in the area of counterespionage.[588]

NOTE: This commission played a role in creating the Board of National Estimates (BNE). The BNE, designed to review and produce National Intelligence Estimates (NIEs), was assisted by an Office of National Estimates (ONE) that drew upon the resources of the entire community.[589]

1949   Central Intelligence Agency Act of 1949

- Further expanded the authorities of the CIA. Admin authorities such as the establishment of procurement authority and travel and training of personnel.
- Transfer and receive funds from other government agencies.
- DCI responsible for protecting sources and methods.
- CIA exempted from laws requiring disclosure of its operations (organization, people, function, salary, number of employees).
- DCI could admit up to 100 aliens per year
- DCI could certify appropriated funds expenditures. Did not have to conform to other reporting laws.[590]

Eisenhower Administration 1953-1961

1954   Doolittle Report

Major Findings/Comments:

- CIA properly placed in the organization and laws relating to CIA functions were sufficient.[591]

---

[586]Dulles-Jackson-Correa Report 129, 134 CRS Report, Appendix C, IC21 February 1996.

[587]Dulles-Jackson-Correa Report 11 CRS Report, Appendix C, IC21 February 1996.

[588]Dulles-Jackson-Correa Report 58 CRS Report, Appendix C, IC21 February 1996.

[589] The work of the BNE is described in Donald P. Steury ed., *Sherman Kent and the Board of National Estimates: Collected Essays* (Washington: Center for the Study of Intelligence, 1994) (citation as noted in Best and Boerstling, 9).

[590]David F. Rudgers, *Creating the Secret State: The Origins of the Central Intelligence Agency, 1943-1947* (Lawrence: KS: University Press of Kansas, 2000), 166.

[591] The Report on the Covert Activities of the Central Intelligence Agency, 30 September 1954, Appendix A, 54 (citation as noted in Best and Boerstling, 11). Cited hereafter as Doolittle Report, CRS Report, Appendix C, IC21 February 1996.

Recommendations (9):

- Called for more efficient internal administration...natural tendency to over classify documents originating in the Agency.[592]

- Increase cooperation between the clandestine and analytical sides of the CIA.[593]

1955   Second Hoover Commission (Task Force on Intelligence Activities)

Selected Major Finding/Comment:

- Need to reform CIA's internal organization

Recommendations (9):

- Day-to-day administration of CIA delegated to executive officer or chief of staff so DCI can concentrate on issues affecting the entire Community.[594]

- Establish a congressional oversight committee and a presidential advisory committee.[595]

- Systematic rechecking of all personnel every five years...to make certain that none has succumbed to some weakness of intoxicants or sexual perversion.[596] NOTE: This is the first time, the term "intelligence community" linked departmental agencies and the CIA.[597]

1958   NSCID 1 Revisions

- Eisenhower approved the first major revisions to NSCID 1 adding a preamble stressing the need for efficiency across the entire national security effort. Also, added community responsibilities and created the United States Intelligence Board (USIB).[598]

1959   Bruce-Lovett

---

[592] Doolittle Report 14, CRS Report, Appendix C, IC21 February 1996.

[593] Doolittle Report 17, CRS Report, Appendix C, IC21 February 1996.

[594] Commission on Organization of the Executive Branch of the Government, A Report to Congress, Intelligence Activities, June 1955, 70-71 (citation as noted by Best and Boerstling, 10). Cited hereafter as Clark Task Force Report, CRS Report, Appendix C, IC21 February 1996

[595] Clark Task Force Report, 71, CRS Report, Appendix C, IC21 February 1996.

[596] Clark Task Force Report, 74, CRS Report, Appendix C, IC21 February 1996.

[597] Commission on Organization of the Executive Branch of the Government, A Report to the Congress, Intelligence Activities, June 1955, 13 (citation as noted in Best and Boerstling, 10).

[598] Warner, 8.

Major Findings/Comments:

- Criticized the CIA for being too heavily involved in Third World intrigues while neglecting the hard intelligence on the Soviet Union.[599]

Recommendations:

- U.S. reassess its approach to covert action programs, and a permanent authoritative position be created to assess the viability and impact of covert action programs.[600]

1959   National Security Act of 1959

Kennedy Administration 1961-1963

1961   Taylor Commission

Major Findings/Comments:

- Evenly critical of the White House, the CIA, the State Department and the Joint Chiefs of Staff for their roles in Operation Zapata (Bay of Pigs).[601]

Recommendations:

- Creation of the Strategic Resources Group (SRG)—mechanism for planning and coordination of overall Cold War strategy,

- Seek JCS opinions in planning paramilitary operations,

- Review of policy constraints placed upon U.S.

- Reaffirmed its commitment to ousting Castro from power.[602]

---

[599] Peter Grose, *Gentlemen Spy: The Life of Allen Dulles* (Boston: Houghton Mifflin, 1994), 445-458 (citation as noted in Best, 12). Cited hereafter as Bruce-Lovett, CRS Report, Appendix C, IC21 February 1996.

[600] Bruce-Lovett, 447-448, CRS Report, Appendix C, IC21 February 1996.

[601] Bruce-Lovett, 532 CRS Report, Appendix C, IC21 February 1996.

[602] The report was published as *Operation Zapata: The "Ultrasensitive" Report and Testimony of the Board of Inquiry on the Bay of Pigs* (Frederick, MD: University Publications of America, Inc., 1981) 40 (citation as noted in Best and Boerstling, 14).

1961   Kirkpatrick Report

Major Findings/Comments:

- CIA IG internal investigation which criticized the CIA Directorate of Plans for not having consulted the CIA's Cuban analysts before the invasion. CIA bore the blame.[603]

Recommendations:

- No recommendations were identified in source material. CIA viewed the report as a personal attack on CIA and DCI Dulles. The few at CIA who read the report characterized it as professionally shabby.[604]

Johnson Administration 1963-1969

Due to the U.S. preoccupation with Vietnam, with the exception of the Warren Commission investigating the Kennedy assassination, there were no major investigations.

Nixon Administration 1969-1974

1971   A Review of the Intelligence Community (Schlesinger Report)

Major Findings/Comments (47):

- Noted the community's "impressive rise in...size and cost" with the "apparent inability to achieve a commensurate improvement in the scope and overall quality of intelligence products."[605]

- Criticized unproductively [sic] duplicative collection systems and the failure in forward planning to coordinate the allocation of resources.[606]

---

[603] Evan Thomas, *The Very Best Men, Four Who Dared: The Early Years of the CIA* (New York: Simon and Schuster, 1995), 268 (citation as noted in Best and Boerstling, 15).

[604] John Ranelagh, *The Agency: The Rise and Decline of the CIA* (New York: Simon and Schuster, 1987), 278 (citation as noted in Best and Boerstling, 14).

[605] A Review of the Intelligence Community, 10 March 1971, 1 (citation as noted in Best, 16). Cited hereafter as Schlesinger Report, CRS Report, Appendix C, IC21 February 1996.

[606] Schlesinger Report, 8-9, CRS Report, Appendix C, IC21 February 1996.

Recommendations:

- Considered the creation of Director of National Intelligence (DNI), enhancing DCI's authority, and establishing a Coordinator of National Intelligence (CNI) as White House-level overseer of the IC.[607]

NOTE: The Schlesinger Report led to a limited reorganization of the IC under presidential directives dated 5 November 1971. This directive called for: An enhanced leadership role for the [DCI] in planning, reviewing, and evaluating all intelligence programs and activities, and in the production of national intelligence.[608] Two boards were established—Intelligence Resources Advisory Committee (IRAC) to advise the DCI on the preparation of a consolidated IC budget and the Intelligence Community Staff (ICS) to assist the DCI in guiding the staff. Nonetheless, both boards lacked statutory authority necessary; the IRAC did not have statutory authority to bring the intelligence budget under DCI control and the ICS did not have statutory authority necessary for an expanded community-wide role.[609]

1972   NSCID 1 Revisions

- Nixon issued a directive based on the Schlesinger Report granting DCI more authority. NCS approved second major revision to NSCID 1.
- Added four major DCI responsibilities:
  - Plan and review all intelligence activities and spending, submitting annually to the White House the IC's overall program/budget;
  - Produce national intelligence for the President and policymakers;
  - Chair all community-wide advisory panels;
  - Establish intelligence requirements and priorities.[610]

---

[607] Schlesinger Report, 25-33, CRS Report, Appendix C, IC21 February 1996.

[608] "Reorganization of the U.S. Intelligence Community," Weekly Compilation of Presidential Documents, 4 November 1971, 1467-1491, 1482 (citation as noted in Best, 16).

[609] Memorandum for the Director of Central Intelligence, 16 January 1962; quoted in Prados, 89-414F, 46 (citation as noted in Best and Boerstling, 17).

[610] Warner, 9.

Ford Administration 1974-78

1975   Commission on the Organization of the Government for the Conduct of Foreign Policy (Murphy Commission)

Major Findings/Comments:

- Noted the fundamental difficulty that while the DCI has line authority over the CIA he only has limited influence over other intelligence agencies, but the Commission did not think this arrangement should be changed.[611]

Recommendations:

- DCI have an office close to the White House and be accorded regular and direct contact with the President.[612]
- Strengthen PFIAB and more intensive review of covert operations prior to their initiation but although Congress should be notified the President should not sign such notification since it is harmful to associate "the Head of State so formally with such activities."[613]
- Intelligence requirements and capabilities process needs to be established at the NSC-level in a officially approved five-year plan. Need to prepare a consolidated foreign intelligence budget[614]
- Replacement of BNE with eleven National Intelligence Officers (NIOs) to draft the NIEs.[615]

1975   Commission on CIA Activities within the United States (Rockefeller Commission)

Major Findings/Comments:

- Concerned with CIA internal security activities—infiltration of domestic organizations, collection of information about U.S. citizens domestic activity and drug use and communications equipment testing on unsuspecting persons.

---

[611] U.S., Commission on the Organization of the Government for the Conduct of Foreign Policy, Report, June 1975, 92 (citation as noted in Best and Boerstling, 17). Cited hereafter as Murphy Report, CRS Report, Appendix C, IC21 February 1996.

[612] Murphy Report, 98-99, CRS Report, Appendix C, IC21 February 1996.

[613] Murphy Report, 100-101, CRS Report, Appendix C, IC21 February 1996.

[614] Murphy Report, 101, CRS Report, Appendix C, IC21 February 1996.

[615] CRS Report, Appendix C, IC21 February 1996.

- Concerned with efforts by previous White House staff to use CIA resources improperly.[616]

Recommendations:

- Number of proposals to delimit CIA's authority to collect foreign intelligence within the United States.
- Consideration given to appointing DCIs from outside of CIA and that no DCI serve longer than 10 years. Also, two deputies should be appointed; one to serve as administrative officers and the other as military officer.
- FBI and CIA submit to NSC a detailed agreement setting forth jurisdictions of each agency and proposal for effective liaisons between the two.
- All intelligence agencies review their classified holdings and declassify as much as possible.[617]

1975 Senate Select Committee to Study Governmental Operations with Respect to Intelligence Activities (Church Committee)

Major Findings/Comments:

- Concentrated on illegalities and improprieties by the CIA in light of revelations about assassination plots organized by the CIA. However, its mandate extended to all intelligence agencies.[618]

Recommendations (183):

- Omnibus legislation be enacted to spell out purposes of national intelligence activities and define the relationship between these activities and Congress; urged intelligence agencies charters, roles and responsibilities; and prohibitions or limitations on certain intelligence activities.
- Presidential authorization and congressional committee notification for covert action activities.
- DCI should be recognized by statute as the President's principal foreign advisor and responsible for preparing the national intelligence

---

[616] CRS Report, Appendix C, IC21 February 1996.

[617] CRS Report, Appendix C, IC21 February 1996.

[618] CRS Report, Appendix C, IC21 February 1996.

requirements, preparing the national intelligence budget, and for providing guidance to intelligence operations.

- Monies for national intelligence budget should be appropriated to the DCI rather than to IC directors.
- Deputy DCI for the IC should be established.
- Recommended barring political assassinations, efforts to subvert democratic governments, and support for police/internal security forces in violations of human rights.

1976   House Select Committee on Intelligence (Pike Committee)

Major Findings/Comments:

Recommendations:

- Except in time of war, covert actions should not include assassination; congressional oversight committee notified within 48 hours of presidential approval of covert actions; and that, covert actions terminate no later than 12 months from the date of approval or reconsidered.
- All intelligence-related items must be included in the President's budget and that this figure be disclosed.
- Prohibit transfer of funds between intelligence agencies and any reprogramming of funds within agencies would require congressional approval.
- DCI should be separate from managing the CIA.
- DIA should be abolished and its functions split between the CIA and OSD.
- CIA should be divided into two separate agencies, one for analysis and one for clandestine and covert operations.[619]

1976   Senate Committee on Government Operation Hearings (Clifford and Cline Proposals)

Recommendations (Clifford):

- Create the position of Director of General Intelligence to serve as the President's chief advisor on Intelligence matters and as principal point of contact with congressional intelligence committees.[620]

---

[619] CRS Report, Appendix C, IC21 February 1996, 23-25.

[620] U.S. Congress, Senate, 94th Congress, 2nd session, Committee on Government Operations, Oversight of U.S. Government Intelligence, Functions, Hearings, 21 January – 6 February 1976, 203-204 (citation as noted in Best and Boerstling, 25).

Recommendations (Cline):

- DCI given broad powers over the entire IC and that CIA be divided into two agencies—one for analysis and one for clandestine work.
- DCI be elevated to cabinet-rank.[621]

1976   Executive Order 11095

- Identified DCI as the President's primary intelligence advisor and principal spokesperson for the IC. Responsible for developing the NFIP.
- Delineated responsibilities of each intelligence agency.
- Established three-member Intelligence Oversight Board (IOB).
- Placed restrictions on physical and electronic surveillance of American citizens.[622]

Carter Administration 1976-80

1978   Executive Order 12036

- Superseded EO 11905.
- Formally recognized the establishment of the NFIP.[623]
- DCI now had full and exclusive responsibility for approval of NFIP budget.[624] Note: During the Carter Administration, DCI Stansfield Turner was given budget authority over the DIA and Pentagon intelligence arms. However, this EO was rescinded by President Reagan.[625]

1978-80 Proposed Charter Legislation

Recommendations:

- The draft National Intelligence Reorganization and Reform Act of 1978 would have provided statutory charters to all intelligence agencies and created a Director of National Intelligence (DNI) to serve as head of the entire IC but it was never reported out of either the House

---

[621] CRS Report, Appendix C, IC21 February 1996.

[622] Executive Order 11905, 18 February 1976, United States Foreign Intelligence Activities, as summarized in Alfred B.Prados, Intelligence Reform: Recent History and Proposals, CRS Report 88-562 F, 18 August 1988, 18.

[623] Executive Order 12036, 24 January 1978, United States Intelligence Activities.

[624] Warner, 10.

[625] "Can Spy Agencies Ever Work Together," *Christian Science Monitor,* 21 July 2004.

or Senate Intelligence Committees. However, the Foreign Intelligence Surveillance Act (FISA) of 1978 (P.L.95-811) was enacted.

- 96th Congress introduced charter legislation as well but only stand-alone legislation passed such as the bill reducing the number of committees requiring notification of covert actions. [626]

1978   Foreign Intelligence Surveillance Act

- Established comprehensive legal standards and procedures for the use of electronic surveillance to collect foreign intelligence and counterintelligence within the United States. This was the first legislative authorization for wiretapping and other forms of electronic surveillance for intelligence purposes against foreign powers and foreign agents. Created the Foreign Intelligence Surveillance Court (FISC).[627]

Reagan Administration 1980-88

1981   Executive Order 12333

- Detailed the roles, responsibilities, missions, and activities of the IC.
- Designated the DCI as the primary intelligence advisor to the President and NSC on national foreign intelligence.
- Granted the DCI full responsibility for the production and dissemination of national foreign intelligence. [628]
- Granted the DCI more explicit authority over the development, implementation, and evaluation of the NFIP.[629]

1985   Turner Proposal

Recommendations:

- Reduce the emphasis on covert action.
- Implement a charter of the IC.
- Separate the DCI and Director, CIA; create Director of National Intelligence.[630]

---

[626] CRS Report, Appendix C, IC21 February 1996, 25-26.

[627] U.S. Congress, Senate Select Committee on Intelligence, *Special Report of the Select Committee on Intelligence 4 January 1995 to 3 October 1996*, 105th Cong. 1st sess., 1997. S. Rept 105-1, 15-16.

[628] Section 1.5 (a, d,e,h,k), Executive Order 12333, 4 December 1981, United States Intelligence Activities (citation as noted in Best and Boerstling, 27).

[629] Mark M. Lowenthal, *U.S. Intelligence: Evolution and Anatomy* (Westport, CT: Praeger, 1992), 107.

[630] CRS Report, Appendix C, IC21 February 1996.

Recommendations (Tower Commission):

- Establish procedures for covert actions.

Recommendations (Congressional Select Committees):

- Presidential findings should be made prior to initiation of covert action, in writing, and should be made known to select members of Congress no later than 48 hours after approval.
- If extremely sensitive then only four congressional members need be notified instead of the existing requirement for eight.[631]

---

[631] U.S. Congress, 100th Congress, 1st session, Senate Select Committee on Secret Military Assistance to Iran and the Nicaraguan Opposition and U.S. House of Representatives Select Committee to Investigate Covert Arms Transactions with Iran, Report of the Congressional Committee Investigating the Iran-Contra Affair with Supplemental, Minority, and Additional Views, S. Rept 100-216/H. Rept. 100-433, 17 November 1987, 423-427 (citation as noted in Best and Boerstling, 28).

Appendix C — Post-Cold War Intelligence Reform 1990-2000[632]

Bush Administration, 1989-1993

1992   Boren-McCurdy

These were separate plans for omnibus restructuring of the IC introduced by the Senate (Boren) and the House (McCurdy). These plans, the Senate's Intelligence Reorganizations Act of 1992 and the House's companion bill, were to serve as an intelligence counterpart to the Goldwater-Nichols Department of Defense Reorganization Act of 1986, commonly known as the Goldwater-Nichols Act. Both proposals recommended:

- Creating Director of National Intelligence with authority to program and reprogram intelligence funds throughout the IC to include the DOD and to direct their expenditures; task intelligence agencies and temporarily transfer personnel;
- Creating two Deputy Directors of National Intelligence (DDNIs)— one for analysis and estimates and the other for IC affairs;
- Creating a separate Director, CIA, subordinate to DNI;
- Consolidating analytical and estimative efforts of the IC;
- Creating a National Imagery Agency within DOD to collect, exploit, and analyze imagery. (House version would divide these efforts into two separate agencies)
- Authorizing the Director, DIA to task defense agencies with collection requirements and to shift personnel, funds, functions from one DOD intelligence agency to another.[633]

The effort would have provided statutory mandates for agencies where operational authority was created by executive branch mandates. However, this legislation was not adopted, although provisions were added to FY1994 Intelligence Authorization Act (P.L. 102-496) that provided basic charters for intelligence agencies and set forth in law the DCI's coordinative responsibilities vis-à-vis

---

[632] Richard A. Best, Jr., "Proposals for Intelligence Reorganization, 1949-2004," *CRS Report for Congress,* RL32500, Washington, D.C.: Congressional Research Service, Library of Congress, 29 July 2004, CRS-30, >URL:*http://www.fas.org/irp/crs/RL32500.pdf*>>, accessed 25 August 2004. Cited hereafter as CRS Report, July 2004. Note: The is an updated version of a previous compilation entitled, Appendix C, IC21: The Intelligence Community in the 21st Century by Richard A. Best, Jr., and Herbert Andrew Boerstling.

[633]CRS Report, July 2004, CRS-30.

intelligence agencies other than the CIA. Strong opposition from the DOD and Armed Services Committee inhibited its passage.[634]

1992　　Intelligence Organization Act

- This Act passed as part of the Intelligence Authorization Act of 1993; much of its text came from the S.2198 introduced by Senator Boren (see above).

- Specified the roles of the DCI for the first time (as opposed to duties).

- Codified the DCI's budget powers by requiring DCI approval of IC budgets before incorporating into NFIP and prior approval before reprogramming any NFIP funds.

- Upon approval of White House, Congress, and affected agency's head, the DCI could shift funds and personnel from one NFIP program to another.[635]

Clinton Administration, 1993-2000

1995　　Presidential Decision Directive (PDD-35)[636]

- Increasing number of military deployments necessitated the need for tactical intelligence support. The IC support of this directive resulted in a diversion of shrinking national, strategic intelligence resources to growing, tactical missions.[637]

- Divided intelligence priority into hard targets, upper tier groups such as the rogue states and transnational issues and global coverage (lower tier) includes everything else.

---

[634]CRS Report, July 2004, CRS-31.

[635] Michael Warner, *Central Intelligence: Origin and Evolution* (Washington, DC: Center for the Study of Intelligence, 2001), 12.

[636] Intelligence Community officers told the Joint Inquiry in U.S. Congress, Senate, Select Committee on Intelligence and House, Permanent Select Committee on Intelligence, *Joint Inquiry into Intelligence Community Activities Before and After the Terrorist Attacks of September 11, 2001*, 107th Cong., 2nd sess., S.Rept. 107-351 and H. Rept. 107-792, December 2002, C. Systemic Findings, 49 that the lack of adequate separation between tiers made it difficult to choose between priorities and intelligence prioritization was often confusing. An NSA official described PDD-35 as cumbersome. For example, NSA had some 1,500 formal requirements by 11 September 2001 covering virtually covering every situation and target. Almost 200,000 Essential Elements of Information (EEIs) were reflective of these requirements.

[637] Warner, 13.

1995-96   Commission on the Roles and Capabilities of the U.S. Intelligence Community (Aspin-Brown Commission)

Report titled "Preparing for the 21st Century: An Appraisal of U.S. Intelligence but was commonly known as the Aspin-Brown Report. The Committee was formed to assess the future direction, priorities, and structure of the IC in the post-Cold War environment. P.L. 103-359 set forth nineteen separate issues for the commission to address, including determination of intelligence needs and priorities in the post-Cold War world, whether or not existing organizational arrangements provide the most effective and efficient framework to meet those needs, and what resources would be necessary to satisfy these requirements.[638]

- Designating the Attorney General to coordinate law enforcement (LE) response to global crime. Sharing of information between LE and IC should be improved.
- Establishing two new DCI deputies—one for IC and one for day-to-day management of CIA. Both would be Senate-confirmed positions.
- DCI would concur with appointments of heads of national intelligence elements within DoD and evaluate their performance.
- Realignment of intelligence budgeting procedures with discipline (SIGINT, IMINT, HUMINT) managers.
- Recommended disclosing the intelligence budget.
- With regard to congressional oversight, appointments to intelligence committees should be treated like appointments to other congressional committees rather than set number of years. [639]

1995-96   IC21: Intelligence Community in the 21st Century (a HPSCI Staff Study)

House Intelligence Committee Staff Study undertook a major review of the roles, functions and structure of the Intelligence Community. Specific IC21 recommendations initially called for a major restructuring of the Community. Following are selected recommendations:

- DCI stronger voice in appointment of directors of NFIP agencies.
- DCI should have greater programmatic control of intelligence budgets and intelligence personnel.
- Establish within the NSC a Committee on Foreign Intelligence

---

[638]CRS Report, Appendix C, February 1996, 29-30.
[639]CRS Report, July 2004, CRS-32.

- Create two additional DDCIs—one to manage all IC analysis and production and one for IC-wide budgeting, requirements and collection management and tasking, consolidated infrastructure management and system acquisition.
- Create a Director of Military Intelligence (DMI) to serve as program manager of JMIP and program coordinator for TIARA.
- Establish a Community Management Staff (CMS) with IC-wide authority over, and coordination of, requirements, resources, and collection.
- Separate the Clandestine Service (all human intelligence) from the CIA and report directly to the DCI.
- Establish a Technical Collection Agency.
- Establish common standards and protocols for technical collection systems, from collection through processing, exploitation and dissemination.
- Establish a Technology Development Office to perform Community R&D functions.
- House Intelligence Committee should be made a standing committee without tenure limits.[640]

1997   Intelligence Renewal and Reform Act of 1996

- Required the SecDef to win concurrence of DCI for appointing directors to NSA, NIMA, and NRO; DCI would also write performance appraisals for these directors.
- DDCI for Community Management and ADCI for Collection, Analysis and Production, and Administration.

According to Odom, this Act did not change the basic structure of the IC, so its changes, while probably beneficial, must be regarded as largely cosmetic. *Modernizing Intelligence: Structure and Change for the 21st Century* (Fairfax, VA: National Institute for Public Policy, 1997), 6.

1999-01   Report of the U.S. Commission on National Security/21st Century (Hart-Rudman Commission)

The Hart-Rudman Commission did not specifically address intelligence reform. This Commission looked at the United States government as a whole. The final reports of this Committee encompassed three and one-half years of effort, which culminated in three substantive reports published separately Phase I (1999), Phase II (2000), and Phase III (2001).

---

[640]CRS Report, July 2004, CRS-33.

**1999   Phase I Report Emerging Global Security Environment for the
           First Quarter of the 21st Century (15 September 1999)**

The Commission articulated 12 beliefs about the future that laid the foundation upon which their conclusions were drawn.

Conclusions for the next twenty-five years:

1. America will become increasingly vulnerable to hostile attack on our homeland, and our military superiority will not protect us.

2. Rapid advances in information and biotechnologies will create new vulnerabilities for U.S. security.

3. New technologies will divide the world as well as draw it together.

4. The national security of all advanced states will be increasingly affected by the vulnerabilities of the evolving global economic infrastructure.

5. Energy will continue to have major strategic significance.

6. All borders will be more porous; some will bend and some will break.

7. The sovereignty of states will come under pressure, but will endure.

8. Fragmentation or failure of states will occur, with destabilizing effects on neighboring states.

9. Foreign crises will be replete with atrocities and the deliberate terrorizing of civilian populations.

10. Space will become a critical and competitive military environment.

11. The essence of war will not change.

12. U.S. intelligence will face more challenging adversaries, and even excellent intelligence will not prevent all surprises.

13. The United States will be called upon frequently to intervene militarily in a time of uncertain alliances and with the prospect of fewer forward-deployed forces.

14. The emerging security environment in the next century will require different military and other national capabilities.[641]

---

[641] Hart and Rudman Phase I Report, 4-7.

The Commission indicated that to preserve American liberties and fulfill these goals in a new age, America's priority objectives and key policy objectives must be these:

- Defend the United States and ensure that it is safe from the dangers of a new era.
- To maintain America's social cohesion, economic competitiveness, technological ingenuity, and military strength.
- To assist the integration of key major powers, especially China, Russia, and India, into the mainstream of the emerging international system.
- To promote, with others, the dynamism of the new global economy and improve the effectiveness of international institutions and international law.
- To adapt U.S. alliances and other regional mechanisms to a new era in which America's partners seek greater autonomy and responsibility.[642]

The Hart-Rudman Commission stipulated the five kinds of military capabilities that United States requires in this new environment:

- Nuclear capabilities to deter and protect the United States and its allies from attack
- Homeland security capabilities
- Conventional capabilities necessary to win major wars
- Rapid employable expeditionary/intervention capabilities
- Humanitarian relief and constabulary capabilities.[643]

2001   Phase III Report Road Map for National Security: Imperative for Change (published 15 February 2001)

The Commission proposed structural changes with recommendations in five key areas:

- Ensuring the security of the American homeland
- Recapitalizing key institutions in science and education
- Redesigning key institutions of the Executive Branch
- Overhauling the U.S. government's military and civilian personnel systems
- Reorganizing Congress's role in national security affairs.[644]

---

[642]Hart and Rudman Phase II Report Key Objectives, 8-12.

[643] Hart and Rudman Phase II Report, Implications for National Security, 14.

[644] Hart-Rudman Phase III Report, viii.

The Commission concluded that the structure of the Intelligence Community did not require change. However, it did look at the supporting role intelligence plays and identified three areas of emphasis, "steps," that when undertaken would promote successful implementation of the other report recommendations.

- Recommend that the President order the setting of national intelligence priorities through National Security Council guidance to the DCI.
- IC should emphasize the recruitment of HUMINT sources on terrorism as one of its highest priorities, and ensure that existing operational guidelines support this policy.
- The Community should place new emphasis on collection and analysis of economic and science/technology security concerns, and incorporate more open source intelligence into its analytical products.[645]

Phase III Recommendations

These fifty recommendations are listed in order of presentation in the original document, Appendix 1, The Recommendations, The United States Commission on National Security/21st Century. The original document was color coded to indicate recommendations that could be implemented via Congressional action (red), Executive Order (blue) or agency head or congressional leadership (green).

Phase III Recommendations- Securing the Homeland

1. The President should develop a comprehensive strategy to heighten America's ability to prevent and protect against all forms of attack on the homeland, and to respond to such attacks if prevention and protection fail.

2. The President should propose, and Congress should create, a National Homeland Security Agency (NHSA) with responsibilities for planning, coordinating, and integrating various U.S. government activities involved in homeland security. The Federal Emergency Management Agency (FEMA)should be a key building block in this effort.

3. The President should propose to Congress the transfer of the Customs Service, the Border Patrol, and Coast Guard to the NHSA, while preserving them as distinct entities.

---

[645] Road Map for National Security: Imperative for Change—The Phase III Report of the U.S. Commission on National Security/21st Century, 15 February 2001, URL: *http://www.nssg.gov*, accessed 1 November 2003. Hereafter cited as Hart-Rudman Phase III Report.

4. The President should ensure that the National Intelligence Council: include homeland security and asymmetric threats as an area of analysis; assign that portfolio to a National Intelligence Officer; and produce National Intelligence Estimates on these threats.

5. The President should propose to Congress the establishment of an Assistant Secretary of Defense for Homeland Security within the Office of the Secretary of Defense, reporting directly to the Secretary.

6. The Secretary of Defense, at the President's direction, should make homeland security a primary mission of the National Guard, and the Guard should be organized, properly trained, and adequately equipped to undertake that mission.

7. Congress should establish a special body to deal with homeland security issues, as has been done with intelligence oversight. Members should be chosen for their expertise in foreign policy, defense, intelligence, law enforcement, and appropriations. This body should also include members of all relevant Congressional committees as well as ex-officio members from the leadership of both Houses of Congress.

Phase III Recommendations-Recapitalizing America's Strengths in Science and Education

8. The President should propose, and the Congress should support, doubling the U.S. government's investment in science and technology R&D by 2010.

9. The President should empower his Science Advisor to establish non-military R&D objectives that meet changing national needs, and to be responsible for coordinating budget development within the relevant departments and agencies.

10. The President should propose, and the Congress should fund, the reorganization of the national laboratories, providing individual laboratories with new mission that minimize overlap.

11. The President should propose, and Congress should pass, a National Security Science and Technology Education Act (NSSTEA) with four sections: reduced-interest loans and scholarships for students to pursue degrees in science, mathematics, and engineering; loan forgiveness and scholarships for those in these fields entering government or military service; a National Security Teaching Program to foster science and math

teaching at the K-12 level; and increased funding for professional development of science and math teachers.

12. The President should direct the Department of Education to work with the states to devise a comprehensive plan to avert a looming shortage of quality teachers. This plan should emphasize raising teacher compensation, improving infrastructure support, reforming the certification process, and expanding existing programs targeted at districts with especially acute problems.

13. The President and Congress should devise a targeted program to strengthen the historically black colleges and universities in our country, and should particularly support those that emphasize science, mathematics, and engineering.

Phase III Recommendations-Institutional Redesign

14. The President should personally guide a top-down strategic planning process and delegate authority to the National Security Advisor to coordinate that process.

15. The President should prepare and present to the Congress an overall national security budget to serve the critical goals that emerge from the NSC strategic planning process. Separately, the President should continue to submit budgets for individual national security departments and agencies for Congressional review and appropriations.

16. The NSC should be responsible for advising the President and for coordinating the multiplicity of national security activities, broadly defined to include economic and domestic law enforcement activities as well as the traditional national security agenda. The NSC Advisor and staff should resist the temptation to assume a central policymaking and operational role.

17. The President should propose to the Congress that the Secretary of Treasury be made a statutory member of the National Security Council.

18. The President should abolish the National Economic Council, distributing its domestic economic policy responsibilities to the Domestic Policy Council and its international economic responsibilities to the National Security Council.

19. The President should propose to Congress a plan to reorganize the State Department, creating five Under Secretaries, with the responsibility

for overseeing the regions of Africa, Asia, Europe, Inter-America, and Near East/South Asia, and redefining the responsibilities of the Under Secretary for Global Affairs. These new Under Secretaries would operate in conjunction with the existing Under Secretary for Management.

20. The President should propose to the Congress that the U.S. Agency for International Development be consolidated into the State Department.

21. The Secretary of State should give greater emphasis to strategic planning in the State Department and link it directly to the allocation of resources through the establishment of a Strategic Planning, Assistance, and Budget Office.

22. The President should ask Congress to appropriate funds to the State Department in a single integrated Foreign Operations budget, which would include all foreign assistance programs and activities as well as all expenses for personnel and operations.

23. The President should ensure that Ambassadors have the requisite area knowledge as well as leadership and management skills to function effectively. He should therefore appoint an independent, bipartisan advisory panel to the Secretary of State to vet ambassadorial appointees, career and non-career alike.

24. The Secretary of Defense should propose to Congress a restructuring plan for the Office of the Under Secretary of Defense for Policy that would abolish the office of Assistant Secretary for Special Operations and Low-Intensity Conflict (SOLIC), and create a new office of an Assistant Secretary dedicated to Strategy and Planning (S/P).

25. Based on a review of core roles and responsibilities of the staffs of the Office of the Secretary of Defense, the Joint Staff, the military services, and the CINCs, the Secretary of Defense should reorganize and reduce those staffs by ten to fifteen percent.

26. The Secretary of Defense should establish a ten-year goal of reducing infrastructure costs by 20 to 25 percent through outsourcing and privatization as many DoD support agencies as possible.

27. The Congress and the Secretary of Defense should move the Quadrennial Defense Review (QDR) to the second year of a presidential term.

28. The Secretary of Defense should introduce a new process that would require the Services and defense agencies to compete for the allocation of some resources within the overall defense budget.

29. The Secretary of Defense should establish and employ a two-track acquisition system, one for major acquisitions and a second, "fast-track" for a limited number of potential breakthrough systems, especially those in the area of command and control.

30. The Secretary of Defense should foster innovation by directing a return to the pattern of increased prototyping and testing of selected weapons and support systems.

31. Congress should implement two-year defense budgeting *solely* for the modernization element of the DoD budget (R&D/procurement) because of its long-term character, and its should expand the use of multiyear procurement.

32. Congress should modernize Defense Department auditing and oversight requirements by rewriting relevant sections of U.S. Code, Title 10, and the Federal Acquisition Regulations.

33. The Secretary of Defense should direct the DoD to shift from a threat-based force sizing process to one which measures requirements against recent operational activity trends, actual intelligence estimates of potential adversaries' capabilities, and national security objectives, once these are formulated in the new administration's national security strategy.

34. The Defense Department should devote its highest priority to improving and furthering expeditionary capabilities.

35. The President should establish an Interagency Working Group on Space (IWGS) at the National Security Council to coordinate all aspects of the nation's space policy, and place on the NSC staff those with the necessary expertise in this area.

36. The President should order the setting of national intelligence priorities through National Security Council guidance to the Director of Central Intelligence.

37. The Director of Central Intelligence should emphasize the recruitment of human intelligence sources on terrorism as one of the Intelligence Community's highest priorities, and ensure that operational

guidelines are balanced between security needs and respect for American values and principles.

38. The Intelligence Community should place new emphasis on collection and analysis of economic and science/technology security concerns, and incorporate more open source intelligence into analytical products. Congress should support this new emphasis by increasing significantly the National Foreign Intelligence Program (NFIP) budget for collection and analysis.

Phase III Recommendations-The Human Requirements for National Security

39. Congress should significantly expand the National Security Education Act (NSEA) to include broad support for social sciences, humanities, and foreign languages in exchange for military and civilian service to the nation.

40. The Executive and Legislative Branches should cooperate to revise the current Presidential appointee process by reducing the impediments that have made high-level public service undesirable to many distinguished Americans. Specifically, they should reduce the number of Senate confirmed and non-career Senior Executive Service (SES) positions by 25 percent; shorten the appointment process; and revise draconian ethics regulations.

41. The President should order the overhauling of the Foreign Service system by revamping the examination process, dramatically improving the level of on-going professional education, and making leadership a core value of the State Department.

42. The President should order the elimination of recruitment hurdles for the Civil Service, ensure a faster and easier hiring process, and see to it that strengthened professional education and retention programs are worthy of full funding by Congress.

43. The Executive Branch should establish a National Security Service Corps (NSSC) to enhance civilian career paths, and to provide a corps of policy experts with broad-based experience throughout the Executive Branch.

44. Congress should significantly enhance the Montgomery GI Bill, as well as strengthen recently passed and pending legislation supporting

benefits—including transition, medical, and homeownership—for qualified veterans.

45. Congress and the Defense Department should cooperate to decentralize military personnel legislation dictating the terms of enlistment/commissioning, career management, retirement, and compensation.

46. The Congressional leadership should conduct a thorough bicameral, bipartisan review of the Legislative Branch relationship to national security and foreign policy.

47. Congressional and Executive Branch leaders must build programs to encourage individual members to acquire knowledge and experience in both national security and foreign policy.

48. Congress should rationalize its current committee structure so that it best serves U.S. national security objectives; specifically, it should merge the current authorizing committee with the relevant appropriations subcommittee.

49. The Executive Branch must ensure a sustained focus on foreign policy and national security consultation with Congress and devote resources to it. For its part, Congress must make consultation a higher priority and form a permanent consultative group of Congressional leaders as part of this effort.

50. The President should create an implementing mechanism to ensure that the major recommendations of this Commission result in the critical reforms necessary to ensure American national security and global leadership over the next quarter century.

Appendix D—Talking Heads Intelligence Reform

This appendix contains a collection of reform recommendations from selected intelligence and national security specialists. Their respective musings have been provided for informational purposes. Interested readers are encouraged to review original source for more information. Also, a membership listing is provided whenever the committee composition was identified. Interestingly, many commissioners are repeat performers such as Brent Scowcroft, Gary Hart, Lee Hamilton, Bob Kerrey, James Schlesinger (now deceased), R. James Woolsey, and Warren B. Rudman. *The Washington Post* refers to these wise men—elite corps of former government luminaries—as a small club of professional chin-strokers who are called in to take over where our elected representatives find an issue too dangerous to handle. *The Post* reports, "As the federal government in Washington punts its problems to commissions, the commission-sitters proffer their Solomonic advice, which is then generally ignored—until the next crisis demands the formation of a new commission."[646]

1994/95 Colloquium The Intelligence Community: Is it Broken? How to Fix It?[647]

Robert Gates' suggestions for a starting agenda:

- Areas of greatest savings for the intelligence budget lie in the military intelligence arena. DMI should be created. Keep decentralized targeting functions.
- Do not duplicate military intelligence analysis in the Community. Give DIA the CIA military analysis efforts.
- Eliminate the differentiation between the NFIP and TIARA. When it comes to technical collection systems, national systems are tactical systems.
- Complete the vertical integration of stovepipes—the collection systems. Create the National Imagery Agency.
- Build an open-source gateway.
- Need a new requirements and evaluation process.
- CIA needs to be smaller and more focused. Covert, paramilitary capability should be moved out of CIA and into DoD.

---

[646]Dana Milbank, "The Small Bundle of Names Tied Up With Blue Ribbons," The Washington Post, 4 February 2004, C9.

[647] John H. Hedley, A Colloquium: The Intelligence Community: Is it Broken? How to Fix It? URL: http://www.cia.gov/csi/studies/96unclass/index.htm.

- Need greater integration of the Community. Need to consolidate administrative structures.
- DCI should continue to be head of CIA.
- IC needs to accelerate move toward greater openness.
- If IC doesn't change, it will be forced upon the Community.

Colloquium Members:
Chairman, The Honorable Howard H. Baker, Jr.

The Honorable Robert M. Gates	The Honorable Dan Glickman
The Honorable Lee Hamilton	LTG William E. Odom (Ret)
Gen Brent Scowcroft (Ret)	Anthony Arend
Les Aspin	Charles Battaglia
Charles Cogan	Chester Crocker
Carl Ford	Gary Foster
Alton Frye	Tobi Gati
Allan Goodman	David Gries
John Hollister Hedley	Jim Hoagland
Sarah Holmes	William G. Hyland
Max M. Kapelman	Richard J. Kerr
Brian Latell	Douglas MacEachin
John M. McMahon	Cranwell Montgomery
Walter Pincus	Elizabeth Rindskopf
Britt Snider	Christopher Straub
George Tenet	Thomas G. Weston
Casimir A. Yost	

1995   Aspin-Brown Commission

The Commission was formed to assess the future direction, priorities, and structure of the IC in the post-Cold War environment.

Committee Members:

Chairman, Harold Brown	Former Chairman, Les Aspin (Deceased)
Vice-Chairman, Warren B. Rudman	Gen Lew Allen, Jr., USAF, (Ret)

Zoe Baird	Ann Z. Caracristi
Tony Coelho	David H. Dewhurst
Representative Norman D. Dicks	Senator J. James Exon
Wyche Fowler, Jr.,	Stephen Friedman
Representative Porter J. Goss	Anthony S. Harrington
Robert J. Hermann	Lt Gen Robert E. Pursley, USAF, (Ret)
Senator John Warren	Paul D. Wolfowitz

1996   LTG James R. Clapper, Jr.(Ret) Radical Ruminations:[648]

Radical Ruminations Premise:

- Conduct all national collection as a coherent, unitary activity
- Designate/empower a single national collection "czar"
  - —Bring all intelligence resources to bear operationally, regardless of stovepipe "INTs"

  - —Enable systematic, meaningful trade-off between/among collection disciplines

  - —Don't end individual/unique endeavors of "INTs"

Structure/organization:

- "Re-invent" DIRNSA as collection czar
- Transition gradually
  - —Technical/open source collection first

  - —HUMINT later

- Reassign INFOSEC missions
  - —Free "protective IW" role of "spy baggage"

  - —Let NSA focus on homogeneous intelligence missions

---

[648] LTG James R. Clapper, Jr. (RET), "A Proposed Restructuring of the Intelligence Community," Briefing presented at Center for Information Policy Research, Harvard University, Guest Presentations, Spring 1996, Incidental Paper: Seminar on Intelligence, Command and Control, January 1997, URL: http://pirp.harvard.edu/pubs_pdf/clapper/clapper-i97-1.pdf>, accessed 1 April 2004.

Reform acquisition with a single R&D/acquisition authority for all collection endeavors, regardless of regime/medium

Processes:

- "One-stop shopping" for collection requirements
- Customers express one intelligence need—not in four discipline-unique languages
- Conduct all national production as a coherent, unitary activitiy
- Designate/empower a single national production "czar"
  - —Maintain institutional integrity of production centers, but collocate resources where appropriate
  - —Designate authoritative executive agents

Infrastrucuture:

- Establish infrastructure "czar," but retain information management within collection/production elements
- Infrastructure officer also heads national services staff that centrally manages and decentrally executes:
  - —Security
  - —Personnel
  - —Administration
  - —Pay and finances
  - —Logistics
  - —Training and education
  - —Etc.

1999-2001 The United States Commission on National Security/21st Century

Committee Members:

Executive Director, Gen Charles G. Boyd (Ret)

Co-Chairman, Gary Hart   Co-Chairman, Warren B. Rudman

Commissioners:

Anne Armstrong   Norman R. Augustine
John Dancy   John R. Galvin
Leslie H. Gelb   Newt Gingrich

Lee H. Hamilton	Lionel H. Olmer
Donald B. Rice	James Schlesinger
Harry D. Train	Andrew Young

2002   Joint inquiry into Intelligence Community Activities Before and After the Terrorist Attacks of September 11, 2001

Senate Select Committee on Intelligence (SSCI 107th Congress)[649]

Chairman, Bob Graham (D-FL)

Vice Chairman, Richard C. Shelby (R-AL)

Carl Levin (D-MI)	Jon Kyl (R-AZ)
John D. Rockefeller (D-WV)	James M. Inhofe (R-OK)
Dianne Feinstein (D-CA)	Orrin Hatch (R-UT)
Ron Wyden (D-OR)	Pat Roberts (R-KS)
Richard J. Durbin (D-IL)	Mike DeWine (R-OH)
Evan Bayh (D-IN)	Fred Thompson (R-TN)
John Edwards (D-NC)	Richard Lugar (R-IN)
Barbara Mikulski (D-MD)	

House Permanent Select Committee on Intelligence (HPSCI 107th Congress)[650]

Chairman, Porter J. Goss (R-FL)

Ranking Democrat, Nancy Pelosi (D-CA)

Doug Bereuter (R-NE)	Sanford D. Bishop (D-GA)
Michael N. Castle (R-DE)	Jane Hartman (D-CA)
Sherwood L. Boehlert (R-NY)	Gary A. Condit (D-CA)
Jim Gibbons (R-NV)	Tim Roemer (D-IN)
Ray LaHood (R-IL)	Silvestre Heyes (D-TX)
Randy "Duke" Cunningham (R-CA)	Leonard L. Boswell (D-IA)
Peter Hoekstra (R-MI)	Collin C. Peterson (D-MN)

---

[649]U.S. Congress, Senate, Select Committee on Intelligence and House, Permanent Select Committee on Intelligence, Joint Inquiry into Intelligence Community Activities Before and After the Terrorist Attacks of September 11, 2001, 107th Cong., 2nd sess., S.Rept. 107-351 and H. Rept. 107-792, December 2002, viii. Cited hereafter as Joint Inquiry Report.

[650] Joint Inquiry Report, ix.

Richard Burr (R-NC)　　　　　　　Bud Cramer (D-AL)

Saxby Chambliss (R-GA)

Terry Everett (R-AL)

Joint House/Senate Inquiry Staff[651]

Director, Eleanor Hill	Previous Director, Britt Snider
Deputy Director, Rick Cinquegrana	
David Barton	Ann Barton
Daniel Byman	Michael Davidson
George Ellard	Rahul Gupta
Kay Holt	John Ivicic
Michael Jacobson	Everette Jordan
Miles Kara	John Keefe
Thomas Kelley	Dana Lesemann
Patti Littman	Catherine Lotrionte (departed summer 2002)
Arthur Menna	Lewis Moon
Patrica Ravalgi	Alonzo Robertson
Robert Rosenwald	Michael Smith
Catherine Williams	

2003　　LTG (Ret) William E. Odom's Recommendations[652]

Extracted from his book *Fixing Intelligence: For a More Secure America*. However, the book is based principally on a study supported and published by the National Institute for Public Policy in 1997 entitled, *Modernizing Intelligence: Structure and Change for 21st Century*. Odom was Chairman of the Study Panel.

- Make no statutory changes in the DCI's authority.
- Strengthen the role of the National Intelligence Council (NIC).
- Relocate the Directorate of Intelligence.
- Restructure the CMS.
- Retain the National Foreign Intelligence Board and the Intelligence Community Executive Committee.

---

[651] Joint Inquiry Report, x.

[652] William E. Odom, *Fixing Intelligence: For a More Secure America* (New Haven, CT: Yale University Press, 2003).

- Require Periodic Structural Review.
- Keep the Defense Human Intelligence Service as a single DoD organization under the operational control of the director of operations of the CIA.
- Create an overt human intelligence organization within the DoD as a joint activity that coordinates its activities with the CIA as the national human intelligence manager.
- Put all the DIA's electronic intelligence collection under NSA. Put its imagery intelligence collection under NIMA (now NGA).
- Create a DoD counterintelligence management center with operational control and policy, and program management authority over the military service counterintelligence capabilities.
- Abolish the National Reconnaissance Office and transfer its program offices to NSA and NIMA. Alternately, retain the NRO but give it no independent budget. It would sell its procurement services to NSA and NIMA, which would include funds for satellite procurement in their own budgets. …Major collection agencies should not have large portions of their operating assets funded through an independent DoD program. All of the foregoing changes are essential to make the DoD intelligence structure fit the reforms of the IC at large. What additional structure changes make sense within the DoD?
- Make the director of DIA the coordinating manager of all intelligence support to material and force development—both joint and by the services.
- Create within the DIA a "net assessment" center, responsible directly to the secretary of defense, which makes judgments about the strength of U.S. forces versus potential adversary forces as a basis for deciding military force requirements.

National Institute for Public Policy Participants:[653]

Dr. William R. Graham	LTG Harry E. Soyster, USA (Ret)
Mr. Robert E. Rich	Dr. Gregory F. Treverton
Ms. Elisabeth R. Rindskopf, Esq.	Lt Gen James R. Clapper, USAF (Ret)

2004   National Commission on Terrorist Attacks Upon the United States (9/11 Commission Report)

---

[653] *Modernizing Intelligence: Structure and Change for the 21st Century* (VA: National Institute for Public Policy, 1997), cover page.

Committee Members:

Chair, Thomas H. Kean

Vice Chair, Lee H. Hamilton

Richard Ben-Veniste   Bob Kerry

Fred F. Fielding   John F. Lehman

Jamie Gorelick   Timothy J. Roemer

Slade Gorton   James R. Thompson

Commission Staff: Seventy-eight staffers contributed to this effort.

Executive Director, Phillip Zelikow

Deputy Executive Director, Christopher A. Kojm

General Counsel, Daniel Marcus

Appendix E — Post-9/11 Intelligence Reform Reports

2002   **Joint Inquiry into Intelligence Community Activities Before and After the Terrorist Attacks of September 11, 2001 (Joint Inquiry)**

In February 2002, the Senate Select Committee on Intelligence and the House Permanent Select Committee on Intelligence agreed to conduct an unprecedented Joint Inquiry into the activities of the U.S. Intelligence Community. This committee was limited to approximately one year's duration.[654]

These findings are presented verbatim from the Joint Inquiry Committee source document.[655]

Factual Findings:

1. Finding: While the Intelligence Community had amassed a great deal of valuable intelligence regarding Usama Bin Laden and his terrorist activities, none of it identified the time, place, and specific nature of the attacks that were planned for September 11, 2001. Nonetheless, the Community did have information that was clearly relevant to the September 11 attacks, particularly when considered for its collective significance.

2. Finding: During the spring and summer of 2001, the Intelligence Community experienced a significant increase in information indicating that Bin Laden and al Qa'ida intended to strike against U.S. interests in the very near future.

3. Finding: Beginning in 1998 and continuing into the summer of 2001, the Intelligence Community received a modest, but relatively steady, stream of intelligence reporting that indicated the possibility of terrorist attacks within the United States. Nonetheless, testimony and interviews confirm that it was the general view of the Intelligence Community, in the spring and summer of 2001, that the threatened Bin Laden attacks

---

[654] U.S. Congress, Senate, Select Committee on Intelligence and House, Permanent Select Committee on Intelligence, Joint Inquiry into Intelligence Community Activities Before and After the Terrorist Attacks of September 11, 2001, 107th Cong., 2nd sess., S.Rept. 107-351 and H. Rept. 107-792, December 2002, Part One-Findings and Conclusions, 1. Cited hereafter as Joint Inquiry Report (section).

[655] Joint Inquiry Report III. Findings and Conclusions, 7-10.

would most likely occur against U.S. interests overseas, despite indications of plans and intentions to attack in the domestic United States.

4. Finding: From at least 1994, and continuing into the summer of 2001, the Intelligence Community received information indicating that terrorists were contemplating, among other means of attack, the use of aircraft as weapons. This information did not stimulate any specific Intelligence Community assessment of, or collective U.S. Government reaction to, this form of threat.

5. Finding: Although relevant information that is significant in retrospect regarding the attacks was available to the Intelligence Community prior to September 11, 2001, the Community too often failed to focus on that information and consider and appreciate its collective significance in terms of a probable terrorist attack. Neither did the Intelligence Community demonstrate sufficient initiative in coming to grips with the new transnational threats. Some significant pieces of information in the vast stream of data being collected were overlooked, some were not recognized as potentially significant at the time and therefore not disseminated, and some required additional action on the part of foreign governments before a direct connection to the hijackers could have been established. For all those reasons, the Intelligence Community failed to capitalize fully on available, and potentially important, information.

Note: the Joint Inquiry Committee report further identified ten additional sub-findings which elaborated on the Intelligence Community's analytical deficiencies annotated in Finding 5.

Systematic Findings:

The Joint Inquiry identified a number of systemic weaknesses within the IC. According to the Inquiry, "if not addressed, these weaknesses will continue to undercut U.S. counterterrorist efforts." The systemic findings are presented verbatim from the Joint Inquiry source document:

1. Finding: Prior to September 11, the Intelligence Community was neither well organized nor equipped, and did not adequately adapt, to meet the challenge posed by global terrorists focused on targets within the domestic United States. Serious gaps existed between the collection coverage provided by U.S. foreign and U.S. domestic intelligence capabilities. The U.S. foreign intelligence agencies paid inadequate attention to the potential for a domestic attack. The CIA's failure to watchlist suspected terrorists aggressively reflected a lack of emphasis on a process

designed to protect the homeland from terrorist threat. As a result, CIA employees failed to watchlist al-Mihdhar and al-Mazmi. At home, the counterterrorism effort suffered from the lack of an effective domestic intelligence capability. The FBI was unable to identify and monitor effectively the extent of activity by al-Qa'ida and other international terrorist groups operating in the United States. Taken together, these problems greatly exacerbated the nation's vulnerability to an increasingly dangerous and immediate international terrorist threat inside the United States.

2. Finding: Prior to September 11, 2001, neither the U.S. Government as a whole nor the Intelligence Community had a comprehensive counterterrorist strategy for combating the threat posed by Usama Bin Laden. Furthermore, the Director of Central Intelligence (DCI) was either unwilling or unable to marshall the full range of Intelligence Community resources necessary to combat the growing threat to the United States.

3. Finding: Between the end of the Cold War and September 11, 2001, overall Intelligence Community funding fell or remained even in constant dollars, while funding for the Community's counterterrorism efforts increased considerably. Despite those increases, the accumulation of intelligence priorities, a burdensome requirements process, the overall decline in Intelligence Community funding, and reliance on supplemental appropriations made it difficult to allocate Community resources effectively against an evolving terrorist threat. Inefficiencies in the resource and requirements process were compounded by problems in Intelligence Community budgeting practices and procedures.

4. Finding: While technology remains one of this nation's greatest advantages, it has not been fully and most effectively applied in support of U.S. counterterrorism efforts. Persistent problems in this area included a lack of collaboration between Intelligence Community agencies, a reluctance to develop and implement new technical capabilities aggressively, the FBI's reliance on outdated and insufficient technical systems, and the absence of a central counterterrorism database.

5. Finding: Prior to September 11, the Intelligence Community's understanding of al-Qa'ida was hampered by insufficient analytic focus and quality, particularly in terms of strategic analysis. Analysis and analysts were not always used effectively because of the perception in some quarters of the Intelligence Community that they were less important to agency counterterrorism missions than were operations personnel. The quality of counterterrorism analysis was inconsistent, and many analysts were inexperienced, unqualified, under-trained, and without access to

critical information. As a result, there was a dearth of creative, aggressive analysis targeting Bin Laden and a persistent inability to comprehend the collective significance of individual pieces of intelligence. These analytic deficiencies seriously undercut the ability of U.S. policymakers to understand the full nature of the threat, and to make fully informed decisions.

6. Finding: Prior to September 11, the Intelligence Community was not prepared to handle the challenge it faced in translating the volumes of foreign language counterterrorism intelligence it collected. Agencies within the Intelligence Community experienced backlogs in material awaiting translation, a shortage of language specialists and language-qualified field officers and a readiness level of only 30% in the most critical terrorism-related languages.

7. Finding: Prior to September 11, the Intelligence Community's ability to produce significant and timely signals intelligence on counterterrorism was limited by NSA's failure to address modern communications technology aggressively, continuing conflict between Intelligence Community agencies, NSA's cautious approach to any collection of intelligence relating to activities in the United States, and insufficient collaboration between NSA and the FBI regarding the potential for terrorist attacks within the United States.

8. Finding: The continuing erosion of NSA's program management expertise and experience has hindered its contribution to the fight against terrorism. NSA continues to have mixed results in providing timely technical solutions to modern intelligence collection, analysis, and information sharing problems.

9. Finding: The U.S. Government does not presently bring together in one place all terrorism-related information from all sources. While the CTC does manage overseas operations and has access to most Intelligence Community information, it does not collect terrorism-related information from all sources, domestic and foreign. Within the Intelligence Community, agencies did not adequately share relevant counterterrorism information, prior to September 11. This breakdown in communications was the result of a number of factors, including differences in the agencies' missions, legal authorities and cultures. Information was not sufficiently shared, not only between different Intelligence Community agencies, but also within individual agencies, and between the intelligence and the law enforcement agencies.

10. Finding: Serious problems in information sharing also persisted, prior to September 11, between the Intelligence Community and relevant

non-Intelligence Community agencies. This included other federal agencies as well as state and local authorities. This lack of communication and collaboration deprived those other entities, as well as the Intelligence Community, of access to potentially valuable information in the "war" against Bin Laden. The Inquiry's focus on the Intelligence Community limited the extent to which it explored these issues, and this is an area that should be reviewed further.

11. Finding: Prior to September 11, 2001, the Intelligence Community did not effectively develop and use human sources to penetrate the al-Qa'ida inner circle. This lack of reliable and knowledgeable human sources significantly limited the Community's ability to acquire intelligence that could be acted upon before the September 11 attacks. In part, at least, the lack of unilateral (i.e., U.S.-recruited) counterterrorism sources was a product of an excessive reliance on foreign liaison service.

12. Finding: During the summer of 2001, when the Intelligence Community was bracing for an imminent al-Qa'ida attack, difficulties with FBI applications for Foreign Intelligence Surveillance Act (FISA) surveillance and the FISA process led to a diminished level of coverage of suspected al-Qa'ida operatives in the United States. The effect of these difficulties was compounded by the perception that spread among FBI personnel at Headquarters and the field offices that the FISA process was lengthy and fraught with peril.

13. Finding: Redacted. Unclassified version not available.

14. Finding: Senior U.S. military officials were reluctant to use U.S. military assets to conduct offensive counterterrorism efforts in Afghanistan, or to support or participate in CIA operations directed against al-Qa'ida prior to September 11. At least part of this reluctance was driven by the military's view that the Intelligence Community was unable to provide the intelligence needed to support military operations. Although the U.S. military did participate in [redacted] counterterrorism efforts to counter Usama Bin Laden's terrorist network prior to September 11, 2001 most of the military's focus was on force protection.

15. Finding: The Intelligence Community depended heavily on foreign intelligence and law enforcement services for the collection of counterterrorism intelligence and the conduct of other counterterrorism activities. The results were mixed in terms of productive intelligence, reflecting vast differences in the ability and willingness of the various foreign services to target Bin Laden and al-Qa'ida network. Intelligence Community

agencies sometimes failed to coordinate their relationships with foreign services adequately, either within the Intelligence Community or with broader U.S. Government liaison and foreign policy efforts. This reliance on foreign liaison services also resulted in a lack of focus on the development of unilateral human sources.

16. Finding: The activities of the September 11 hijackers in the United States appear to have been financed, in large part, from monies sent to them from abroad and also brought in on their persons. Prior to September 11, there was no coordinated U.S. Government-wide strategy to track terrorist funding and close down their financial support networks. There was also a reluctance in some parts of the U.S. Government to track terrorist funding and close down their financial support networks. As a result, the U.S. Government was unable to disrupt financial support for Usama Bin Laden's terrorist activities effectively.

17. Finding: Despite intelligence reporting from 1998 through the summer of 2001 indicating that Usama Bin Laden's terrorist network intended to strike inside the United States, the United States Government did not undertake a comprehensive effort to implement defensive measures in the United States.

18. Finding: Between 1996 and September 2001, the counterterrorism strategy adopted by the U.S. Government did not succeed in eliminating Afghanistan as a sanctuary and training ground for Usama Bin Laden's terrorist network. A range of instruments was used to counter al-Qa'ida, with law enforcement often emerging as a leading tool because other means were deemed not to be feasible or failed to produce results. Although numerous successful prosecutions were generated, law enforcement efforts were not adequate by themselves to target or eliminate Bin Laden's sanctuary. While the United States persisted in observing the rule of law and accepted norms of international behavior, Bin Laden and al-Qa'ida recognized no rules and thrived in the safe haven provided by Afghanistan.

19. Finding: Prior to September 11, the Intelligence Community and the U.S. Government labored to prevent attacks by Usama Bin Laden and his terrorist network against the United States, but largely without the benefit of an alert, mobilized and committed American public. Despite intelligence information on the immediacy of the threat level in the spring and summer of 2001, the assumption prevailed in the U.S. Government that attacks of the magnitude of September 11 could not happen here. As a

result, there was insufficient effort to alert the American public to the reality and gravity of the threat.

Recommendations:

These recommendations were condensed by the present author from the Joint Inquiry Report, Recommendations, December 10, 2002.[656] In most cases, the Joint Inquiry Report offered specific steps to accomplish a particular recommendation, as outlined below.

1. Congress should amend the National Security Act of 1947 to create and sufficiently staff a statutory Director of National Intelligence who shall be the President's principal advisor on intelligence and shall have the full range of management, budgetary and personnel responsibilities needed to make the entire U.S. intelligence Community operate as a coherent whole. Note: All subsequent recommendations referring to DNI imply that this first recommendation has been adopted; otherwise, DCI should be replaced for DNI.

2. Current efforts by the NSC to examine and revamp existing intelligence priorities should be expedited, given the immediate need for clear guidance in intelligence and counterterrorism efforts.... Finally, the establishment of IC priorities, and the justification for such priorities, should be reported to both the House and Senate Intelligence Committees on an annual basis.

3. The NSC should prepare a U.S. government-wide strategy for combating terrorism, both at home and aboard....Consistent with applicable law, the strategy should effectively employ and integrate all capabilities available to the IC against those threats.

4. The position of National Intelligence Officer for Terrorism should be created.

5. Congress and the Administration should ensure the full development within the Department of Homeland Security of an effective all-source terrorism information fusion center.

6. The FBI should strengthen and improve its domestic capability as fully and expeditiously as possible.

7. Congress and the Administration should carefully consider how to best structure and manage U.S. domestic intelligence responsibilities. Con-

---

[656]Joint Inquiry Report, Recommendations, 1-17.

gress should review the scope of domestic intelligence authorities to determine their adequacy in pursuing counterterrorism at home and ensuring the protection of privacy and other rights guaranteed under the Constitution.

8. The Attorney General and the Director, FBI should take necessary action to ensure FBI and other IC members receive in-depth training in use of the Foreign Intelligence Surveillance Act (FISA) to address terrorist threats to the United States; FISA search results are disseminated in a timely manner; and FBI assesses the threat of international terrorism within the U.S.

9. The House and Senate Intelligence and Judiciary Committee should continue to examine FISA and its implementation thoroughly to determine whether its provisions adequately address present and emerging threats.

10. Director, NSA should present to the DNI and Secretary of Defense by June 30, 2003 and report to the House and Senate Intelligence Committees a detailed plan that describes the solutions for the technological challenges for signals intelligence (SIGINT) and the products and costs associated with this get-well program (author's naming convention). Also, NSA collaborates with CIA and FBI within limits of law.

11. DNI should require measures be implemented to greatly enhance the recruitment and development of workforce with the intelligence skills and expertise needed for success in counterterrorist efforts. Specifically, expand and improve counterterrorism training programs; build upon provisions of Intelligence Authorization Act for FY 2003 regarding the development of language capabilities; expand existing IC Reserve Corps; expand and improve educational grant programs focused on intelligence-related fields; enhance recruitment of a more ethnically and culturally diverse workforce; and Congress should consider enacting legislation, modeled on the Goldwater-Nichols Act of 1986, to instill the concept of jointness throughout the IC.

12. Steps should be taken to increase and ensure the greatest return on this nation's substantial investment in intelligence, including budgeting for long-term counterterrorism capabilities; consider a separate classified IC budget; counterterrorism investment should be accompanied by sufficient flexibility; and outside agency to conduct cost-benefit analysis on the resources spent.

13. The State Department should review and report to the President and Congress by June 30, 2003 on the extent to which revisions in bilateral and multilateral agreements would strengthen U.S. counterterrorism efforts.

14. Congress should maintain vigorous, informed, and constructive oversight of the IC. To achieve this, the National Commission on Terrorist Attacks Upon the United States should consider: changes in the budgetary process; changes in the rules regarding membership in the oversight committees; whether oversight should remain separate committees or be a joint committee; extent that classification decisions impair congressional oversight; and how congressional oversight can best contribute to the continuing need of the IC to evolve and adapt to changes in the subject matter of intelligence and the needs of policymakers.

15. President should review and consider amendments to the Executive Orders, polices and procedures that govern national security classification of intelligence information, in an effect to expand access to relevant information to federal agencies outside the IC, for state and local authorities, and for the American public. Congress should review the statutes, policies and procedures that govern the national security classification of intelligence information and its protection from unauthorized disclosure.

16. The DCI should report to the House and Senate Intelligence Committees no later than June 30, 2003 as to the steps taken to implement a system of accountability throughout the IC, to include processes for identifying poor performance and affixing responsibility for it, and for recognizing and rewarding excellence in performance.

17. The Administration should review and report to the House and Senate Intelligence Committees by June 30, 2003 regarding what progress has been made in reducing the inappropriate and obsolete barriers among intelligence and law enforcement agencies engaged in counterterrorism, what needs to be done and what legislative measures are required.

18. Congress and the Administration should ensure the full development of a national watchlist center that will be responsible for coordinating and integrating all terrorist-related watchlist systems.

19. The IC, and in particular the FBI and the CIA, should aggressively address the possibility that foreign governments are providing support to or are involved in terrorist activity targeting the United States and U.S. interests.

DCI Written Statement

On 24 March 2004, DCI George Tenet submitted a written Statement for the Record before the 9/11 Commission. He stated that the Joint Inquiry Report had made 19 recommendations to improve the nation's ability to combat terrorism and that the IC has taken action on all that are within the IC's control. The present author indicates in parentheses the number associated with the above-listed recommendation she believed the IC action addressed. The following actions are extracted verbatim from the DCI's written statement:[657]

1. The President signed National Security Presidential Directive 26 to create a dynamic process for articulating and reviewing intelligence priorities. DCI Directive 2/3 established a National Intelligence Priorities Framework as a mechanism to translate the national foreign intelligence objectives and priorities approved by the National Security Council into specific guidance and resource allocations for the Intelligence Community. (2)

2. In February 2003 the President issued the National Strategy for Combating Terrorism, incorporating strategic planning elements of national security, homeland security, combating weapons of mass destruction, securing cyberspace, and protecting critical infrastructure. (3)

3. The Position of National Intelligence Officer for Transnational Threats has been established and an officer and deputy are in place. (4)

4. The Terrorist Threat Integration Center was established in May 2003 to enable the full integration of terrorist threat-related information and analysis. The Center is a joint-venture composed of officers from five major partners (CIA, FBI, Department of Homeland, Department of Defense, Department of State), as well as from organizations such as the Nuclear Regulatory Commission, Department of Energy, and Capital Police. The Center reports directly to the DCI in his or her statutory capacity as head of the Intelligence Community. (5)

5. The FBI is making considerable progress strengthening and improving its domestic capability in such fields as counterintelligence, counterterrorism, and analysis and reports. The Bureau has developed a strategic plan outlining its top counterterrorism priorities, increased hiring and

---

[657]George Tenet, "Written Statement for the Record of the Director of Central Intelligence Before the National Commission on Terror Attacks Upon the United States," 24 March 2004. http://www.9-11commission.gov//hearings/hearing8/tenet_statement.pdf, accessed 1 May 2004.

training and reassigned agents to high-priority programs, and expanded the number of Joint Terrorism Task Forces to all 56 Field Offices and to 28 Resident Agencies. (6)

6. An Interagency FISA Panel has been established to prioritize foreign intelligence collection pursuant to the Foreign Intelligence Surveillance Act when resources are not sufficient to permit timely processing of FISA requests. (8)

7. A plan to resolve SIGINT technical challenges, provide quarterly reviews of products and funding, and integrate collection and analytic capabilities of NSA, CIA, and FBI has been submitted to the House and Senate Intelligence Committees. (10)

8. Measures to enhance recruitment and development of a Counterterrorism workforce are underway. These include signing the Strategic Direction for Intelligence Community Language Activities directive to provide objectives for investment decisions in language training; launching a five-year, $15 million investment in new computer-delivered proficiency tests used by the Intelligence Community; and making watchlist training mandatory for all Counterterrorist Center line officers. (11)

9. A DCI Directive was issued to address intelligence information security in the context of providing expanded access to intelligence information outside the Intelligence Community. (15)

10. The Information Sharing Workshop Group was established under the authority of the Deputy Director of Central Intelligence for Community Management and the Intelligence Community Deputies Committee to develop a comprehensive strategy for sharing information among intelligence and law enforcement agencies engaged in counterterrorism. (17)

11. Homeland Security Presidential Directive 6 established the Terrorist Screening Center to integrate all terrorist-related watchlist systems. (18)

12. Finally, the CIA and the FBI, as well as other Intelligence Community agencies, continue collection and analysis programs to try to determine the extent to which foreign governments are providing support to or are engaged in terrorist activity targeting the U.S. (19)

2004   The National Commission on Terrorists Attacks Upon the United States (9/11 Commission Report)

Congress and the President created the National Commission on Terrorist Attacks Upon the United States (Public Law 107-306) on 26 November 2002, to investigate "facts and circumstances relating to the terrorists attacks of September 11, 2001," including those relating to intelligence agencies, law enforcement agencies, diplomacy, immigration issues and border control, the flow of assets to terrorist organizations, commercial aviation, the role of congressional oversight and resource allocation, and other determined relevant by the Commission.[658]

Recommendations:

How to Do It?

These recommendations were extracted verbatim from the 9/11 Commission Report, Chapter 13, entitled, "How to Do It? A Different Way of Organizing the Government."[659] Because this chapter reflected those recommendations that affect the IC organization, the author choose to present these recommendations first. Chapter 12, "What to Do? A Global Strategy" provided recommendations of what should be considered in U.S. national strategy. These recommendations follow the list associated with Chapter 13.

Unity of Effort Across the Foreign-Domestic Divide

- We recommend the establishment of a National Counterterrorism Center (NCTC), built on the foundation of the existing Terrorist Threat Integration Center (TTIC). Breaking the older mode of national government organization, this NCTC should be a center for joint operational planning *and* joint intelligence, staffed by personnel from the various agencies. The head of the NCTC should have authority to evaluate the performance of the people assigned to the Center.

Unity of Effort in the Intelligence Community

- The current position of Director of Central Intelligence should be replaced by a National Intelligence Director with two main areas of responsibility: (1) oversee national intelligence centers on specific

---

[658] *The 9/11 Commission Report: Final Report of the National Commission on Terrorist Attacks Upon the United States*, (New York: W.W. Norton & Company, 2004), xv. Cited hereafter as 9/11 Report.

[659] 9/11 Report, Chapter 13, 362-428.

subjects of interest across the U.S. government and (2) manage the national intelligence program and oversee the agencies that contribute to it.

- The CIA Director should emphasize (a) rebuilding the CIA's analytic capabilities; (b) transforming the clandestine service by building its human intelligence capabilities; (c) developing a stronger language program, with high standards and sufficient financial incentives; (d) renewing emphasis on recruiting diversity among operations officers so they can blend more easily in foreign cities; (e) ensuring a seamless relationship between human source collection and signals collection at the operational level; and (f) stressing a better balance between unilateral and liaison operations.

- Lead responsibility for directing and executing paramilitary operations, whether clandestine or covert, should shift to the Defense Department. There it should be consolidated with the capabilities for training, direction, and execution of such operations already being developed in the Special Operations Command.

- Finally, to combat the secrecy and complexity we have described, the overall amounts of money being appropriated for national intelligence and to its component agencies should no longer be kept secret. Congress should pass a separate appropriation act for intelligence, defending the broad allocation of how these tens of billions of dollars have been assigned among the varieties of intelligence work.

Unity of Effort in Sharing Information

- Information procedures should provide incentives for sharing, to restore a better balance between security and shared knowledge.
- The President should lead the government-wide effort to bring the major national security institutions into the information revolution. He should coordinate the resolution of the legal, policy, and technical issues across agencies to create a "trusted information network."

Unity of Effort in the Congress

- Congressional oversight for intelligence—and counterterrorism—is now dysfunctional. Congress should address this problem. We have considered various alternatives: A joint committee on the old model of the Joint Committee on Atomic Energy is one. A single committee in each house of Congress, combining authorizing and appropriating authorities, is another.

- Congress should create a single, principal point of oversight and review for homeland security. Congressional leaders are best able to judge what committee should have jurisdiction over this department and its duties. But we believe that Congress does have the obligation to choose one in the House and one in the Senate, and that this committee should be a permanent standing committee with a nonpartisan staff.

- Since a catastrophic attack could occur with little or no notice, we should minimize as much as possible the disruption of national security policy making during the change of administration by accelerating the process for national security appointments. We think the process could be improved significantly so transitions can work more effectively and allow new officials to assume their new responsibilities as quickly as possible.

Organizing America's Defenses within the United States

- A specialized and integrated national security workforce should be established at the FBI consisting of agents, analysts, linguists, and surveillance specialists who are recruited, trained, rewarded, and retained to ensure the development of an institutional culture imbued with a deep expertise in intelligence and national security.

- The Department of Defense and its oversight committee should regularly assess the adequacy of Northern Command's strategies and planning to defend the United States against military threats to the homeland.

- The Department of Homeland Security and its oversight committees should regularly assess the types of threats the country faces to determine (a) the adequacy of the government's plans—and the progress against those plans—to protect America's critical infrastructure and (b) the readiness of the government to respond to the threats that the United States might face.

What to Do?

These recommendations were extracted verbatim from the 9/11 Commission Report, Chapter 12, entitled, "What to Do? A Global Strategy.[660]

---

[660]9/11 Report, Chapter 12, 361-398.

Attack Terrorists and Their Organizations

- The U.S. government must identify and prioritize actual or potential terrorist sanctuaries. For each, it should have a realistic strategy to keep possible terrorists insecure and on the run, using all elements of national power. We should reach out, listen to, and work with other countries that can help.

- If Musharraf [Pakistan President] stands for enlightened moderation in a fight for his life and for the life of his country, the United States should be willing to make hard choices too, and make the difficult long-term commitment to the future of Pakistan. Sustaining the current scale of aid to Pakistan, the United States should support Pakistan's government in its struggle against extremists with a comprehensive effort that extends from military aid to support for better education, so long as Pakistan's leaders remain willing to make difficult choices of their own.

- The President and the Congress deserve praise for their efforts in Afghanistan so far. Now the United States and the international community should make a long-term commitment to a secure and stable Afghanistan, in order to give the government a reasonable opportunity to improve the life of the Afghan people. Afghanistan must not again become a sanctuary for international crime and terrorism. The United States and the international community should help the Afghan government extend its authority over the country, with a strategy and nation-by-nation commitments to achieve their objectives.

- The problems in the U.S.-Saudi relationship must be confronted, openly. The United States and Saudi Arabia must determine if they can build a relationship that political leaders on both sides are prepared to publicly defend—a relationship about more than oil. It should include a shared commitment to political and economic reform, as Saudis make common cause with the outside world. It should include a shared interest in greater tolerance and cultural respect, translating into a commitment to fight the violent extremists who foment hatred.

Prevent the Continued Growth of Islamist Terrorism

- The U.S. government must define what the message is, what it stands for. We should offer an example of moral leadership in the world, committed to treat people humanly, abide by the rule of law, and be generous and caring to our neighbors. America and Muslim friends can agree on respect for human dignity and opportunity. To Muslim parents, terrorists like Bin Laden have nothing to offer their children but visions of violence and death. America and its friends have a crucial advantage—we can offer these parents a vision that might give their children a better future. If we heed the views of thoughtful leaders in the Arab and Muslim world, a moderate consensus can be found.

- Where Muslim governments, even those who are friends, do not respect these principles, the United States must stand for a better future. One of the lessons of the long Cold War was that short-term gains in cooperating with the most repressive and brutal governments were too often outweighed by long-term setbacks for America's status and interests.

- Just as we did in the Cold War, we need to defend our ideals abroad vigorously. America does stand for its values. The United States defended, and still defends, Muslims against tyrants and criminals in Somalia, Bosnia, Kosovo, Afghanistan, and Iraq. If the United States does not act aggressively to define itself in the Islamic world, the extremists will gladly do the job for us.

- Recognizing that Arab and Muslim audiences rely on satellite television and radio, the government has begun some promising initiatives in television and radio broadcasting to the Arab world, Iran, and Afghanistan. These efforts are beginning to reach large audiences. The Broadcasting Board of Governors has asked for much larger resources. It should get them.

- The United States should rebuild the scholarship, exchange, and library programs that reach out to young people and offer them knowledge and hope. Where such assistance is provided, it should be identified as coming from the citizens of the United States.

- The U.S. government should offer to join with other nations in generously supporting a new International Youth Opportunity Fund. Funds will be spent directly for building and operating primary and secondary schools in those Muslim states that commit to sensibly investing their own money in public schools.

- A comprehensive U.S. strategy to counter terrorism should include economic policies that encourage development, more open societies, and opportunities for people to improve the lives of their families and to enhance prospects for their children's future.

- The United States should engage other nations in developing a comprehensive coalition strategy against Islamic terrorism. There are several multilateral institutions in which such issues should be addressed. But the most important policies should be discussed and coordinated in a flexible contact group of leading coalition governments. This is a good place, for example, to develop joint strategies for targeting terrorist travel, or for hammering out a common strategy for the places where terrorists may be finding sanctuary.

- The United States should engage its friends to develop a common coalition approach toward the detention and humane treatment of captured terrorists. New principles might draw upon Article 3 of the Geneva Conventions on the law of armed conflict. That article was specifically designed for those cases in which the usual laws of war did not apply. Its minimum standards are generally accepted throughout the world as customary international law.

- Our report shows that Al Qaeda has tried to acquire or make weapons of mass destruction for at least ten years. There is no doubt the United States would be a prime target. Preventing the proliferation of these weapons warrants a maximum effort—by strengthening counterproliferation efforts, expanding the Proliferation Security Initiative, and supporting the Cooperative Threat Reduction program.

- Vigorous efforts to track terrorist financing must remain front and center in U.S. counterterrorism efforts. The government has recognized that information about terrorist money helps us to understand their networks, search them out, and disrupt their operations. Intelligence and law enforcement have targeted the relatively small number of financial facilitators—individuals al Qaeda relied on for their ability to raise and deliver money—at the core of al Qaeda's revenue stream. These efforts have worked. The death or capture of several important facilitators has decreased the amount of money available to al Qaeda and has increased its costs and difficulty in raising and moving that money. Captures have additionally provided a windfall of intelligence that can be used to continue the cycle of disruption.

Protect Against and Prepare for Terrorists Attacks

- Targeting travel is at least as powerful a weapon against terrorists as targeting their money. The United States should combine terrorist travel intelligence, operations, and law enforcement in a strategy to intercept terrorists, find terrorist travel facilitators, and constrain terrorist mobility.

- The U.S. border security system should be integrated into a larger network of screening points that includes our transportation system and access to vital facilities such as nuclear reactors. The President should direct the Department of Homeland Security to lead the effort to design a comprehensive screening system, addressing common problems and setting common standards with system wide goals in mind. Extending those standards among other governments could dramatically strengthen America and the world's collective ability to intercept individuals who pose catastrophic threats.

- The Department of Homeland Security, properly supported by the Congress, should complete, as quickly as possible, a biometric entry-exit screening system, including a single system for speeding qualified travelers. It should be integrated with the system that provides benefits to foreigners seeking to stay in the United States. Linking biometric passports to good data systems and decisionmaking is a fundamental goal. No one can hide his or her debt by acquiring a credit card with a slightly different name. Yet today, a terrorist can defeat the link to electronic records by tossing away an old passport and slightly altering the name in the new one.

- The U.S. government cannot meet its own obligations to the American people to prevent the entry of terrorists without a major effort to collaborate with other governments. We should do more to exchange terrorist information with trusted allies and raise U.S. and global border security standards for travel and border crossing over the medium and long term through extensive international cooperation.

- Secure identification should begin in the United States. The federal government should set standards for the issuance of birth certificates and sources of identification, such as drivers' licenses. Fraud in identification documents is no longer just a problem of theft. At many entry points to vulnerable facilities, including gates for boarding aircraft, sources of identification are the last opportunity to ensure that people are who they say they are and to check whether they are terrorists.

- Hard choices must be made in allocating limited resources. The U.S. government should identify and evaluate the transportation assets that need to be protected, set risk-based priorities for defending them, select the most practical and cost-effective ways of doing so, and then develop a plan, budget, and funding to implement the effort. The plan should assign roles and missions to the relevant authorities (federal, state, regional, and local) and to private stakeholders. In measuring effectiveness, perfection is unattainable. But terrorists should perceive that potential targets are defended. They may be deterred by a significant chance of failure.

- Improved use of "no-fly" and "automatic selectee" lists should not be delayed while the argument about a successor to CAPPS continues.

This screening function should be performed by the TSA, and it should utilize the lager set of watchlists maintained by the federal government. Air carriers should be required to supply information needed to test and implement this new system.

- The TSA and the Congress must give priority attention to improving the ability of screening checkpoints to detect explosives on passengers. As a start, each individual selected for special screening should be screened for explosives. Further, the TSA should conduct a human factors study, a method often used in the private sector, to understand problems in screener performance and set attainable objectives for individual screeners and for the checkpoints where screening takes place.

- As the President determines the guidelines for information sharing among government agencies and by those agencies with the private sector, he should safeguard the privacy of individuals about whom information is shared.

- The burden of proof for retaining a particular governmental power should be on the executive, to explain (a) that the power actually materially enhances security and (b) that there is adequate supervision of the executive's use of the powers to ensure protection of civil liberties. If the power is granted, there must be adequate guidelines and oversight to properly confine its use.

- At this time of increased and consolidated government authority, there should be a board within the executive branch to oversee adherence to the guidelines we recommend and the commitment the government makes to defend our civil liberties.

- Homeland security assistance should be based strictly on an assessment of risks and vulnerabilities. Now, in 2004, Washington, D.C., and New York City are certainly at the top of any such list. We understand the contention that every state and city needs to have some minimum infrastructure for emergency response. But federal homeland security assistance should not remain a program for general revenue sharing. It should supplement state and local resources based on the risks or vulnerabilities that merit additional support. Congress should not use this money as a pork barrel.

- Emergency response agencies nationwide should adopt the Incident Command System (ICS). When multiple agencies or multiple jurisdictions are involved, they should adopt a unified command. Both are proven frameworks for emergency response. We strongly support the decision that federal homeland security funding will be contingent, as of October 1, 2004, upon the adoption and regular use of ICS and unified command procedures. In the future, the Department of Homeland Security should consider making funding contingent on aggressive and realistic training in accordance with ICS and unified command procedures.

- Congress should support pending legislation which provides for expedited and increased assignment of radio spectrum for public safety purposes. Furthermore, high-risk urban areas such as New York City and Washington, D.C., should establish signal corps units to ensure communications connectivity between and among civilian authorities, local first responders, and the National Guard. Federal funding should be given high priority by Congress.

- We endorse the American National Standards Institute's recommended standard for private preparedness. We were encouraged by Secretary Tom Ridge's praise of the standard, and urge the Department of Homeland Security to promote its adoption. We also encourage the insurance and credit-rating industries to look closely at a company's compliance with the ANSI standard in assessing its insurability and creditworthiness. We believe that compliance with the standard should define the standard of care owed by a company to its employees and the public for legal purposes. Private-sector preparedness is not a luxury; it is a cost of doing business in the post-9/11 world. It is ignored at a tremendous potential cost in lives, money, and national security.

2004   Executive Orders

The following four Executive Orders (EOs) were issued by President Bush on 27 August 2004. Many of the provisions of these EOs—strengthening management of IC and creation of the NCTC—are interim measures to be taken until Congress enacts legislation.

Executive Order Strengthening Management of the Intelligence Community[661]

- Amended EO 12333. Until the NID is created, the DCI has all of the responsibilities outlined in this EO.

- Acts as principal advisor to the President for intelligence.

---

[661] U.S. President, "Executive Order Strengthened Management of the Intelligence Community," 27 August 2004, URL: www.whitehouse.gov/news/releases/2004/08/20040827-6.html, accessed 2 September 2004.

- Develop objectives and guidance for IC collection, processing, analysis, and dissemination of intelligence of whatever nature and source
- Coordinate the annual consolidated NFIP budget and report to President the effectiveness of implementation of NFIP by IC
- Recommend and concur in selection of IC heads
- Supervise the newly created NCTC
- Set standards and qualifications for training, education, career development of personnel and the establishment of common security policies within IC
- Determine intelligence collection priorities, manage collection tasking, and resolve conflicts in tasking of national collection assets
- Ensure integrated intelligence collection against enduring and emerging national security threats

Executive Order for a National Counterterrorism Center[662]

- Serve as the primary organization in the U.S. Government for analyzing and integrating terrorism and counterterrorism information, excepting purely domestic counterterrorism information.
- Conduct strategic operational planning for counterterrorism activities integrating all instruments of national power
- Assign operational responsibilities to lead agencies for counterterrorism activities
- Ensure that agencies have access to and receive all source intelligence to execute their counterterrorism plans or perform independent, alternative analysis.
- Serve as central knowledge bank on known and suspected terrorists and international terror groups

Executive Order Strengthening the Sharing of Terrorism Information with the Public[663]

- Agencies that possess or acquire information must give access to terrorism information to other agency heads with counterterrorism functions while protecting individual privacy under the law

---

[662] U.S. President, "Executive Order National Counterterrorism Center,"27 August 2004, URL: www.whitehouse.gov/news/releases/2004/08/20040827-5.html, accessed 2 September 2004.

[663] U.S. President, "Executive Order Strengthening the Sharing of Terrorism Informationn to Americans,"27 August 2004, URL: www.whitehouse.gov/news/releases/2004/08/20040827-4.html, accessed 2 September 2004.

- Establish common standards for terrorism information within the IC. Improve information sharing by: protecting sources and methods while also creating unclassified versions whenever possible; minimizing compartmentalization whenever possible; being free of originator controls whenever possible; creating incentives for information sharing

Establish Information Systems Council to plan for and oversee the proposed interoperable terrorism information environment to facilitate the sharing of terrorism information among appropriate agencies

Executive Order Establishing the President's Board on Safeguarding Americans' Civil Liberties[664]

- Advance the policy of protecting the legal rights of all Americans, including freedoms, civil liberties, and information privacy guaranteed by federal law
- Board advises President on effective means to implement the Policy
- Board is Chaired by Deputy Attorney General and Vice-Chair is Undersecretary for Border and Transportation Security DHS. Members include senior officers from DOJ, FBI, DHS, CIA, NSA, DoD, OMB, Treasury, TTIC

---

[664] U.S. President, "Executive Order Establishing the President's Board on Safeguarding Americans' Civil Liberties,"27 August 2004, URL: <www.whitehouse.gov/news/releases/2004/08/20040827-3.html>, accessed 2 September 2004.

APPENDIX F — GAO Human Capital Management Reference Tables

Table 7-3 Key Practices and Implementation Steps for Mergers and Transformations*

Practice	Implementation Steps
Ensure top leadership drives the transformation.	■ Define and articulate a succinct and compelling reason for change. ■ Balance continued delivery of services with merger and transformation activities.
Establish a coherent mission and integrated strategic goals to guide the transformation.	■ Adopt leading practices for results-oriented strategic planning and reporting.
Focus on a key set of principles and priorities at the outset of transformation	■ Embed core values in every aspect of the organization to reinforce the new culture.
Set implementation goals and a timeline to build momentum and show progress from day one.	■ Make public implementation goals and timeline. ■ Seek and monitor employee attitudes and take appropriate follow-up actions. ■ Identify cultural features of merging organizations to increase understanding of former work environments. ■ Attract and retain key talent. ■ Establish an organizational knowledge and skills inventory to exchange knowledge among merging organizations.
Dedicate an implementation team to manage the transformation process.	■ Establish networks to support implementation team. ■ Select high-performing team members.
Use the performance management system to define the responsibility and assure accountability for change.	■ Adopt leading practices to implement effective performance management systems with adequate safeguards.
Establish a communication strategy to create shared expectations and report related progress.	■ Communicate early and often to build trust ■ Ensure consistency of message. ■ Encourage two-way communication. ■ Provide information to meet specific needs of employees.
Involve employees to obtain their ideas and gain ownership for the transformation.	■ Use employee teams. ■ Involve employees in planning and sharing performance information. ■ Incorporate employee feedback into new policies and procedures. ■ Delegate authority to appropriate organizational levels.
Involve employees to obtain their ideas and gain ownership for the transformation.	■ Adopt leading practices to build a world-class organization.

* Government Accountability Office, Human Capital Considerations Critical to 9/11 Commission's Proposed Reforms (Washington, D.C: GPO, 14 September 2004), 5. Cited hereafter as GAO Human Capital Report.

Table 7-4 Key Practices for Effective Performance Management**

1. Align individual performance expectations with organizational goals. . An explicit alignment helps individuals see the connection between their daily activities and organizational goals.

2. Connect performance expectations to crosscutting goals. Placing an emphasis on collaboration, interaction, and teamwork across organizational boundaries helps strengthen accountability for results.

3. Provide and routinely use performance information to track organizational priorities. Individuals use performance information to manage during the year, identify performance gaps, and pinpoint improvement opportunities.

4. Require follow-up actions to address organizational priorities. By requiring and tracking follow-up actions on performance gaps, organizations underscore the importance of holding individuals accountable for making progress on their priorities.

5. Use competence to provide a fuller assessment of performance. Competencies define the skills and supporting behaviors that individuals need to effectively contribute to organizational results.

6. Link pay to individual and organizational performance. Pay, incentive, and reward systems that link employee knowledge, skills, and contributions to organizational results are based on valid, reliable, and transparent performance management systems with adequate safeguards.

7. Make meaningful distinctions in performance. Effective performance management systems strive to provide candid and constructive feedback and the necessary objective information and documentation to reward top performers and deal with poor performance.

8. Involve employees and stakeholders to gain ownership of performance management systems. Early and direct involvement helps increase employees' and stakeholders' understanding and ownership of the system and belief in its fairness.

9. Maintain continuity during transitions. Because cultural transformations take time, performance management systems reinforce accountability for change management and other organizational goals.

** GAO Human Capital Report, 8

Appendix G — Intelligence Reform and Terrorism Prevention Act of 2004

The following outline and highlights were extracted from the United States Senate Committee on Governmental Affairs *Summary of Intelligence Reform and Terrorism Prevention Act of 2004*.[665] With the exception of ZERO provisions for congressional oversight reform, this Act provided agency- and department-wide reform provisions. For brevity, only selected elements relating to the IC are highlighted; only headings are provided for all others. For a more comprehensive review of this Act, see U.S. Congress, Senate, *Intelligence Reform and Terrorism Prevention Act of 2004 Conference Report*, 108th Cong. 2nd sess. S-2845 or the Governmental Affairs Committee Summary.

TITLE I

Director of National Intelligence

Establishes a Senate-confirmed Director of National Intelligence (DNI). The DNI cannot serve as the Director of the CIA or as the head of any other element of the IC. The DNI shall not be located in the Executive Office of the President.

National Intelligence Program

The National Foreign Intelligence Program is re-designated as the National Intelligence Program (NIP).

Authorities of the DNI

Budget Build: DNI shall "develop and determine" the annual NIP based on proposals provided by respective IC agency and organization heads. The IC agency and organization heads must also furnish the DNI any additional requested budgetary information.

Budget Execution: DNI shall "ensure the effective execution" of the annual intelligence and intelligence-related activities budget. The Director OMB must apportion NIP funds at the "exclusive direction" of the DNI for IC allocation. The DNI "directs the allotment or allocations" of such appropriations. Department comptrollers are then responsible for allocating, reprogramming, or transferring NIP funds "in an expeditious manner." The DNI "shall monitor the implementation and execution of the NIP by the heads of elements of the IC". If a department

---

[665]United States Congress, Senate, Committee on Governmental Affairs, Summary of Intelligence Reform and Terrorist Prevention Act of 2004, 108th Cong. 2nd sess., 6 December 2004

comptroller acted in a manner not consistent with the direction of the DNI, the DNI must notify the President and Congress within 15 days of such discovery.

Transfer and Reprogramming of Funds: DNI directs all transfers and reprogramming of NIP funds under the following guidelines: 1) must be for a higher priority intelligence activity; 2) must support an emergent need, improve program effectiveness, or increase efficiency; and 3) may not involve funds from the CIA Reserve for Contingencies or a DNI Reserve for Contingencies. This NIP fund transfer or reprogram must be approved by OMB after consulting with the affected department heads and must be less than $150 million or less than 5 percent of the department's or agency's NIP funds for a single fiscal year. Furthermore, it cannot terminate an acquisition program. If the affected department head concurs then these limits do not apply.

Transfer of Personnel: The DNI is authorized 500 new personnel billets. Also, the DNI may transfer 150 NIP personnel to the Office of the DNI for not more than two years. Within the first year after the creation of the national intelligence center, the DNI may transfer 100 Community personnel to that center. OMB Director must approve and appropriate Congressional committees must be notified of such transfers. DNI can transfer unlimited numbers of personnel within the Community providing these transfers 1) are to higher priority intelligence activities; 2) support an emergent need, improve program effectiveness, or increase efficiency. Appropriate Congressional committees must be notified of such transfers.

Tasking and Analysis: DNI established objectives and priorities for the IC and manages and directs tasking of collection, analysis, production, and dissemination of national intelligence. DNI approves requirements for collection and analysis. DNI may establish national intelligence centers as necessary.

Personnel Management: DNI, in consultation with heads of other IC agencies, develops personnel policies and programs. Rotation policies should seek to duplicate within the IC the joint officer management policies established by the Goldwater-Nichols Department of Defense Reorganization Act of 1986.

Protection of Sources and Methods: DNI shall protect sources and methods from unauthorized disclosure and is responsible for classification guidelines.

Foreign Liaison: DNI coordinates relationships between intelligence or security services for foreign governments or international organizations.

Acquisition/Milestone: DNI has same acquisition and appropriation authorities given the CIA Director in the CIA Act of 1949 with the exception of using funds without regard to any law or regulation concerning the expenditure of funds. DNI has exclusive milestone decision authority for NIP-funded major systems with the exception of those DoD programs for which the DNI has joint authority with the SecDef. If DNI and SecDef cannot reach agreement then the President resolves.

Common Services: DNI consults with heads of other IC agencies to determine if common concern efforts can be accomplished more efficiently in a consolidated manner.

Appointments: DNI recommends to the President nominees for Principal Deputy DNI and for CIA Director. DNI has right to concur in the appointment or recommendation for the heads of NSA, NRO, and NGA; the Assistant Secretary of State for INR; the Directors of the Offices of Intelligence and Counterintelligence at DOE; the Assistant Secretary for Intelligence and Analysis and the Department of Treasury; the Executive Assistant Director for Intelligence at the FBI; and the Assistant Secretary for Homeland Security for Information Analysis. Also, the DNI must be consulted for appointments or recommendations for the Director of DIA and the Deputy Assistant Commandant of the Coast Guard for Intelligence.

Office of the DNI

Staff: CMS will transfer to Office of the DNI.

Co-Location: Beginning 1 October 2008, the Office of the DNI will not be co-located with any other IC element.

Deputy Directors: Senate-confirmed Principal Deputy DNI. Principal Deputy DNI may appoint not more than four additional deputies.

National Intelligence Council: Is established in the Office of the DNI.

General Counsel: Senate-confirmed General Counsel in the Office of the DNI.

Civil Liberties Protection Officer: Appointed by the DNI.

Director of Science and Technology: Established within the Office of the DNI.

National Counterintelligence Executive: Moved to the Office of the DNI.

Inspector General: Established within the Office of the DNI.

Definition of National Intelligence

Revised definition of national intelligence includes information gathered in the U.S. or abroad that pertains to more than one agency and involves threats to the U.S., its people, property, or interests; the development, proliferation, or use of weapons of mass destruction; or any other matter bearing on national or homeland security.

Information Sharing

Requires the President to establish an Information Sharing Environment (ISE) to facilitate the sharing of terrorism information among all appropriate Federal, State, local, tribal and private sector entities. This provision calls for specific implementation of information sharing activities to be completed by a specified date, e.g., within 180 days of enactment, agency-wide capabilities review must be completed; within 270 days President must issue guidelines for acquiring, accessing, sharing and using information, and in consultation with the Privacy and Civil Liberties Oversight Board provide guidelines to protect privacy and civil liberties.

President will designate a Program Manager who is responsible for information sharing across the Federal Government and who will oversee the implementation and management of the ISE. An interagency panel, based on the Information Sharing Council created by EO 13356, will be established to advise the President and Program Manager and to facilitate interagency coordination.

Privacy and Civil Liberties

Privacy and Civil Liberties Oversight Board: Created within the Executive Office of the President to ensure that privacy and civilian liberties concerns are considered in the implementation of laws, regulations, and executive branch policies related to efforts to protect the nation against terrorism. Board will comprise a Senate-confirmed chairman and Senate-confirmed vice chairman as well as three other members appointed by the President. All members serve at the pleasure of the President.

Analysis

Alternative Analysis: DNI shall establish a process and assign an individual or entity the responsibility of ensuring that IC elements conduct alternative analysis.

Safeguarding Objectivity in Intelligence Analysis: DNI shall identify an individual with the Office of the DNI who is available to analysts within the Office of the DNI to counsel, conduct arbitration, offer recommendations, and as appropriate, initiate inquiries into real or perceived problems of analytical tradecraft or politicization, biased reporting, or lack of objectivity in intelligence analysis.

Analytical Integrity: DNI shall assign an individual or entity to ensure that finished intelligence products produced by any IC element are timely, objective, independent of political considerations, based on all sources of available intelligence, and employ the standards of proper analytic tradecraft. The individual or entity assigned this responsibility, on a regular basis, shall conduct detailed reviews of IC's finished intelligence product to determine whether product was based on all sources of available intelligence, properly described the quality and reliability of underlying sources, properly caveated and expressed uncertainties or confidence in analytic judgments, and properly distinguished between underlying intelligence and the assumptions and judgments of analysts.

Preservation of Authorities

President shall issue guidelines to ensure effective implementation of the authorities provided to the DNI in a manner that does not abrogate the statutory responsibilities of the Director of OMB or heads of executive branch departments.

National Counterterrorism Center

National Counter Terrorism Center is established in the Office of the DNI. Director is Senate-confirmed and may not simultaneously serve in any other capacity in the executive branch. Director reports to the DNI on budget and intelligence matters, but to the President on the planning and progress of joint counterterrorism operations (other than intelligence operations). NCTC conducts "strategic operational planning"—defined as the mission, the objectives to be achieved, the tasks to be performed, interagency coordination of operational activities, and the assignment of roles and responsibilities. NCTC Director monitors the implementation of strategic operational plans and obtains relevant information from departments and agencies on the progress of such entities in implementing the plans.

National Counterproliferation Center

National Counterproliferation Center shall be established within 18 months after enactment or President may waive this requirement if President determines that it does not materially improve the government's ability to halt the proliferation of weapons of mass destruction. Waiver must be in writing and submitted to Congress.

National Intelligence Centers

DNI is authorized to establish National Intelligence Centers (NICs) to address intelligence priorities. Within their areas of intelligence responsibility, these centers will have primary responsibility for providing all-source analysis and for identifying and proposing to the DNI intelligence collection and production requirements. DNI will ensure the NICs are sufficiently staffed and that the IC shares information to facilitate their mission. Each will have a separate budget account.

Joint Intelligence Community Council

Chaired by the DNI. Membership includes the Secretaries of State, Treasury, Defense, Energy, and Homeland Security, the Attorney General and other presidential-designees. JICC assists the DNI by advising on budget and other matters and by ensuring the timely execution of the programs, policies, and directives of the DNI.

Education and Training

DNI develops a comprehensive education, recruitment, and training plan to meet linguistic requirements for the IC. DNI will bring together Community educational components to promote joint education and training. DNI established an IC Scholarship Program for students in exchange for IC service.

Open Source Intelligence

DNI ensures that the IC makes efficient and effective use of open source information and analysis.

Effective Date/Implementation Plan

Title I is to take effect no later than six months after enactment (NLT 17 June 2005). President will submit to Congress an implementation plan NLT 180 days after effective date. Within 60 days of the DNI's initial appointment, the DNI will appoint individual to Office of the DNI positions.

"Lookback" Provision

DNI will submit to the Congressional intelligence committees NLT one year after the effective day of the Act, a report on the progress made to implement this title and such recommendations for additional legislative or administrative action as the DNI considers appropriate.

TITLE II

Federal Bureau of Investigation

FBI is given authority to raise the mandatory retirement age to 65 years of age for 50 FBI employees per fiscal year through 30 September 2007 (basically two years after enactment). FBI has discretionary authority to establish and train a reserve service for the temporary reemployment of up to 500 former FBI employees during periods of emergency.

TITLE III

Security Clearances

President designates a single entity to oversee the security clearance process and develop uniform standards and policies for access to classified information. The President also designates a single entity to conduct clearance investigations. Establishes a national database to track clearances.

TITLE IV —TRANSPORTATION SECURITY

Subtitle A-National Strategy for Transportation Security

Subtitle B-Aviation Security

Subtitle C-Air Cargo Security

Subtitle D-Maritime Security

TITLE V — BORDER PROTECTION, IMMIGRATION AND VISA MATTERS

Subtitle A-Advanced Technology Northern Border Security Pilot Program

Subtitle B-Border and Immigration Enforcement

Subtitle C-Visa Requirements

Subtitle D-Immigration Reform

Subtitle E-Treatment of Aliens Who Commit Acts of Torture, Extrajudicial Killings, or Other Atrocities Abroad

TITLE VI — TERRORISM PREVENTION

Subtitle A-Individual Terrorists As Agents of Foreign Powers ("Lone Wolf" Provision)

Subtitle B-Money Laundering and Terrorist Financing

Subtitle C-Money Laundering Abatement and Financial Antiterrorism Technical Corrections

Subtitle D-Additional Enforcement Tools

Subtitle E-Criminal History Background Checks

Subtitle F-Grand Jury Information Sharing

Subtitle G-Providing Material Support to Terrorism

Subtitle H-Terrorist and Military Hoaxes

Subtitle I-Weapons of Mass Destruction Prohibition Improvement Act

Subtitle J-Prevention of Terrorist Access to Destructive Weapons Act of 2004

Subtitle K-Pretrial Detention of Terrorists

TITLE VII — 9/ll COMMISSION IMPLEMENTATION ACT OF 2004

Subtitle A-The Role of Diplomacy, Foreign Aid, and the Military in the War on Terrorism

Subtitle B-Terrorist Travel and Effective Screening

Subtitle C-National Preparedness

Subtitle D-Homeland Security Grants

Subtitle E-Public Safety Spectrum

Subtitle F-Presidential Transition

Subtitle G-Improving International Standards and Cooperation to Fight Terrorist Financing

Subtitle H-Emergency Financial Preparedness

TITLE VIII – GENERAL PROVISIONS

Subtitle A-Intelligence Matters

The NID shall establish a formal relationship, including information sharing, between elements of the IC and the National Infrastructure Simulation Center.

Subtitle B-Department of Homeland Security Matters

Subtitle C-Homeland Security Civil Rights and Civil Liberties Protection

Subtitle D-Other Matters

Acronyms

ADCI	Assistant Deputy Director Central Intelligence
AFCEA	Armed Forces Communications and Electronics Association
ASA	Army Security Agency
BNE	Board of National Estimates
CBJB	Congressional Budget Justification Book
CIA	Central Intelligence Agency
CIG	Central Intelligence Group
CIO	Central Imagery Office
CIRAS	Corporate Information Retrieval System
CMS	Community Management Staff
CP	Command Post
CPI	Corruption Perceptions Index
CSI	Center for the Study of Intelligence
CTC	Counterterrorism Center
C41	Command and Control, Communications, Computers, Intelligence
DARO	Defense Airborne Reconnaissance Office
DCI	Director Central Intelligence
DCSINT	Deputy Chief of Staff for Intelligence
DDNI	Deputy Director for National Intelligence
DDPO	Defense Dissemination Program Office
DI	Directorate of Intelligence
DIA	Defense Intelligence Agency
DMA	Defense Mapping Agency
DMI	Director of Military Intelligence
DNI	Director for National Intelligence
EO	Executive Order
FBI	Federal Bureau of Investigation
EEI	Essential Elements of Information
FEMA	Federal Emergency Management Agency
GAO	Government Accountability Office
GDP	Gross Domestic Product
HAC	House Appropriations Committee
HI	Horizontal Integration
HSTL	Harry S. Truman Library
HPSCI	House Permanent Select Committee on Intelligence
HSPD	Homeland Security Presidential Directive
HUMINT	Human Intelligence
IRAC	Intelligence Resources Advisory Committee

IC	Intelligence Community
ICS	Intelligence Community Staff
IG	Inspector General
IAAFY	Intelligence Authorization Act Fiscal Year
IMINT	Imagery Intelligence
IOB	Intelligence Oversight Board
IT	Information Technology
IWGS	Interagency Working Group on Space
JCS	Joint Chiefs of Staff
JITF-CT	Joint Intelligence Task Force-Counterterrorism
JMIP	Joint Military Intelligence Program
MASINT	Measurement and Signals Intelligence
NCTC	National Counterterrorism Center
NDI	National Director for Intelligence
NFIP	National Foreign Intelligence Program
NGA	National Geospatial-Intelligence Agency
NHSA	National Homeland Security Agency
NIA	National Intelligence Authority
NIAD	National Intelligence Authority Directive
NIC	National Intelligence Council
NIMA	National Imagery and Mapping Agency
NIE	National Intelligence Estimate
NIO	National Intelligence Officers
NMIA	National Military Intelligence Association
NPIC	National Photographic Interpretation Center
NRO	National Reconnaissance Office
NSA	National Security Agency
NSCID	National Security Council Intelligence Directive
NSEA	National Security Education Act
NSSC	National Security Service Corps
NSSG	National Security Study Group
OMB	Office of Management and Budget
ONE	Office of National Estimates
ONI	Office of Naval Intelligence
OPM	Office of Personnel Management
OSD	Office of Secretary of Defense
OSS	Office of Strategic Services
OOTW	Operations Other Than War
PE	Program Element
PFIAB	President's Foreign Intelligence Advisory Board
PL	Public Law

RIA	Revolution in Intelligence Affairs
RMA	Revolution in Military Affairs
SAC	Senate Appropriations Committee
SES	Senior Executive Service
SIGINT	Signals Intelligence
SIPRNET	Secret Internet Protocol Router Network
SMO	Support to Military Operations
SOLIC	Special Operations Low-Intensity Conflict
SRG	Strategic Resources Group
SSCI	Senate Select Committee on Intelligence
TRADOC	Training and Doctrine Command
TSA	Transportation Security Agency
TSC	Terrorist Screening Center
TIARA	Tactical Intelligence and Related Activities
UN	United Nations
USIB	United States Intelligence Board
WMD	Weapons of Mass Destruction

Bibliography

"A Special Relationship? The US and UK Spying Alliance Is Put Under the Spotlight." *London Financial Times,* 6 July 2004.

Ackerman, Robert K. "Horizontal Integration Challenges Intelligence Planner." *Signal* 58, no. 2, October 2003. Accessed via ProQuest, 22 January 2004.

"Airport Security Still Lacking." *Washington Post,* 23 September 2004, E2.

Allen, Charles E. "Intelligence: Cult, Craft, or Business?" Briefing presented at Center for Information Policy Research, Harvard University, Guest Presentations, Spring 2000. Incidental Paper: Seminar on Intelligence, Command and Control, July 2001. URL: *http://pirp.harvard.edu/pubs_pdf/allen/allen-i01.pdf>.* Accessed 1 April 2004.

Allen, Mike and Dan Eggen. "Bush May Move Soon on 9/11 Report: President Close to Announcing Plans for Revamping Intelligence System." *Washington Post,* 29 July 2004, A6.

———."Bush Backs off Limit on 9/11 Questioning: Talk to Panel Leaders to be Open-Ended." *Washington Post,* 10 March 2004, A3.

Alliot-Marie, Michele. "Afghanistan's Drug Boom: The Opium Problem Could Undo Everything That's Being Done to Help the Afghan People." *Washington Post,* 6 October 2004, A27.

Appendix I of *Results of the 1973 Church Committee Hearings on CIA Misdeeds, and the 1984 Iran/Contra Hearings.* URL: <http://pw1.netcom./ ncoic/cia_info.htm. Accessed 3 August 2004.

Ashcroft, John C. "Transcript: 9/11 Commission Hearing." *Washington Post,* online ed., 13 April 2004, URL: *<http://www.washingtonpost.com/ac2/wp-dyn/A9088-2004Apr13?language=printer>.* Accessed 14 April 2004.

Babington, Charles. "Hill Wary of Intelligence Oversight Changes, Lawmakers from Both Parties Resist Recommendations of 9/11 Commission." *Washington Post,* 12 September 2004, A5.

Baenen, Jeff. "9/11 Report Is Up for National Book Award." *Washington Post,* 14 October 2004, C4.

Bainbridge,W.S. Speech presented at 2003 Nanotechnology Conference and Trade Show, "Converging Technologies." San Francisco, CA, 23-27 February 2003.URL: *<http://mysite.verizon.net//william.bainbridge/dl/nbic.htm>.* Accessed 13 October 2004.

Baker, Peter and Walter Pincus. "Bush Signs Intelligence Reform Bill: President Now Must Find an Experienced Hand to Guide 15 Agencies." *Washington Post,* 18 December 2004, A1.

Bamford, James. *The Puzzle Palace: A Report on America's Most Secret Agency.* Boston: Houghton Mifflin Company, 1982.

Bardach, A.L. "Interrogation: Listen to the Admiral." *Slate,* online ed., 16 December 2004, URL: <http://.slate.msn.com>. Accessed 17 December 2004

Barger, Deborah G. "It is Time to Transform, Not Reform, U.S. Intelligence." *SAIS Review*, 24, no. 1 Winter-Spring 2004: 23-31.

Barnett, Thomas P.M. *The Pentagon's New Map*. New York: G.P. Putnam's Sons, 2004.

———."The Pentagon's New Map: It Explains Why We're Going to War, And Why We'll Keep Going to War." *Esquire*, 1 March 2003. Accessed via ProQuest 11 May 2004.

Barr, Stephen. "GAO Chief Refuses to Stop Doing the Math." *Washington Post*, 18 January 2004, C2.

———."NSA Makes No Secret of Stepped-Up Recruitment Effort." *Washington Post*, 22 April 2004, B2.

———."Pentagon Can Hire 2,500 Experts for National Security." *Washington Post*, 26 March 2004, B2.

———."Talk of 9/11 Report Centers on Importance of People, Rather Than Structure." *Washington Post*, 15 September 2004, B2.

Bender, Bryan. "US Intelligence Shake-Up Meets Growing Criticism." *Boston Globe*, 2 January 2004, A1.

Berkowitz, Bruce. "Better Ways to Fix Intelligence." *Orbis*, 45, no. 4 (Fall 2001): 609-619.

———."The DI and "IT:" Failing to Keep Up With the Information Revolution," *Studies in Intelligence* 47, no. 1. (2003): 67-74.

———. *The New Face of War: How War Will Be Fought in the 21st Century*. New York: The Free Press, 2003.

Berkowitz, Bruce D. and Allen E. Goodman. *Best Truth: Intelligence in the Information Age*. New Haven, CT: Yale University Press, 2000.

———. *Strategic Intelligence for American Security*. Princeton: Princeton University Press, 1989.

Best, Richard A., Jr. "Proposals for Intelligence Reorganization, 1949-2004." *CRS Report for Congress*. RL32500. Washington, D.C.: Congressional Research Service, Library of Congress, 29 July 2004.>URL: *http://www.fas.org/irp/crs/RL32500.pdf*>. Accessed 25 August 2004.

———."Reforming Defense Intelligence." *CRS Report for Congress*, 91-475 F. Washington, D.C.: Congressional Research Service, Library of Congress, 1 June 1991.

Best, Richard A., Jr. and Herbert Andrew Boerstling. "Appendix C, IC21: The Intelligence Community in the 21st Century," *CRS Report for Congress*. Washington, D.C.: Congressional Research Service, Library of Congress, 28 February 1996. *URL:<http://www.access.gpo.gov/congress/house/intel/ic21/ic21018.html>*. Accessed 11 May 2004.

Betts, Richard K. "Fixing Intelligence." *Foreign Affairs*. 81, no. 1 (January/February 2002): 43-59.

Bhagwati, Fagdish. "Coping with Antiglobalization: A Triology of Discontents." *Foreign Affairs*, 81, no.1 (January/February 2002): 2-7.

"Bin Laden Lieutenant Admits to September 11 and Explains Al-Qa'ida's Combat Doctrine." *Middle East Review of International Relations,* Special Dispatch Series No. 344, 10 February 2002. URL: <http://www.memri.org/bin articles.cgi?Page=subjects&Area=jihad&ID=SP34402.

Black, Cofer. "Investigation of Sept 11 Intelligence Failures." 26 September 2002. Accessed via LexisNexis, 12 January 2004.

Book World. "Washington Area Bestsellers." *Washington Post,* 12 September 2004,11.

Borch, Fred L. "Comparing Pearl Harbor and "9/11": Intelligence Failure? American Unpreparedness? Military Responsibility? *Journal of Military History,* 67, no. 3 (July 2003). Accessed Proquest 4 December 2003.

Boren, David L., Sen. (D-OK). "The Intelligence Community: How Crucial?" *Foreign Affairs,* 71, no.3 (Summer 1992): 52-62.

Bowens, Gregory J. "Clinton Accepts Budget Freeze, Vows to Fight Deeper Cuts." *Congressional Quarterly Weekly Report,* 31 July 1993, 2077.

Bowers, Faye. "The New Top in Redrawn US Intelligence." *Christian Science Monitor,* 15 December 2004, 2.

Breitweiser,Karen. "Investigation of Sept 11." 18 September 2002. Accessed via Lexis Nexis, 12 January 2004.

Brezinski, Zbigniew. *Choice: Global Domination or Global Leadership.* New York: Basic Books, 2004.

Budget of the United States Government, Fiscal Year 2005 Budget Reform Proposals, U.S. *Government Printing Office.* URL: *<http://frwebgate4.access.gpo.gov/cgi-bin/waisgate.cgi?WAISdocID=08729814703+41+0+...>.* Accessed 21 August 2004.

Central Intelligence Agency. *Global Trends 2015: A Dialogue About the Future with Non government Experts.* NIC2000-02, December 2000, <http: //www.cia.gov/cia/reports/globaltrends2015 >. Accessed 29 September 2004.

———. *Intelligence for a New Era in American Foreign Policy.* Presented in Center for the Study of Intelligence Conference Report, January 2004.

Christensen, Clayton M. *The Innovator's Dilemma: When New Technologies Cause Great Firms to Fail.* Boston: Harvard Business School Press, 1997.

Clapper, James R. Clapper, Jr., Lt Gen, USAF (Ret). "A Proposed Restructuring of the Intelligence Community." Briefing presented at Center for Information Policy Research, Harvard University, Guest Presentations, Spring 1996. Incidental Paper: Seminar on Intelligence, Command and Control, January 1997. URL: http://pirp.harvard.edu/pubs_pdf/clapper/clapper-i97-1.pdf>. Accessed 1 April 2004.

———.Director, National Geospatial-Intelligence Agency. E-mail to NGA workforce. Subject: "D-MAIL #16 – D/NGA Testimony Before HPSCI on 9/11Commission Report." 19 August 2004.

Cline, Ray. *Secrets, Spies, and Scholars.* Washington, DC: Acropolis Books, 1976.

Cloud, David S. "Huge Challenge Awaits Intelligence Chief." *Wall Street Journal,* 21 December 2004, A4.

Cohen, William S. "Restructuring: From the Top...." *Washington Post,* 1 August 2004, B1+.

Cohen, Richard. "Bonne Chance." *Washington Post Magazine,* 11 July 1993, 3.

Colby, William. *Honorable Men.* New York: Simon and Schuster, 1978.

Commercial Observation Satellites: At the Leading Edge of Global Transparency. Eds. John C. Baker, Ray A. Williamson, and Kevin M. O'Connell. Arlington, VA: RAND, 2001.

Congressional Research Service. *H.R. 10 (9/11 Recommendations Implementation Act) and S.2845 (National Intelligence Reform Act of 2004): A Comparative Analysis.* Updated 21 October 2004.

Cronin, Audrey Kurth. "Behind the Curve: Globalization and International Terrorism. *International Security* 27, no.3 (Winter 2002/03): 30-58.

Davies, Frank. "Graham, 2 Allies Introduce Overhaul of U.S. Intelligence." Miami Herald, 1 August 2003, 17A.

DeBose, Brian. "House OKs Intelligence Reform Bill," *The Washington Times,* 8 December 2004, A1+.

———."Senate Approves Intelligence Bill." *The Washington Times,* 9 December 2004, A1+.

Dewar, Helen. "Another Congress to Return for Another Lame-Duck Stint: Post-Election Meetings to Finish Work Set for Mid-November." *Washington Post,* 27 October 2004, A23.

———."Senators Offer New Oversight Structure: Intelligence Panels Would be Reworked." *Washington Post,* 5 October 2004, A4.

Diamond, John. "Intelligence Impasse Mainly a Question of Control: But Civilians, Military Share Power Already." *USA Today,* 29 November 2004, 6.

Dionne, E.J., Jr. "A Lesson From 9/11: Openness." *Washington Post,* 23 July 2004, A29.

Dowd, Maureen "Head Spook Sputters." *New York Times,* online ed., 15 April 2004. URL: *http://www.nytimes.com/2004/04/15/opinion/15DOWD.html?th=&page wanted=print& pos....* Accessed 19 April 2004.

Drogin, Bob. "THE NATION: Two Agencies Melding Minds on Intelligence." *Los Angeles Times,* 31 December 2004. Accessed via Proquest, 7 January 2005.

Duffy, Michael."So Much For The WMD." *Time.* 9 February 2004, 42-46.

_____, "How to Fix Our Intelligence." *Time,* 26 April 2004, online ed., URL: *http://www.time.com/time/magazine/printout/0,8816,1101040426-612372.html.* Accessed 27 April 2004.

Eggen, Dan. "FBI Backlogged in Translation of Counterterrorism Wiretaps." *Washington Post,* 28 September 2004, A25.

————."FBI Names 6th Counterrorism Chief Since 9/11." *Washington Post,* 29 December 2004, A17.

————. "For the Record: While House vs. 9/11 Panel: Resistance, Resolution," *Washington Post,* 9 March 2004, A2.

————.GOP Plan Calls for Revamping Intelligence: Pentagon, CIA Would Give Up Many Duties." *Washington Post,* 23 August 2004, A1+.

————."9/11 Panel Chronicles U.S. Failures: Final Report Faults Two Administrations and Calls for Broad Reform." *Washington Post,* 23 July 2004, A1+.

Dan Eggen and Charles Barrington. "Many are Cool to Intelligence Plan: Bush Expresses Reservation; Tenet Says GOP Proposal Would 'Gut the CIA.'" *Washington Post,* 24 August 2004, A3

Dan Eggen and Helen Dewar. "Intelligence Reforms May be Stalled: 9/11 Panel Chief Fears Momentum Loss; Victims' Kin Critical." *Washington Post,* 15 October 2004, A13.

Dan Eggen and Susan Schmidt. "Data Show Different Spy Game Since 9/11." *Washington Post,* 1 May 2004, A1.

Dan Eggen and Walter Pincus. "House Member Seeks Gorelick's Resignation." *Washington Post,* 15 April 2004.

Dan Eggen and Walter Pincus. "Key Idea of 9/11 Panel is Faulted: Commission Seeks Intelligence Chief in White House." *Washington Post,* 31 July 2004, A1+.

Eilperin, Juliet. "U.S. Firms Look Ahead to Emissions Cuts Overseas: Whether Russia Ratifies Treaty is Key." *Washington Post,* 3 October 2004, A13.

Elkins, Dan, LDCR, USN (Ret.). *An Intelligence Resource Manager's Guide.* 5th ed. Washington, D.C.: Defense Intelligence Agency, 1997.

Farah, Douglas and Richard Shultz. "Al Qaeda's Growing Sanctuary." *Washington Post,* 14 July 2004, A19.

Fessler, Pamela. "Chairman Boren, McCurdy Urge Leaner, Revamped Operations." *Congressional Quarterly Weekly Report,* 8 February 1992: 316-317.

Flynn, Stephen E. "The Neglected Home Front." *Foreign Affairs,* 83, no. 5 (September/ October 2004): 20-33.

"Foreign Policy Association: DDO's Remark." 24 June 2004, URL: http://www.americanintelligence.us/modules.php?name=News&file=article&sid=18>. Accessed 26 June 2004.

"Framing the Problem of PPBS." *BENS Tail-to-Tooth Commission Report,* January 2000. URL: *http://www.bens.org/images/PPBS2000-Framing.pdf.* Accessed 10 November 2004.

Friedman, Thomas L. "Small and Smaller." New York Times, online ed., 4 March 2004. URL: http://www.nytimes.com/2004/03/04/opinion/04FRIE.html. Accessed 4 March 2004.

————. *The Lexus and the Olive Tree.* New York: Farrar, Straus and Gioux, 1999.

Francis Fukuyama and others. "Second Thoughts: The Last Man in the Bottle Responses." *The National Interest* 56 (Summer 1999). Accessed via Proquest, 24 November 2003.

Garcia, Michelle. "Nearly 100 Families are Suing Over 9/11: Federal Compensation is Forsaken." *Washington Post,* 23 January 2004, A9.

Gates, Robert M. *From The Shadows: The Ultimate Insider's Story of Five Presidents and How They Won The Cold War.* New York: Simon & Schuster, 1997.

"Global Terrorism, Strategy, and Naval Forces," Chapter 5 in *Globalization and Maritime Power.* Ed. Sam J. Tangredi. Washington, D.C.: National Defense University, 2002.

Globalization and Maritime Power. Ed. Sam J. Tangredi. Washington, D.C.: National University Press, 2002.

Goodman, Jr., Glenn W. "Interview with Stephen Cambone." Defense News. Online ed., 8 December 2003, *URL: http://www.defensenews.com/story.* Accessed 9 December 2003.

Goo, Sara Kehaulani. "Hundreds Report Watch-List Trials: Some Ended Hassles at Airports by Making Slight Change to Name." *Washington Post,* 21 August 2004, A8.

Gorelick, Jamie S. "The Truth about 'the Wall'." *Washington Post,* 18 April 2004, B7.

Gorman, Siobhan. "On Guard, But How Well?" *National Journal* (6 March 2004): 696-703.

Goss, Sen. Porter (R-FL). "An Inquiry That's Awash in Disputes at the Outset."Interview by Douglas Jehl. In New York Times, on line ed., 2 February 2004. URL: www.nytimes.com/2004/02/02international/middleeast/02ASSE.html. Accessed 2 February 2004.

Government Accountability Office, *Department of Defense: Status of Financial Management Weaknesses and Progress Towards Reform.* Washington, DC: GPO, 25 June 2003.

————. *Human Capital Considerations Critical to 9/11 Commission's Proposed Reforms.* Washington, D.C: GPO, 14 September 2004.

————. *Major Management Challenges and Program Risks: A Government Perspective.* Washington, DC: GPO, January 2003.

Graham, Bob, Sen. (D-FL). "Past Intelligence Failures Set Us Up For More." Interview by Marie Cocco. *Long Island Newsday,* 17 February 2004."

Graham, Bradley. "Intelligence Changes Concern Pentagon: Creation of New Director-May Hurt Military Operations, Officials Warn." *Washington Post,* 11 August 2004, A19.

Grier, Peter and Faye Bowers. "Can Spy Agencies Ever Work Together," *Christian Science Monitor,* 21 July 2004, 01

Grose, Peter. *Gentlemen Spy: The Life of Allen Dulles.* Boston: Houghton Mifflin, 1994.

Grove, Andrew. *Only the Paranoid Survive: How to Exploit the Crisis Points that Challenge Every Company and Career.* New York: Doubleday, 1996.

Haass, Richard. "Policymakers and the Intelligence Community: Supporting US Foreign Policy in the Post-9/11 World." *Studies in Intelligence* 46, no. 3 (2002). URL: *http://www.cia.gov/csi/studies/vol46no3/article01.html.* Accessed 24 March 2005.

Hagel, Sen. Chuck (R-NE). "Intelligence Reform and False Urgency." *Washington Post,* 3 August 2004, A17.

Haines, Gregory K. "Looking for a Rogue Elephant: The Pike Committee Investigations and the CIA." *Studies in Intelligence* (Winter 1998-1999): 81-90.

Hamilton, Lee H. Government Affairs Committee Hearing. *C-SPAN.* Airdate 30 July 2004.

Hart, Gary. "A Paul Revere No One Wants to Hear From." Salon.com, 6 April 2004.

———."Heeding the 9/11 Panel." Interview by David S. Broder. *Washington Post,* 8 August 2004, B07.

———. Speaker at the World Affairs Council of Northern California symposium, "Intelligence Community Reform." San Francisco, CA., 18 November 2003. Videotape viewed in the John T.Hughes Library on 1 June 2004.

Hayden, Michael V., LtGen, USAF. "Testimony before the Joint Inquiry of the Senate Select Committee on Intelligence and the House Permanent Select Committee, 17 October 2002." URL:http://www.fas.org/irp/congress/2002_hr/ 101702hayden.html.

"Headlines Over the Horizon: Analysts at the RAND Corporation Lay Out Ten International-Security Developments that Aren't Getting the Attention They Deserve." *Atlantic,* 292, no. 1 (July/August 2003): 84-90.

Heisbourg, Francois. "How the West Could Be Won." In "One Year After: A Grand Strategy for the West?" *Survival* 44, no 3 (Winter 2002-03): 145-155.

Hedley, John Hollister. Institute for the Study of Diplomacy, School of Foreign Service, Georgetown University. *ISD Occasional Paper 1: Checklist for the Future of Intelligence.* Gaithersburg, MD: Reproductions, Inc., 1995.

———."A Colloquium: The Intelligence Community—Is It Broken? How to Fix It? *Studies in Intelligence* 39, no. 5 (1994): 11-18.

Herrington, Keith E. "Inside DIA: Horizontal Integration—The Transformation Roadmap for U.S. Intelligence and the National Security Community." *Communiqué,* August 2004, 10.

Hersh, Seymour M. "Huge CIA Operation Reported in U.S. against Antiwar Forces, Other Dissidents in Nixon Years." *New York Times,* 22 December 1974, 1, 26.

Hill, Eleanor. "Investigation of Sept 11." 17 October 2002. Accessed via LexisNexis, 12 January 2004.

"Homeland Security Oversight." Editorial. *Washington Post,* 28 December 2004, A18.

"How a Bill Becomes Law. *Washington Post,* 18 August 2004, C14.

Hsu, Spencer S. "Anti-terror Network Launched: Agencies across Country to Share Computer Data." *Washington Post,* 25 February 2004, B1+.

Huband, Mark. "Ex-CIA Officer Dismisses Reforms." *London Financial Times,* 12 December 2004, A6.

Hubbard, Robert L. "Another Response to Terrorism: Reconstituting Intelligence Analysis for *21st* Century Requirement." *Defense Intelligence Journal,* 11, no. 1 2002): 71-80.

Hughes, Patrick M. "Future Conditions: The Character and Conduct of War, 2010 and 2020." Briefing presented at Center for Information Policy Research, Harvard University, Guest Presentations, Spring 2003. Incidental Paper: Seminar on Intelligence, Command and Control, July 2003. URL: <http://pirp.harvard.edu/Pubs-pdf/Hughes/Hughes-i03-1.pdf>. Accessed 1 April 2004.

Huntington, Samuel P. "The Hispanic Challenge." *Foreign Policy,* 141(March/April 2004): 30-53.

Hutchings, Robert. Chairman National Intelligence Council. Keynote speech presented at the International Security Management Association, "Terrorism and Economic Security." Scottsdale, AZ, 14 January 2004. Printed in National Intelligence Council Speeches/Statements via online. URL: <http://www.odci.gov/nic/speeche _terror_and_econ_sec.html. Accessed 13 October 2003.

Ignatius, David. "Hypocrisy on Spy Reform." Washington Post, 8 October 2004, A35.

"Intelligence." *Time*. 4 February 1946, 24.

"Intelligence Agency to 'Tunnel' Into Pentagon Information Database." *Inside the Pentagon,* 29 January 2004.

"Intelligence Resource Management." *Potomac Strategies & Analysis, Inc.,* December 2003, 64.

"Intelligence and the Law," Chapter 7 of *Strategic Intelligence: Theory and Application.* 2d rev ed. Eds. Douglas H. Dearth and R. Thomas Goodden. Carlisle Barracks, PA: United States Army War College Center for Strategic Leadership, 1995.

"Intelligence and Military Misfortunes," Chapter 11 of *Strategic Intelligence: Theory and Application.* 2d rev ed. Eds. Douglas H. Dearth and R. Thomas Goodden. Carlisle Barracks, PA: United States Army War College Center for Strategic Leadership, 1995.

"Intelligence, Ethics, and Open Society," Part IV of *Strategic Intelligence: Theory and Application.* 2d rev ed. Eds. Douglas H. Dearth and R. Thomas Goodden. Carlisle Barracks, PA: United States Army War College Center for Strategic Leadership, 1995.

"Introduction," in *Globalization and Maritime Power.* Ed. Sam J. Tangredi. Washington, D.C.: National Defense University Press, 2002.

"Iran's Missles Can Now Hit Europe, Ex-Official Says." *Washington Post,* 6 October 2004, A21.

Jablonsky, David. *Paradigm Lost? Transitions and the Search for a New World Order.* Westport, CT: Praeger, 1995.

Jaffe, Gregg. "At the Pentagon, Quirky Powerpoint Carries Big Punch: In a World of 'Gap' States, Mr. Barnett Urges Generals to Split Force in Two; Austin Powers on Soundtrack." *The Wall Street Journal,* 11 May 2004, A1.

Jeffreys-Jones, Rhodri. *The CIA and American Democracy* New Haven, CT: Yale University Press, 1989.

Jehl, Douglas. "Boeing Lags in Building Spy Satellites." *New York Times,* 4 December 2003, C1.

———."CIA Report Finds Its Officials Failed in Pre-911 Efforts," *New York Times,* 7 January 2004, A1+.

Joint House and Senate Intelligence Committee. "September 19, 2002 Committee Hearing: Brent Scowcroft and Samuel R. Berger." URL: *http://www.complete911timeline.org/2002/Congressionalinquiry091902b.html>.* Accessed 21 October 2003.

Jordan, Amos A. and others. *American National Security,* 5th ed. Baltimore: The Johns Hopkins University Press, 1999.

Jordan, Mary. "Pit Stop on the Cocaine Highway: Guatemala Becomes Favored Link for U.S.-Bound Drugs." *Washington Post,* 6 October 2004, A20.

Kady, Martin II and John Donnelly. "Many Decisions Ahead After Intelligence Bill Clears." *CQ TODAY,* 7 December 2004.

Kagan, Robert. "Strategic Dissonance." In "One Year After: A Grand Strategy for the West?" *Survival* 44, no. 4 (Winter 2002-03): 135-156.

Kamen, Al. "In the Loop: There's No Place Like Zone." *Washington Post,* 8 October 2004, A23.

———."In the Loop: Millions of Secrets." *Washington Post,* 3 May 2004, A19.

Kaplan, David E. and Kevin Whitelaw, "Intelligence Reform—At Last." *U.S. News and World Report.* 20 December 2004, 31-32.

Kaplan, Robert K. "The Coming Anarchy: How Scarcity, Crime, Overpopulation, Tribalism, and Disease are Rapidly Destroying the Social Fabric of Our Planet." *Atlantic,* online ed., February 1994. URL: <http://www.theatlantic.com/Politics/foreign/anarchy.htm>. Accessed 22 June 2004.

Kean, Thomas H. and Lee H. Hamilton. "Intelligence Reform Can Wait No Longer." *Washington Post,* 8 September 2004, A23.

Kennicott, Philip. "Remembering: A Novel Approach." *Washington Post,* 1 August 2004, B1+.

Kent, Sherman. *Strategic Intelligence for American World Policy.* Princeton, NJ: Princeton University Press, 1949.

Kerr, Richard J. "The Evolution of the U.S. Intelligence System in the Post-Soviet Era." Briefing presented at Center for Information Policy Research, Harvard University, Guest Presentations, Spring 1992. Incidental Paper: Seminar on Intelligence, Command and Control, August 1994. URL: *http://pirp.harvard.edu/pubs_pdf/Kerr/kerr-i94-4.pdf.* Accessed 1 April 2004

Kindsvater, Larry C. "A Senior Officer's Perspective: The Need to Reorganize the Intelligence Community." *Studies in Intelligence* 47, no. 1 (2003): 33-37.

Kobyakov, Julius Major General (Ret.). Email to Intelligence Forum listserv. Subject: "U.S. Intelligence Reform." 23 August 2004.

Komarow, Steven. "Army Studies Lessons of Iraq: Report Lays Out Strengths, Weaknesses Revealed in War." *USA Today*, 18 February 2004, 8.

Kraus, Clifford. "Oklahoman Who Opposed Foley to Lose House Intelligence Post." *New York Times*, 9 January 1993. A1.

Krim, Jonathan. "FBI Rejects Its New Case File Software: Database Project Has Cost Nearly $170 Million." *Washington Post*, 14 January 2005, A5.

Lardner, Jr., George. "McCurdy No 'Shrinking Violet: Intelligence Panel to Swear in Witnesses, Push for Reorganization." *Washington Post,* 7 February 1991, A17.

Leary, William M. Ed. *The Central Intelligence Agency: History and Documents.* University of Alabama Press, 1984

Lee, Christopher. "Agencies Getting Heavier on Top: 17 Executive Titles Created Since 1960." *Washingon Post,* 23 July 2004, A27.

———."GAO Again Finds Fault With the Federal Books: Auditors Say That Government's Records Are So Inadequate They Cannot be Evaluated, but Bush Official Cites Progress." *Washington Post*, 21 December 2004, A23.

Lenczowski, Roberta E. "NIMA and the Intelligence Community." Briefing presented at Center for Information Policy Research, Harvard University, Guest Presentations, Spring 2003. Incidental Paper: Seminar on Intelligence, Command and Control, July 2003. URL:*http://pirp.harvard.edu/pubs_pdf/lenczow-i03-1.pdf>*. Accessed 1 April 2004.

Levine, Samantha. "Spinning Terror's Rolodex: Creating a Master List of Bad Guys is Turning Out to be a Tall Order." *U.S. News & World Report*, 2 February 2004, 31.

Linden, Ian. "What is Globalisation?" *Geographical* 75, no. 10 (October 2003): 44-45.

Linzer, Dafna. Rules Still Hinder Intelligence Sharing." *Associated Press,* online ed., 28 March 2004, URL: *<http://www.mercurynews.com>*. Accessed 29 March 2004.

Lohr, Steve. "Many New Causes for Old Problem of Jobs Lost Abroad." *New York Times,* online ed. 15 February 2004. <http://www.nytimes.com/2004/02/15 business/15JOBS.html?>. Accessed 17 February 2004.

Lord, Carnes. "NCS Reform for the Post-Cold War Era." *Orbis* 44, no. 3 (Summer 2000): 433-450.

Loven, Jennifer. "President Signs Measure Overhauling Intelligence: Aiming to Improve Spy Network in Wake of 9/11 Attacks, Bill Creates Counterterror Center, New Director." *Associated Press,* 17 December 2004. Accessed via *http://www.baltimoresun.com/news/custom/attack/bal-bush1217,0,6868674.story.*

Lowenthal, Mark M. *Intelligence: From Secrets to Policy.* 2nd ed. Washington, D.C.: CQ Press, 2003.

———. *U.S. Intelligence: Evolution and Anatomy.* Westport, CT: Praeger, 1992.

Mallaby, Sebastian. "The World Bank's Force of Nature." *Washington Post,* 27 September 2004, A19.

Mamdani, Mahmood. *Good Muslim, Bad Muslim.* New York: Pantheon, 2004.

Markle Foundation. *Creating a Trusted Network for Homeland Security: Protecting America's Freedom in the Information Age: Second Report of the Markle Foundation Task Force.* 2 December 2003. Accessed via *http://www.markletaskforce.org,* 1 July 2004.

————.*Protecting America's Freedom in the Information Age: The First Report of the Markle Foundation Task Force.* 7 October 2002. Accessed via *http://www.markletaskforce.org,* 1 July 2004.

Marsan, Carolyn Duffy. "Management Strategies—Worth the Wait: Security Clearances Take More Than a Year to Obtain, But Federal IT Work Pays Well." *Network World,* 7 June 2004, 65.

Matthews, William. "U.S. Army Cites Deficiencies With Data Collection." *Defense News.* Online ed., 12 April 2004, URL: <http://www.defensenews.com/story. Phy?F=280391&C=America>. Accessed 10 November 2004.

May, Ernest R. "The Intelligence Community: How Crucial?" *Foreign Affairs,* 71, no.3 (Summer 1992): 63-72.

McCarthy, Ellen. "Dealing With Clearance Insecurity." *Washington Post,* 15 April 2004, E1+.

————."Homeland Security Wants Better Integration." *Washington Post,* 25 March 2004, E4.

————."NSA is Making No Secret of Its Technology Intent." *Washington Post,* 24 June 2004, E1+.

McCutcheon, Chuck. "Push for Intelligence Overhaul Losing Momentum on the Hill." *CQ Weekly,* 27 April 2002, 1109-1110.

McDonald, Mark. "As Heroin Flourishes, So Could Terror." *Philadelphia Inquirer,* 10 May 2004, A1.

McFarlane, Robert. "Restructuring: From the Top…." *Washington Post,* 1 August 2004, B1+.

Measuring Globalization: Economic Reversals, Forward Momentum. *Foreign Policy* 141 (March/April 2004): 54-69.

Melymuka, Kathleen. "Premier 100 Panel Weighs Infrastructure Hype, Reality: Changes Are Coming, But Not as Fast as Vendors Like to Think." *Computerworld,* online ed., 9 March 2004. URL: <http://www.computerworld. Com/printthis/2004/ 0,4814,90931.html. Accessed 11 March 2004.

Merle, Renae. "Army Raises Cost of Combat Modernization: Futuristic Project Includes Drones, Unmanned Vehicles, "Smart' Munitions." *Washington Post,* 23 July 2004, A23.

Milbank,Dana. "The Small Bundle of Names Tied Up With Blue Ribbons."*Washington Post,* 4 February 2004, C1+.

Miles, Anne Daugherty. Joint Military Intelligence College. Occasional Paper Number Nine. *The Creation of the National Imagery and Mapping Agency: Congress's Role as Overseer.* Washington, DC: Joint Military Intelligence College, 2002.

Miles, Marc A., Edwin J. Feulner, and Mary Anastasia O'Grady. 2004 Index of Economic Freedom. Washington, DC: The Heritage Foundation, 2004 and New York: Wall Street Journal, 2004. URL: *<http://www.heritage.org/research/features/index/countries.html>.* Accessed 14 January 2004.

Miller, Abraham H. and Brian Alexander. "Structural Quiescence in the Failure of IC21 and Intelligence Reform." *International Journal of Intelligence and Counterintelligence,* 14, no. 2 (Summer 2001): 234-261.

Mitchell, Jeff. Intelligence analyst at 1st Information Operations (IO) Command. Interview by the author, 1 March 2004.

Mitchell, Russ. "The Ghosts in the Machine: Can Technology Find Terrorists?" *The American Spectator* 34, no. 8 (Nov/Dec 2001). Accessed via ProQuest, 4 December 2003.

Modernizing Intelligence: Structure and Change for the 21st Century. VA: National Institute for Public Policy, 1997.

Morgan, Dan. "Overhaul of Congressional Panels Urged: Report Finds Responsibility, Accountability Lacking." *Washington Post,* 23 July 2004, A21.

Morgenthau, Hans J. *Politics Among Nations: The Struggle for Power and Peace.* 4th ed. New York: Knopf, 1967.

Mousseau, Michael. "Market Civilization and Its Clash with Terror." *International Security* 27, No. 3 (Winter 2002/03): 5-21.

Nakashima, Ellen. "U.N. Cites Record in HIV Cases, Faults Prevention as Inadequate." *Washington Post,* 7 July 2004, A1+.

"Nation in Brief." *Washington Post,* 5 November 2004, A4.

National Security Act of 1947, as amended. <http://www.history-matters.com/archive/church/rockcomm/html/Rockefeller_0144a.htm>. Accessed 3 August 2004.

News Reports. "Terrorist Profiting in Illicit Goods: Interpol Chief Warns About Counterfeiting." *International Herald Tribune,* 26 May 2004.

Nichols, John. "Flawed Intelligence Bill." *The Nation,* 3 January 2004, 6.

Nye, Joseph. "Globalisation and Discontent." *The World Today,* 57, nos. 8/9, (Aug/Sep 2001). Accessed via ProQuest, 14 January 2004.

———.and William A. Owen. "America's Information Edge." *Foreign Affairs.* 75, no. 2 (March/April 1996): 20-36.

Oakley, Phyllis. "Restructuring: From the Top...." *Washington Post,* 1 August 2004, B1+.

O'Connell, Kevin and Robert R. Tomes. "Keeping the Information Edge," *Policy Review* 122 (Dec 2003/Jan 2004). Accessed via ProQuest, 14 June 2004.

Odom, William E. *Fixing Intelligence for a More Secure America.* New Haven, CT: Yale University Press, 2003.

O'Harrow, Jr., Robert. "Senate Bill Proposes Anti-Terror Database: Civil Liberties Groups Express Concern." *Washington Post*, 28 September 2004, A4.

Ostroff, Frank. *The Horizontal Organization: What the Organization of the Future Actually Looks Like and How It Delivers Value to Customer.* New York: Oxford University Press, Inc., 1999.

——.*The Horizontal Organization: What the Organization of the Future Actually Looks Like and How It Delivers Value to Customer.* New York: Oxford University Press, Inc., 1999. Review by Bert A. Spector. *The Academy of Management Executives,* May 1999, 97-98.

Paltrow, Scot J. "White House Hurdles Delay 9/11 Commission Investigation: Documents and Interviews are Subject of Tense Talks as Tight Deadline Looms." *Wall Street Journal*, online ed., 8 July 2003, <http: online.wsj.com/public/us>. Accessed 9 July 2003.

Pappas, Aris A. and James M. Simon, Jr. "Daunting Challenges, Hard Decisions: The Intelligence Community—2001-2015." *Studies in Intelligence* 46, no. 1 (2002): 39-47.

Pavitt, James. *"Change and the CIA." Washington Post,* 6 August 2004, A19.

——."Testimony of James L. Pavitt Before the National Commission on Terrorist Attacks Upon the United States."14 April 2004, URL: <http: //www.9-commission.gov/hearings/hearing8/staff_statement_5.pdf>. Accessed 20 April 2004.

Peters, Tom. *Re-Imagine! Business Excellence in a Disruptive Age.* London: DK, 2003.

Pincus, Walter. "Analysis: Bush's Intelligence Moves Don't Attain Scope Urged by 9/11 Panel." *Washington Post*, 2 September 2004, A4.

——. "Bush's Plan Limits Intelligence Chief: Others Would Carry Out Operation.," *Washington Post*, 11 September 2004, A4.

——."CIA Alters Policy after Iraq Lapses." *Washington Post*, 12 February 2004,A1.

——. "Congress Resists Key Recommendation of 9/11 Panel: Without Consolidation, Homeland Security Department Officials Report to 88 Panels on Capitol Hill." *Washington Post*, 1 January 2005, A4.

——. "Goss Pick Withdraws From CIA Consideration." *Washington Post*, 5 October 2004, A10.

——. "Intelligence Bill Clears Congress: Bush Expected to Approve Post 9/11 Reforms Next Week." *Washington Post*, 9 December 2004, A4.

——. "Iraq Called 'Springboard' for Insurgency Figure: Intelligence Experts Say Jordanian Militant Zarqawi Wants Broader Role in Jihad Movement." *Washington Post*, 21 October 2004, A25.

——. "McLaughlin Defends CIA, Cites Reform in Speech: Deputy Director Rejects Idea of Intelligence Czar." *Washington Post*, 7 July 2004, A21.

——. "National Intelligence Director Proves to be Difficult Post to Fill: Uncertainties Over Role, Authority are Blames for Delay." *Washington Post*, 31 January 2005, A4.

———. "No Intelligence Compromise Seen: Lawmakers See Slim Chance for Passage in December Session." *Washington Post,* 22 November 2004, A9.

———. "Passage of Intelligence Bill Called Doubtful: Lawmakers Say Bush, Cheney Need to Lobby," *Washington Post,* 22 November 2004, A3.

———. "President Gets to Fill Ranks of New Intelligence Superstructure: Reform Legislation is Set to Be Signed into Law on Friday." *Washington Post,* 16 December 2004, A35.

———. "Senate Realigns Intelligence Procedures; New Reform Statue Calls for Some Changes." *Washington Post,* 23 December 2004, A21.

———. "September 11 Commission Critics Question Panel's Study of New Measures: Report Said to Overlook Changes." *Washington Post,* 10 August 2004, A3.

———. "Skepticism About Defector's Weapons Allegations Ignored." *Washington Post,* 13 July 2004, A12.

———. "Support for Intelligence Plan: Powell, Ridge Back One Director But Defer to Bush on Specifics." *Washington Post,* 14 September 2004, A4.

———. "Turf War Stalls Intelligence Bill: Pentagon Allies at Odds with Advocates of New Director." *Washington Post,* 27 October 2004, A4.

———. "9/11 Panel's Plan Would Reduce Influence of CIA: Experts Predict Realignment of Roles." *Washington Post,* 29 July 2004, A6.

Pincus, Walter and Dana Milbank. "Bush Plan Draws on Advice of 9/11 Panel: New Proposal Gives Intelligence Chief More Budget Power." *Washington Post,* 9 September 2004, A1+.

Pincus, Walter and Dana Priest. "Goss Brings 4 Staffers From Hill to CIA: New Director Quickly Makes His Mark on Agency with Personnel Decision." *Washington Post,* 5 October 2004, A3.

Priest, Dana. "Retired Official Defends the CIA's Performance." *Washington Post,* 5 November 2004, A23.

Priest, Dana and Dafna Linzer. "Panel Condems Iraq Prewar Intelligence: Senate Report Faults 2002 Estimate Sent to Hill, Accuses the CIA of "Group-Think." *Washington Post,* 10 July 2004, A1+.

Priest, Dana and Walter Pincus. "Analysis: Director's Control is a Concern." *Washington Post,* 8 December 2004, A1.

Radi, David A. "Intelligence Inside the White House: The Influence of Executive Style and Technology." Briefing presented at Center for Information Policy Research, Harvard University, Guest Presentations, March 1997. Incidental Paper, URL: *http://pirp.harvard.edu/pubs_pdf/radi/radi-i97-3.pdf*>. Accessed 1 April 2004.

"Records Gap Leaves Borders Vulnerable: Report Says U.S. Border Patrol Won't Get Complete FBI Fingerprint Files for Years." *Washington Post,* 3 March 2004, A11.

Reddy, Anitha. "Local Firms Respond to a Changing U.S. Military." *Washington Post,* online ed., 26 April 2004. URL: http://www.washingtonpost.com/ac2/wp-dyn/A40181-2004Apr25?>. Accessed 29 April 2004.

Reno, Janet. "Transcript: 9/11 Commission Hearing." *Washington Post,* online ed., 13 April 2004. URL: <http://www.washingtonpost.com/ac2/wp-dyn/A9088-2004Apr13?>. Accessed 14 April 2004.

Report of the Commission on the Roles and Capabilities of the United States Intelligence Community. *Preparing for the 21st Century: An Appraisal of U.S. Intelligence.* Washington: Government Printing Office, 1996, *http://www.access.gpo.gov/int/int001.html.* Accessed 1 December 2004.

Results of the 1973 Church Committee Hearings on CIA Misdeeds, and the 1984 Iran/Contra Hearings. *URL: <http://pw1.netcom/ ncoic/cia_info.htm.* Accessed 3 August 2004. ed., 8 April 2004. *URL: http://www.washingtonpost.com/ac2/wp-dyn/A61252-04Apr8>.* Accessed 14 April 2004.

Roberts, Sen. Pat (R-KS). "Perspectives." *Newsweek,* 19 July 2004.

Rood, Justin. "Ashcroft, Mueller and Ridge En Route to Hill Spotlights." *CQ Homeland Security – Intelligence,* 1 June 2004 via *http://homeland.cq.com/hs/news.do.* Accessed 2 June 2004.

Rudgers, David F. *Creating the Secret State: The Origins of the Central Intelligence Agency, 1943-1947.* Lawrence, KS: University Press of Kansas, 2002.

Rudman, Warren B. "Perspectives on National Security in the Twenty-First Century." Briefing presented at Center for Information Policy Research, Harvard University, Guest Presentations, Spring 2002. Incidental Paper: Seminar on Intelligence, Command and Control, June 2003. URL: http://www/pirp.harvard.edu/pubs_pdf/udman/rudman.i02.pdf>. Accessed 1 April 2004.

Rumsfeld, Donald. Secretary of Defense. "Rumsfeld: Use Caution in Intelligence Reform." *The Washington Post,* 18 August 2004, A1+.

Sachs, Jeffrey D. *The Geography of Economic Development.* Newport: Naval War College, 2000. URL: <http://www.nwc.navy.mil/press/review/2000/ Autumn/art6%2DA00.htm>. Accessed 29 June 2003. Samuelson, Robert J. "Seduced by 'Reform." *Washington Post,* 2 June 2004, A25.

Sanger, David E. and William J. Broad. "Pakistani's Nuclear Earnings: $100 Million." *New York Times,* online ed., 16 March 2004, URL: <http://www//nytimes.com/2004/03/16/international/asia/16NUKE.html?>. Accessed 17 March 2004.

Sangillo, Gregg and Siobhan Gorman, "Smarter Intelligence a Post-9/11 Priority." *National Journal* (22 May 2004): 1572-1579.

Savage, Marcia. "No Rave Reviews." CRN, 14 October 2002. Accessed via ProQuest, 28 January 2004.

Schumer, Charles, Sen. (D-NY). "U.S. Senator Charles Schumer (D-NY) Holds News Conference on 9/11, 9 July 2003. Accessed via LexisNexis, 12 January 2004.

Sen, Amartya. "If It's Fair, It's Good: 10 Truths About Globalization." *Canadian Dimension,* 14 July 2001. Accessed via LexisNexis, 30 September 2004.

Shays, Christopher, Reps. (R-CN) and Carolyn Maloney (D-NY). "Congress, Reorganize Thyself." *Washington Post,* 22 December 2004, A27.

Shelby, Richard C., Sen. (R-AL). "September 11 and the Imperative of Reform in the U.S. Intelligence Community: Additional Views of Senator Richard C. Shelby." 10 December 2002l, URL: *http://intelligence.senate.gov/Shelby.pdf.* Accessed 21 October 2003.

Shenon, Philip. "Next Round is Set in Push to Reorganize Intelligence." *New York Times,* 20 December 2004, A19.

————."9/11 Panel is Said to Urge New Post for Intelligence." *New York Times,* online ed., 17 July 2004. URL: <htpp://www.nytimes.com/2004/17/olitics/17panel.html >. Accessed 19 July 2004.

Shenon, Philip and Carl Hulse. "House Leadership Blocks Vote on Intelligence Bill." *New York Times,* 21 November 2004, A1.

Shenon, Philip and Eric Lichtblau. "Sept.11 Panel Cites CIA for Failures in Terror Case." *New York Times,* online ed., 15 April 2004. URL: *http://www.nytimes.com/2004/ 04/15/politics/15PANE.html.* Accessed 19 April 2004.

Shrader, Katherine Pfleger. "Analysts Are in Great Demand: Intelligence Agencies Scramble for Talent." *Washington Post,* 30 December 2004, A24.

Simpson, Glenn R. Language Lessons for Pentagon: Lack of Arabic Speakers Hinders Commanders in Battle for Iraq." *Wall Street Journal,* 3 December 2003, A4.

Sipress, Alan. "An Indonesian's Prison Memoir Takes Holy War Into Cyberspace: In Sign of New Threat, Militant Offers Tips on Credit Card Fraud." *Washington Post,* 14 December 2004, A19.

Slevin, Peter. "New 2003 Data: 625 Terrorism Deaths, Not 327." *Washington Post,* 23 June 2004, A1.

Smith, Jeffrey R. "Senate Panel Rejects Request to Increase Intelligence Budget." Washington Post, 17 July 1993. A2.

————."State Dept. Concedes Errors in Terror Data." *Washington Post,* 10 June 2004, A17.

Smist, Frank J. Jr. *Congress Oversees the United States Intelligence Community.* 2n^d ed. Knoxville: The University of Tennessee, 1994.

Sniffen, Michael J. "Secrets Perplex Panel: Classified Data Growing to Include "Comically Irrelevant." *Washington Post,* 3 September 2004, A17.

Stern, Christopher. "So Long to Long Distance? Calling Packages, Internet Phoning Swiftly Ending a High-Cost Category." *Washington Post,* 5 August 2004, E1+.

Strohm, Chris. "Senators Ask Who's in Charge of Homeland Intelligence." GovExec.com, 25 March 2004. *URL:<http://www.govexec.com/dailyfed/0304/032504c1.htm.* Accessed 29 March 2004.

Tenet, George. "DCI's Worldwide Threat Briefing: The Worldwide Threat 2004: Challenges in a Changing Global Context." Presented to Senate Armed Services Committee, 9 March 2004.

————. "Investigation of Sept 11." 17 October 2002. Accessed via LexisNexis, 12 January 2004.

———."Transcript: 9/11 Commission Hearing on Intelligence." *Washington Post,* online ed., 14 April 2004. URL: http://www.washingtonpost.com/ac2/wp-dyn/A11115-2004Apr14?>. Accessed 15 April 2004.

———. "Testimony on World-Wide Threats." 7 February 2001. Accessed via Lexis Nexis, 5 February 2004.

———. "Written Statement for the Record of the Director of Central Intelligence Before the National Commission on Terror Attacks Upon the United States." 24 March 2004. URL: <http://www.9-11commission.gov/hearings/hearing8/tenet_Statement.pdf>. Accessed 1 May 2004.

"Terrorism Center Wrestles Technology, Secrecy," *Reuters,* 28 April 2004.

The 9/11 Commission Report: The Final Report of the National Commission on Terrorist Attacks Upon the United States. New York: W.W. Norton & Company, 2004.

The Global Century: Globalization and National Security. Ed. Richard Kugler and Ellen L. Frost. Washington, DC: National Defense University Press, 2000.

"Time to Rethink – America's Intelligence Services." *The Economist Newspaper Ltd.,* 20 April 2002. Accessed via Lexis-Nexis, 28 January 2004.

"Transcript: 9/11 Commission Hearing on Intelligence." *Washington Post.* online ed., 14 Apil 2004. <URL: *www.washingtonpost.com/ac2wp-dyn/*A11115-2004Apr14?>. Accessed 15 April 2004.

"Transcript: 9/11 Commission Hearing on Law Enforcement, Counterterrorism" *Washington Post.* Online ed., 14 Apil 2004. <URL: www.washingtonpost.com/ac2wp-dyn/ A12238-2004Apr14?. Accessed 15 April 2004.

Treverton, Gregory F. "Intelligence: The Achilles Heel of the Bush Doctrine." *Arms Control Today.* 33, no. 6. (Jul/Aug 2003). Accessed via Proquest, 6 November 2003.

———.*Reshaping National Intelligence in an Age of Information.* Cambridge: Cambridge University Press, 2001.

United States Commission on National Security/21st Century. *New World Coming: American Security in the 21st Century Major Themes and Implications Phase I Report on the Emerging Global Security Environment for the First Quarter of the 21st Century.* 5 September 1999. URL:< *http://www.nssg.gov*>. Accessed 1 November 2003.

United States Commission on National Security/21st Century. *Road Map for National*

Security: Imperative for Change—The Phase III Report of the U.S. Commission on National Security/21st Century. 15 February 2001. URL: <*http://www.nssg.gov*>. Accessed 1 November 2003.

United States Commission on National Security/21st Century. *Seeking a National Strategy: A Concert for Preserving Security and Promoting Freedom Phase II Report on a U.S. National Strategy for the 21st Century.* 15 April 2000. URL: <*http:// www.nssg.gov*>. Accessed 1 November 2003.

U.S. Congress, House, (Democratic Members) House Select Committee on Homeland Security, *America at Risk: The State of Homeland Security Initial Findings,* 108th Cong., 2nd sess., January 2004.

U.S. Congress, House, Armed Services Committee, Terrorism, Unconventional Threats and Capabilities Subcommittee. *C4I Interoperability: New Challenges in 21st Century Warfare.* 108 th Cong., 2nd sess., 21 October 2004.

U.S. Congress, House, Permanent Select Committee on Intelligence, Staff Study. *IC21: Intelligence Community in the 21st Century.* 104th Cong., 9 April 1996. URL:<http://www.fas.org/irp/congress/1996_rptIc21/ic21001.html>. Accessed 21 October 2003.

U.S. Congress, House, Permanent Select Committee on Intelligence. *Intelligence Authorization Act for Fiscal Year 2004.* 108th Cong., 2nd sess., 2004.H.Rept 108-558.

U.S. Congress, House, Permanent Select Committee on Intelligence, Hearing. *The Current and Future State of Intelligence.* 103rd Cong., 2nd sess., 24 February 1994. URL: <http://www.fas.org/irp/congress/1994_hr/hpsci022494.pdf>. Accessed on 1 June 2004.

U.S. Congress, House, Permanent Select Committee on Intelligence, Subcommittee on Terrorism and Homeland Security. Counterterrorism Intelligence Capabilities and Performance Prior to 9-11. Report, 107th Cong., 2 sess., 17, July 2002. URL: http://www.fas.org/irp/congress/2002_rpt/hpsci_ths0702.html. Accessed 21 October 2003.

U.S. Congress, Senate, Select Committee on Intelligence, Confirmation Hearings of John Deutch, 104th Congress, 2nd sess., 26 April 1995.

U.S. Congress, Senate, Select Committee on Intelligence and House, Permanent Select Committee on Intelligence. Joint Inquiry on Counterterrorist Center Customer Perspective, 19 September 2002. Accessed via LexisNexis, 12 January 2004.

U.S. Congress, Senate, Select Committee on Intelligence and House, Permanent Select Committee on Intelligence. Joint Inquiry into Intelligence Community Activities Before and After the Terrorist Attacks of September 11, 2001. 107th Cong., 2nd sess., S.Rept. 107-351 and H. Rept. 107-792, 20 December 2002.

U.S. Congress, Joint House and Senate Intelligence Committee, "September 19, 2002 Committee Hearing: Brent Scowcroft and Samuel R. Berger." URL: http://complete911timeline.org/2002/Congressionalinquiry091902b.html>.Accessed 21 October 2003.

U.S. Congress, Select Committee on Intelligence and House, Permanent Select Committee on Intelligence. Investigation of September 11, Hearings, 107th Cong., 2nd sess., 18 September, 17 October 2002, 2. Accessed via LexisNexis, 12 January 2004.

U.S. Congress, Senate, Committee on Armed Services. Fiscal Year 2005 Joint Military Intelligence Program (JMIP) and Army Tactical Intelligence and Related Activities (TIARA). Hearings, 108th Cong., 2nd sess., 7 April 2004, 13.

United States Congress, Senate, Committee on Governmental Affairs, Summary of Intelligence Reform and Terrorist Prevention Act of 2004, 108th Cong. 2nd sess., 6 December 2004.

U.S. Congress, Senate, Select Commission on Intelligence. *Special Report of the Select Committee on Intelligence United States Senate January 4, 1995 to October 3, 1996.* 105th Cong., 1st sess. S. Rept.105-1, 22 January 1997. URL: <www.emergency.com/int03.htm>. Accessed 21 October 2003.

U.S. President. "Executive Order Strengthened Management of the Intelligence Community." 27 August 2004. URL: <www.whitehouse.gov/news/releases/2004/08/20040827-6.html>. Accessed 2 September 2004.

U.S. President. "Executive Order National Counterterrorism Center. 27 August 2004. URL: <www.whitehouse.gov/news/releases/2004/08/20040827-5.html>. Accessed 2 September 2004.

U.S. President. "Executive Order Strengthening the Sharing of Terrorism Information to Americans." 27 August 200. URL: <www.whitehouse.gov/news/releases/2004/8/20040827-4.html>. Accessed 2 September 2004.

U.S. President. "Executive Order Establishing the President's Board on Safeguarding Americans' Civil Liberties." 27 August 2004. URL: <www.whitehouse.gov/News/releases/2004/08/20040827-3.html>. Accessed 2 September 2004.

Verton, Dan. "Rice Grilled on Information-Sharing Shortfalls." ComputerWorld, Online ed. 8 April 2004, URL: <http://www.computerworld.com. Accessed 14 April 2004.

Von Drehle, David. "Analysis: The Findings—America's Failings, in Depressing Details." *Washington Post*, 23 July 2004, A1+

"Washington in Brief: Terrorism Expert Calls Seaports Vulnerable." *Washington Post*, 28 January 2004, A04.

Warner, Michael. *Central Intelligence: Origin and Evolution*. Washington, DC: Center for the Study of Intelligence, 2001.

Waterman, Shaun. "Intelligence Community Reform Stalls." United Press International, 11 December 2003. Accessed via LexisNexis, 28 January 2004.

Watkins, Michael D. and Max H. Bazerman, "Predictable Surprises: The Disasters You Should Have Seen Coming," *Harvard Business Review* (March 2003): 72-80.

Webster's II New College Dictionary, 2001.

Weisman, Johnathan. "Bush Economic Aide Says Government Lacks Vision." *Washington Post,* 13 December 2003, A1+.

Weisman, Jonathan and Robin Wright. "Funds to Rebuild Iraq are Drifting Away from Target: State Department to Rethink U.S. Effort." *Washington Post,* 6 October 2004, A18.

Wertheimer, Michael A. "Crippling Innovation—and Intelligence." *Washington Post*, 21 July 2004, A19.

Wirth, Kevin E. *The Coast Guard Intelligence Program Enters the Intelligence Community: A Case Study of Congressional Influence on Intelligence Community Evolution*, Unpublished MSSI Thesis, Washington, D.C.: Joint Military Intelligence College, 2002

"World in Brief." *Washington Post,* 6 October 2004, A22.

"World in Brief," *Washington Post,* 7 October 2004, A26.

Zegart, Amy B. *Flawed By Design: The Evolution of the CIA, JCS, and NSC.* Stanford, CA: Stanford University Press, 1999.

"9/11 Report to Be TV Mini-Series." *New York Times,* 15 November 2004, B2.

About the Author

Melanie M.H. Gutjahr has recently completed a year as an Intelligence Research Fellow at the Joint Military Intelligence College on sabbatical from the National Geospatial-Intelligence Agency, where she is a systems engineer. Ms. Gutjahr has more than twenty-six years of wide-ranging experience in signals intelligence (SIGINT) operations, computer operations, financial management and technical training. At NGA, she has served as a senior financial manager and deputy division chief.

Prior to joining NGA in 1999, Ms. Gutjahr worked as a principal engineer, systems analyst and senior technical trainer for civilian firms whose clients were other Intelligence Community and U.S. government agencies. Additionally, Ms. Gutjahr has served as an adjunct faculty member at Aiken Technical College.

Ms. Gutjahr is a Colonel in the U.S. Army Reserves (USAR) and is assigned as the Deputy G2 for United States Army Pacific (USARPAC). As a SIGINT officer, she has served in command and staff level positions in both strategic and tactical environments. Colonel Gutjahr is a graduate of the U.S. Army Command and General Staff College. She was mobilized to active duty in support of Operation DESERT SHIELD/DESERT STORM and most recently, Operation NOBLE EAGLE.

Ms. Gutjahr holds a BS from the University of Missouri-Columbia, an EdM from Boston University, and a CSS (Certificate of Special Studies in Administration and Management) from Harvard University Extension School. She was an honor graduate from the National Defense University Information Resources Management College and is a Department of Defense-certified Chief Information Officer and Chief Information Assurance Officer. Ms. Gutjahr holds certification from the National Security Agency as an Education and Training Officer.

Ms. Gutjahr has been active in community affairs, having served as a volunteer counselor and on the Board of Directors for a county-wide social service organization. In addition, she held elected office for a community organization that interfaced with county and state legislative officials. She has received three Maryland gubernatorial appointments to an advisory committee and served over twelve years as chairperson. The author may be contacted at *gutjahrm@nga.mil.*

www.ingramcontent.com/pod-product-compliance
Lightning Source LLC
Chambersburg PA
CBHW070629290526
45790CB00001B/48